TM

# References for the Rest of Us!®

## BESTSELLING BOOK SERIES

Do you find that traditional reference books are overloaded with technical details and advice you'll never use? Do you postpone important life decisions because you just don't want to deal with them? Then our *For Dummies*® business and general reference book series is for you.

For Dummies business and general reference books are written for those frustrated and hard-working souls who know they aren't dumb, but find that the myriad of personal and business issues and the accompanying horror stories make them feel helpless. *For Dummies* books use a lighthearted approach, a down-to-earth style, and even cartoons and humorous icons to dispel fears and build confidence. Lighthearted but not lightweight, these books are perfect survival guides to solve your everyday personal and business problems.

> *"More than a publishing phenomenon, 'Dummies' is a sign of the times."*
>
> — The New York Times

> *"A world of detailed and authoritative information is packed into them..."*
>
> — U.S. News and World Report

> *"...you won't go wrong buying them."*
>
> — Walter Mossberg, Wall Street Journal, on For Dummies books

Already, millions of satisfied readers agree. They have made For Dummies the #1 introductory level computer book series and a best-selling business book series. They have written asking for more. So, if you're looking for the best and easiest way to learn about business and other general reference topics, look to For Dummies to give you a helping hand.

Wiley Publishing, Inc.

# Entrepreneurship
## FOR
# DUMMIES®

by Dr. Kathleen Allen

Wiley Publishing, Inc.

**Entrepreneurship For Dummies®**

Published by
**Wiley Publishing, Inc.**
909 Third Avenue
New York, NY 10022
www.wiley.com

For general information on our other products and services or to obtain technical support, please contact our Customer Care Department within the U.S. at 800-762-2974, outside the U.S. at 317-572-3993, or fax 317-572-4002.

Wiley also publishes its books in a variety of electronic formats. Some content that appears in print may not be available in electronic books.

*Library of Congress Cataloging-in-Publication Data:*

Library of Congress Control Number: 00-105667

ISBN: 0-7645-5262-7

Manufactured in the United States of America

10 9 8 7 6 5 4

1O/RZ/QY/QS/IN

# *About the Author*

**Kathleen R. Allen Ph.D.**

Dr. Allen is an authority on entrepreneurship and small business technology and is the author of *The Complete MBA For Dummies* (with Peter Economy), *eBusiness Technology Kit For Dummies* (with Jon Weisner), *Entrepreneurship and Small Business Management, Launching New Ventures,* and *Growing and Managing an Entrepreneurial Business,* as well as several other books. She has also written for popular business magazines and newspapers (*Inc., Los Angeles Times, Los Angeles Business Journal,* and *The New York Times*) and is called upon by the *Wall Street Journal,* CNN, CNBC, and a variety of other media, for expert opinion in the field of entrepreneurship.

As a professor of entrepreneurship at the Lloyd Greif Center for Entrepreneurial Studies at the Marshall School of Business at the University of Southern California, she helps hundreds of young entrepreneurs start new ventures. Allen is actively involved in academic research, most recently in issues related to the unique environment of high tech start-up companies. She is also a founding member of the Entrepreneurship Research Consortium, a national research organization consisting of leading universities around the world, which is conducting groundbreaking research on nascent entrepreneurs.

At the University of Southern California, she is leading an initiative to form an alliance between the business and engineering schools to commercialize intellectual property developed at the university. She has developed a number of courses in the area of technology commercialization and serves on the university's technology board.

As an entrepreneur, Allen has been involved in commercial real estate development for the past ten years, having cofounded a development firm specializing in apartment, office, and industrial space; and a brokerage — American Pacific Investments — which she sold. She is presently the cofounder and CFO of Gentech Corporation, a technology-based manufacturing company that recently launched a line of patented, intelligent, industrial power source machines. She is also consulting to a number of technology-based ventures, including three medical technology companies with patented products.

In the past three years, with the assistance of Microsoft Corporation, Allen has been working to educate small business owners and entrepreneurs on the value of technology as a competitive advantage, and to educate software manufacturers and resellers to the mindset and needs of small business owners.

# Dedication

To my students at the Greif Entrepreneurship Center at the University of Southern California, who never cease to amaze me with their entrepreneurial efforts.

# Author's Acknowledgments

I would like to give my sincere thanks and appreciation to the talented publishing team at Hungry Minds, particularly Mark Butler, Norm Crampton, Neil Johnson, and Pam Mourouzis. I would also like to thank my family for their unconditional love and support during a time when I was doing two books at once.

## Publisher's Acknowledgments

We're proud of this book; please send us your comments through our online registration form located at www.dummies.com/register.

Some of the people who helped bring this book to market include the following:

*Acquisitions, Editorial, and Media Development*

**Project Editor:** Norm Crampton

**Acquisitions Editor:** Mark Butler

**Copy Editor:** Neil Johnson

**Acquisitions Coordinator:** Tonia Morgan-Oden

**Technical Editor:** Robert L. Newhart II

**Editorial Manager:** Pam Mourouzis

**Editorial Assistant:** Carol Strickland

*Production*

**Project Coordinator:** Maridee Ennis

**Layout and Graphics:** Beth Brooks, Tracy K. Oliver, LeAndra Johnson, Brian Torwelle, Jeremy Unger, Erin Zeltner

**Proofreaders:** Laura Albert, John Bitter, Laura L. Bowman, Susan Moritz, Carl Pierce, Charles Spencer

**Indexer:** Liz Cunningham

*Publishing and Editorial for Consumer Dummies*

**Diane Graves Steele,** Vice President and Publisher, Consumer Dummies

**Joyce Pepple,** Acquisitions Director, Consumer Dummies

**Kristin A. Cocks,** Product Development Director, Consumer Dummies

**Michael Spring,** Vice President and Publisher, Travel

**Brice Gosnell,** Publishing Director, Travel

**Suzanne Jannetta,** Editorial Director, Travel

*Publishing for Technology Dummies*

**Richard Swadley,** Vice President and Executive Group Publisher

**Andy Cummings,** Vice President and Publisher

*Composition Services*

**Gerry Fahey,** Vice President of Production Services

**Debbie Stailey,** Director of Composition Services

# Contents at a Glance

*Introduction* ..........................................................................*1*

*Part I: Getting Started in Entrepreneurship* .................*7*
Chapter 1: What's an Entrepreneur, Anyway? ................................................9
Chapter 2: Moving at the Speed of E-Business ...............................................21
Chapter 3: Preparing to Hear When Opportunity Knocks ............................33
Chapter 4: Testing an Opportunity Before You Leap ....................................45

*Part II: Developing Your Business Concept* ..................*57*
Chapter 5: Listening to What Your Industry Tells You ................................59
Chapter 6: What Your Customers Can Tell You ............................................73
Chapter 7: Designing Products and Services for a New Marketplace .........87
Chapter 8: Protecting Your Products and Services ....................................103
Chapter 9: Getting Products and Services to Customers: Distribution .....121
Chapter 10: Putting Together Your Start-up Team ......................................131
Chapter 11: Assessing Your Start-up Financial Needs ...............................149

*Part III: Creating a Company* .....................................*169*
Chapter 12: Getting Ready to Do a Business Plan ......................................171
Chapter 13: Finding Money to Start and Grow Your Venture ...................187
Chapter 14: Starting with the Right Legal Structure ..................................205
Chapter 15: Developing a Business Model for a Digital World ..................219

*Part IV: Growing a Company* .......................................*233*
Chapter 16: Planning for Growth ..................................................................235
Chapter 17: Organizing Your Business for Growth .....................................253
Chapter 18: Reaching the Customer ..............................................................269
Chapter 19: Proving You Can Make Money: The Financial Plan ...............289
Chapter 20: Planning for Things That Go Bump in the Night ...................311

*Part V: The Part of Tens* ..............................................*329*
Chapter 21: Ten Reasons Not to Start a Business ......................................331
Chapter 22: Ten Ways to Spark Your Entrepreneurial Spirit ....................335
Chapter 23: Ten Ways to Use the Internet to Grow Your Business ...........339
Chapter 24: Ten Best Resources for Gathering Competitive Intelligence ....345

*Index* ...........................................................................*349*

# Cartoons at a Glance

*By Rich Tennant*

page 7

page 57

page 169

page 233

page 329

*Fax:* 978-546-7747
*E-mail:* richtennant@the5thwave.com
*World Wide Web:* www.the5thwave.com

# Table of Contents

*Introduction* ...................................................... 1

How Entrepreneurship Has Changed ........................................1

How Entrepreneurs Define Success .......................................2

About This Book ........................................................3

Foolish Assumptions ....................................................3

Icons Used in This Book ...............................................4

How This Book Is Organized .............................................4

Part I: Getting Started in Entrepreneurship ..........................4

Part II: Developing Your Business Concept ............................5

Part III: Creating a Company .........................................5

Part IV: Growing a Company ...........................................5

Part V: The Part of Tens .............................................5

How to Use This Book ...................................................6

*Part I: Getting Started in Entrepreneurship* ..................... 7

**Chapter 1: What's an Entrepreneur, Anyway?** ....................9

Understanding Entrepreneurship .........................................9

Recognizing an entrepreneurial venture ...............................10

Putting together the pieces of an entrepreneurial venture ...........12

Distinguishing entrepreneurial ventures from small
businesses .........................................................14

Tasting the Many Flavors of Entrepreneurship ..........................15

The home-based entrepreneur ..........................................15

The virtual entrepreneur .............................................16

The serial entrepreneur ..............................................17

The traditional entrepreneur .........................................17

Deciding to Become an Entrepreneur ....................................18

Consider your personal goals .........................................18

Look ahead ...........................................................20

**Chapter 2: Moving at the Speed of E-Business** ....................21

Everyone Runs an E-Business ...........................................22

The Internet Gives You an Edge ........................................22

Scaling out = Competitive advantage ..................................23

Harnessing technology = Competitive advantage ........................23

Turning information into knowledge = Competitive advantage ....24

Breaking the Link between Information and Things .......................25

Sharing Information (And Everything Else) .............................26

Communication keeps getting easier, freer ............................26

Hierarchy is out, network is in ......................................27

Everyone's Value Chain Is Shorter ...................................................27
Making Yourself Obsolete (Before Someone Else Does It for You) ........28
Changing the Way You Buy Things .................................................29
Deconstructing the Company .........................................................30
    Giving up control ...................................................................31
    Getting flexible and fast ........................................................31
Technology Disrupts; That's Good ..................................................32

**Chapter 3: Preparing to Hear When Opportunity Knocks** .........33

Starting to "Cook" on an Idea ........................................................34
    1. Changing a business .........................................................34
    2. Solving a problem with creativity .......................................35
Spotting Obstacles in Your Path .....................................................35
    You think you're not creative (Think again!) ...........................36
    You loathe criticism (Well don't we all?) ................................36
    You're a creature of habit ......................................................36
    You lack confidence ..............................................................37
    You're overconfident (jumbo ego) ..........................................37
Clearing Away the Obstacles ..........................................................37
    Going back to familiar territory ..............................................38
    Finding a problem and solving it ............................................38
    Using your personal network .................................................39
    Making time to be creative .....................................................41
    Finding a favorite thinking space ...........................................41
    Playing with toys, games, and kids ........................................41
Growing Ideas with Outside Help ...................................................42
Finding Opportunity in Failure ......................................................43
Finding Opportunity in the Unconventional .....................................43
Finding the Right Place for Innovation ............................................44
    Making the environment friendly ...........................................44

**Chapter 4: Testing an Opportunity Before You Leap** ..............45

Starting with a Personal Assessment ..............................................46
Turning an Opportunity into a Business Concept ...............................47
    Benefits versus features: What does the customer buy? ..............48
    Why isn't money part of the concept? .....................................49
Quick-Testing Your Concept ..........................................................50
Getting Serious: Doing Feasibility Analysis ......................................51
    Feasibility versus business plan: Double the work? ....................53
    An overview of feasibility analysis .........................................54

*Part II: Developing Your Business Concept* ...................57

**Chapter 5: Listening to What Your Industry Tells You** ............59

Understanding Your Industry .........................................................60
    Using a framework of industry structure ..................................61
    Deciding on an entry strategy ................................................64

Researching an Industry ........................................66
     Checking out the status of your industry ..............67
     Competitive intelligence: Checking out the competition ..............68
Benchmarking Against the Perfect Industry ..............72

## Chapter 6: What Your Customers Can Tell You ...............73

Defining Your Niche .......................................73
     Narrowing your market ..............................74
     Developing a niche strategy ........................76
Researching Your Customers ...............................77
     Figuring out what data you need ....................77
     Looking at secondary sources first .................78
     Doing primary research to get the best information ..............79
     Putting together a customer profile ................82
Forecasting Demand: Tough but Crucial ....................83
Triangulating to Demand ..................................85
     Using substitute products and services to gauge demand ..............85
     Interviewing customers and intermediaries ..........85
     Going into limited production with a test market ...........86

## Chapter 7: Designing Products and Services for a
## New Marketplace ........................................87

Zeroing-in on a New Product ..............................88
     Become an inventor .................................88
     Team with an inventor ..............................89
     License an invention ...............................89
Thinking Realistically about Product Development .........91
     Finding the money ..................................91
     Developing new products: The process ...............95
Moving Fast to Prototype Stage ...........................99
     Designing right ....................................99
     Sourcing your materials ...........................101
     Making your product ...............................102
The One-Minute Product Plan .............................102

## Chapter 8: Protecting Your Products and Services ..............103

Patenting Your Better Mousetrap .........................104
     Timing is everything ..............................104
     Is it patentable? .................................105
     Types of patents ..................................106
     The patent process ................................107
Copyrighting Your Original Work of Authorship ...........110
     Claiming copyright ................................110
     Things you can't copyright ........................111
Protecting Your Logo: A Trademark .......................112
Guarding Your Interests .................................113
     Contracts .........................................113
     Nondisclosure agreements ..........................114

Strategies for Protecting Your IP ................................................115
    Offensive strategies ...........................................................116
    Defensive strategies ..........................................................118

**Chapter 9: Getting Products and Services to Customers: Distribution** .............................................**121**

Outsourcing Logistics ...................................................................122
Creating Your Distribution Strategy .........................................123
Distributing through Market Channels ......................................125
    Consumer channels ..........................................................125
    Industrial channels ...........................................................127
Using Intermediaries .....................................................................127
Evaluating Your Channel ...............................................................128
    The cost of the channel ....................................................128
    Channel coverage ..............................................................130
    Distribution control ..........................................................130

**Chapter 10: Putting Together Your Start-up Team** ...............**131**

Finding Your Start-up Partners ...................................................132
    The rules with family and friends .................................132
    Covering all the bases ......................................................133
    Putting everything in writing .........................................133
    Benchmarking the perfect team .....................................134
Forming a Board of Advisors ......................................................134
    Yes, you need attorneys ..................................................135
    Accountants can help you survive ................................136
    Your banker can be your friend .....................................138
    Don't forget your insurance broker ..............................139
    Putting together an advisory board ..............................140
Forming a Board of Directors ......................................................142
    Deciding when you need a formal board ......................142
    Creating a personal board — your mentors .................144
Pulling Yourself Up by the Bootstraps .....................................144
    Outsourcing savvy .............................................................146
    Leasing your staff ..............................................................146

**Chapter 11: Assessing Your Start-up Financial Needs** ...........**149**

Estimating How Much You Will Sell ...........................................150
    Getting a three-way fix on demand ...............................151
    Forecasting your sales .....................................................151
Calculating How Much You Will Spend .....................................152
    Cost of goods produced ..................................................152
    General and administrative expenses ...........................153
    Taxes ....................................................................................153
Preparing Financial Statements ..................................................153
    Calculating profit and loss — the income statement ....154
    Forecasting your cash flow .............................................157
Planning to Break Even .................................................................162

Figuring How Much Money You Need .......................................162
    Taking a virtual tour of your business ..........................163
    Looking at the money you
        will need to spend ...................................................164
    Thinking about your business in stages ........................165
Putting It All Together ...............................................................165
    The one-minute financial plan .......................................168

## Part III: Creating a Company ........................ 169

### Chapter 12: Getting Ready to Do a Business Plan ..............171
Drawing a Conclusion about Feasibility ..................................171
Looking at the Who, What, Where, and Why of Business Plans ..........172
    Addressing the needs of your audience .......................173
    Using a guideline-outline ..............................................177
Getting Started with a Vision .....................................................181
Finding the Big Mission ..............................................................182
Looks Count: Preparing and Presenting the Plan ...................182
    Making the plan look good ............................................183
    Presenting your plan ......................................................184
    The one-minute business plan .......................................186

### Chapter 13: Finding Money to Start and Grow Your Venture ......187
Starting with a Plan ....................................................................188
    When you're financing a traditional business ...............189
    When you're financing for e-commerce ........................190
Tapping Friends, Family, and Lovers ........................................191
Finding an Angel ..........................................................................192
    How to spot an angel .....................................................192
    How to deal with angels .................................................193
Daring to Use Venture Capital ...................................................194
    Calculating the real cost of money ...............................195
    Tracking the venture capital process ...........................196
Selling Stock to the Public: An IPO ...........................................198
    Considering the advantages and disadvantages
        of going public ..........................................................199
    Deciding to go for it .......................................................200
Finding Other Ways to Finance Growth ....................................202

### Chapter 14: Starting with the Right
### Legal Structure ...........................................205
Deciding on the Best Legal Form for Your Business ...............205
    Understanding the factors
        that affect your choice .............................................206
Going It Alone: The Sole Proprietorship ..................................207
    Advantages of sole proprietorships .............................207
    Disadvantages of sole proprietorships ........................208

Choosing a Partner: The Partnership ..................................................209
    Forming a partnership ............................................................210
    The partnership agreement ....................................................210
Going for the Gold: The Corporation ..............................................211
    Enjoying the benefits of a corporation ..............................212
    Weighing the risks ..................................................................213
    Where and how to incorporate ..........................................214
Looking for Flexibility: The S Corporation, the LLC, and the
    Nonprofit Corporation ............................................................215
    Sizing up the S Corporation ..................................................215
    Comparing the S Corporation with the LLC ..................216
    Making profits in a nonprofit organization ....................217
Benchmarking Your Best Choice ......................................................218

**Chapter 15: Developing a Business Model for a Digital World ....219**

Producing Several Models from One Product or Service ............219
    Your consulting company ......................................................220
    Your software company ........................................................220
    Your movie theater ................................................................221
    Your restaurant ......................................................................221
Looking for Another Gillette ............................................................222
Improving on the Bricks-and-Mortar Model ..................................223
    Providing a service with an upside ....................................223
    Making money while you sleep ............................................227
Flying High and Fast with Internet Models ....................................228
    Taking a chance on clicks and hits ....................................228
    Using a subscription-based model ....................................229
    Growing a hybrid with clicks and bricks ..........................230
    Having it all with clicks and mortar ..................................231
    Thinking small ........................................................................232

*Part IV: Growing a Company* ........................................*233*

**Chapter 16: Planning for Growth ...........................235**

Identifying Factors That Affect Growth ..........................................236
Starting with Some Basic Growth Strategies ................................237
Growing within Your Current Market ..............................................239
    Building out your customer base ........................................239
    Developing your market ........................................................239
    Developing your product ......................................................241
    Branding your company ........................................................241
Growing within Your Industry ..........................................................242
    Moving vertically in your channel ....................................243
    Moving horizontally in your channel ................................243
    Creating a network in your industry ..................................244

Diversifying Outside Your Industry .............................................244
    Capitalizing on the synergy of like businesses .................244
    Acquiring an unrelated business ......................................245
Going Global to Grow .................................................................245
    Deciding if you're ready ..................................................246
    Finding great global markets .........................................247
    Getting help ..................................................................248
    Using the Internet to go global .....................................249
Growing as a High Tech Company ..............................................250
    Finding the early adopters .............................................251
    Getting to mainstream adoption ....................................251
    Surviving mainstream adoption .....................................251

**Chapter 17: Organizing Your Business for Growth** .............253
Moving from Entrepreneurship to Professional Management ..............254
    Discovering your company's culture ..............................255
    Developing a human resource policy .............................256
Organizing for Speed and Flexibility .........................................258
    Organizing around teams ..............................................258
    Taking your company online ..........................................260
Finding and Keeping Great People .............................................261
    Recruiting the right people ...........................................262
    Choosing the right candidate ........................................264
    Recruiting an experienced CEO for an e-business ..........267

**Chapter 18: Reaching the Customer** ..........................269
Marketing to Customers, One at a Time ....................................270
    Using the customer to build your market strategy .......271
    Using technology to build your market strategy ..........272
    Using the Internet to build a market strategy ..............273
Creating a Marketing Plan .........................................................276
    Preparing to plan ..........................................................277
    Writing a one-paragraph marketing plan ......................277
    Defining your customer ..................................................279
    Doing your market research ...........................................280
    Building and protecting your brand ...............................280
Keeping Your Best Customers ....................................................282
    Creating your promotional mix ......................................283
    Building relationships ....................................................286

**Chapter 19: Proving You Can Make Money: The Financial Plan** ...289
Identifying the Components of a Successful Financial Plan ................290
    Starting with goals ........................................................291
    Looking at capital budgeting .........................................291
    Budgeting for operations ...............................................292
    Financial forecasts and ratios .......................................294

Building the Financial Statements ........................................295
    Reviewing the income statement ................................295
    Developing the balance sheet ....................................296
    Creating the cash flow from operations statement .........298
    Preparing the statement ...........................................299
    The bottom line on cash ...........................................301
Using Financial Ratios to Judge Performance .....................302
    Liquidity ratios .....................................................303
    Profitability ratios .................................................304
    Leverage ratios .....................................................304
Cash Planning: Managing Your Working Capital .................305
    Planning for accounts receivable ..............................305
    Managing your accounts payable .............................309

**Chapter 20: Planning for Things That Go Bump in the Night** ......**311**
Preparing for the Unknown: When Bad Things Happen to
    Good Companies ....................................................312
    Protecting your company from lawsuits ....................312
    Handling a decline in sales .....................................314
    Surviving the loss of a key employee .......................315
    Dealing with the economy and Uncle Sam .................316
    Coping with product liability ...................................317
Harvesting the Wealth with a Graceful Exit .......................318
    Selling your business .............................................319
    Selling out but staying involved ..............................320
When You Think You Can't Exit Gracefully ........................323
    Facing bankruptcy ..................................................324
    Avoiding bankruptcy ...............................................326
Stepping Back from the Brink ..........................................326

*Part V: The Part of Tens* .............................................**329**

**Chapter 21: Ten Reasons Not to Start a Business** ...............**331**
Because Everyone Is Doing It ...........................................331
Because You Want to Be a Millionaire ...............................331
Because You're Looking for a Secure Job ...........................332
Because You Don't Want to Work for Someone Else .............332
Because You Just Came into Some Money ..........................333
Because If the Kid Down the Street Did It, So Can You .........333
Because You Want to Give Everyone in Your Family a Job ....333
Because You've Got a Great Idea .......................................334
Because It's Too Risky ....................................................334
Start a Business Because It's What You Most Want to Do .....334

**Chapter 22: Ten Ways to Spark Your Entrepreneurial Spirit** . . . . . .335

Start Reading about Great New Businesses ...........................................335
Join a Community Business Organization ...........................................336
Hang around a University Business School ...........................................336
Tell a Friend ...........................................337
Do a Feasibility Study ...........................................337
Leave Your Job (or Get Laid Off) ...........................................337
Discover an Industry ...........................................337
Spend Time with an Entrepreneur ...........................................338
Find a Mentor ...........................................338
Do Something — Anything ...........................................338

**Chapter 23: Ten Ways to Use the Internet to
Grow Your Business** . . . . . . . . . . . . . . . . . . . . . . . . . . . . . . . . . . . . . . . .339

Get Started Quickly ...........................................339
Become a Virtual Business ...........................................340
Join a Network of Business Colleagues ...........................................340
Stay in Touch with Your Customers ...........................................341
Communicate with Your Strategic Partners ...........................................341
Gather Competitive Intelligence ...........................................341
Promote Your Company ...........................................342
Reach Global Customers ...........................................342
Create an Intelligent Company ...........................................343
Develop New Products and Services ...........................................343

**Chapter 24: Ten Best Resources for Gathering
Competitive ntelligence** . . . . . . . . . . . . . . . . . . . . . . . . . . . . . . . . . .345

Pounding the Pavement ...........................................345
Shopping Your Competitors' Turf ...........................................346
Skimming the Industry Journals ...........................................346
Surfing the Web ...........................................347
About.com ...........................................347
OneSource.com ...........................................347
IndustryLink.com ...........................................347
Dun & Bradstreet ...........................................348
Hoover's Online ...........................................348
Lexis-Nexis ...........................................348
Government Sources ...........................................348

*Index* ................................................*349*

# Introduction

● ● ● ● ● ● ● ● ● ● ● ● ● ● ● ● ● ● ● ● ● ● ● ● ● ● ● ● ● ● ● ● ● ● ● ● ● ● ● ● ● ● ● ● ● ●

*E*ntrepreneurship is a personal thing. It isn't really about money or start-ing businesses — sure, entrepreneurs like to make money and start busi-nesses, but that's not the reason they are entrepreneurs. It's much more than that. For entrepreneurs, it's about having a passion for doing something you love; that's the entrepreneurial spirit.

Entrepreneurs like to do things that excite the world, bend the rules a bit, and make us look at something in an entirely new way. They are opportunis-tic, finding new possibilities at every turn. So entrepreneurship is also about creativity, innovation, and change.

Although stereotyped as risk takers, the truth is that entrepreneurs take calcu-lated risks — they are not the gamblers people make them out to be. In their businesses, they assess their options and choose their course based on their probability of success. They're not afraid to fail because they tend to measure their real success by how many times they learn from their mistakes and go on to try again. Entrepreneurship involves challenge, persistence, and planning.

These days, finding any aspect of life that isn't in a state of change is difficult. In the world of business, you discover companies going in and out of busi-ness, customer loyalty as ephemeral as the wind, jobs disappearing overnight and replaced by jobs that never existed before, and technology changing the way we do things in every aspect of our lives. Times are exciting if you enjoy change and know how to deal with it. Dealing with change is one of the important things entrepreneurs do best. They thrive on it because they know that with change comes opportunity. Those kinds of opportunities are among the many reasons to think about developing the entrepreneurial spirit and mindset.

## How Entrepreneurship Has Changed

For the past two decades or longer, entrepreneurship has been viewed simply as a process for starting new businesses. Only recently have those of us who study this phenomenon concluded that entrepreneurship is more impor-tantly about an opportunistic mindset and spirit. That's a significant distinc-tion, because it means that everyone has the potential to benefit from understanding the mind of the entrepreneur. Whether you work in a large cor-poration, own a business, run a nonprofit organization, or are at home raising children, you can find opportunities to improve your situation by applying this way of thinking to your life and work.

So, my approach to entrepreneurship starts with a mindset and spirit. Then it guides you in discovering the strategies, skills, and tools you must find and use to turn ideas into opportunities and opportunities into successful business concepts. You find out that being small and flexible has distinct advantages in the new digital economy, that you can have a global presence with the click of a mouse button, and that it's customers who define what a business is, what products and services it produces, and how successful it becomes.

# How Entrepreneurs Define Success

If I ask you to describe a successful entrepreneur, chances are you'll point to the size of his or her business, how much money it makes, how much its investors earn. Those certainly are ways to describe a successful business, but entrepreneurs typically take a much more personal view when defining success. Ask Wally Amos of Uncle Noname Cookies, and he tells you that success is "turning lemons into lemonade." Others say that being happy with what you're doing and feeling like you're accomplishing something is a measure of success. Every entrepreneur's definition of success is different and personal, but in the listing below I categorize the more common responses so you can see that success is not always about money.

- ✔ **Purpose:** Entrepreneurs must feel a sense of purpose or direction in what they're doing. Success is a journey not a destination, but knowing the direction you're heading and why seems to be a common component of success.

- ✔ **Failure — the other half of success:** No one denies that life is full of ups and downs. Most entrepreneurs experience failure of one sort or another, but knowing that failure is a possibility doesn't frighten them. If trying something doesn't have the potential for failure, it isn't worth doing because no risk is attached to it. Anyone can try something that is guaranteed to be a success. That's why entrepreneurs find opportunity where no one else does; they're not afraid to go where the risk is.

- ✔ **Sense of satisfaction:** Most successful entrepreneurs are doing what they love, so it doesn't feel like work.

- ✔ **No free lunch:** Success comes from hard work. Even entrepreneurs you read about, you know, the ones who seem to have appeared out of nowhere to become hugely successful, have spent years you don't hear about struggling to become that overnight success.

In *Entrepreneurship For Dummies,* you discover that entrepreneurship is an exciting, sometimes scary, roller-coaster ride — a way of life that you may decide to enjoy.

# About This Book

*Entrepreneurship For Dummies* contains practical information, tips, and check-lists that can be used by anyone who aspires to start a business, work as an entrepreneur inside a large corporation, or just become more opportunistic by acquiring an entrepreneurial attitude. It doesn't matter whether you have ever owned a business or even have any business experience. You can use this book to think about the world of the entrepreneur and decide if it's right for you.

This book is definitely grounded in the real world. It is based on research I have conducted in the field of entrepreneurship, the work I have done with hundreds of entrepreneurs starting new ventures, and my own experiences as an entrepreneur, so there are no hypothetical situations here. I have pulled together the best information, the best tips, and the best examples of how to make entrepreneurship work for you.

*Entrepreneurship For Dummies* is a guide to everything you ever wanted to know about the entrepreneur and the entrepreneurial process. Don't know where to get started? I'll help you. Don't know how to find an opportunity and test it? I'll give you the information you need to put yourself in a position to find that great business idea and then test it in the marketplace before you commit to starting a business to turn that idea into reality.

This book is organized so that whatever you're looking for is easy to find.

 ✔ Suppose you want to figure out how much money you need to start your business. Just go to that chapter and the specific section you need, and you'll find exactly what you're looking for.

 ✔ Or, if you really want to get serious about becoming an entrepreneur, you can start on page one and work your way to the end.

Whichever route you choose, I'm certain that this book and its real-world examples are going to inspire you to think about entrepreneurship as a way of life.

# Foolish Assumptions

Before I began this book, I made some assumptions about you — the reader. (I know that's not always wise, but I'm an entrepreneur — I'm not afraid to take a risk!) I assumed that you want to understand what entrepreneurs do to create those exciting e-businesses you read about and see on TV. And I also assumed that you're ready to make an investment in your future. Finally, I assumed that you want to know how to use entrepreneurial skills and attitudes in whatever endeavor you decide to undertake.

## Icons Used in This Book

I use little pictures, called icons, next to blocks of text throughout the book. They're designed to draw your attention to things I want you to remember.

A good idea, trick, or shortcut that can save you time and money.

A piece of information you shouldn't forget.

A tip that can help you avoid disasters.

An example from the real world to illustrate my point.

# How This Book Is Organized

*Entrepreneurship For Dummies* is organized into five parts, and each chapter within a part goes into detail on a specific topic. This organization makes it easier for you to find what you're looking for. I think I've covered everything you need to know to put together a winning entrepreneurial strategy.

## Part I: Getting Started in Entrepreneurship

In this part, you get an introduction to the world of the entrepreneur and the new environment in which businesses are being started. You also consider how entrepreneurs discover those great opportunities and find out how to increase your creative abilities so you can become more opportunistic yourself. Finally, this part deals with how to turn an opportunity into a great business concept that you can test in the marketplace.

## Part II: Developing Your Business Concept

This part gets you started in the nuts and bolts of feasibility analysis, which is a way to test your business opportunity in the real world before you spend time and money starting a business to make it happen. In this part are lots of strategies and tactics for researching your industry and target market, and for testing your customer, product or service, and distribution channel. You also find out how to put together an effective start-up team and figure out how much money it will take to start your venture.

## Part III: Creating a Company

Once you've determined that you have a business concept that is feasible, you need to create a company to execute the plan for your business. In this part, you find out everything you want to know about business plans and how to develop them. You also discover the best legal form for your business and the best business model to make money. And speaking of money, you also find out a variety of different ways to tap into financial resources, so that you can start and grow your business.

## Part IV: Growing a Company

One of the byproducts of a successful start-up is growth. This part focuses on how to take your business beyond start-up to successfully grow it to a new level. You discover how to plan for growth, organize your business so that it can handle growth, develop a marketing plan that gets your message to customers, create a financial plan that tracks your business's health, and plan for those unexpected events that happen to every business.

## Part V: The Part of Tens

In this part, I give you some of my best tips for reasoning why you maybe shouldn't start a business, motivating yourself to get started with a business idea if you should start a business, and using technology to grow your business. I finish this part with the best industry resources on the Web to help you gather competitive intelligence.

# How to Use This Book

If you want the most from this book, I suggest you start at the beginning and work your way to the end. This book contains a wealth of information for you to explore, and I don't want you to miss any of it.

But, if you already have some business experience and not much time (like so many of us), you can skip from topic to topic depending on what interests you. The Table of Contents is organized to help you find what you need easily and quickly.

No matter how you approach this book, I'm sure you'll enjoy it. If you have any questions or comments, I'd like to hear from you. Please contact me at `kallen@marshall.usc.edu`.

# Part I
# Getting Started in Entrepreneurship

**The 5th Wave** By Rich Tennant

"Oh, we're doing just great. Philip and I are selling decorative jelly jars on the Web. I run the Web site and Philip sort of controls the inventory."

# In this part . . .

The best way to understand the world of the entrepreneur is to jump right in and swim with it. This part gives you a quick introduction to that world and starts you on the road to changing your mindset — your attitudes and way of looking at the world — to a more entrepreneurial, opportunistic one. You also get your first taste of how entrepreneurs come up with those great business ideas and test them in the market before they take the leap and start a business.

# Chapter 1

# What's an Entrepreneur, Anyway?

### In This Chapter
▶ Understanding what entrepreneurship really means
▶ Discovering the many types of entrepreneurs
▶ Deciding to become an entrepreneur

The term *entrepreneur* has been overused, misused, abused, and tacked onto practically anything and everything from owning a business to holding a particular view of the world.

Everyone from the corner shoe repair guy to the hotshot software designer claims to be an entrepreneur.

Entrepreneurs grace the covers of popular magazines and are guests on TV shows beamed to thousands of other entrepreneur hopefuls.

As a matter of fact, entrepreneurs come in an amazing variety of types and styles. And they *are* a unique breed. The ventures they create disrupt the economy. That's because an entrepreneur changes the way you and I do things — usually for the better.

Entrepreneurs create *value* in the marketplace in a wonderful variety of interesting new ways. This book shows you how they do it, so that you can, too.

## Understanding Entrepreneurship

Who exactly are these people at the center of *entrepreneurship?* In simple terms, an entrepreneur is someone who creates a new opportunity in the world of business and assembles the resources necessary to successfully exploit that opportunity — money, people, and organization. This broad definition is essential to include all the different kinds of entrepreneurial ventures and different ways for you to approach entrepreneurship.

If you want to become an entrepreneur, the odds are pretty good that you can. Check this statistic: One out of three U.S. households is home to at least one adult with some level of experience as a founder or owner in an entrepreneurial or small business venture. It's true. What's more, in nearly 7 million U.S. households, one or more persons is involved in a new start-up business venture. That's a lot of new entrepreneurs every year!

But even those figures pale in comparison to what happened during the past five years. The world of entrepreneurship was given a new shot of energy by the amazing expansion of the World Wide Web. In 1993, no Web sites existed on the Internet. By June 1996, 200,000 sites had been launched, but by September 1997, only 15 months later, the Internet was home to 1,400,000 Web sites and more than 25,000,000 users. In early 2000, 15.7 million domain names were registered on the Internet.

As you can see, the Internet and e-commerce have turned the world of business upside down in only a few short years. Entrepreneurs on the Web have changed the way people spend their time, find information, meet other people, take care of personal matters, and even start a business.

## Recognizing an entrepreneurial venture

You can spot an entrepreneurial business by the way it shakes up the market and changes the way things are done. Look at what Starbuck's did to coffee. The Seattle coffee company transformed the everyday routine of having a cup of coffee into a totally new experience, attracting millions of people to the social pleasure of enjoying coffee. Starbuck's *value proposition* — that customers would enjoy an experience with their top grade coffee — permitted the company to charge more than consumers had ever paid for coffee before. The result was a rapidly growing company with an international scope. That's what I mean by entrepreneurship. Entrepreneurial ventures are usually improvements on things we're familiar with. Entrepreneurs usually carve out little market niches at first with a relatively small number of customers. They start with limited resources and differentiate their businesses through their personal efforts. If they move fast and run the business right, they can gain a foothold in the market before they have to go head-to-head with much bigger competitors.

Entrepreneurs are ordinary people who do extraordinary things. They take everyday ideas and give them some magic. You don't need a lot of experience or resources to be an entrepreneur. You need passion and persistence.

# Check your entrepreneurial instincts

Just for fun, take this little quiz to see if you have the right stuff to become an entrepreneur. But don't take the results too seriously. I assure you that your answers will not determine whether you can succeed as an entrepreneur, but they may help you decide if entrepreneurship is right for you. The answers provided are the most common answers given by entrepreneurs.

1. Are you:

   - Married?
   - Single?
   - Widowed?
   - Divorced?

2. Are you:

   - Male?
   - Female?

3. Why do you want to start a business?

   - To make a lot of money
   - To be independent
   - To give myself a job
   - To gain power
   - To become famous

4. How comfortable are you with uncertainty?

   - Very comfortable
   - Somewhat comfortable
   - Not comfortable

5. To become successful as an entrepreneur, what will you need?

   - Money
   - Luck
   - Hard work

   - A good idea
   - All of these

6. Concerning your willingness to take risk, are you :

   - A high risk taker
   - A moderate risk taker
   - One who avoids risk

**Answers**

1. The most common response is _married._ This doesn't mean that all entrepreneurs are married when they start their businesses or stay married for the duration (that's a different question). It does appear, however, that many entrepreneurs are married by the time they start a venture, possibly because having a spouse gives them a steady income while they're risking time and capital starting a new venture. However, these days, you notice growing numbers of single entrepreneurs starting dot-com ventures at early ages.

2. It still is true that more men start new ventures than women, but that too is changing. Women are starting businesses at a much faster rate than men, typically while they're in their 20s before they get married and start families or after their children are grown.

3. The common reason entrepreneurs give for wanting to start a business is to be independent. For most entrepreneurs, money is a by-product of operating a venture they are passionate about. However, money motivates a certain class of entrepreneurs. And when the media touts the riches of dot-com entrepreneurs, people flock to e-commerce as a possible way to quickly create wealth. But even the allure of quick riches is changing as venture capitalists shift their focus to

_(continued)_

*(continued)*

technology companies that create value and make a profit within about three years.

4. Most entrepreneurs are comfortable with uncertainty, because they understand intuitively that uncertainty brings opportunity with it. In general, people who must have a high degree of predictability in their lives are uncomfortable in the world of the entrepreneur.

5. To be successful as an entrepreneur, you probably need a little of all these things — money, luck, hard work (you need lots of that), and a good idea. Entrepreneurs will tell you, however, that they make their own luck by taking calculated risks and building a network of contacts.

6. Entrepreneurs are neither high risk takers nor do they avoid risk. They are moderate or calculated risk takers. They manage risk and make decisions based on what they believe their chances of success to be. Entrepreneurship is inherently risky, but so is driving a car and most everything else we do in life that has any significance. Entrepreneurs are just better at judging risk and finding ways to manage it.

## *Putting together the pieces of an entrepreneurial venture*

Entrepreneurial ventures are complex animals. They have numerous parts, and the parts interact in a variety of ways. Look at Figure 1-1 to see all the major components of the entrepreneurial environment.

Take a closer look at each of the parts:

- **The Entrepreneur:** Though just one component, the entrepreneur is the driving force and coordinator of all the activities, resources, and people that need to be brought together to start a new venture. The entrepreneur's passion and vision give life to the business. The entrepreneur brings to the business experience, education, skills, a value system, and a network of people to rely on for help in getting the business started.

- **Legal, Government:** Every aspect of an entrepreneurial venture is affected by the law to some degree, from the legal form of the venture (see Chapter 14), to the intellectual property it develops (see Chapter 8), to the contracts it writes, and to the employees it hires (see Chapter 17). Government — federal, state, and local — adds regulations to the mix in the form of taxes, fees, tariffs, and penalties for non-compliance.

- **Suppliers:** Suppliers provide, among many other things, inventory, raw materials, parts, and even labor. Suppliers also help finance the new business by providing lines of credit and extending payment periods.

- **Competitors:** Competitors help determine if the market is hostile or friendly to the new venture. They have a huge impact on pricing, marketing strategy, and distribution-channel strategy (see Chapter 9).

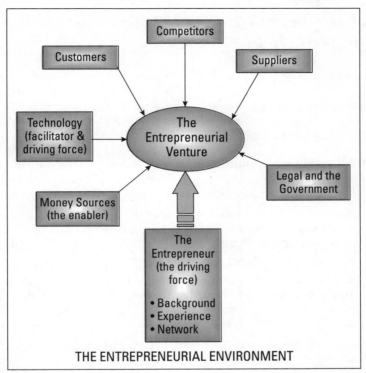

**Figure 1-1:**
The entre-
preneurial
venture.

✔ **Customers:** Customers are the lifeblood of the business — without them,
no business exists. Customers influence everything the business does,
from the development of new products and services, to designing
market strategies, to support services, and to the nature and quality of
customer service.

✔ **Technology:** Only a few years ago, no one described technology as a
facilitator and driving force of an entrepreneurial venture. But now, technology is a prime facilitator of business processes, creating efficiencies
and capabilities that businesses never experienced before. Think about
it: How many businesses five years ago expected to be conducting some
or all of their business on the Internet today?

✔ **Money:** For most entrepreneurial ventures, money is the enabler. When
all the other components of a successful business concept are in place —
customer, value proposition, product/service, and distribution (you find
out about these in Chapter 4) — then money comes into play as a
resource that makes everything happen. I say "for most entrepreneurial
ventures" for a reason. Some entrepreneurial ventures, like those in
biotechnology where product development times are long and costly, are
naturally driven by money. Without sufficient capital, you can't survive
the research and development phase long enough to actually put
together a venture to commercialize the technology.

## Distinguishing entrepreneurial ventures from small businesses

As this chapter begins, I suggest that many small, start-up ventures are likely to be called *entrepreneurial* even if they aren't. Let's face it, nearly every new business starts small, so physical size alone doesn't separate entrepreneurs from businesspeople who simply want to support a lifestyle. The differences lie much deeper. In general, people who start entrepreneurial ventures are

- ✔ **Driven by opportunity.** Entrepreneurs see opportunities where others don't. They strive to satisfy a need that is not being served, or create a new product or technology that changes the way things are done.

- ✔ **Focused on innovation.** Entrepreneurs are creative and find ways to innovate in every aspect of their business, from the product or service, to marketing and distribution, to the business model (see Chapter 17).

- ✔ **Determined to create new value by shaking up the marketplace.** Entrepreneurs change the economic environment of the marketplace they enter. One example: Instead of pulling trained workers from other businesses, entrepreneurs are inclined to create entirely new jobs and new opportunities. Thus they add new value.

- ✔ **Determined to grow.** Entrepreneurs seek to grow their businesses and exploit opportunity to the fullest.

By comparison, people who start small, what I call *lifestyle businesses,* generally do so to provide a job for themselves and an income for their families. These businesses tend to remain small and geographically bound — they serve a local community. Most small businesses have the potential to grow and innovate and become entrepreneurial ventures, but their founders typically don't want to do that. The corner shoe repair shop, the pizza parlor, the consultant in business for herself, and the local manufacturer of rebuilt engines are examples of small, lifestyle businesses. And although such businesses represent the vast majority of all businesses in the U.S., they are not the prime source of new jobs in the economy. Entrepreneurs generate the jobs.

So, decide what kind of business you want to start, because that decision will affect all the others. If you plan to build an enterprise with a global presence, you'll set different goals and make different decisions than if you want to confine your activity to the community.

# Tasting the Many Flavors of Entrepreneurship

If anyone tells you that all entrepreneurs take risks, that all entrepreneurs are optimists, that all entrepreneurs are anything, ignore this wisdom. No traits define all entrepreneurs. You can find a variety of entrepreneurial types in the marketplace — they are as diverse a group of people as you'll ever see. But they have some things in common. For example, surveys find that virtually all entrepreneurs have cofounders, so starting the venture as a team is important.

*Inc.* magazine, in a recent study of the fastest growing private companies, found these facts about entrepreneurs and their ventures:

- ✔ Median age of entrepreneur at time of company founding, 33

- ✔ Average time the entrepreneur spends on the computer per week, 20 hours

- ✔ Average number of vacation days the entrepreneur takes per year, 13

- ✔ Average percentage of revenues from international sales, 6 percent

What these few facts tell you is that the average entrepreneur is young, technically savvy, works hard, and builds a global business. In the following sections of this chapter, you find out about the many ways to become an entrepreneur.

## The home-based entrepreneur

More than 14 million people are involved in home-based businesses. Why is starting a business from home so popular? I find several reasons:

- ✔ Because of technology, in particular the Internet, people can run their business from anywhere just by going on-line.

- ✔ Because more resources are available to entrepreneurial businesses than ever. Web sites like Microsoft's bCentral (www.bcentral.com) and AllBusiness (www.allbusiness.com) provide much of the information and resources a growing entrepreneurial business needs to operate successfully.

- ✔ Because tax laws have grown friendlier to home-based businesses. On your personal tax return, you can deduct the portion of your home devoted to business along with all your business expenses.

Sometimes entrepreneurs start from home for an obvious reason: The rent is cheap. Jack Panzarella moved back home at age 21 so he could realize his dream of commercializing an invention. Panzarella is a rare blend of inventor and entrepreneur — the two don't often go together in the same person. Usually, inventors team with entrepreneurs to get their inventions to market.

Panzarella's parents, both entrepreneurs, welcomed their inventor son back into the fold. The young man was working as a repossessor of cars when he came up with the invention. One of the cars he reclaimed had a neon tube attached to its undercarriage. The glow looked terrific at auto shows when the car was parked and the wiring was plugged into an electrical outlet. Panzarella wondered if there wasn't a way to run the neon off the car battery.

After much trial and error, he found a way to do it. Promoting customer awareness, he drove his car with the Undercar Neon around town. Onlookers swarmed around asking where they could buy the light set. Slowly, Panzarella put together a network of dealers to carry his product and landed two big mail order catalog accounts.

With his business launched, Panzarella didn't waste any time. He created more products with the neon theme. In 1998, he introduced neon lights for in-line skates. His company has three divisions, Undercar Neon, Sport-Neon, and Home-Neon, carrying a line of 200 products and employing 200 people. Sales are in excess of $16 million a year. Panzarella obviously doesn't work from home any more — his company is one of New Jersey's fastest growing companies. You can learn more about this business by visiting its Web site at `www.streetglow.com/site/company`.

## The virtual entrepreneur

The Internet has given rise to a new kind of entrepreneur, the virtual entrepreneur — businesses that have no traditional, bricks-and-mortar location for customers to visit. Like Amazon.com, some may have employees, offices, and warehouse space, but their only contact with customers occurs in cyberspace. Some virtual entrepreneurs do everything in cyberspace — work with strategic partners, employ experts, develop products, and deliver the goods to customers, all via the Internet.

Carley Roney wouldn't go through her 1993 wedding again for anything — that is, unless she had the benefit of her own company, The Knot Inc. Planning her own nuptials, Roney quickly realized that the fairy-tale wedding preparations portrayed in bridal magazines don't paint an accurate picture of what most brides-to-be experience. Roney wanted to solve that problem. She came up with an Internet-based solution to the real problems people face when planning weddings. She calls her Web site TheKnot.com, and it has become the source of information and ideas for anything related to tying the knot.

In 1996, Roney and spouse presented their concept to America Online (AOL). The first round of seed money arrived shortly thereafter, and the business has provided an exciting ride ever since. TheKnot.com receives more than a million first-time visitors every month. They can search for everything from wedding gowns to cakes. The site also has its own gift registry. While the company is a virtual one, Roney & Partners are doing a few things to dip their toes into the real world. They introduced a magazine, negotiated a three-book deal with a publisher, and are at work on a series for PBS. You can learn more about this company by visiting its Web site at www.theknot.com.

## The serial entrepreneur

Many entrepreneurs enjoy recognizing an opportunity and turning it into a business, but they don't enjoy running a business day-to-day. They prefer, instead, to leave that job to others who are more capable. Once the business is up and running, these entrepreneurs move on to the next opportunity.

Wayne Huizenga is the classical serial entrepreneur. Starting with a single garbage truck (which he drove himself), he grew his company truck by truck to become Waste Management, the largest garbage hauler and waste management service in the world. But on the way to reaching that entrepreneurial success, Huizenga had another idea, prompted by a conversation with a friend about the video rental business. That conversation led to Blockbuster Entertainment, Huizenga's second billion-dollar business. Upon selling Blockbuster to Time-Warner, this serial entrepreneur decided to professionalize the used car industry by founding Auto Nation, his third billion-dollar venture.

## The traditional entrepreneur

Traditional entrepreneurs start bricks-and-mortar businesses and build them to a point where they can harvest the value they have created. Before the Internet and e-commerce changed the face of things, that's how entrepreneurship usually worked. Actually, the traditional model is still the most common, but an increasing number of these mainstream business owners reinvent their enterprise by adding a Web component.

Jack Shin started a little lifestyle business in 1977 called Camera World, in downtown Portland, Oregon. As Bronwyn Fryer reports in *Inc. Technology,* Shin worked painstakingly to build his little business. He targeted the serious photographer and built strong relationships with his suppliers. In addition to the retail outlet, Shin developed a mail order catalog, which became so popular that it accounted for 70 percent of the business's revenues. In 1992, Shin computerized the fulfillment and shipping function of his company, and this gave him better information about his customers. Camera World was wisely built on customer relationships and repeat sales.

At some point in every business, it's time to infuse the business with new life. That happened for Camera World around 1995, when sales flattened and digital cameras were on the horizon. Shin, who had never taken a vacation, decided to sell the company. The buyer, Alessandro Mina, owned an investment fund whose goal was to take old-fashioned companies and turn them into high-flying Internet companies. Camera World was perfect for him because it had an established and happy customer base that was accustomed to purchasing products via mail order, it had back-end systems that worked, and it was a profitable company. Mina and his partners bought Camera World Co. and named the Internet arm cameraworld.com.

Camera World's annual revenues grew from $80 million in 1998 to more than $115 million in 1999. You can check them out at www.cameraworld.com.

# Deciding to Become an Entrepreneur

This chapter gives you a taste of what entrepreneurship is all about. Are you still interested? Good! It's time to introduce you to the skills you need to succeed. The one thing that I can't give you is the passion, that fire in the belly, that certain something that keeps you going when all the odds appear to be against you. Entrepreneurs have it; so do great people in every profession. If you feel the passion, it's time for you to get started.

## Consider your personal goals

If the business you launch doesn't complement your personal values and goals, it won't be a source of satisfaction to you, and chances are, you won't be as successful as you may be in an area that you care deeply about. Before starting a new business, ask yourself the questions that follow. They can help you know yourself better and point you toward the right match.

### Why do you want to start a business?

I know this is a deep question, but it's important and fundamental to your success as an entrepreneur. If, for example, you're thinking that starting a business provides financial security, you need to remember that most entrepreneurs take no money out of the business for the first year or so, not until they can draw a salary and still leave the company with a positive cash flow (see Chapter 19 for more on cash flow). Likewise, remember that entrepreneurial wealth typically comes from appreciation in the value of the business, which takes time. Sure, some dot-com entrepreneurs strike it rich from the proceeds of initial public offerings. But for the vast majority of businesses, building value and wealth for the founders takes time. I never recommend starting a business just to make money. Start a business that you love (you'll have to spend a lot of time at the business, so you'd better at least like it), give it your best, and you'll increase your chances of creating wealth through your entrepreneurial venture.

### How is starting a business going to affect your personal life?

If you're young and have no special responsibilities other than to yourself, you can afford to take chances that an older person may not be able to take. You can afford to fail and lose money because you have more time to start again. By contrast, if you're starting a business at an older age, you may want to look for an opportunity that pays off faster or that's especially attractive to growth capital from outside sources.

You also want to consider the needs of your family and the responsibilities you have that won't go away when you start a business. You need the support of your family, and they need to understand what starting a business is going to mean to your family life.

### Are you in physical shape to start a business?

A new venture demands long hours and focused effort. Are you up to it? Are you taking care of your health and getting the exercise you need to give you the stamina required to successfully launch this venture? I know too many entrepreneurs who work 14-hour days, 7 days a week to get their new ventures to the survival stage. That kind of work requires that you take care of your health — eat properly and exercise — or you may not be able to enjoy the fruits of your labor.

### What aspects of business make you really uncomfortable?

We all have things that bother us or working situations that we don't particularly enjoy. It's important to recognize what your issues are so that you don't have to confront the same matters on a daily basis. If you don't like to carry any debt, for example, you probably don't want to start a business that requires debt, like the clothing business. How do you feel about being a boss? If you don't like to deal with the issues related to employees, you probably want to consider starting a virtual company that outsources its personnel needs to other companies. If you don't work well under stress, you may want to stay away from advertising or a pure dot-com company. Look carefully at your attitudes about the way you like to work before you start a business.

### How will your feelings about business affect the potential growth of your business?

As an entrepreneur, you have the biggest impact on whether your business grows. You need to examine your attitudes about growth in general and all the ramifications of growing. For example, how do you feel about ownership issues like how much of the company you want to retain as your own? What about your ability to delegate control to other people? Do you plan to build a company that will endure over a long period or do you want to get in and out quickly? Recognizing your attitudes about business helps you steer around the hazards.

## Look ahead

Entrepreneurial opportunities rarely drop out of the blue. You need to cultivate them. I talk about that in Chapter 3 (among other places) — things you can do to enhance your creative powers and coax opportunity out of hiding. I also talk about how to create a business concept and test it in the marketplace, and how to build a business that lets you execute the concept. This book is organized so that you can take a random walk through all the topics, dipping into chapters on a need-to-know basis, whether that means creating a concept, conducting a feasibility study, or plunging into the business planning process. So, welcome aboard! Feel free to go wherever you want — that's the entrepreneurial way.

# Chapter 2

# Moving at the Speed of E-Business

## In This Chapter

▶ Satisfying customers in the Internet environment

▶ Gaining competitive advantage

▶ Leveraging the power of information

▶ Deconstructing and streamlining your entrepreneurial venture

*Y*ou've heard it a thousand times: The Internet has forever changed the way we do business. But what does that really mean to an entrepreneur? If you operate a cute little boutique in Kennebunkport, Maine, how has the Internet changed what you do? If you provide machined parts to a major manufacturer in Oakland, California, why do you have to change the way you operate? Business has been fine so far.

Business also has been fine until recently for a number of bricks-and-mortar enterprises that seemed unlikely to be affected by Internet companies. But that was yesterday. Check this sampling of traditional business types that are being chased by Internet start-ups.

| *Old Business* | *New Business* |
| --- | --- |
| Florist | 1-800-Flowers, www.1800flowers.com |
| Furniture store | Furniture.com, www.furniture.com |
| Gardening store | Garden Escape, www.garden.com |
| Employment agency | Monster.com, www.monster.com |
| Mortgage broker | QuickenMortgage, www.quickenmortgage.com |

I don't say that the Internet affects every business equally, but certainly every business is affected by the *perception* that all things now happen in *Internet time* — almost instantaneously. In this chapter you find new fundamental truths about being in business today. These truths result from the impact of the Internet on businesses and on people's lives.

# Everyone Runs an E-Business

An e-business is one that uses electronic commerce, the Internet, and technology in general to create competitive advantages for itself. When I use the term *e-business,* I'm speaking of the *new* entrepreneurship and the new business models that have resulted from the technology revolution and the Internet. E-businesses are not necessarily pure Internet businesses. They may, in fact, be fairly traditional businesses that have used technology and the Internet to reinvent themselves and to provide their customers with more value. So, the Internet may be just one component of the overall e-business, or it may be the entire business.

Now back to the two questions posed at the beginning of this chapter. If you own that boutique in Kennebunkport, how has the Internet changed what you do? It has made you more accessible to your customers and given you a broader reach. You don't have to wait until customers visit Maine to show them your wares; you can do that from your Web site, giving prospects the flavor of Kennebunkport wherever they are. In addition, the Web site will let you create long-term relationships with your customers so they will return often and recommend your company to their friends.

If you supply machined parts to a major manufacturer, on the other hand, going online may not be your decision alone. Your buyers may require that you go online to receive purchase orders, invoices, and reorders. Huge companies like Wal-Mart require their suppliers — no matter what their size — to link to the Wal-Mart inventory system electronically so that the supplier knows immediately when Wal-Mart is running low on a particular item. The supplier can then restock the big retailer in plenty of time.

The Internet can be an extension of your business or it can be the entire basis of your business. Either way, you need it today to be successful tomorrow.

# The Internet Gives You an Edge

How does the Internet, as a critical component of your technology strategy, give your entrepreneurial venture a competitive advantage? In four big ways:

- The Internet provides easy, fast access to vital information.
- The Internet lets you build sustainable size quickly.
- The Internet encourages the synergy of working with virtual partners.
- The Internet lets your company focus on what it does best, while you outsource other functions to companies that can do those things better.

# Scaling out = Competitive advantage

Businesses are getting smaller in terms of infrastructure and physical assets. Smaller? That may sound contrary to one of the basic tenets of entrepreneurial ventures — that they are growth oriented. The kind of *smaller* that I mean isn't opposed at all to that notion. Entrepreneurial e-businesses form partnerships with other businesses to help them scale out functions that they aren't equipped to handle in-house. The Internet has made it possible to manage all those partnership relationships online, creating time and space for the entrepreneur to concentrate on what she or he does best — the core processes that they do well.

When you start a new venture today, you don't think, "How am I going to make money on the Web?" Instead, you think, "How do I make money in the business I'm starting?" Every great business starts small, with a notion of what the customer wants, how much money it's going to take to build a company to provide what the customer wants, where the money will come from, and how success will be measured.

So, the fundamental economics of start-ups have not changed. What has changed is the speed at which businesses are started, products are developed, and business is transacted. That speed is referred to as *Internet time,* and it has ramifications for everything from product development to service and delivery.

If you want to move as fast as possible, keep your business as small as you can.

# Harnessing technology = Competitive advantage

Recently I've been studying the effects of technology on small businesses and comparing the results against businesses in the same industries that do not use technology as a competitive advantage. The differences are striking. Businesses that use technology to improve their competitive profile see opportunities and potential for their businesses that they were never able to see before.

One engineering design firm I worked with thought of itself as a small shop serving a limited market in its seaside town in Southern California. The company thought its biggest project capabilities were in a range between $5 million to $10 million. However, after installing and learning to use network technology and developing a Web site, the company found that it had sped up its processes enough to begin bidding on much bigger projects. Technology gave the company the speed it needed to compete against much larger companies and to do more complex projects.

Another company I know was offering office suites for lease to business tenants. The owner saw a need for space that provides services that companies need but maybe can't afford to own themselves. She spent some time investigating what technology was able to do for her business and its customers. As it turned out, technology totally transformed her already quite successful, but traditional, property management company into a state-of-the-art solution provider for businesses that need high-speed Internet access, a client/server network, video-conferencing, and so forth. Adding technology to the product/service mix not only made this entrepreneur more efficient and effective, it created value for her customers and a huge competitive advantage in her marketplace.

What's the message in these stories? Companies that attach technology to their processes achieve quantum leaps in productivity, leaps that are hard for competitors to match. That's why we're seeing huge differences in the performance levels of businesses that use technology and those that don't.

## *Turning information into knowledge = Competitive advantage*

You probably know how to get information. What's more, you are probably being bombarded by more information than you care to receive, and it comes from every source imaginable. But are you using that information to build company intelligence — *knowledge?* Are you sharing information across every function of your business so that you can take advantage of the synergy of multiple sources of intelligence? Or are you beginning to think that information in and of itself is almost useless because it's not generally organized, filtered, or put into perspective in terms of the needs of your business?

If you want to build a company that uses its *knowledge* to create a competitive advantage, shift the spotlight away from information and focus it on brains and intelligence. Technology is the enabler in the process of creating knowledge. (Later in this chapter you'll see that at times technology can be a driving force, but that's another matter.) As an entrepreneur who wants to create a successful e-business, you can use technology in four key ways:

- ✔ To leverage knowledge — company intelligence — across the entire company

- ✔ To speed up collaboration among employees, strategic partners, and customers

- ✔ To organize around the customer and to be able to mass customize and mass personalize the products and services you provide

- ✔ To make your operations more efficient

In Chapter 3, I have more to say about employing technology to exploit opportunity.

# Breaking the Link between Information and Things

In the e-business world, new ideas and new companies seem to have more value than traditional ideas and ways of doing things. That notion alone is a good reason why the Internet is a friendly environment for a new business start-up, because everyone who surfs the Web is looking for the latest and greatest thing. If you have it, whether "it" is information, products, or services, customers will find you.

Selling things, or products, is not the same as selling information, however. The economics of the two are very different. When you sell a product, you no longer own it. But when you sell an idea, or a piece of music, or a blueprint, you still own it and can sell it again and again. The exciting thing about information is that it can be replicated at virtually zero cost and sold an unlimited number of times. This means that, unlike many other "things," information is not generally subject to the law of diminishing returns. Theoretically, you can continue to sell information over and over, forever.

What the Internet did for information was to separate it from the economics of things. We no longer need physically intensive media, like books, magazines, and newspapers, to deliver information. Breaking the link between information and things has freed information to go wherever it wants to go. So when the people in your company are electronically connected, information flows in every direction, for use by anyone who needs it.

You can create value for your e-business by taking advantage of the freedom and mobility of information to create new products and services for your customers.

Perhaps you are particularly good at something — maybe it's gardening or growing orchids. If you have picked up on important techniques and tricks over the years that are of value to other people interested in orchids, you can share those ideas through an online newsletter, a Web site, branded products, consulting, and so forth. The possibilities are limited only by your imagination.

# Sharing Information (And Everything Else)

The beauty of the Internet is its *open architecture*. The Internet is perfectly designed to let all sorts of participants coexist in harmony. No one company can claim control. That wasn't the original idea. Way back when (15 or 20 years ago), experts predicted the supreme reign of private computer networks on the Internet, and many companies that believed that idea were stuck with a lot of useless hardware when the Internet took off at warp speed — much more rapidly than anyone expected.

We are moving "back to the future" in some ways. One of the reasons companies came into existence originally was to reduce the hassle of having to deal with individual vendors for each and every thing you wanted to buy. For example, if you wanted to build a house, you had to find all the specialized labor and materials yourself — lumber, bricks, bricklayers, carpenters, painters, and all the other essentials — and then supervise the construction. At some point, a savvy entrepreneur decided there was an opportunity here to solve a problem, and construction companies came into being.

The Internet has restored the option of doing business one-on-one by sharing information and taking on partners in our customers, suppliers, and even competitors. People now expect to get their information from the original source rather than going through a filtering process conducted by intermediaries. Just as there is nowhere to hide on the Internet, information is becoming less and less secret. The potential value of that information depends on how you package it and use it to create intelligence.

Share company information to increase the intelligence of your business.

## Communication keeps getting easier, freer

E-mail, chat rooms, and the Internet in general have empowered people to reach out to others all over the world, forming communities of the like-minded. Entrepreneurial e-businesses are finding that they can bring their customers together to strengthen their joint ties to the businesses with which they deal. When customers get together, even under the auspices of a business, they begin to take charge of their own community by letting the company know what they want, and by communicating and getting help from one another.

One great example is PlumbNet, www.plumbnet.com, which bills itself as "the interactive plumbing network." It creates a forum for people who have problems with pipes, drains, and other plumbing issues. Thus, people who are plumbing-challenged can tap the wisdom of Bob Allen, the cyber-plumber, and share solutions to common plumbing problems. Remarkably, professional plumbers have joined the crowd as well, dispensing free advice for which they normally charge as much as $100 an hour.

But free and easy communication also has a downside. The Internet empowers everyone, including people who oppose what your company is doing. A disgruntled customer can rapidly mobilize a guerrilla protest group that can hit your Web site with complaints and tirades that will discourage others from doing business with you. Even if the complaints are unfounded, they spread like wildfire in the cyberworld and do their damage before you can marshal your defenses.

Use the Internet to build a community of customers. Then listen to your customers and give them a stake in your company.

## Hierarchy is out, network is in

Organizational structures are changing. The top-down, hierarchical mode has never been the choice of entrepreneurs, who prefer flatter, team-based organizational styles. In successful e-businesses, ideas percolate up from everyone in the company; ideas are tested in the real world as quickly as possible, even when they're not perfect. And e-business entrepreneurs also let their customers tell them how to change the products and services to work better.

To survive, entrepreneurial e-businesses rely on networks, those elaborate webs of partnerships that allow a venture to achieve scale quickly. Operating within a network, a very small business gains very big clout and the capability to do more than what it can do alone. Even venture capitalists, those powerful icons of money, are creating networks of the companies they invest in. One such company in Silicon Valley forms networks of the companies it funds. The companies share information, technology, resources, and labor. In a sense, they all work for their common success. The venture capitalist has an equity stake of 25 to 30 percent in each company of the 175 companies in its network and sits on the board of directors of each company.

You don't have to do it alone. There is safety, power, and success in numbers, so create a network of people and businesses.

# Everyone's Value Chain Is Shorter

A value chain is a distribution channel. It's the highway for delivering your product or service to the end user. The traditional value chain looks something like Figure 2-1.

Figure 2-1:
The
traditional
value chain.

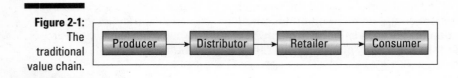

At each point along the channel, someone provides a service that increases the value of the product and allows that intermediary to mark up the price of the product or service. In the 1990s, we saw the shortening of the value chain by discounters like Price Club and Home Depot. They merged the retailer function into the warehousing operation (part of the distributor function), resulting in lower prices to the consumer.

But the Internet has now taken out the distributor as well, reducing a complex channel to a direct one where the consumer or end-user deals directly with the producer. Thus, many value chains now look like Figure 2-2.

Figure 2-2:
The Internet
shortens the
value chain.

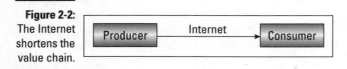

Now, industries like travel, real estate, and financial services are seeing their traditional products and services being taken over by their customers who have the power to access the information they need via the Internet and control the transaction from start to finish with the click of a mouse. Businesses everywhere have to reinvent themselves before they find they are out of business.

# Making Yourself Obsolete (Before Someone Else Does It for You)

The need for speed has been instigated by information technology in general and e-mail and the Internet specifically. Because communications can now occur instantaneously, there is the perception that everything *must* occur at Internet speed. That's why the first question one business owner asks another is, "May I have your e-mail and Web addresses?" If you're not using e-mail or the Web, you're immediately classified as a business owner who doesn't "get it," one who's behind the times.

Similarly, the pace of introducing new products and services is breathtaking. Today, before your first product is out the door and into the marketplace, you had better have the next version on the drawing board, with all the latest bells and whistles attached. Internet time waits for no one, even those companies (and they're in the majority) that do most of their business off the Internet.

If you don't find ways to make your current products or services obsolete, someone else will.

With the rapid pace of change in today's digital world, and recognizing that change is inevitable, every business needs to think about ways to put itself out of business, ways to make obsolete its current products and services before they become commodities. Here's a process that will help you do that:

- Get your key decisionmakers together in one group.
- Identify the ways in which you are currently doing business.
- Find all the holes in your current strategies that can be penetrated by technology in one form or another.
- Develop ways to respond to these threats.
- Do rapid experimentation in small ways and get immediate responses from your customers.
- Keep experimenting and modifying the product or service until you achieve what your customers want.

# Changing the Way You Buy Things

Businesses are increasingly making all their purchases online, forming huge buying groups and forcing manufacturers to lower their prices. Consumers are also buying more things online than ever before.

One entrepreneur saw an opportunity to solve a convenience problem for people living in major metropolitan areas. Tim DiMello of Boston knew from experience that working professionals don't have time to do their grocery shopping, and they don't want to spend their precious weekend time in a grocery store. So he founded Streamline, which fills online orders from customers directly from its 56,000-square-foot warehouse and delivers each order to a special refrigerated container installed in the customer's garage. Streamline also offers other common services like video rentals, laundry and dry cleaning, and film processing. While this new way of purchasing is in the earliest of stages and not yet as cheap as going to the grocery store, it does solve a convenience problem for many people.

Entrepreneurs are finding that they can take care of a lot of their purchasing activities online:

- ✔ Small business suppliers like Office Max and Staples receive your order online and deliver the goods to your door, often at no charge.
- ✔ Kinko's receives your e-mailed design of a new promotional brochure, prints it, and delivers the finished product to you.

The new ways to buy products and services offer many opportunities for entrepreneurs to solve transaction problems for other companies. If, for example, the industry in which you're interested has not yet taken advantage of online purchasing, you may want to create a business that makes it easy for people in your industry to find what they need online.

Wherever there's a customer need that hasn't been filled, there's an opportunity for an entrepreneur to satisfy that need.

# Deconstructing the Company

To survive and prosper in a digital world, entrepreneurial companies are deconstructing — taking themselves apart and rebuilding — so that they can move faster and get new products to market in Internet time. This dynamic environment is tailor-made for entrepreneurial e-businesses that start small and stay small and flexible as long as possible. There has never been a better time than now to start a business.

Because of technology and the Internet, barriers to entry are low when you identify a niche that is not being served. But you had better get going fast, because it won't be that way for long! Entrepreneurial start-ups typically bootstrap and outsource their way in the beginning, making the most of their limited resources. This frugality actually gives them a competitive advantage over bigger companies in the same markets because newcomers don't have as much overhead to cover. They can also experiment and test new ideas without it costing the company too much.

Being frugal has another benefit. On the Internet, price matters. Customers, whether they're other businesses or consumers, can use the powerful database that is the Internet to comparison shop. The Internet has made every product or service a commodity, so price is pretty much all that matters. Those companies that can keep their overhead down and operate lean and smart have a fighting chance. Those that can add value to a commodity in the minds of customers can win at this game. Entrepreneurs are good at creating value with limited resources, so the Internet is one start-up environment that is perfect for them.

# Giving up control

Entrepreneurs have often been called "control freaks" because they work with such passion and persistence — with such a sense of focus — that it's difficult for them to delegate anything to other people and feel comfortable that the assignment will be done the way they want. But the speed and complexity of today's start-up environment has taught entrepreneurs that they can't do it alone. The fact is that the most successful start-ups today have been founded by teams — two, three, or four people with different areas of expertise and different networks of contacts. The new entrepreneurial teams willingly outsource tasks that they can't or don't know how to accomplish, because they know they will get their business up and running much faster that way. In fact, most Internet start-ups bring on professional management teams before they ever get started: They know that growth will typically come fast, and they want to be ready for it.

# Getting flexible and fast

In the old days, you took your time planning for your business, and your plans looked forward maybe three to five years. No more. Today you'd better plan on a horizon of about 12 to 18 months, which means you'll have to plan much more quickly and rely more often on intuition and gut feeling. You'll try things based on the notion that they may work or that the timing "feels" right. You will experiment and test new ideas with actual customers as fast as you can get a prototype ready.

If you have a start-up venture in mind, this is a great time for you because the Internet has leveled the playing field for all businesses by creating standards and providing access to markets, customers, and information. You have easier access than ever before to capital in the earliest stages, and you can tap into global markets the minute you hit the Net.

If you have a start-up venture, you're also in a better position to innovate and create new products and services — certainly much faster and with more creativity than much larger companies that are bogged down in bureaucracy. The biggest companies are dealing with long-established systems that make it difficult for them to maneuver effectively. As a small company, you are closer to your customers, and this means that you are also closer to their needs and desires. You have the upper hand when it comes to developing new products and services that customers want. Customers actually get involved in the development of your new products, and that is a significant competitive advantage for any company.

# Technology Disrupts; That's Good

I'm one of the many people who are rethinking the idea that technology is "an enabler." In light of the impact of the Internet on business and life in general, what appears to be true is that technology is also "a disrupter." Technology doesn't always solve business problems; sometimes, it creates them. But in the right hands, the new problem usually becomes a new benefit.

I'm reminded of the often-quoted "Moore's Law," conceived by Gordon Moore, founder of Intel Corp., the semiconductor company. It says that every 18 months, computer-processing power will double while costs will decline by half. In simple terms, this means that technology always moves toward smaller, cheaper, and faster. That's why the processing power of huge main-frame computers of years ago can now be found in palm-sized video games.

To satisfy customers today, you have to provide more than products and services; you must provide your customers with information, and you need to gather information from your customers. Technology can provide your business with ways to reach customers on an individual level, gather their specific information, let them give you feedback, analyze that feedback, and feed it directly into a customized and personalized product or service. In doing so, you give your customer control of the process — your customer has direct access to your company's information and resources.

To be able to operate in a fast-paced market, you will also probably need to develop strategic partnerships and outsource some tasks to other companies that do those things particularly well. Managing those relationships is facilitated by the use of technology.

For example, you may choose to outsource your fulfillment functions (packaging, shipping, and logistics) because you don't have expertise in that area and it costs too much to set up the function. Being able to communicate and share information with your fulfillment company will be critical to the successful delivery of products to your customers. You will also want to track the status of your shipments in real time without having to pick up a telephone and call someone.

Everywhere, businesses are looking for ways to use technology to push back-office functions out the back door, so that they can focus on what they do best and remain quick on their feet.

# Chapter 3

# Preparing to Hear When Opportunity Knocks

*In This Chapter*

▶ Stimulating your creative juices

▶ Dealing with obstacles (real and imaginary)

▶ Developing new product ideas with outside help

▶ Preparing an environment for innovation

*Y*ou may wonder where all those great business ideas that pepper the media come from. How is it that some people just seem to know which ideas will be successful and which won't? You may also wonder why some very simple and obvious ideas claim huge investment dollars while your much more interesting idea goes wanting.

I don't claim to answer those questions absolutely, because there really is no one right answer for any of them. But in this chapter, I show you how to unleash your creative skills and how to listen very carefully for opportunity.

In fact, why don't you test your creative abilities by trying the following exercise? It's a classic:

> Choose a product that is part of your everyday life — for example, a jar. Then, list all the possible products you could make from the jar. Use your imagination and be as creative as possible.

I have seen people come up with at least 30 different product ideas. You may not be able to match that number on the first try, but over time you'll find that you get increasingly better at looking at an object from a completely different point of view. Some typical products suggested for the jar are flower pot, fish bowl, and pencil holder. (Did you think to break the jar to do something with the pieces?)

Ideas for businesses can come from anywhere. Zalman Silber can tell you that his more than $9 million entertainment business sprang from the simple notion that people need something to do with their spare time. Silber's story was told in *Inc.* a few years ago. In 1991, Silber worked in an office in the venerable Empire State Building, which is visited by 3.4 million tourists every year. He reasoned that weather often prevented many of those tourists from getting the view from the top. So, he thought, what if tourists could experience the Big Apple in a virtual way? His concept was a simulated helicopter tour of the city, and he did such an effective job of describing his idea that he managed to raise $6.2 million before he had even built what was to become the New York Skyride. When the ride opened in 1996, he managed to garner 19 percent of the tourists who visited the Empire State Building at $11.50 a ticket.

One of the first things you need to understand is that ideas and opportunities are not the same breed of animal. You probably generate dozens of ideas every day without even realizing it. Every time you solve a problem, it involves an idea on your part or someone else's. Every time you plan to do something, it involves an idea of one sort or another. But not all those ideas — in fact few of them — have the potential to become opportunities.

An opportunity (in a business sense) is an idea that has commercial potential. You can make money with it, develop a business around it, or in some other way create value.

# Starting to "Cook" on an Idea

You need to get started somewhere, so why not right here? I want to get your creative juices going so that you are opportunity-focused in this chapter. Try these two exercises and see how creative you can be.

## 1. Changing a business

Choose a business in your community. Make sure it's one that you understand. Then figure out a way to do that business differently from the way it is currently operating. For example, suppose you choose a restaurant that is operating in the traditional manner as a retail location where people come to eat. You could put the restaurant on the Internet, let people click through a menu and order online. The food is then delivered to their homes. In this exercise, you're applying creative thinking to an existing business.

## 2. Solving a problem with creativity

Examine your home environment carefully to find a problem that needs to be solved. Ideally, it will be something that requires a better process. This is an opportunity — an opportunity to solve a problem. *Now create an opportunity that will solve the problem.* For example, suppose you discover that you often miss deadlines for paying bills because when the mail comes in, you stack it up in a corner to get to later. Unfortunately, you never get to it, and the stack grows increasingly higher. This is definitely a problem and an opportunity. Chances are you are not the only person in the world who has this problem. What if you could devise a product that enabled people to sort their mail quickly and easily? Would that be the basis for a business opportunity?

How did you do? Was it easy or difficult to do these exercises? If you struggled trying to come up with some ideas, you may be facing obstacles that you have inadvertently set up for yourself.

# Spotting Obstacles in Your Path

It may surprise you to discover that you are often your own worst enemy when it comes to improving your ability to be creative. Ask yourself a few questions:

- ✔ Do I let myself get so busy that I never have any time to think?
- ✔ Am I afraid of being criticized?
- ✔ Am I having problems that seem to be constantly on my mind?
- ✔ Am I under a lot of stress?
- ✔ Do I believe that I'm not a creative person?

If you answered yes to any of the above questions, you have identified an issue that could be stifling creativity for you. Actually, the fourth one is the real killer of creativity, because it makes you less productive and less effective. If you are experiencing any of these five conditions, you probably won't do the things you need to do to become more creative.

Additional obstacles — real or imaginary — that may keep you from being your creative best are addressed in the following sections.

## You think you're not creative (Think again!)

Maybe in your family your brother or sister was always referred to as "the creative one," because he or she could draw or play a musical instrument. You, on the other hand, were not creative, and that belief is one that you carried with you throughout your life. Being artistic or musically inclined are two types of creativity, but there are degrees of creativity within each. Still, they are not the only kinds of creativity. The kind of creativity we're talking about here has to do with your ability to view things in new ways, to think about things in unusual ways, and to generally "think outside the box."

## You loathe criticism (Well don't we all?)

Many times people don't try new things because they're afraid that people will criticize them or think they're crazy. Unfortunately, that attitude keeps these same people from realizing their full potential, because they're always being held back by their need to be accepted by others as rational human beings. Creativity doesn't often have anything to do with rationality; on the contrary, it is often the seemingly irrational idea that ends up being the very solution you're seeking. Certainly, Gary Dahl wasn't thinking about what people would think of him when he came up with the idea of The Pet Rock. He just knew that he was tired of all the chores related to a pet like a dog or cat, so he decided that people needed a pet that was no trouble at all. He packaged the rocks with a "Pet Rock Training Manual" that he spent months writing and sold 1.5 million of them in 1975 for $3.95 a piece ($11.25 in 2000 dollars).

And what about Harvard graduate Ken Hakuta, who discovered another fad-type product when his mother sent him a rubber, octopus-shaped toy from Japan? What was unusual about this toy was that when you would throw it at a wall, it would stick; but then gravity would cause it to crawl down the wall. Hakuta licensed the North American rights to distribute the toy, called it the Wacky Wallwalker, and sold more than 250 million of the little beasts in the 1980s. He made more than $20 million.

## You're a creature of habit

Routines certainly have value. They let you complete regular and repetitive tasks more effectively. But if you rely too much on routines, you limit your thinking to those routines and you miss out on all those other ways of looking at things outside your routines. In other words, you restrict the possible responses in a particular situation. That keeps you from improving, finding new and better ways of doing things, and generally keeping up with change.

# You lack confidence

Closely tied to a fear of being criticized is lack of confidence in expressing new and unusual ideas. If you are the kind of person who generally seeks approval from others for the things you do or the ideas you generate, you are putting curbs on your ability to be creative. Many of the products we depend on today would never have existed if the people who invented them didn't have the courage to risk the "slings and arrows" of people who didn't have the inventor's vision. For example, Andrew Wilson, a Boston-based investment banker, was traveling through Memphis to visit the legendary home of Elvis Presley when he saw an amphibious military vehicle from the World War II era known as "the duck." It had been converted into a tour bus, but what Wilson saw was that it was perfectly suited to land and water tours in Boston. Convincing city officials in Boston wasn't easy because at the time he didn't even own a duck that he could show them. But Wilson had confidence that he had found his dream opportunity. Finally, after much searching, he discovered Manuel Rogers, a collector of military vehicles, who owned a duck. Rogers loved the idea and helped Wilson raise the money to get started in 1994. By 1996, Boston Duck Tours was earning revenues of $3.4 million and looking for other cities to expand to.

# You're overconfident (jumbo ego)

The opposite of a lack of confidence is having an ego so big that you think you already have all the answers, so you don't consider new ways of thinking. It's fine to have strong beliefs and values that guide your thinking and decision making, but you also need to suspend the limitations on your thinking once in a while so that you can be creative and grow.

Your author is fond of saying that the best opportunities are often found where MBAs don't go. In other words, blue-collar, unglamorous industries are often the source of tremendous opportunities. Todd Smart saw an opportunity to consolidate the independent towing industry when he sold his car, bought his first tow truck, and founded Absolute Towing and Trucking in Southern California in 1987. Absolute Towing's annual sales for 1997 reached $5 million. In 1998, his company merged with seven other national companies to form United Road Service, which went public in May of that year.

# Clearing Away the Obstacles

So what can you do to overcome all the obstacles you may have created for yourself that will keep you from being creative enough to become a successful entrepreneur? Help is on the way. You can do several things right now to start on the road to more creative thinking. You may first want to visit a Web site aptly called *Creativity Web*. It's at www.ozemail.com.au.

If you're not familiar with the au extension after the .com, it means that the site is based in Australia, where it appears they are very much interested in creativity. On this site, you'll find many articles on various aspects of creativity. It is a one-stop shop for resources on creativity.

## Going back to familiar territory

Most ideas actually come from environments and things with which you're familiar — your neighborhood, a comment from a friend, a suggestion of an employee, or a problem identified by a customer. Too often people think they have to look for opportunity outside what they know — it's the grass-is-always-greener syndrome. Actually, quite the opposite is true. Most ideas have very common roots in things we know and are comfortable with. What turns these ideas into opportunities is the ability of the entrepreneur to look at the common from an uncommon point of view, to juxtapose two things that normally are not associated with each other, to tear things apart and put them back together in a new way.

Research supports this notion that the bulk of our new ideas come from our prior experience. The work of entrepreneurship professor Gerald Hills at the University of Illinois at Chicago points to the following sources of new venture ideas:

- ✔ Prior experience (73%)
- ✔ Business associates (33%)
- ✔ Seeing a similar business (26%)
- ✔ Friends or relatives (19%)
- ✔ Hobby/personal interest (17%)
- ✔ Market research (11%)
- ✔ Serendipity (11%)
- ✔ Other sources (7.4%)

John Sanchez was a first year law student at UC Hastings College of Law in San Francisco, California, when he realized that law students spend too much time trying to find everything from summer law clerk jobs to roommates to used books and much more. He and his partner founded Jdpost.com in the summer of 1999 as an Internet community for law students. Law firms use it as well to screen applicants for law clerk positions and positions after graduation.

CASE STUDY

## Doing what you do best

It is not only scientists and engineers whose products become the genesis for an entrepreneurial venture. Many artists have also become entrepreneurs by sharing their works with the world. One such artist is Donna Mae Montgomery who has worked in a number of media, from photography to ceramics, sculpture, and painting. Perhaps her best-known works are her collages dating back to the 1970s when she was a member of the Xerox-Mail and Rubber Stamp Artist movement. Those designs can be found in the Whitney Museum in New York.

Montgomery faced more challenges than most in becoming an entrepreneur. In addition to suffering from dyslexia and epilepsy, she began working from the age of 17 but couldn't manage to hold a job because of her disabilities. Finally at the age of 48, she sought help from a therapist and it was then that she began to really focus on her art. She was particularly interested in plastic as a creative medium and began creating photocopy-inspired pieces that feature characters developed in a naïve or surreal style. With the photocopier, she can print her designs directly onto plastic and then cut and bake them to shrink them to the size she wants. Each piece has a personal story attached to it.

To get the business help she needed to become an entrepreneur, Montgomery became a member of the San Francisco Women's Initiative for Self Employment where she learned how to write a business plan and got the consulting help she needed to launch the business.

## Finding a problem and solving it

Every day, you probably run across little annoyances, little problems that you wish you could solve. Why not pick one and see if you can actually solve it. You probably do that without knowing it every day. For example, how many times have you not had the appropriate tool for something you wanted to do, so you improvised and used something else in its place? That's actually being creative. Now, just take it one step further and find a new solution to an old problem.

CASE STUDY

Kristin Penta was always fascinated by cosmetics. According to Don Debelak, who profiled her in *Business Start-Ups* in May 2000, from the time she was a kid, she was cooking her own cosmetic formulas, so it was no surprise that when she graduated from college, she wanted to work for a cosmetics manufacturer. After much searching she found Pentech International, Inc., which manufactures private label, low cost cosmetic pencils. Penta was brimming with ideas for low-cost cosmetics for teenagers. She started building her product base in her division of the company. In 1997, when Pentech decided to focus on writing instruments rather than cosmetics, Penta found some investors who bought out her product line and helped her start Fun Cosmetics of which she owns 20 percent.

## Using your personal network

As you saw in the research discussed in an earlier section, business associates was the second most popular source of new ideas for business ventures. Personal networks are a critical component in the opportunity recognition process and serve to open your mind to a variety of thoughts and ideas, of which one may become that great opportunity you were looking for.

CASE STUDY

# Meet Doug Hall: New product guru extraordinaire

It has been said that Doug Hall, the unabashed guru of product innovation and creativity, can pull new-product ideas literally out of thin air like magic. In just three days he can get product companies like PepsiCo, Procter & Gamble, and Nike to come up with 30 viable products. That's a process that normally takes these companies three months. In fact, on average, you have about 18 products in your home that were first conceived at RSI, Hall's remarkable company based outside Cincinnati, Ohio.

Hall's base of operations is a grand old house he has dubbed Eureka! Mansion to celebrate the Eureka! Stimulus Response, which is what you experience when you come up with what he calls a "wicked-good idea." The mansion is home to anything and everything that gets people to have fun and loosen up, from Nerf Ballzookas to whoopee cushions. Hall firmly believes that if you're laughing, you will come up with better ideas.

With tactics like the "Mind Dumpster," "Bulging," and "Smash Association," Hall can get his clients to suspend their old ways of thinking and embrace his wackiness. And while clients are focusing on ideas, Hall's "trained brains" (his team of creative people) wander through the room adding ideas, drawing packaging solutions, and sparking creativity wherever they feel it's lacking.

Food is a critical component of his creative strategy. According to Hall, "if corporations would double their food budgets, they'd get

more than double their return on investment." So at Hall's invention fests, food and drink are plentiful, as is music, which he uses to stimulate ideas — Dixieland jazz to get acquainted, classic rock and roll to get things moving, and funky tunes like the theme from Gilligan's Island for his brain dump.

Hall's invention style has been studied to compare it with other methods in terms of effectiveness. Arthur VanGundy of the University of Oklahoma ran a comparison group of Hall's people and his own and challenged them to come up with ideas for snack foods. Van Gundy's groups averaged 6.5 marketable ideas in 45 minutes, while Hall's groups averaged 36.3 marketable ideas or 558% more. From this experience, VanGundy learned that to successfully generate a greater volume of ideas, you must do three things:

✔ You have to believe that anything is possible.

✔ You have to create an environment that stimulates creativity.

✔ You have to use a variety of stimuli, both related and unrelated to the particular problem you're trying to solve.

According to Hall's Web site, Eureka Ranch is a place where Eureka! Trailblazer Training leverages quantitative science and gritty street smarts to help managers think smarter, faster, and more imaginatively. Check out Hall's Eureka Ranch Web site at www.eurekaranch.com/default1.htm.

## Making time to be creative

One of the big reasons you've never seen yourself as a creative person is that you've never allowed yourself time to be creative. Countless distractions occur on any given day, and if you let yourself be pulled away from what you're concentrating on by every little distraction that comes along, from e-mail announcements to boring work and coworkers who take any opportunity to get away from their work and bother you, you will never find enough time to develop your creative skills.

Set aside some time for yourself to focus on building your latent creative tendencies. Here are some examples of things you can do during that precious time.

## Finding a favorite thinking space

Put on some thinking music (anything Mozart is good for this), sit in a comfortable chair or stretch out on a couch, close your eyes, and just free-associate for a while. Let ideas and thoughts come in and out of your mind in any order. The more you do this the more interesting and creative your thoughts will become. Alternatively, you can do this while running, doing yoga, or floating in your swimming pool. Any activity that lets you meditate will work. You need to find the one that allows you to be your most creative.

## Playing with toys, games, and kids

Toys like Legos and K'NEX are great for stimulating creativity in a physical way. Various kinds of games, computer simulations, and video games also call for some creative thinking. They may kindle the more playful side of your creative thinking ability. Of course, playing with kids will let you see creativity and imagination in action. Kids can take the simplest tools — sticks, blocks, paper bags, and so forth — and turn them into props in an elaborate fantasy they build and act out. Suspend your adult intellect for a bit and try being a kid again. It will surprise you how easily you can look at your very familiar world in a new light.

Here's a list of some additional ways that you can enhance your creative ability:

 ✔ **Keep an idea file or notebook.** You never know when an idea will strike, and even though you think it's the greatest idea you've ever had and you couldn't possibly forget it, write it down! In fact, keep a journal of all your ideas. You may not be able to make one happen right now, but who knows, sometime in the future may be perfect for turning that idea into an opportunity.

✔ **Read, read, read.** Newspapers, magazines, and trade journals are great sources of ideas and trends. You may even learn about some new regulation that could mean an opportunity for you.

✔ **Try thinking in opposites.** Pick something you're familiar with and then think about what it isn't. For example, a telephone is something you can't eat — or can you? AT&T brainstormed that opposite when their marketing people asked themselves what a telephone is NOT. As a result, they decided to create chocolate telephones to send to their best customers.

✔ **Find new uses for old things.** 3M scientist Arthur Fry was working on developing bookshelf arranger tape when the idea for Post-it Notes, the sticky-backed bookmarkers, came to him.

# Growing Ideas with Outside Help

Have you ever thought of going to an invention nursery to find a new product idea that may spark a new business venture? What is an invention nursery, you say? Well, it's a place that focuses on research and development (R&D) of new products, and they are thriving today. Some examples are such venerable organizations as Arthur D. Little in Cambridge, Massachusetts; SRI International in Menlo Park, California; and Battelle Memorial Institute in Columbus, Ohio. In fact, 50 years ago, Batelle, a nonprofit organization, invented the electrophotographic copying process that Xerox ultimately commercialized.

Today everyone is looking for new ideas, new solutions, and new products and processes, but for most businesses, doing R&D is an expensive proposition, one few can afford. Consequently, one of the biggest trends is outsourcing invention to one of the 20 big nurseries. Of course, small entrepreneurial companies still can't afford to outsource to expensive invention labs, so they often seek out university professor/scientists or independent engineers. Still, some of the big invention houses take on small clients. For example, Batelle, which is working on cancer therapies and new types of fuel-efficient cars, also invented LavaBuns, a pad to keep bottoms of football fans warm in cold-weather stadiums, for a small company. One entrepreneur went to Design Partners in Concord, California and almost turned around and walked out after looking at all the prize-winning designs displayed on their walls. His humble product was a tote bag that college students would use to carry toiletries between their dorm room and the shower. Design Partners was happy to work with him, saying that even a tote bag requires good design skills.

At some invention nurseries you'll pay $20,000 to $30,000 for a fairly simple design project. Others will take equity in your company, betting that you will be a huge success. Still another option is a company like Invent Resources, www.weinvent.com, which charges nothing up front but when your product goes to market, takes a royalty of 4 percent to 7 percent. Of course, of the hundreds of products they look at, only about 10 percent ever see the marketplace. That's because sometimes a product that you can design and build in a shop cannot be mass-produced easily and for a cost that allows you to make a profit.

Do not use invention services that advertise in TV infomercials or in magazines with offers to help you patent and commercialize your invention. You don't need an invention service to patent your invention. You do need a good patent attorney. And you need an entrepreneur to help you commercialize your product.

# Finding Opportunity in Failure

You have probably heard the oft-quoted phrases, "learn from your failures," and "you can't succeed without first failing." Trite but true. The Ford Edsel was undoubtedly the biggest new car failure in automobile history. And what's surprising is that Ford did its homework before introducing the car — or at least Ford thought that it had researched its market. What happened, in fact, was that customers no longer were segmented based on income groups, as Ford had assumed. Instead, customers had become differentiated based on lifestyle. Ford's failure actually turned out to be the basis on which it then created the biggest new-car win in history with the Mustang. Ford learned from its failure.

The problem is that most people do not learn from their failures; instead, they head off in an entirely new direction only to fail again because they didn't apply the lessons learned from the previous experience.

# Finding Opportunity in the Unconventional

In 1984, Virgin Atlantic Airways stunned the industry when it defied logic and took out its first-class seats and service. But Virgin was not acting precipitously without having done its homework. On the contrary, Virgin had figured out that they earned more profit on business class than first class. So they added value for their customers by putting in sleeper-recliner seats that their competitors didn't have, and providing free transportation to and from the airport. As Virgin's competitors began to copy its innovations, Virgin didn't rest on its laurels; it added state-of-the-art lounges where business passengers could do everything — take a shower, get their clothes pressed, and use the latest office equipment. Virgin saw itself as a solution provider rather than an airline, and that made all the difference.

Sometimes, doing what no one else is willing to do provides a huge opportunity and some space in which to exploit it before the skeptics discover that you were right.

# Finding the Right Place for Innovation

Too often entrepreneurs think that it takes a great idea — a great product — to build a great company. But that's not true at all. Thomas Edison's greatest invention wasn't the lightbulb; it was the modern research and development lab. Walt Disney's greatest creation wasn't Disneyland; it was Disney imagineering, the source of all their great ideas. Successful companies create environments that stimulate creativity and produce a continuing flow of superb ideas. Why is your company's environment so important to creativity? Simply put, it's because environments have the ability to either stimulate your senses or dull them. Consider the following:

- If you regularly work in an environment that is *rigid and hierarchical* (many layers of management), chances are your ability to think outside the box will be very limited because ways of doing things will tend to be standardized.

- If your environment is hectic, *fast-paced, with many deadlines* — something you find in the world of advertising — you will probably have little opportunity to spend in contemplation, an activity that is generally necessary for creativity to happen.

## Making the environment friendly

The following are some actions you can take to handle your environment and make it more conducive to creativity:

- Find new and interesting ways to minimize the distractions in your life. Be sure to make time for some quiet time for yourself on a regular basis.

- At the very least, you should devote some time each day to quiet contemplation to train your mind to be more attentive to creative opportunities.

- Some people have found that a certain room or place allows them to relax and meditate. Dr. Yoshiro Naka Mats, the prolific Japanese inventor (with over 2,300 patents for such things as the floppy disk, compact disk and player, and the digital watch), has developed an entire process to spark his creativity. He created some unique environments; for example, he starts his creativity process by sitting calmly in a room in his home — a sort of meditation room with only natural things in it — then he moves to a dynamic room, which is a dark room with the latest in audio/video equipment. Finally, he heads for the swimming pool where he swims underwater for long periods.

I'm not suggesting that you need to copy Dr. Naka Mats to become creative. Find the process and location that works for you. The important thing to remember is that you will be more creative in some environments than others.

# Chapter 4

# Testing an Opportunity Before You Leap

*In This Chapter*

▶ Passing the entry exam

▶ Converting an idea into a business concept

▶ Running your concept past the critics

▶ Taking stock with a feasibility analysis

*Y*ou may get the impression that today's entrepreneurs come up with an idea over coffee one evening and by the next day or so, they're in business. At least, that's the way it seems from all the media stories, particularly those about Internet businesses. The reality is something quite different, however. The vast majority of businesses take a lot of time and preparation before they're ready to see the marketplace.

While it is true that companies like Yahoo! Store, www.yahoostore.com, have made it theoretically possible for you to be doing business on the Internet in a matter of minutes, that doesn't mean that just because you have your Web site up, people will automatically come flocking to it. And even if they land on your site through a search engine or just by accident, it doesn't mean they'll stay, and it doesn't mean they'll buy.

Every new business idea needs to be tested and proven in the marketplace, and that takes time and money. It's particularly difficult when your concept is very new and you don't have any benchmarks against which to judge its feasibility.

In this chapter, you discover ways to take an idea that has been percolating in your mind and develop it into a form that lets you test it in the marketplace to find out whether it's feasible before you spend hours of time and a lot of money trying to make an unfeasible business succeed.

# Starting with a Personal Assessment

Actually, you need to do some homework before you begin to consider your opportunity further and turn it into a business concept. You need to ask yourself several questions and (here's the important part) answer them honestly. These are simple yes/no questions found in Table 4-1. Don't spend too much time thinking about them — just circle your answers quickly.

If you find that you're circling a bunch of *yes* replies, the chances are good that you have what it takes to start an entrepreneurial venture. If, on the other hand, you are answering *no* to several of the questions, it doesn't automatically mean that you'd better quit while you're ahead. What it does mean is that you may find some aspects of entrepreneurship uncomfortable or not compatible with the way you behave. Often you can resolve these issues by bringing partners on board who are good at doing what you are not.

Questions 1–5 pertain to your personality and ability to adapt to new situations. Questions 6–10 address the stresses and challenges of being an entrepreneur. Questions 11–15 deal with skills and experience. Just circle yes or no in answer to each of the questions. You'll find out a lot about your ability to deal with an entrepreneurial environment.

| Table 4-1 | Personal Inventory | |
|---|---|---|
| *Question* | *Answers* | |
| 1. Do you enjoy making your own decisions? | Yes | No |
| 2. Are you persistent in the face of challenges? | Yes | No |
| 3. Do you regularly meet deadlines? | Yes | No |
| 4. Do you like change? | Yes | No |
| 5. Do you enjoy competing? | Yes | No |
| 6. Are you willing to work 12–14 hours a day 7 days a week to get your business started? | Yes | No |
| 7. Do you have excellent physical stamina? | Yes | No |
| 8. Do you deal well with stress? | Yes | No |
| 9. Are you willing to risk your savings? | Yes | No |
| 10. Are you willing to change your lifestyle to make this business go? | Yes | No |
| 11. Do you have the skills needed to run this venture? | Yes | No |

| Question | Answers | |
|---|---|---|
| 12. Do you have the skills required to conduct the feasibility analysis? | Yes | No |
| 13. Do you have a network of people you can tap for assistance and funding? | Yes | No |
| 14. Do you have sufficient money to at least start the business? | Yes | No |
| 15. Is this venture compatible with your life and career goals? | Yes | No |

# Turning an Opportunity into a Business Concept

You already know what an *opportunity* is. But what exactly is a *business concept?* Put simply, a business concept is a way to define an opportunity so that it can be tested through a process known as *feasibility analysis*. Stick with me — I walk you through this maze of terms.

A business concept, whether it's for an Internet business, a service business, or a manufacturing business, has four parts: the customer, the product or service, the value proposition, and the distribution channel. Assume for a minute that the business you want to start involves developing a portal site for manufacturers and retailers in the apparel industry who want to buy and sell from each other. Questions you can ask that lead you to completely defining the business concept include:

- ✔ **What is the product or service you are offering?** In this case, you are providing a Web site that will link small apparel manufacturers with retail outlets.

- ✔ **Who is your customer?** Your customer is the person or business that pays you, in other words, the source of your revenues. In this case, your customer is the small manufacturer who pays a subscription fee to be listed on the site and have its products displayed.

- ✔ **What is the value proposition?** The value proposition is the benefit that is being provided to the customer. In other words, why will the customer buy from you — what's in it for them? Here the benefit is that retailers will more easily find the products they want to sell and small apparel manufacturers will have more outlets for their products.

- ✔ **How will the benefit be delivered to the customer?** The distribution channel for this concept is the Internet. That's how you will reach the customer and deliver the benefit.

# Benefits versus features: What does the customer buy?

Entrepreneurs often confuse benefits with features. Features are the particular characteristics of a product or service, like color, accessories, ergonomics, and so forth. You take care to design in all the features that you think your customers want, and you're justly proud of the result.

But customers typically don't buy features. Oh, sure, they check to make sure all the features are present and accounted for. But the decision to buy is usually based on the *benefits* provided by the service or product. Here's an example to make this concept clearer. Suppose you own a clothing boutique. Some of the *features* of your business are:

- Excellent location with lots of parking
- Designer clothes not found in department stores
- Great salespeople who learn what your needs are

Those are important features that describe the business, but they tell us nothing about the benefits to the customer because they're not presented from the customer's point of view. They're presented from the company's point of view. Now think how a customer *benefits* from these features. From the customer's perspective, those features are

- The customer *saves time* by being able to easily park right next to the boutique.
- The customer will be able to *conveniently* find *in one location* the designer clothes he or she wants.
- The customer will *not have to waste time* trying to figure out what works on her and what piece of clothing goes with what. She will receive personal attention.

An easy way to try to view the benefits of the product or service you're offering is to put yourself in the customer's shoes and ask, "What's in it for me?" In other words, "Why should I shop at this boutique?"

If you know what the customer values — saving time by going to one location and getting expert help — you are better able to design your business concept to meet those needs. And that will result in loyal customers.

# Why isn't money part of the concept?

Recall that the four components of the business concept are the product or service, customer, value proposition, and distribution channel. Why doesn't the business concept include anything related to money? Isn't it important to know how much money the business will make, or how much it will need to get started? That's a good question, because money is certainly important to the start-up of any business, but we're developing a concept and doing feasibility analysis because we don't yet know that we have a viable business. We don't know yet whether customers are interested in what we have to offer. If we don't know that, then we have no way of calculating how much our revenues will be because we don't know what demand is.

Money is really an *enabler*. It enables you to get a feasible business started. It doesn't, however, help you test for feasibility. Most entrepreneurs start businesses with limited resources, mostly their own. So, more businesses start small and grow relatively slowly depending on the personal resources of the entrepreneur. Money is important, but you need to first find out whether you have a business that has customers.

## Try out your business concept skills

The best way to experience anything is to do it. Looking at the concepts of other entrepreneurs helps you see how they differentiated themselves, creating niches in the market where they can enter and survive long enough to build successful businesses.

What we have here is a simple exercise that will test your ability to identify the four components of a business concept so that you can understand completely what a business is about. Take a look at the PrivaSeek Web site, www.privaseek.com, and list what you believe to be its product/service, customer, value proposition, and distribution channel.

Now, let's see how you did. PrivaSeek provides technology that helps consumers protect their privacy on the Internet. Customers access the technology at the Web site. So, the customer is the consumer; the product is privacy technology; the benefit or value proposition is the ability to protect your name when you do transactions on the Internet; and the product/service is delivered over the Internet.

Let's try one more — a different type of business. Go to www.streamline.com and answer the same questions.

This time, the product/service is brand names, fresh foods, and services. The customers are busy families in Boston, Chicago, and New Jersey. The value proposition is saving time, and providing the convenience of online shopping and delivery of food and services. The benefit is delivered directly to the customer's home.

# Quick-Testing Your Concept

Once you have your business concept in place, you can do a preliminary test quickly at little cost. Doing this will tell you whether you ought to take the time and spend the money to do a full-blown feasibility study. Steps you need to take for a quick, gut test of your business concept include:

- Talking with a few trusted friends to get their feedback. Don't be surprised or discouraged if they tell you that you're crazy. People thought Fred Smith was joking when he said he boasted about the ability to deliver a package anywhere in the United States overnight. They stopped laughing when he showed them how to do it in his new enterprise, Federal Express.

- Running a checklist on the forces in favor of your concept and the forces against it. You may have done this kind of test when you were trying to make a major decision. You looked at the advantages and disadvantages to see which there were more of. You can do the same with your business concept. Ask yourself whether more forces are working for your concept than against it.

- Asking yourself some critical questions:

    - **Am I really interested in this opportunity?** You had better be passionate about your concept because it's going to take a lot of time, energy, and money to make it happen. If you're not thinking about it day and night, maybe you don't want to do it badly enough.

    - **Is anyone else interested in this opportunity?** You can't do a business alone — you need customers, employees, cofounders, investors, and others. If no one seems interested in what you're proposing, you need to reconsider or revamp your concept statement based on the feedback you get.

    - **Will people pay for what I'm offering?** It's one thing for a person to tell you your concept is great, but is that person willing to write a check? And how much are people willing to pay for your product or service? Remember, your product or service must be perceived as sufficiently valuable so that you can charge enough to pay your costs and make a profit.

- Now ask yourself two final questions:

    - **Why me?**

    - **Why now?**

These two questions are simple, but they get at the heart of what you're trying to do. Why should you be the one to execute this business concept? Why are you better than anyone else who comes up with the same concept?

This question addresses your level of confidence in yourself and your ability to execute. It's one thing to come up with an idea and turn it into an opportunity. It's quite another to make it happen. Both talents are needed, and if they're not found in the same person, then you need to find a partner who can fill the gap. If you're an idea person — an inventor type — you will probably want to team with someone who has business skills and knows how to successfully start a business.

Why is this concept doable now? Why hasn't anyone done it before? The *why now* questions get at the uniqueness and viability of the concept. If no one has ever done this before, is it because it's inherently not doable, or is it because you really have come up with something unique? You will have to check out both possibilities.

# Getting Serious: Doing Feasibility Analysis

So you have a concept that you're passionate about, one that other people are interested in, and they've told you that they would actually pay money for what you're about to offer. Before you get too excited and think that it's time to start finding space and hiring people, sit down for a minute and take stock of the fact that your homework has just begun. There is much more to be done before you ever see that customer getting out his or her checkbook.

For one thing, you've only done a quick test of your concept. There's a lot more that you need to find out about before you can feel confident enough to start dealing in the marketplace. What you need to do now is a feasibility analysis. A feasibility analysis is a process whereby you can test the various components of your business concept and arrive at the conditions under which you are willing to go forward with this business. No matter what type of business you intend to start — restaurant, manufacturer, retail outlet, Internet business — you will go through the same feasibility process. Of course, if you're looking to test a pure Internet concept, you will probably go through the process much faster, but you will still do it.

At this point, you may be asking yourself why you wouldn't just do a business plan. It seems like that's what everyone says you need to be doing. Let's talk about the differences for a minute.

# It takes more than passion: It takes persistence

The story of the entrepreneur who falls blindly in love with his concept is not a new one — in fact, it's a common tale that often ends in failure and despair. It's not always a good idea to love your concept so much that you fail to see the fatal flaws. But sometimes, passion will get you through the setbacks, failures, and rejections long enough to triumph. Such is the case of Tom Ashbrook, Rolly Rouse, and their baby, HomePortfolio.com. HomePortfolio is billed as the leading Internet destination for premium home design products. They feature top-of-the-line and hard-to-find products and direct you to your nearest retailers. It is also an online solution for technology and marketing, and a commerce site for makers and merchants of home-design products.

But, it wasn't always so. Going from idea to opportunity to a real business was a long and windy road. As Ashbrook reported in *Fortune Small Business,* back in 1995, Ashbrook and Rouse had just discovered an idea that caught fire and took over every aspect of their lives. They lived and breathed The Idea and were determined that this would be their big hit. They definitely had passion going for them, but they also had several things working against them:

- No money

- No business degrees

- No technology background

- No acquaintances in the venture capital area

- No claim to young innocence — they were turning 40 at the time

- Tons of prior claims on their time and attention — wives, kids, mortgages, and well-used credit cards

Most people with any sense and good jobs would probably back off after looking at this list of negatives, but Ashbrook and Rouse were in love and were clueless about the challenges. They had bought into the hype over the Internet and felt that they had to "digitize or die." They had the vision; they had the passion; after several months, they had the business plan; what they needed was the money. It always comes back to money.

They began making the rounds of trade shows pitching their concept to the biggest names in the design world to positive feedback. Finally in 1996, they landed the seed money — $500,000 — not as much as they really needed, but it validated their belief that the business would work. By March of 1997, however, the seed money had run out and things really started to get tough. Credit cards (they had collected a lot of them) became their backup as they sought for money to pay bills that had soared to over a half million dollars. They had mortgaged their homes and had to borrow from relatives to survive.

Their full site finally went live in January 1998 to the high praise of the *New York Times.* As manufacturers began to sign up, the venture money that had shunned them until now, stepped up to the plate. Scripps Ventures put up a first round of $5 million. Today the site hosts a network of more than 1,200 top brands and 50,000 retailers. HomePortfolio has over 100 employees and offices in five cities. To date they have raised over $25 million in venture funding. You can check out the site at www.homeportfolio.com.

# Feasibility versus business plan: Double the work?

I've said that performing a feasibility study is a way to test your business concept to see whether it has market potential. Doesn't a business plan do the same thing? Actually, no, it doesn't. A business plan describes not only a business concept but also the infrastructure that needs to be put in place to successfully execute the business concept. In other words, the business plan describes the company you are going to create. Take a look at Table 4-2 to see a comparison of the components of the feasibility study with the additional components that you find in the business plan.

| Table 4-2 | Feasibility Study versus Business Plan |
|---|---|
| *Feasibility Analysis* | *Business Plan (What's New?)* |
| Executive Summary | Process Analysis or Operation Plan |
| The Business Concept | Organization Plan |
| Genesis or Founding Team | Marketing Plan |
| Industry/Market Analysis-Test of Customer | Financial Plan |
| Product/Service Development Plan | Growth Plan |
| Financial Plan — Start-up requirements | Contingency Plan |
| Feasibility Decision: Conditions under which to go forward | |
| Timeline to launch | |
| Bibliography | |
| Appendix (A,B,C,and so forth) | |

As you can see, the business plan assumes that you have a feasible business concept and can now add the operational pieces needed to execute the concept. I devote Chapter 12 to the business plan, but for now focus on the feasibility study. In this chapter, you will get an overview of the parts of the feasibility analysis, but if you want more detail on each of the components, check out Chapters 5–12.

# An overview of feasibility analysis

Feasibility analysis consists of a series of tests that you will conduct as you discover more and more about your opportunity. After each test, you ask yourself if you still want to go forward. Is there anything here that prevents you from going forward with this business? Feasibility is a process of discovery and during that process you will probably modify your original concept several times until you get it right. That's the real value of feasibility — the way that it helps you refine your concept — fine tune it — so that you have the highest potential for success when you launch your business.

Today, you can often go for financing on the strength of a feasibility study alone. Certainly in the case of Internet businesses, speed is of the essence, so many an Internet company has gotten first-round financing on its proof of concept alone and then done a business plan before it had to go for bigger dollars in the form of venture capital.

## Executive summary

The executive summary is probably the most important piece of a feasibility analysis because, in two pages, it presents the most important and persuasive points from every test you did during your analysis. An effective executive summary captures the reader's attention immediately with the excitement of the concept. It doesn't let the reader get away; it draws the reader deeper and deeper into the concept as it proves your claim that the concept is feasible and will be a market success.

The most important information to emphasize in the executive summary is your proof that customers want what you have to offer. This proof comes from the primary research you do with the customers to find out what they think of your concept and how much demand there is. The other key piece on which to place emphasis is your description of your founding team. Even the greatest ideas can't happen without a great team, and investors put a lot of stock in a founding team's expertise and experience.

If you're doing an Internet type business, you may want to prepare what's called a *proof of concept*. This is essentially a one-page statement of why your concept will work, emphasizing what you have done to prove that customers will come to your site. That may be in the form of showing hits to your beta site or a list of customers signed up and ready to go when the site is finished. Similarly, if you're developing a new product, your proof of concept is your market quality prototype.

## Business concept

In this first part of the feasibility analysis, you are developing your business concept as we talked about in the beginning of this chapter. Essentially you are answering the questions:

- ✔ What is the business?
- ✔ Who is the customer?
- ✔ What is the value proposition?
- ✔ How will the benefit be delivered?

It's important to be able to state your business concept in a couple of clear, concise, and direct sentences that include all four of the components of the concept. This is what is often called your "elevator pitch" — a conversation that begins when the elevator door closes and ends when the door opens at your floor. That means you only have a few seconds to capture your listener's attention, so you better be able to get it all out quickly and confidently. If you're preparing a feasibility analysis that will be shown to investors, you will want to state your business concept right up front in the concept section. Then you can elaborate on each point as a follow-up. Here's an example:

> Gentech is in the power equipment business, providing contractors and developers solutions to power needs in remote areas through rental equipment outlets.

As you find out more about your business concept, you'll also want to consider the various spin-off products and services you may be able to offer.

One-product businesses have a much more difficult time becoming successful than multi-product/service companies. You don't want to put all your eggs into one basket, and you want to give your customer choices.

### Industry analysis

Testing whether or not the industry in which you will be operating will support your concept is an important part of any feasibility analysis. Here you look at the status of your industry, identify trends and patterns of change, and look at who the major players in terms of competitors may be. Also, don't forget that one way to find a great opportunity is to study an industry first. For more details on how to do an industry analysis, check out Chapter 5.

### Market/customer analysis

Here you will be testing your customer. Inside your industry, you will find a market segment appropriate to your business, then identify a niche that is not being served so that you have an entry strategy with the lowest barriers possible and the highest probability of success. In this part of the analysis, you will also look at what your potential customer wants and what the demand for your product/service is. You will also consider a variety of different distribution channels to deliver the benefit to the customer. To find out more, see Chapter 6.

### Genesis or founding team analysis

We said earlier that investors look very carefully at the founding team because even the best concept won't happen without a team that can execute. In this part of the analysis, you want to consider the qualifications, expertise, and experience of your founding team. If you are planning to do this as a solo entrepreneur, we urge you to reconsider. The vast majority of successful start-ups are done by teams, and the reason is that today's business environment is so complex and so fast-paced that no one person has all the skills, time, and resources to do everything him or herself. Having said that, you can find in Chapter 10 lots of ways to make up for skills and people you lack.

### Product/service development analysis

Whether you're planning to offer a product or a service or both (and that's usually the case), it's going to take some planning. Consider which tasks must be accomplished to prepare the product or service for market, whether that be developing a product from raw materials and going through the patent process or developing a plan for implementing a service concept. Identify tasks and figure out a timeline for completion of them. Chapter 8 shows many ways to do a product/service analysis.

### Financial analysis

Once you know you have a market and a team, it's finally time to consider money. (You probably thought we were never going to get to it!) In this part of the feasibility analysis, you figure out how much money you need to start the business and carry it to a positive cash flow. You also distinguish among the types of money, which will be important in defining your financial strategy. You can find out how to do this analysis in Chapter 12.

### Feasibility decision

Once you have gone through all the various tests that comprise the feasibility analysis, you are ready to make a decision about going forward. Of course, throughout the process of doing the tests, you may have decided to stop — because of something you found out from analysis of the industry, market, product/service, and so forth. But if you're still on the mission, now's the time to define the conditions under which you go forward.

### Timeline to launch

You always need to end a feasibility analysis with an action plan so that you're sure that at least something will happen. Establishing a list of tasks to be completed and a time frame for completing the tasks will increase the probability that your business will be launched in a timely fashion. The research you have done along the way will help you make wise decisions about the length of time it takes to complete everything and open the doors to your business.

# Part II
# Developing Your Business Concept

The 5th Wave          By Rich Tennant

BLUBBER IN·A·CUP

OUT OF BUSINESS

"It's hard to figure. The concept was a big hit in Nome."

## In this part . . .

You're swimming in entrepreneurial waters in this part, focusing on all the activities entrepreneurs do to test business opportunities in the marketplace. You discover how to research your industry and target market, then test your customer, product or service, and distribution channel. You also figure out what type of start-up team is best for your venture — and how much money all this is going to take.

# Chapter 5

# Listening to What Your Industry Tells You

*In This Chapter*

▶ Looking at today's industries

▶ Checking out an industry

▶ Selecting an industry

*E*very successful business operates inside an environment that affects everything it does. The environment includes the industry in which the business operates, the market that the business serves, the state of the economy, and the various people and businesses with which the business interacts. The industry is the focus of this chapter. Now, more than ever before, understanding your industry is a critical component of the success of your entrepreneurial venture. If you position your company well inside a growing, healthy industry, you have a better chance of building a successful venture. By contrast, if your business niche is a weak position in a hostile, mature industry, your fledgling business may be doomed.

Industries have lifecycles, just like people. They emerge, grow, go through difficult times, and reach maturity. Then they die or are reborn by some new technology or some other force that gives them new life. The stages in the life cycle of a business basically look like this:

- ✔ **Birth.** A new industry emerges, usually based on some new technology. The PC is one example.

- ✔ **Adaptation.** The initial firms in the new industry go through a lot of experimentation and changes as they adapt to customer expectations during the time that they have proprietary rights that exclude others from competing.

- ✔ **Differentiation, competition.** Over time, as the industry grows and more firms enter, you begin to see intense product differentiation. Less uncertainty is evident because standards have been established and proprietary rights have become less exclusive. The industry becomes competitive.

✓ **Shakeout.** At the most intense point of competition, there is a shakeout, and those companies that are unable to successfully compete leave.

✓ **Maturity.** The industry matures and a few firms dominate.

The point at which you enter the industry determines your strategies and your ability to succeed. Ahead, I talk about how to discover the wealth of opportunity and possibilities in your industry.

# Understanding Your Industry

We are in a time when new industries are emerging on a regular basis. In fact, with e-commerce holding so much of the attention of young entrepreneurs today, you may ask, "Is e-commerce an industry?" That's a great question. If we define an industry as a group of related businesses, then all e-commerce businesses have one thing in common — the Internet. But we know that on the Internet there are retail businesses, manufacturers, wholesalers, and service companies, so every member of the value chain (which I discuss in Chapter 2) is found in one location.

All retail businesses have retail in common, and all manufacturers have manufacturing in common. Are retail and manufacturing industries as well? Within retail, there are clothing retailers and book retailers among many others. Is clothing an industry? Is publishing an industry? The answer to all these questions is yes.

Actually, there are layers of industries, starting with the broadest terms and working down to the more specific terms. As an example, let's take an e-commerce business that almost everyone knows: Amazon.com. Figure 5-1 shows how Amazon.com is positioned.

**Figure 5-1:**
Amazon.com is in the CD-book-toy subsector of the retail business sector of the e-commerce industry.

You can easily see that if we consider e-commerce to be an industry, a grouping of like businesses, then Amazon is definitely part of that industry. Within e-commerce, Amazon is also a retail business that happens to be using the Internet as its marketing/distribution channel. Within retail, it operates in the publishing, music, toys, and video industries, among others. What this means to you is that when you study Amazon's industry, you're really looking at three distinct industries, and it's important to understand what's going on in each. You will need to do the same with the industry you have chosen for your feasibility study. Start at the broadest level of industry definition and work your way down to the segment that includes the product or service that you are providing.

## Using a framework of industry structure

One way to begin to look at the industry in which you're interested is to use a common framework. One framework that I particularly like is based on the work of W.H. Starbuck and Michael E. Porter, two experts on organizational strategy. I adapt their ideas in Figure 5-2, where you see how entrepreneurs must be constantly on the lookout for forces that affect every area of their businesses.

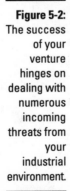

**Figure 5-2:** The success of your venture hinges on dealing with numerous incoming threats from your industrial environment.

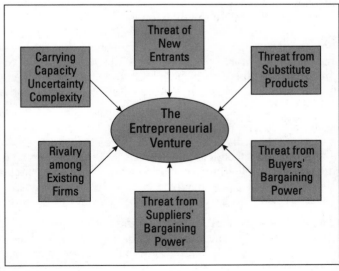

If the entrepreneurial environment looks to you like a battlefield — well it often is! But for every threat there's a countermeasure. The first step is to look at what these outside forces really are.

### Carrying capacity, uncertainty, and complexity

This first environmental factor explains why so many industries today are changing, moving more rapidly, and making it more difficult for businesses to succeed. *Carrying capacity* refers to the extent to which an industry can accept more businesses. It may not have occurred to you that industries can become oversaturated with too many businesses. When that happens, the capacity of businesses to produce their products and services exceeds the demand for them. Then it becomes increasingly difficult for new businesses to enter the industry and survive.

*Uncertainty* refers to the predictability or unpredictability of the industry — stability or instability. Typically volatile and fast changing, computer and many other technology industries produce more uncertainty. But these same industries often produce more opportunities for new ventures to take advantage of.

*Complexity* is about the number and diversity of inputs and outputs in the industry. Complex industries cause businesses to have to deal with more suppliers, customers, and competitors than other industries. Biotechnology and telecommunications are examples of industries with high degrees of complexity in the form of competition and government regulation.

### Threat to new entrants

Some industries have barriers to entry that are quite high. These barriers come in many forms. Here are the main ones:

- **Economies of scale:** These are product volumes that enable businesses to produce goods more inexpensively than a new business can. A new business can't compete with the low costs of the established firms. To combat economies of scale, new firms often form alliances that give them more clout.

- **Brand loyalty:** If you're a new business, you face competitors that have achieved brand loyalty, which makes it much more difficult to entice customers to your products and services. That's why it's so important to find a market niche that you can control — a need in the market that is not being served. That will give you time to establish some brand loyalty of your own. Check out Chapter 6 to find out more about niches.

- **High capital requirements:** In some industries, there are high costs for the advertising, R&D, and plant and equipment you need to compete with established firms. Again, new companies often overcome this barrier by outsourcing expensive functions to other firms.

- **Buyer switching costs:** Buyers don't generally like to switch from one supplier to another unless there's a good reason to do so. That's why once a person invests the time to learn and use the Windows environment, for example, he or she is reluctant to start all over with a different platform. Entrepreneurs must match the need that is not being met with the current product to get the customer to switch.

✔ **Access to distribution channels:** Every industry has established methods for getting products to customers. New companies must have access to those distribution channels if they are going to succeed. The one exception is where the new business finds a new method of delivering a product or service that the customer accepts, for example, the Internet.

✔ **Proprietary Factors:** Established companies may own technology or a location that gives them a competitive advantage over new companies. However, new ventures have often entered industries with their own proprietary factors that enable them to enjoy a relatively competition-free environment for a brief time.

✔ **Government regulations:** In some industries, a long and expensive governmental process, like FDA approval for foods and drugs, can be prohibitive for a new business. That's why many new ventures form strategic alliances with larger companies to help support the costs along the way.

✔ **Industry hostility:** In some industries, rival companies make it difficult for a new business to enter. Because they typically are mature companies with many resources, they can afford to do what it takes to push the new entrant out. Again, finding that niche in the market where you're giving the customer what your competitors are not helps your company survive, even in a hostile industry.

## Threat from substitute products/services

Remember that your competition comes not only from companies that deal in the same products and services that you do, but also from companies that have substitute products. These products accomplish the same function but use a different method. For example, restaurants compete with other restaurants for consumer dollars, but they also compete with other forms of entertainment that include food.

## Threat from buyers' bargaining power

Buyers have the power to force down prices in the industry when they are able to buy in volume. For example, companies like Price/Costco, Toys 'R' Us, and Best Buy have this kind of buying power. New entrants can't purchase at volume rates; therefore, they have to charge customers more. Consequently, it's more difficult for them to compete.

## Threat from suppliers' bargaining power

In some industries, suppliers have the power to raise prices or change the quality of products that they supply to manufacturers or distributors. This is particularly true where there are few suppliers relative to the size of the industry and they are the primary source of materials in the industry. Don't forget that labor is also a source of supply, and in some industries like software, highly skilled labor is in short supply; therefore the price goes up.

### Rivalry among existing firms

Highly competitive industries force prices down and profits as well. That's when you see price wars, the kind you find in the airline industry. One company lowers its prices and others quickly follow. This kind of strategy hurts everyone in the industry and makes it nearly impossible for a new entrant to compete on price. Instead, savvy entrepreneurs find an unserved niche in the market where they don't have to compete on price.

## Deciding on an entry strategy

The structure of your industry will largely determine how you enter the industry. Failing to consider the structure of your industry can mean that you spend a lot of time and money only to find that you have chosen the wrong entry strategy. By then, you may have lost your window of opportunity. For the most part, new ventures have three broad options as entry strategies: differentiation, niche strategy, and cost superiority.

### Differentiation

With a differentiation strategy, you attempt to distinguish your company from others in the industry through product/process innovation, a unique marketing or distribution strategy, or through branding. If you are able to gain customer loyalty through your differentiation strategy, you will succeed in making your product or service less sensitive to price because customers will perceive the inherent value of dealing with your company.

What do you do when your company is stuck in one spot and not growing? If you're Jerry Kohl, CEO of Leegin Creative Leather, you don't sit around waiting for something to happen. In an industry where it's difficult to stand out in a crowd, Kohl found a way to differentiate his company. Leegin makes leather belts — a pretty boring business. So how did Kohl differentiate the company? Through technology and the reinvention of his company. Kohl saw that the industry had a terrible reputation for sloppiness in operations, lost orders, poor manufacturing quality, and poor shipping. That's what had to change. He set out to create a new kind of belt company — lean and mean and customer oriented. And he did just that. Today, his salespeople can tap into industry reports on their laptops when they're in the field with customers. Those stats on how certain types of belts are selling provide credibility when you're trying to convince a customer that one color is selling better than another. The computer also helps the salesperson customize customers' inventories, so they are more efficient, ordering only what they need, when they need it. Salespeople can send in orders online and check the status of orders for their customers.

For Kohl, using technology has meant keeping a better handle on what his 60 salespeople are doing each day. He was so pleased with the success in transforming the sales department that he went on to transform every other function in the business. The result? A company that is a moving target for its competitors — agile and ready for change at a moment's notice. Today, Leegin, which has more than 600 employees in a state-of-the-art manufacturing facility in California, manufactures 20,000 belts a day and ships to 8,000 of the best retailers in the U.S. You can find Leegin at its Web site, http://brighton.com.

## Niche strategy

The niche strategy is perhaps the most popular entrepreneurial strategy for new ventures. It involves identifying and creating a place in the market where no one else is — serving a need that no one else is serving. This niche gives you space and time to compete without going head to head with the established players in the industry. It lets you own a piece of the market where you can establish the standards and create your brand.

Spencer Newman found a niche in the market that suited him perfectly. An avid adventure vacation person, Newman discovered that there were lots of other people like him who liked to hike the Appalachian Trail, ski down volcanoes in the Pacific Northwest, and backpack in Bolivia. Donna Fenn reports in *Inc.* magazine that in 1994, Newman started a mail-order catalog, offering a one-stop shop for adventure-travel books. Soon after starting the business, he was offered an opportunity that changed the future of his business. Outdoor Adventure Online was an Internet site that was interested in putting his catalog offerings on their site. Newman felt that he had nothing to lose, so he did it. Then just a few months later, he was contacted by another Internet business — Great Outdoor Recreation Pages (GORP) — that promised him more than just a listing of his offerings. It promised an interactive shopping cart and would take a percentage of all Newman's online sales. Newman made the move, and by 1997, his tiny company was raking in $1.4 million in sales.

However, before he rested on his laurels, 1998 brought to the forefront a little-known online retailer called Amazon.com that was selling Newman's inventory for 20 percent less. Newman realized that competing on price would never work; he had to give his unique customers what Amazon wasn't able to; he gave them real-time contact with people who actually had experience doing the things that his customers enjoyed. He also offered an online newsletter, maps, videos, and posters. He is now tracking sales generated by his online partners and rewards them with commissions. Recently, Newman opened a small retail outlet, and created a lectures series. He intends to continue responding quickly to changes in his industry — finding new niches to conquer. You can check out his business at www.gorp.com/atbook.htm.

### Cost superiority

Being the low-cost leader is typically difficult for a new venture because it relies heavily on volume sales and low-cost production. A new venture can take advantage of providing the lowest cost products and services when it's part of an emerging industry where everyone shares the same disadvantage.

How does a computer parts business survive anymore in a super-competitive industry that practically gives away the hardware in favor of the software? EBC Computers Inc. does just that, and it does it better than most. The Salt Lake City-based company was ranked on the *Inc 500* as one of the fastest growing private companies in 1999. In an industry that takes no prisoners, Edy Bedoya, EBC's founder, manages to scrape out a net profit of 3 percent. He does it by being a fanatic about keeping costs low. With the prices for computer parts falling rapidly, even a one-day delay can cost a lot of money.

*Inc.* magazine reports that Bedoya keeps inventories at next to nothing and moves a high volume of product. Time is of the essence in this business. For example, in February of 1999, Pentium III 450 chips sold for $510 each at wholesale; they were $289 in May, $262 in June, and $225 in mid July — that's a 56 percent drop in about five months. So for EBC, `www.ebccomputers.com/`, to make any money, they have to sell quickly before prices drop. Bedoya found out two important things about his industry: You have to move fast, and you have to develop trust with the people you deal with.

# Researching an Industry

Getting to understand your industry inside and out is critical to developing any business strategies you may have. Yes, it's a lot of work, but it will pay off many times.

Today, it's much easier to research an industry because of all the sources available on the Internet. But, I must caution you that not everything posted on a Web site is necessarily true or from a creditable source. Anyone can easily put up a Web site, tout that he or she is an expert in whatever, and if you don't do any checking, you may be relying on an unreliable source. So, how do you check on your sources? Here are some things you can do:

✔ Ask yourself if the site or author is a recognized expert in the field.

✔ Ask people who are familiar with the industry you're researching if they've ever heard of that site or that person.

✔ Compare what that site or person has said with what others are saying. If you find a number of sources that seem to agree, you're probably okay. Of course, don't assume that just because many people are saying something, it's necessarily true; that's how rumors get started.

When you present information that you've gathered from someone else's research in your feasibility study or business plan, you need to give credit to that person with a full citation of the title, author, source, date, and page. Things become a bit trickier with Internet sites because sometimes all they give is the URL. Great sites like *Inc.* Online and *BusinessWeek* Online always attribute articles to their authors and the hard copy source. Be wary of sites that do not do this. Always be aware that not all sites archive information, so what you find one week may be gone the next. That's why it's important to have a citation that includes more than just the URL.

When it's time to analyze your industry, you'll find that you can access a wealth of information out there. One good place to start is with the Standard Industrial Classification Index at `www.wave.net/upg/immigration/sic_index.html`. This site lets you search for your industry and industry segment and then gives you the 4-digit SIC code that represents that portion of the industry. This is useful for finding information at many sites you may choose.

## Checking out the status of your industry

As you begin to do your research on the industry, you will probably find yourself overwhelmed with data and not knowing which is important and which is not. Here's a list of questions to guide you in defining the critical information about your industry:

- ✔ **Is the industry growing?** Growth can be measured in many ways: number of employees, revenues, units produced, and number of new companies entering the industry.

- ✔ **Who are the major competitors?** You want to understand which companies dominate the industry, what their strategies are, and how your business is differentiated from them.

- ✔ **Where are the opportunities in the industry?** In some industries, new products and services provide more opportunity; while in others, an innovative marketing and distribution strategy will win the game.

- ✔ **What are the trends and patterns of change in your industry?** You want to look backwards and forwards to study what has happened over time in your industry to see if it foreshadows what will happen in the future. You also want to see what the industry prognosticators are saying about the future of the industry. But the best way to find out about the future of your industry is to get close to the new technology that is in the works yet may not hit the marketplace for five years.

- ✔ **What is the status of new technology and Research & Development (R&D) spending?** Does your industry adopt new technology quickly? Is your industry technology-based or driven by new technology? If you look at how much the major firms are spending on research and development of new technologies, you'll get a pretty good idea of how important technology is to your industry. You'll also find out how rapid the product development cycle is, which tells you how fast you'll have to be to compete.

✔ **Are there young and successful companies in the industry?** If you see no new companies being formed in your industry, it's a pretty good bet that it's a mature industry with dominant players. That doesn't automatically preclude your entry into the industry, but it does make it much more expensive and difficult.

✔ **Are there any threats to the industry?** Is there anything on the horizon that you or others can see that makes any part of your industry obsolete? Certainly, if you were in the mechanical office equipment industry in the early 1980s, we hope you saw the handwriting on the wall with the introduction and mass acceptance of the personal computer.

✔ **What are the typical gross profit margins in the industry?** The gross profit margin (or gross margin) tells you how much room you have to make mistakes. Recall that the gross margin is the gross profit (revenues minus cost of goods sold) as a percentage of sales. If your industry has margins of 2 percent like the grocery industry (sometimes even less), you have little room for error, because 98 percent of what you receive in revenues goes to pay your direct costs of production. You only have 2 percent left to pay overhead. On the other hand, in some industries gross margins run at 70 percent or more, so you end up with a lot more capital to expend on overhead and profit.

## Competitive intelligence: Checking out the competition

One of the most difficult tasks you face is finding information about your competitors. I'm not talking about the obvious things that you can easily find by going to a competitor's physical site or Web site. I'm talking about the really important stuff that can affect what you do with your business concept — things like how much competitors spend on customer service, what their profit margins are, how many customers they have, what their growth strategies are, and so forth. If you're in competition with private companies (which is true most of the time), your task is that much more difficult because private companies don't have to disclose the kinds of information that public companies do.

Here's some of the information you may want to collect on your competitors:

✔ The management style of the company.

✔ Current market strategies. Also, look at what they've done in the past because history tends to repeat itself.

✔ The unique features and benefits of the products and services they offer.

✔ Their pricing strategy.

✔ Their customer mix.

✔ Their promotional mix.

It's helpful to create a grid or matrix that lists all your competitors — direct, indirect, and emerging — so that you can immediately make comparisons with your company.

With a concerted effort and a plan in hand, you can find out a lot about the companies against which you will be competing. Here's a step-by-step strategy for attacking the challenge of competitive intelligence.

### Pound the pavement

If your competition has physical sites, visit them and observe what goes on. What kinds of customers frequent their sites? What do they buy, and how much do they buy? What is the appearance of the site? How would you evaluate the location? Gather as much information as you can through observation and talking to customers and employees.

### Buy your competitors' products

Buying your competitors' products helps you find out more about how your competition treats its customers and how good its products and services are. If you think that it sounds strange to buy your competitors' products, just remember, as soon as yours are in the marketplace, they will buy them.

### Rev up the search engines

Go to the Internet and hit the search engines. Just type in the name of the companies you're interested in and see what comes up. True, this is not the most effective way to search, but it's a start, and you never know what you'll pull up that you otherwise may not have found. Don't forget, many search engines are available. Some of the more common ones are listed below:

| Search engine | URL |
| --- | --- |
| Yahoo.com | www.yahoo.com |
| MSN.com | www.msn.com |
| GoTo.com | www.goto.com |
| AltaVista | www.altavista.com |
| Lycos | www.lycos.com |
| Northern Light | www.northernlight.com |
| Infoseek | www.infoseek.go.com |

## Check information on public companies

In most industries, public companies are the most established companies and often the dominant players, so it's a good idea to check them out. They can also serve as benchmarks for best practices in the industry. There are a host of online resources related to public companies. Here are some of the best:

- ✔ *Hoover's Online,* www.hoovers.com: This source provides detailed profiles of more than 2,500 public companies, which you can access free if you have AOL. Otherwise, it costs you $9.95 a month. But they'll let you download free half-page profiles of more than 10,000 companies.

- ✔ **U.S. Securities & Exchange Commission,** www.sec.gov: This site contains the SEC's Edgar database. It's not terribly user friendly but has great information. Try Free Edgar, www.freeedgar.com, which is a good place to research public companies and those that have filed to go public.

- ✔ *One Source,* www.onesource.com: This site charges a fee, but you may be able to access it through your local college or university. It is an excellent site that provides in-depth reports on public companies and industries. It's a favorite sight of students needing to do industry reports.

## Use online media and newsgroups

Here are some great online sources that you may want to check out:

- ✔ *Inc 500,* www.Inc.com: This database of the fastest-growing private companies in the U.S. contains information you won't find elsewhere on revenue, profit-and-loss percentages, numbers of employees, and so forth for the past eight years.

- ✔ *NewsDirectory.com,* www.newsdirectory.com: This site provides links to Web sites of more than 2,000 newspapers, business journals, magazines, and computer publications.

- ✔ *The Electric Library,* www.elibrary.com: This is a great site if you're looking for articles, reference works, and news wires. You can try it for 30 days free; then it's $9.95 a month. But, if you are near a local university, you may be able to access it from their library computers.

- ✔ *Deja.com Usenet,* www.deja.com/usenet/: This is the self-proclaimed largest archive of e-mail discussion groups. Similar sites include Remarq, www.remarq.com/, and Liszt, www.liszt.com/.

- ✔ *John Makulowich's Awesome Lists,* http://209.8.151.142/: At this site, you'll be able to link to more than 140 sites for everything from intellectual property to the Library of Congress. By the way, if you're wondering who John Makulowich is, he's the vice president of The Writers Alliance, Inc., trainer.com, a corporation specializing in Internet training and IT writing with offices in Maryland and Northern California.

✔ *ProfNet,* www.profnet.com: This site provides a direct link to experts at universities, colleges, corporations, and national laboratories. You may be able to find an expert in your industry and contact that person. There is no charge.

✔ *The Competitive Intelligence Guide,* www.fuld.com/: This site gives you advice on how to seek competitive intelligence and has many links to information on specific industries.

## Troll for data at government Web sites

You will find an extensive network of government sites with mostly free information on economic news, export information, legislative trends, and so forth. Two sources link to most of these sites. They are

✔ *The Federal Web Locator,* www.infoctr.edu/fwl/

✔ *FedWorld,* www.fedworld.gov/

You may also want to go directly to many other often-used sites like the following:

✔ *STAT-USA,* http://www.stat-usa.gov/: This site bills itself as "*the* site for the U.S. business, economic, and trade community, providing authoritative information from the Federal government."

✔ **U.S. Department of Commerce,** www.doc.gov: Here you'll find everything you ever wanted to know about the U.S. economy.

✔ **U.S. Census Bureau,** www.census.gov/: This is the home of the stats based on the census taken every ten years.

✔ **Bureau of Labor Statistics,** www.bls.gov/: This is another site full of information on the economy, in particular, the labor market.

✔ **Patent & Trademark Office,** www.pto.gov: This site is the home of everything you wanted to know about patents, trademarks, and copyrights.

✔ **U.S. House of Representatives Home Page,** www.house.gov/: If you're tracking any kind of legislation that may affect your industry, this is the place to go.

## Use the best Internet sites

If you're doing an Internet business, you will want to look at some sites that focus on providing statistics relative to the Internet. A few of the better ones are

✔ *CyberAtlas,* www.cyberatlas.com: This is a good jumping off point. It regularly posts the latest stats on the Net. If you access the "stats toolbox" section, you will find specific information on topics like advertising, education, finance, retailing, and so forth.

✔ *Emarketer,* `www.emarketer.com`: The reports from this company are reasonably priced and are based on the company's proprietary research.

✔ *The Industry Standard,* `www.thestandard.com/research/metrics/`: This site maintains an extensive database of information on the Internet; plus, it lets you download PowerPoint slides for presentations.

✔ *Mediamark,* `www.mediamark.com`: This site provides general Internet statistics.

✔ **IDC,** `www.idc.com`: This site also provides general Internet statistics.

### Go offline for more research

The Internet is not the only place you can find important information. Some offline sources that you ought to consider include:

✔ **Industry Trade Associations:** Virtually every industry has its own trade association with a corresponding journal or magazine. Trade associations usually track what's going on in their industries, so they are a wealth of information. If you are serious about starting a business in your particular industry, you may want to join a trade association, so you'll have access to inside information.

✔ **Network, network, network:** Take every opportunity to talk with people in the industry. They are on the front lines on a daily basis and they will give you information that is probably more current than what you'll find in the media or on the Web.

# Benchmarking Against the Perfect Industry

Today, with industry boundaries breaking and changes occurring at a breathtaking pace, it isn't easy to find the perfect industry. But here's a benchmark to start: Generally, you're looking for an industry that has more things working for your business than against it — makes sense! So, look for an industry

✔ With more than $50 billion in sales, and therefore more likely to provide many niche opportunities that you can capture.

✔ That is growing at a rate greater than the GNP (gross national product), in other words, one that's friendly to new entrants.

✔ That will let your company make after-tax profits of more than 5 percent of sales within three to five years.

✔ That is socially and environmentally responsible. You may get the added benefit of special grants and other types of funding given by the federal government to companies that produce products and services that are responsible.

# Chapter 6

# What Your Customers Can Tell You

● ● ● ● ● ● ● ● ● ● ● ● ● ● ● ● ● ● ● ● ● ● ● ● ● ● ● ● ● ● ● ● ● ● ● ● ● ● ● ● ● ● ● ● ● ● ● ●

### In This Chapter
▶ Defining who your customers are
▶ Focusing on your customers
▶ Forecasting customer demand for your products or services

● ● ● ● ● ● ● ● ● ● ● ● ● ● ● ● ● ● ● ● ● ● ● ● ● ● ● ● ● ● ● ● ● ● ● ● ● ● ● ● ● ● ● ● ● ● ● ●

*Y*ou have no business without customers. If that's true — and it is — why do so many entrepreneurs fail to plan their businesses around the needs of their customers? Doesn't it make sense that if you design your business to fulfill a customer need, you have a ready market for your products and services?

Identifying a *target market* — the customers who are more likely to purchase from you — is critical. You do so by conducting a thorough feasibility analysis of your business concept (check Chapter 4 for an overview of feasibility analysis). Everything else about your business may appear viable, but if you can't demonstrate that sufficient customer demand exists, the concept won't fly.

In this chapter, you discover how to research and interact with potential customers so that you can gather enough data to make an informed decision about the future of your business.

## Defining Your Niche

In Chapter 5, the focus is *industries* — groups of businesses that have things in common, do transactions with each other, and compete with each other. *Markets* are groups of customers inside an industry. Take a look at Figure 6-1 and you see that in conducting your feasibility analysis (determining whether your business concept is viable), you work your way down from the broad industry to the narrower market niche.

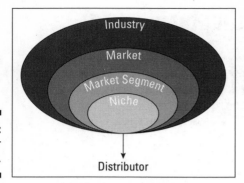

**Figure 6-1:**
Finding your
niche.

Industry

Market

Market Segment

Niche

Distributor

## Narrowing your market

Within each broad market are *segments*. For example, the broad market of people who buy books contains segments of customers for:

- ✔ Travel books (or any other broad category of books)
- ✔ Kids books
- ✔ Books appealing to seniors
- ✔ Audio books

Within a market segment, you can find *niches* — specific needs that aren't being served — such as:

- ✔ Travel books geared toward people with disabilities
- ✔ Kids books that target minorities
- ✔ Books that teach seniors how to deal with technology
- ✔ Audio books that provide current journal articles to professionals

Market niches provide a place for entrepreneurs to enter a market and gain a foothold before bigger companies take notice and begin to compete. Having a niche all to yourself gives you a *quiet period* during which you alone serve a need of the customer that otherwise is not being met. As a result, you get to set the standards for the niche. In short, you're the market leader.

As you zero in on your market, take care that the niche you ultimately choose is big enough to allow your business to make money. The niche you select must have enough customers willing to buy your product from you, enabling you to pay your expenses and turn a profit. I talk about how to do that market research elsewhere in this chapter.

Defining your target market is about identifying the *primary customer* for your products or services — the customer most likely to purchase from you. You want to identify a target market because creating customer awareness of a new product or service is time-consuming and costly, requiring lots of marketing dollars — dollars that few start-ups have at their disposal. So, instead of using a shotgun approach and trying to bag a broad market, aiming at the specific customers who are likely to purchase from you is far more effective. More important still, going to the customer who's easiest to sell to helps you gain a foothold quickly and start to build brand recognition, which makes selling to other potential customers easier.

Your first definition of a target customer will probably be fairly loose — an estimate. For example, suppose your target customers are "professional women." That's a fairly broad estimate. But as you conduct market research, you come to know your primary customer well. In this example, the picture may emerge of "a woman in law, medicine, or business, who is between 35 and 55 years of age, married, with two children."

The basic questions to answer about your potential customers are:

✔ What are their demographics: age, education, ethnicity, income level?

✔ What are their buying habits? What do they buy? When? How?

✔ How do customers hear about your products and services? Do your customers buy based on TV ads, magazines, Internet advertising, word-of-mouth, referrals?

✔ How can your new business meet customers' needs? What customer need is your product now meeting?

Where do you find the answers to these important questions? Your market research — actually talking with potential customers — provides answers. You also discover some techniques for market research later in the chapter.

Not all customers are individuals; many are other businesses. In fact, the greatest dollar volume of transactions conducted on the Internet today is business-to-business. If a distributor, wholesaler, retail store, or manufacturer is paying you, your customer is a business, not an individual consumer. Businesses as customers can be described in pretty much the same way that you describe a person. Businesses come in a variety of sizes and revenue levels. Like consumers, they also have buying cycles, tastes, and preferences.

Don't forget that if your customer is another business, that business may not be the actual end user of your product or service. So then you also have an *end user* to deal with. The end user is the ultimate consumer, the person who uses the product or service. For example, look at Figure 6-2, which depicts a typical channel for distributing a product.

**Figure 6-2:**
Typical
distribution
channel.

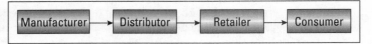

If the distribution channel in Figure 6-2 is filled with your products — refrigerators, for example — who is your customer? It's the distributor who purchases the fridge from you to distribute to retailers. The retailer, in turn, is the distributor's customer. The consumer, who actually uses the fridge, is the retailer's customer and your end user. (The easiest way to identify the customer is to find out who pays you — follow the money!)

Just because the end user is not technically your customer doesn't mean that you can ignore the end user. You need to know as much about the end user as you do about the customer, because you must convince the distributor that a market for the product exists and that the end user will buy enough product so that the distributor and retailer can make a profit. Thus, you must conduct the same kind of research on the end user that you do on the distributor.

## Developing a niche strategy

One primary reason to define and analyze a target market is to find a way into the market so that you have a chance to compete. If you enter a market without a strategy, you're setting yourself up for failure. You are the new kid on the block. If customers can't distinguish you from your competitors, they're not likely to buy from you. People generally prefer to deal with someone they know.

Niche strategy is probably the premier strategy for entrepreneurs because it yields the greatest amount of control. Creating a niche that no one else is serving is the key. That way, you become the leader and can set the standards for those who follow. Niche strategy is important because, as the sole occupant of the niche, you can establish your business in a relatively safe environment (the *quiet period,* as I call it at the top of this chapter) before you develop any direct competitors. Fending off competitors takes a lot of marketing dollars, and when you're a start-up company, you have numerous better uses for your limited resources.

How do you find a niche that no one else has found? By talking to customers. The target market from which your business opportunity comes also holds the keys to your entry strategy. Your potential customers tell you what's missing in your competitors' products and services. They also tell you what they need. Fulfilling that unmet need is your entry strategy.

## Airport niche targets business travelers

You have to go where your customers are; that's where opportunity and your niche in the market are. At least that's what the *Wall Street Journal* reports that Mathias Plank believes. Plank is the founder of Dressmart.com, an online men's clothing retailer. He found his niche in (of all places) airports. Plank is opening Internet sites at several major airports in Europe. His research determined that travelers — particularly business travelers — are often stuck in airports waiting for connections and want to make productive use of their time. Dressmart provides a place where businessmen who have little time, but lots of money, can shop for clothes and have them delivered to their homes. What Plank is betting on is that businessmen will prefer shopping online at airports more than taking time to shop at a traditional store.

Three employees at each airport site take measurements and enter data into the computer. Already, Plank claims to have thousands of fashion profiles of European businessmen in his database.

The question now: Is the market big enough to sustain the business? Certainly, many businessmen travel by plane, and it is generally true that most men don't like to shop by traditional means. But how many will use their downtime at airports to shop rather than to eat, drink, read, or dose? It's always wise to do a test version of your business in a location that is representative of the market. Then, if the first site is successful, you can feel more confident about adding others.

# Researching Your Customers

The research you do on your target market is probably the most important of all, because it helps you determine who your primary customer is. It also helps you determine the level of demand for your product or service. Many new business concepts have failed because entrepreneurs misjudged their marketplace, envisioning more demand than actually existed. That's a costly error that you can avoid, maybe not totally, but substantially.

Market research begins with a plan. The following sections cover components of that plan.

## Figuring out what data you need

Before you take the time to collect data, decide how you're going to use that data and what you need to demonstrate with the data. Do you need to

- ✔ Demonstrate demand for your product or service?
- ✔ Describe the primary customer?
- ✔ Describe the buying patterns of your customers?

Each of these questions requires a different type of data. For example, demonstrating demand for your product or service may require you to find a similar product or service and use its history to estimate demand figures for your enterprise. You can also set up a test site — a temporary, miniature version of the business — to gauge demand. To describe your customer, you need data on demographics like age, income level, and education. To discuss the buying patterns of your customers, you need psychographic data like buying behavior.

These are just a few of the things you may want to achieve through your market research. You want to determine your outcomes first so that you collect the right data. Nothing is more frustrating than doing your analysis and discovering you forgot to gather an all-important piece of information that you needed to present your case.

## Looking at secondary sources first

*Secondary* research involves finding out what others have said about your target market. It's important to do before you go out and talk to people in the market yourself (doing your *primary* research). With the background information you gather from secondary sources, you prepare yourself to ask better, more accurate questions of the people you interview — you don't waste time on the basics.

A good place to start is the U.S. Federal Census Bureau, online at www.census.gov, where you can find all sorts of demographic information, such as age, education, income, and numbers of workers per household. You can define a geographic area and discover whether it is growing, declining, aging, or getting younger. To find some quick facts, just click on the dropdown menu of states and find the one that you're interested in. For example, if you select Colorado, you're directed to links to the 1997 Economic Census, income and poverty statistics, county business patterns for individual years, and many other useful facts. You can see whether the workforce is skilled or unskilled. These kinds of demographics help you determine whether your market has the disposable income you require for your products or services. You can also use census data to figure out how many customers are located within specific geographic boundaries and then segment out customers who meet your requirements.

In your community, you probably have an economic development department and a chamber of commerce that keep statistics on local population trends and economic issues. You may also find an office of the Small Business Development Corp., www.sba.gov/hotlist/sbdc.html. SBDC, a branch of the Small Business Administration, www.sba.gov, that keeps tabs on new ventures and provides funding.

Don't overlook trade associations as a research resource. They give you information about your industry and track customers as well. Online, look at sites like the following associations and publications, to name just a few:

- ✔ *American Demographics,* www.demographics.com/: Contains a wealth of information on consumer markets
- ✔ **American Association for Public Opinion Research,** www.aapor.org/main1.html: Covers every topic imaginable in terms of public views on issues
- ✔ *Market Insights,* www.marketinsights.com/: Deals with the health care market

## *Doing primary research to get the best information*

Doing your own research — called *primary research* — is the best way to get the most current and useful information on your target market. Nothing beats getting out in the marketplace and talking to everyone along your value chain (your distribution channel) about where the needs are.

The biggest challenge of conducting a market analysis is proving that a market for your product or service exists and that it is large enough to make the business concept feasible.

Don't make the mistake made by so many entrepreneurs of assuming they have a winner simply because an assortment of friends and family are over-whelmingly positive about the concept. Maybe these admirers are right, but maybe they're flat out wrong.

To get good data from unbiased responses, you must choose a representative sample of your target market that is unknown to you. That's called a *random sample*. You want people who don't have a personal interest in seeing you succeed, because you want their honest responses. The form of your questions is another crucial concern. Just asking potential customers whether they would buy does not give you the kind of information you need — it's too easy for a respondent to say yes or no without giving you any useful information. You need answers to *why questions,* such as the following:

- ✔ Why will you buy this product or service?
- ✔ Why are you not interested in this product or service?
- ✔ Why do you purchase in these locations?
- ✔ What would it take for you to purchase this product or service?

The answers to why questions give you information that helps you refine your business concept and ensure you're giving customers what they want.

### Surveys by mail and telephone

The first thing many people think of when they hear primary research is doing a survey, either by mail or phone. Despite the advantages of ease and ability to reach many people, mail and phone surveys have significant disadvantages.

✔ Questionnaires are not as easy to develop as you think. Some people spend whole careers studying the most effective ways to question people. If you do choose to use a questionnaire, here are a few tips to make it more effective:

- Keep it short.

- Don't ask leading or biased questions — any question that tends to direct the response.

- Ask the easy questions first.

- Ask the demographic questions last.

- Put answers to multiple-choice questions about age and income (which people resist anyway) into ranges so that respondents don't have to give an exact answer. It is well known that people responding to surveys typically lower their age one category and raise their income one category.

✔ Response rates to mail surveys usually are low, around 15 percent, and achieving even that level usually requires follow-up. A 15 percent response means that about 85 of every 100 persons sampled did not respond. Think about what that non-response rate means: If 15 people responded and 10 of that number (a whopping two-thirds!) said they would buy your product, what do the other 85 think? You have no idea. The only way to resolve the non-response bias is to make an effort to increase the response rate. That, however, takes money. Fortunately, other methods of collecting good data about your customers exist; I discuss those shortly.

✔ With mail and phone surveys, you don't have the benefit of nonverbal communication, like the visual clues to attitudes that you easily pick up in face-to-face interviews. This shortcoming of mail and phone surveys is important, because it has been estimated that 85 percent of all communication is nonverbal.

✔ With mail surveys, you have no way of clarifying a response and no control over the accuracy of the information. (How often have you given a stranger just any old response to a questionnaire that you didn't have time for?)

✔ Phone surveys take much more time to conduct and are prone to interviewer bias.

# Sample questionnaire suitable for mail and phone surveys and interviews

This survey was created by two USC students, David Burlison and Joe Emerson, to obtain information about their potential customers for an Internet concept involving a prepaid purchasing account.

1. Do you have an Internet account?

Yes___ No___

*(This is a screening question so that you don't waste your time on people who don't have Internet access.)*

2. How much time do you spend online each week?_____

*(This question is designed to ascertain how serious an Internet user the respondent is.)*

3. What are your primary uses of the Internet?

a. E-mail

b. Research

c. Shopping

d. News

4. What primary method do you use for making purchases?

a. Cash

b. Check

c. Credit Card

5. Do you have your own credit card?

Yes___ No___

(If no, answer Question 6. If yes, skip Question 6.)

6. Whose credit card do you use to make purchases online?_____

7. Have you ever purchased any goods or services online? Yes___ No___

8. What are your primary concerns with online purchasing?_____

_____

_____

_____

_____

9. If a system allowed you to make secure purchases over the Internet without the need for a credit card, would you be interested in using it?

Yes___ No___Why?_____

_____

_____

_____

_____

_____

To find out more about developing surveys and to see another sample survey, check "How to Prepare a Market Analysis" at
`http://209.241.14.8/fmpro?-db=homepage.fp5&-format=fulltext1.htm&Record=6357&-find`.

### Interviews and focus groups

Personal interviews and focus groups may cost more time and money than mail and phone surveys, but you get what you pay for. These methods can be designed to provide comparatively more valuable market information like:

- ✔ You have more opportunity for clarification and discussion.
- ✔ You gain the advantage of viewing nonverbal communication.
- ✔ The response rate is high.
- ✔ You can ask more open-ended questions.
- ✔ You get the added benefit of being able to network and make new contacts.

A *focus group* is a group interview for which you bring together a representative sample of potential customers to view a presentation of your product or service and discuss its merits. The leader of the focus group (perhaps yourself, but more likely someone specially trained in this interview technique, so that your own biases don't creep in) introduces the product or service you offer, sometimes along with other competing products and services, in an effort to solicit opinions from the group. For example, suppose you're introducing a new kind of beverage. You may do a blind study, offering several beverages (including your product) to the focus group and asking group members to comment on taste, aftertaste, and so forth.

Focus groups can help prevent you from making a costly error in product design or marketing strategy.

## Putting together a customer profile

A customer profile is what you construct from all the data you gather about your prospective buyer. The profile describes your typical customer in great detail, whether the customer is a person or another business, along with demographics, buying habits, and all other factors important to understanding where a buyer is coming from. For example, your typical customer may be "a 35-year-old well-educated female concerned about health issues, who earns $50,000 to $60,000 a year working principally in a management position and has a family with two children."

Knowing that much about your customer (and you certainly can add a lot more to this example) helps you tremendously when you design your marketing plan to reach this customer. The profile also helps you refine your business concept and your product/service design.

## Give customers what they want

Knowing exactly what your customers want can mean not only more sales but also more initial interest in your venture from the people who provide the financing to get it off the ground. At least that's what happened to Gus Conrades and his partner Bryan Murphy. The two launched Wrenchead.com, which sells auto parts and car-care products.

The partners succeeded in raising a first round of $15 million on the strength of their business plan, which summed up their business concept in a simple sentence: "Wrenchead.com sells auto parts to consumers and professionals over the Internet." Investors had no trouble understanding the business. Of course, the partners were also

able to demonstrate that the auto parts market is a hefty $32 billion a year, promising the potential for growth. Conrades and Murphy had both a clear vision of where the company was going and the data to support what they were saying. And they knew the auto parts business inside-out.

The partners also were wise enough to understand that warehousing and distribution is as important (if not more important) than the Internet itself. Their customer-oriented strategy worked: They now sell millions of auto parts and brand-name accessories around the world. (For more details, go to www.fsb.com/fortunesb/ articles/0,2227,662,00.html and www. wrenchead.com.)

# *Forecasting Demand: Tough but Crucial*

One of the more difficult aspects of market research is figuring out how much demand exists for your product or service. The problem is that no one best way to do it exists, so you must approach it from several points of view. This process of using multiple approaches is called *triangulation;* I show you a trio of methods in a moment.

You can certainly extrapolate demand figures from the work of others, but the best numbers come from your personal research in the market. Be forewarned, however, that five people telling you they will buy your product or service is not enough (as I caution you elsewhere in this chapter). You need to know, for example, that five out of six people questioned at random say they will purchase your product or service at a particular price. If you can come up with that kind of result each time you question a focus group, you have a pretty good sense of demand down the road.

If you don't do a good job of forecasting now, you may create huge problems for yourself later, when your attention is occupied by making deadlines, looking for customers, and scrambling to find the people you need to meet demand. Here are a couple of suggestions to help you improve your forecasting:

✔ **Quantify expectations.** You need to know how much you expect your business to grow on an annual basis in terms of sales, profits, and number of employees. For most businesses, growth is fairly predictable, but you can't always control demand. For instance, if you introduce a new technology or product that suddenly catches fire, you can experience what is known as *hockey stick growth* (think of the growth line on a sales chart). If you don't anticipate that growth, you may not have the cash or the human capital available to keep up with demand.

✔ **Ask the right questions and insist on real answers.** You must be able to support the numbers. If you're claiming that sales will grow from $1 million to $5 million by the second year, your banker wants to know what causes that growth? Are you spending more on marketing? Have you reduced costs? What is the basis for the increase? Just be sure that you can explain how you arrive at your figures.

Many factors affect a sales forecast. If any of the items in the following list are relevant to your business, think about them when you calculate sales growth.

✔ **Seasons:** Nearly every business is affected by seasonal demand, that is, months, weeks, days, or even times of the day when customers buy more than at other times.

✔ **Holidays:** In the retail business, holidays are major sales times. By contrast, in manufacturing, holidays may represent a slow time of the year.

✔ **Fashions or styles:** In the clothing industry, for example, you have to know how long a particular fashion is going to be in favor with consumers to be able to judge its economic life.

✔ **Population changes:** Population shifts can cause certain regions, cities, or neighborhoods to change such that a restaurant or boutique no longer has a customer base.

✔ **National developments:** Wars, elections, the stock market, and so forth affect consumers' buying habits.

✔ **Competition:** If you have a lot of competition, for example, you probably have to bring your prices down, meaning you must sell more to make a profit.

✔ **External labor events:** Labor shortages and strikes can depress productivity, and that can depress sales.

✔ **Consumer earnings:** In good times, earnings are high and consumers buy.

✔ **Weather:** Bad weather and catastrophes, like hurricanes can be a boon to businesses like construction, but a bust to sellers of luxury goods.

✔ **Product changes:** Changes in your products mean that customers have to become familiar with something new, so sales may decline for a period of time. By contrast, if the change is welcome, sales may rise precipitously.

✔ **Credit policy changes:** Favorable credit policies may encourage more sales, while no credit may discourage sales.

✔ **Inventory shortages:** Shortages can discourage customers and send them elsewhere to shop, reducing your sales. By contrast, if a product that is in demand experiences a shortage, sales may actually rise at a higher-than-normal pace.

✔ **Price changes:** On goods and services that customers don't require to live or do business, a change in price can directly affect sales — positively if the price goes down and negatively if it goes up.

✔ **Distribution methods:** On any product or service, customers have a preferred way to make their purchases. So if you select the wrong distribution channel, you can lose sales.

Your challenge is to find the best way to gauge demand for your product or service. As you do, don't fool yourself — too much is at stake.

# Triangulating to Demand

Now, back to the business of triangulation. Triangulation involves approaching a demand number from three different sources. You simply get three or more different points of view concerning demand and decide on what appears to be the best information. In this section, I discuss three techniques for developing demand data.

## Using substitute products and services to gauge demand

If you're introducing a product or service that actually is an extension of something already in existence, you may be able to base your demand estimation on the level of demand established by the previous product or service. For example, demand for compact discs was derived from demand for cassette tapes. In other cases, you may be able to substitute another similar product that caters to the same customer base to help you judge demand.

## Interviewing customers and intermediaries

The people who can give you the best estimates are those who work in the market on a daily basis: customers and intermediaries like distributors, wholesalers, and retailers. Spending some time talking with them about the market and what they're seeing in terms of sales levels for products is time well spent. (To find out more about how to talk to industry people, see Chapter 5.)

## *Going into limited production with a test market*

Sometimes the only way to gauge customer demand is to go into limited production so that you can see how customers respond to what you're offering. You may want to do this especially if you've successfully tried the first two techniques I suggest. Putting a product out in the market in a limited fashion lets you get feedback that enables you to modify the product if necessary before it reaches the mass market, where modifications and returns can be costly.

Software companies regularly ship prototype versions to the consumer and business market in not-so-perfect fashion and count on their customers to report bugs to them. Then they create a *patch* to fix the bug and offer it free to download from their Internet site. Although not the best way to do things, that's the nature of that industry, and customers haven't objected too strongly.

If you achieve a successful test market, you can expand to a more formal test market in a specific geographic market that is representative of your customers on a national level. Denver, Colorado, is often used as a test site because of its demographics, which are representative of the U.S. as a whole.

# Chapter 7

# Designing Products and Services for a New Marketplace

## In This Chapter

▶ Finding new product ideas

▶ Developing products like an entrepreneur

▶ Building a prototype

▶ Writing a product plan — in a minute flat!

**R**emember Indiana Jones in *Raiders of the Lost Ark?* At one particularly perilous moment he confides to an impatient colleague, "I'm making this up as I go!"

That's pretty good advice to an entrepreneur on the trail of a new product or service in the new business environment— seize opportunity from the moment, make up the rules as you go. As if you had a choice! Practically everything that used to be considered gospel on the topic of designing new products and services is in the trash can today thanks to technology and a little distribution channel called the Internet.

Yet, some things remain constant: It still costs a lot of money to design and build a working model of a new product. And you still have to satisfy a customer. Today, customers have more choices than ever before and they're grouping themselves in new ways, so it's virtually impossible to mass market to customers in traditional ways. Reaching today's customer is like hitting a moving target, requiring entrepreneurs to embrace the strategies of *mass customization* and *mass personalization*.

Mass customization is giving customers what they want, when they want it, and in the way they want it. One of my companies, for example, produces a combination air-compressor/generator that's usually painted cardinal and gold. But when one of our customers asked that we paint the machines he ordered in yellow and green to match other equipment he had, and to mount a different brand of compressor on the machine, of course we agreed. That's an example of modifying your product to meet the specific needs of your customers. We can do that with our machine because we design the machine with interchangeable parts and mass customization in mind.

Mass personalization, on the other hand, is designing the product in a way that is personal to that customer. For example, when you revisit Amazon.com after registering the first time, the home page greets you using your own name. Over time, Amazon.com tracks your purchases and suggests products for you to look at based on what you have bought previously.

One more thing about the nature of product development today: The boundaries between products and services are fading away. Product companies offer services; service companies develop products; and most companies offer a bundle of products and services. For example, Kinkos, the reprographics company, started by offering copy services, but today also merchandises some office supplies as well — because it made sense that customers might want to see Kinkos as a one-stop shop. However you define your company, think about developing both products and services to offer your customers.

In this chapter, I talk mostly about developing *products*. But you can substitute the word *services* if you want. Services need a development process, too, and it's virtually the same routine that you follow with products. You wouldn't think of opening a new restaurant, for example, without testing your menu first and planning for all the tasks that must be performed smoothly and accurately so that your satisfied customers keep coming back.

# Zeroing-in on a New Product

Many entrepreneurs would like to deal in products, but they're not quite sure how to get started. Of course, you could import products from other countries or buy your products from domestic manufacturers. But if you like the idea of manufacturing and distributing a brand new technology or other type of product, then you have three choices: invent something, team with an inventor, or license an invention.

## Become an inventor

If you're the kind of person who likes to tinker and play around with new ideas that might become inventions, then your role might be to invent a new product. Most entrepreneurs, however, are not inventors — not because they don't have the ability to invent, but because their focus is elsewhere. The mindsets of the entrepreneur and the inventor tend to be quite different and it's unusual to find both in the same person. Not only are the mindsets different, but the skills required by each are very different. In general, pure inventor types aren't interested in the commercial side of things. They invent for the love of invention. Unless an entrepreneur comes along and points out an opportunity, many inventors never see their inventions reach the marketplace.

I work with may types of inventors — engineers, scientists, and so forth — and most would rather spend their time in the laboratory than consider business issues like markets and customers. You have to ask youself what role feels right to you and do that. You can always find the other talents in someone else.

## Team with an inventor

Entrepreneurs often team with inventors to commercialize a new product. That's what my husband and I did with our company (look at the sidebar to see how we recognized our opportunity). Often the opportunity to team with an inventor comes out of the industry in which you're working. You hear about someone who's working on something; you investigate and discover an interesting invention. Do not hesitate to approach an inventor, but remember a couple of important things:

1. **Inventors are paranoid about their inventions. They are sure that someone is out to steal their ideas.**

2. **Inventors typically aren't business oriented and don't want to become business people. Their love is inventing, so don't expect them to be partners in a business sense.**

Structure an arrangement with your inventor that doesn't hamstring your efforts to commercialize the invention. You are each bringing something very important to the mix, so be sure you can work together well.

## License an invention

Companies, universities, the government, and independent inventors are all looking for entrepreneurs to commercialize their inventions. You gain access to these inventions through a vehicle known as *licensing.* Licensing grants you the right to use the invention in an agreed-upon way for an agreed-upon time period. In return, you agree to pay a royalty to the inventor, usually based on sales of the product that results from the invention. You can find out more about licensing in Chapter 8.

The government owns many core technologies developed for the military and the aerospace program, among others. You can license these core technologies and create a new application for use in a different industry. For example, if you go to the NASA technology site at http://nasatechnology. nasa.gov/portal_main.cfm, you can go to the page that highlights their Tech Briefs — summaries of all the technologies available to license.

Alternatively, visit the technology licensing office of most major research universities and you'll find more opportunities. For example, the Stanford University Office of Technology Licensing evaluates, markets, and licenses technology owned by Stanford University. If you go to their site at `http://otl.stanford.edu/industry/index.html`, you would be guided through a process that could potentially lead to your licensing one of their technologies. You would start by familiarizing yourself with their licensing process; then looking for a technology that interests you. Suppose you are interested in medical devices and want to see what kinds of technologies are available. If you go to their list of medical devices `http://availtech.stanford.edu/Scripts/otl.cgi/search?keyword=medical_devices&title=` you find a complete list of all the technologies invented at Stanford University. Click on the docket number and you see a complete description and picture or schematic of the device and the name of the contact person.

Universities are a gold mine of new technology that you can tap into.

CASE STUDY

## Genesis of a product

In the early 1990s, my husband and I were doing commercial real estate development in the San Joaquin Valley in California. We had a group of subcontractors we regularly used on our projects, and one of them was a finish carpenter by the name of Bill Nelson. He had a passion for inventing things. One day he arrived at our home with a very curious looking device in the back of his old pick-up truck. We quickly found out that it was an electric generator and an air compressor sitting on twin four-gallon air tanks, and driven by a small gasoline engine. The concept was simple. When the user starts a power tool, whether air-powered or electric-powered, the machine senses which type of tool is being used and engages either the air compressor or the generator. No one had ever been able to do this before.

We thought the concept intriguing, but at the time, we were busy divesting ourselves of some real estate deals because the market was in a downturn.

A year later, Nelson came back with an improved machine. He confidently attached a hose to the machine with a power tool on the end, walked about 100 feet away, pulled the trigger of the power tool, and the drive motor of the unit started up and the power tool started working. When he lay the tool down, the motor stopped. He also did the same with a small air-powered drill. The machine was designed to allow multiple users of air and electric-powered tools to operate them remotely and simultaneously from one power source, and it provided many other benefits over existing generators and compressors.

Nelson had no business experience and no concept of what it would take to develop his invention to a marketable condition, but we knew it would take a lot. He knew that we had the business experience he needed to commercialize the product. We went into a licensing agreement with him and agreed to fund the development and patenting of the device.

By the time product development was completed and the machine was introduced in the marketplace in 1998, it in no way resembled the original prototype in either design or function. It had now become an intelligent machine with three patents on it. We were able to take his very basic mechanical concept and transform it into a state-of-the-art electronic machine. The inventor continues to develop improvements and work with us.

# Thinking Realistically about Product Development

If you only had to worry about all the changes in the way product development happens, you'd be fine. But as an entrepreneur you have one big issue that big companies don't have — limited resources. Translated, that means not enough money and not enough people to do what you want to do. I don't mean to discourage you right off the bat, but you need to be realistic. It's one thing to start from a concept and build a product that is market-ready when you have a staff of engineers, labor, and unlimited funds to make it happen quickly. It's quite another thing to try to do it when all you have are your own resources.

Because you are working with limited resources, you will probably have to outsource some of the product development tasks. This means you will hire independent contractors to do things like manufacturing, designing, or prototyping. For our product, the intelligent power source, we outsourced everything but final assembly. That meant we worked with 44 vendors, independent contractors, and suppliers. It's like being the ringmaster of a three-ring circus.

You may already feel this will be a daunting task, but I want to encourage you to think of it as a challenge that you can meet. In fact, bootstrapping your way through product development can be a good thing. A lack of resources has propelled many an entrepreneur to seek innovative product and process solutions. In fact, research has found that new entrepreneurial companies are the most successful at introducing break-through innovations — products that change the way we do things. Big companies are better at building sustaining technologies; in other words, technology that is merely an improvement over something that already exists. So, take heart. It may not be easy, but chances are you can develop the next great product.

## Finding the money

I am fond of saying that for entrepreneurs, it's not about the money. And, in general, that's certainly true. You're starting this business because you're passionate about your concept, you want to become independent, or you've always wanted to own your own business. But, if you're interested in starting a business that develops and markets new products, you're in a whole new ball game. Whether you're developing the next great toy, a medical device, or an Internet site, it takes a lot of capital up front. So, for these types of businesses, it really is about the money.

The first thing you should know is that, for the most part, no one is out there waiting to hand you money to turn your product concept (now only on paper) into the next great product. Most entrepreneurs must rely on their own resources to fund product development, at least until they get a working prototype. That's because investors can't conceptualize the value of a product the way the entrepreneur/inventor can until they can see it, touch it, and use it. Then, and only then, might an investor understand the benefit.

The machine that my company developed (see the sidebar) took five years of effort and over $300,000 before it was ready to be marketed. My husband has a background in engineering, so he took the lead on product development, while I did a lot of market research to discover the best applications for the product. We each contributed financially to this process from other things we were doing. We had no outside capital. Remember, this was an industrial machine, not a sexy Internet start-up with people clamoring to contribute money. Five years to develop a product is a long time, but we moved it forward only as fast as the money came in. And we had to live and support our family at the same time. In addition to normal product development costs, we also had to pay for patents to protect what we had developed. It was not easy — there were times when we ran out of money and had to halt product development for a time — but we believed in the product and the benefit it would provide to the user. We resisted asking friends and relatives for help because we knew it would take a long time to build the company, and we didn't want to risk their hard-earned money.

The exception to the rule of needing to use your own resources is generally cutting-edge, new technology — core technology that has the potential to spin off many applications in the form of new products. In this case, you may qualify to apply for government grants or to seek private or professional venture capital.

### Government grants

The government has come to the rescue of many an inventor or company that wanted to develop a new technology from scratch or access a technology that the government developed. I review here the major governmental agencies that provide seed and development capital to private companies.

> ✔ **Small Business Investment Company (SBIC).** These entities are similar to private venture capital funds. Licensed by the Small Business Administration, they provide long-term loans and equity funding (capital in exchange for a stake in the business) to start-up and growing businesses. Each SBIC is different; some focus on certain phases of funding, like early seed funding or growth funding, while others focus on certain types of businesses. You can find them through the SBA Web site at www.sba.gov.

✔ **Venture capital institutes and networks.** Many universities have begun to provide matching services as a way to help local entrepreneurs find investors. The university takes no equity stake in the new venture, but merely acts as a go-between. Typically, the entrepreneur pays an admission fee and submits his or her business plan. The network tries to match the needs of the business with an investor. If an investor is interested in talking to an entrepreneur, contact is made. The success rate of these matching services is not high, but for entrepreneurs who don't have a large network of contacts with investor types, they're a good place to start. Investors sign up with these services voluntarily, so they're looking for good businesses to invest in.

✔ **The Small Business Administration.** If you have previously owned or operated a business, you may qualify for an SBA-guaranteed loan for a new business. The SBA's focus is to provide funding to businesses that may not qualify under traditional banking criteria. If an SBA-backed loan recipient defaults, the SBA guarantees that it will repay the lending institution up to 90 percent of the loan. Although advertisements claim that qualifying criteria for SBA loans are less stringent than for traditional commercial loans, the reality is that most banks judge small, new businesses by the same standards they apply to established businesses. Thus, plan on doing a lot of paperwork if you get one of these loans. The SBA also has a micro loan program (amounts up to $25,000) for entrepreneurs with limited access to capital.

✔ **Small Business Innovative Research (SBIR).** All federal agencies with research and development (R&D) budgets in excess of $100 million must earmark a portion of their budgets to funding grants for small businesses (under 500 employees) devoted to developing technologies in which the government is interested. You can find out what technologies interest the government by checking the solicitations published by the various agencies; the Web site at `www.nttc.edu/solicitations.html`, and the SBA Technology Transfer Program. Agencies like the Department of Energy (`www.oit.doe.gov/inventions/`) describe the kinds of inventions they are supporting. The following are some of the agencies that offer grants:

- Department of Defense

- Department of Energy

- Department of Transportation

- Department of Interior

- Department of Education

- National Aeronautics and Space Administration (NASA)

- Nuclear Regulatory Commission

- Environmental Protection Agency

- Health and Human Services

- National Science Foundation

- Department of Agriculture

Grants provided by the agencies listed here go through three phases, the details of which are described at www.sba.gov/sbir/sbir.html:

- **Phase I (the start-up phase):** Provides awards of up to $100,000 for approximately six months to support and explore the merit or feasibility of an idea or technology.

- **Phase II:** Provides awards of up to $750,000, for as many as two years, to expand the Phase I results. During Phase II, research and development work is performed, and the developer evaluates commercialization potential. Only Phase I award winners are considered for Phase II.

- **Phase III:** Phase III innovation moves from the laboratory into the marketplace. The small business must find funding in the private sector or other non-SBIR federal agency funding.

✓ **State-Funded Venture Capital.** A number of states — Massachusetts, New York, and Oregon, to name a few — provide venture funds to encourage start-ups to locate in their region of the country. For example, Texas has more than 44 state-based venture capital funds. Likewise, states without venture funds may offer special loan or tax incentives to encourage start-ups. Check with the Secretary of State's office in the state you're interested in to see what's available.

### Investor capital

Finding private investors who are willing to take the risk of investing in the very early stages of product development is rare. Unless you've just discovered the next fax machine or PC equivalent, they probably won't even talk to you until you have a working prototype. However, once you have a prototype that's reasonably close to being market ready, some private investor groups — the ones that have carved out a niche in the gap between your personal resources and large-scale private and venture capital — may be willing to provide you with seed capital.

I've sat in on sessions between investors and inventors enough times to know that too often the inventor has no understanding of what it takes to develop a product from the drawing board, the laboratory, or the garage to production quality — something people will buy. They're still too far away from market reality to interest an investor. Take a look at Chapter 13 to find out more about sources of money for starting and growing your business.

### The real truth

If you're thinking the least bit about developing a new product, start saving your money and thinking about potential resources now. Later in this chapter, you find out ways to save money on product development and to get help from others so that you can go through the process more quickly.

## Developing new products: The process

Product development is a process comprised of many tasks. It used to be that you could depict the product development process in a linear fashion that looked similar to Figure 7-1. Each task was completed before the next was started in a logical, orderly process.

**Figure 7-1:**
The traditional product development process.

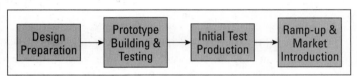

This process works fine in a marketplace that's fairly stable and predictable, but it can't survive in today's dynamic and unpredictable markets. Today, companies focus on fast-cycle product development with a more integrated approach. What I mean by *integrated* is that all the company's functions are represented in the planning, design, and development processes. As a result, you derive input from engineering, manufacturing, marketing, finance, and the customer from the beginning. Dynamic product development looks more like Figure 7-2.

**Figure 7-2:**
Dynamic product development replaces the traditional, linear approach with total, simultaneous input from all company functions.

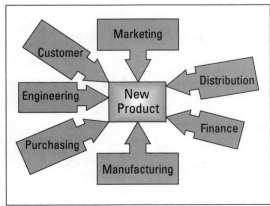

The advantage of getting everyone involved in the process from the beginning is that the ultimate product will reflect each participant's input individually and as a group. For example:

- ✔ **Customer:** Provides valuable information about the product design and functionality so that he gets what he needs.

- ✔ **Engineering:** Uses comprehensive product information to design the product right the first time.

- ✔ **Finance:** Follows production costs and warns developers if they're choosing a component or part that will be too costly in the final product.

- ✔ **Manufacturing:** Makes sure that a viable process for producing the product exists.

- ✔ **Marketing:** Keeps tabs on the marketplace to make sure that the product is well accepted when it's launched.

- ✔ **Purchasing:** Establishes reliable relationships with vendors to make sure that they deliver parts on time.

Notice that although I refer to these functions as if they're major departments in your company, you may outsource many of these functions or have only one person responsible for a particular function. Perhaps your area of expertise is engineering, and your partner's expertise lies in finance. You'll likely have to hire or partner with employees, companies, and other independent contractors to perform the remaining functions to make your project happen.

If you get everyone involved in the process, you can develop your product much faster — and that's important in a world where customers' preferences can change overnight.

### Getting the feedback you need

Here's a checklist of the kinds of feedback you need to solicit from all the people involved in the development of your product:

- ✔ What makes the product better and easier to manufacture?

- ✔ What does the marketplace think of the product?

- ✔ What improves the product, its components, and the way it's built?

- ✔ How reliable is the product? Are any components less reliable than others?

- ✔ Are customers satisfied with the prototype they've seen?

- ✔ Is the product easy to maintain?

- ✔ How will you service the product?

- ✔ How will you handle complaints?

- ✔ How will you get positive publicity for the product?

Answers to these questions are the basic information you need during the process of product development. You may think of more specific questions to ask about your particular product or service.

### Overcoming scarce resources

Many solutions are available to help you overcome the limitations of a start-up company's scarce resources. Here are a few of them:

- ✔ If you have several products in mind, prioritize and start with the one that will bring you the biggest return on investment. Alternatively, if one of the products is the easiest and least costly to develop and has a good-sized market potential, you may want to start with that one.

- ✔ Don't reinvent the wheel. Don't try to manufacture products that others already do very well. Focus your energies on what you do well and out-source everything else. Doing so is called focusing on your *core competencies.* Later, when your company is well established, you can think about bringing some outsourced tasks in-house to save money, control quality better, and speed up your processes.

  Tasks that you may want to outsource include component design, materials specifications, machinery to produce, ergonomic design, packaging design, and assembly drawings.

- ✔ Wherever possible, purchase off-the-shelf parts and components.

- ✔ Look into job shops that can do some of the work for you. Make sure that they will work as quickly as you need and that they're used to working with entrepreneurs.

### Developing in a digital world

The Internet makes it possible to do a complete or partial development of some types of products in cyberspace. Entrepreneurs like Jef Chappell deliver digital products and services to their customers entirely over the Internet. Chappell discovered the power of the Internet for rapid prototyping and testing. He takes advantage of the free hosting services on the Web to put up a prototype Web site featuring his products and services. When the site garners enough customers to begin to show a profit, he shifts the site over to a full-service ISP and invests more significant marketing dollars into the company at that point. That way, if his product or service isn't working the way he wants it to, he has the option to tweak it or shut it down before it costs him a lot of money. You can find a list of those free ISPs by going to the *Free Websites Directory* at http://find.freehosting.net/bizhosts.htm.

Maybe you're not developing completely digital products. Even if you're doing something as traditional as a new toy, a line of apparel, or a mechanical device of some sort, the Internet makes it easier for you to collaborate with partners in any part of the world.

# Designing in digital dreamland

Suppose you have a great idea for a new kind of backpack that is kinder to backs and shoulders — in other words, an ergonomically correct backpack. You've sketched some designs, but now it's time to work with a real designer so the pieces fit together right and the product can be replicated for production purposes. Further, suppose you live in Wyoming and the best designers for this type of item are located in Los Angeles. Flying back and forth is rather awkward, and faxing big design sheets is difficult.

The best solution is e-mail or a Web site. Your designer can e-mail the finished sketches or blueprints to you as a document attachment. You must make sure that you have a compatible program that can read the documents. Otherwise, the designer may be able to take a digital snapshot of the design and send that to you.

Alternatively, the designer can post the product designs on a secure page on his or her Web site and enable you to access it with your browser. The designer may even provide you with access that allows you to mark the design where you have questions or want changes. The two of you can also view the design simultaneously and talk about it.

Design is not the only task you can accomplish by using the Internet. Today you can send your completed designs — say for a new part for your machine — to a rapid prototyping shop, where the design enters a computerized prototyping machine that spits out your part in metal or some other medium.

If your outsourcing partners are online, coordinating work and receiving regular progress updates are a snap. If you want to really go all the way, you and your partners can install digital cameras so that you can actually view what they're doing for you.

Why consider the digital route to product development? Here are some of the many reasons:

- ✔ By outsourcing, you share the resources of other companies and spread the risk of product development.
- ✔ When you link the core competencies of several companies, you get better product innovations because everyone is doing what they do best.
- ✔ By integrating the knowledge and skills of many companies, you can reduce your time to market.
- ✔ Your relationships with other companies give you access to new markets.
- ✔ Solutions are easier to sell than products. Customers really don't buy products; they buy solutions to problems.

Of course, I don't want to make it sound as if partnering in cyberspace has no disadvantages. The fact is that strategic alliances with other companies for product development are like any other partnerships: They can be fraught with problems if you don't choose your partners carefully. So choose partners that believe in what you're doing and have similar company cultures and ways of doing business.

# Moving Fast to Prototype Stage

One critical component of success in product development today is the ability to advance quickly to the prototype stage. When you have a physical model, you can see product features that are sometimes difficult to see in either a blueprint of a design or a computer-simulated model.

*Ergonomics,* the study of how equipment, furniture, and so on affect the human body in workplace situations, is a design feature that becomes more apparent in a physical prototype. When we first designed our PowerSource machine, the design engineer put the handles down low near the wheels. Not until the first prototype was built did we discover that this placement would never work, because even though the prototype handles provided greater leverage to lift the machine, you would hurt your back doing it. The design was not ergonomically correct, so we moved the handles to a better position. We didn't see that problem in the drawings.

One thing you need to know about prototypes: They can cost up to ten times as much as the final product costs to produce, because you're not ordering parts in volume and you're paying your independent contractors a premium for building one or two units instead of 100 or more at a time.

While you're looking for parts for your prototype, try asking manufacturers for samples. Usually, they send a sample for free, because it's more expensive for them to invoice you than it is just to send it.

## Designing right

The design of your new product represents an estimated 8 percent of your budget for the product, but it determines fully 80 percent of the ultimate cost of the product and its subsequent price to the customer. That's an important figure! What that means to you is that if you can make your design right the first time, you'll save a lot of time and money. Redesign — which entails reengineering, new drawings, and a reworking of the prototype — ends up being more costly than the original design, not to mention the potential for a lost opportunity in the marketplace by not getting there quickly.

Estimates indicate that the cost of designing your new product represents only about 8 percent of your overall start-up budget. Nevertheless, that relatively small amount determines fully 80 percent of the ultimate cost of manufacturing the product and, in turn, how much the customer pays for it. That makes design costs an important figure! If you make your design right the first time, you can save a lot of time and money. If not, you face an expensive redesign of your product, which entails reengineering, new drawings, and a reworking of the prototype, adding cost upon cost to the cost of the original design — not to mention the potential for lost opportunity by reaching the marketplace later than expected, or worse, behind someone else.

I can't go into all the technical elements of engineering design, but here are some key elements to ponder when you begin to design your product:

✔ **Start with a good product definition.** A good definition takes feedback from all the functions of your business (I discussed this in the section "Developing new products: The process," earlier in this chapter), especially from your customers. Changing the handlebars on our machine after the first prototype cost us a lot of time and money. Get as much feedback as possible.

✔ **Ask customers what they need, expect, and want.** What customers *need* are the features that they must have to be satisfied with the product. What customers *expect* are the standard features that would be basic to any product of this type. What they *want* are the special features that apply to their individual circumstances — their wish lists.

  You definitely want to prioritize these items, because the cost of putting everything the customer wants into the product may be too high.

✔ **Deploy quality function.** A lengthy discussion of Quality Function Deployment *(QFD)* aside, you may want to consider this method for letting the customer design the product by identifying critical customer preferences and requirements and incorporating them into the design. Software is available to walk you through the process, and some consultants specialize in facilitating QFD.

✔ **Design for manufacturability.** Designing your product with the process of producing it in mind is wise. By doing so, you can significantly reduce manufacturing costs and increase productivity. If you plan to outsource the manufacture of your product, be sure to include that manufacturer in your design phase. Factors you're trying to achieve in designing for manufacturability include

  • Minimizing the number of parts.

  • Simplifying components and using common or standard parts.

  • Designing parts with symmetry.

  • Minimizing electrical cables.

  • Making parts independently replaceable.

- Eliminating adjustments of manufacturing equipment.

- Eliminating fasteners to simplify assembly and reduce direct labor.

- Eliminating jigs and fixtures (devices that hold parts of your product in place while it's being worked on so that each product produced is exactly the same) to reduce changeover costs.

✔ **Design for quality.** If you wait to think about quality until you're manufacturing your product, you're late. Inspecting for quality can raise production costs by as much as 50 percent. If you plan for a quality product and process during the design stage, you can engineer a reliable and stable manufacturing process.

## Sourcing your materials

One product development task that many entrepreneurs overlook in planning the timeframe for product development is the sourcing of materials and parts for their products. Materials and parts account for about 50 percent of total manufacturing cost, so you need to choose them carefully. Locating vendors to supply your materials needs is not a difficult task — there are thousands of them — but finding the best vendors at the right price is the hard part. It took almost a year for my company to source all the components for our machine and arrive at 44 vendors that could give us high-quality parts and components at the best prices. If you don't factor that time and effort into your calculations for how quickly you can get your product to market, you could end up being way off in your timing.

Your first decision is whether to use more than one vendor to supply a single part. A big advantage to using a single vendor to supply as many of your needs as possible is that you'll probably get better service for buying parts in larger quantities and bigger discounts because you're buying more. The main disadvantage is that if something happens to that lone vendor — his warehouse burns down or he raises prices, for example — you won't have a backup that you can turn to quickly. Cover yourself by always having a backup. Perhaps you can purchase 80 percent of your parts from the main vendor and 20 percent from the backup.

Questions to ask yourself when looking for the best vendors include the following:

✔ Can this vendor deliver what I need when I need it?

✔ How much will freight cost using this vendor?

✔ What services does this vendor provide?

✔ Is the vendor familiar with the product lines I'm using?

✔ What are the vendor's maintenance and return policies?

Go online to search for vendors. Most of the good ones have Web sites now. Several sites help you compare prices without having to use the telephone. And be sure to compare prices. A simple bolt can range in price from a few pennies to more than a dollar!

## Making your product

You don't have to be a manufacturer to produce a product. In fact, setting up a manufacturing facility is a pretty expensive undertaking. More and more entrepreneurs are taking advantage of technology and strategic alliances to outsource manufacturing and save money by not having to invest in a plant and equipment at a time when the product is unproven in the market and resources are limited.

Finding someone to manufacture your product is a task that you need to undertake at the same time you're beginning to design the product so that you can integrate product and process in the most effective way. Plenty of manufacturers are able to do what you need in the United States and throughout the world. When you did your industry analysis for feasibility, you probably discovered some of these manufacturers and discovered whether products in your industry are typically manufactured domestically or in foreign countries. Knowing where competitors manufacture their products is important, because if they are manufacturing for a low cost in China and you choose to manufacture domestically at a higher cost, you must find a way to make up the difference so your price to the customer isn't out of line with the rest of the industry.

## The One-Minute Product Plan

A product plan doesn't have to be a long, drawn-out document with pages of information. It should answer the following questions:

- ✔ What is my product?
- ✔ Who will design the product?
- ✔ Who will build the prototype?
- ✔ Will the product require patents?
- ✔ How will the product be produced?
- ✔ Who will manufacture the product?
- ✔ How much will it cost?
- ✔ How long will product development take?

# Chapter 8

# Protecting Your Products and Services

*In This Chapter*

▶ Protecting your mousetrap — patents

▶ Protecting your creative efforts — copyrights

▶ Protecting your brand — trademarks

▶ Protecting everything else — trade secrets

▶ Developing a strategy for intellectual property (IP)

*B*efore the Information Age, assets were mainly things you could touch — tangible things like manufactured products and buildings. In the Roaring Twenties, for example, economists thought the wealth of U.S. companies was based 70 percent on tangible assets and only 30 percent on intangible things like patents, trademarks, copyrights, and trade secrets.

How times have changed! Today, the experts say, the tangible-intangible ratio has reversed. Company value today is based only 37 percent on tangible assets but 63 percent on the intangibles, which as a group are called *intellectual property,* or IP. Intellectual property has become the ultimate asset in the Information Age. In other words, the most important things companies own today are not bricks and mortar and warehouses full of products but intellectual property — patents, trademarks, copyrights, and trade secrets.

Big companies are now stockpiling this IP in a way they've never done before. They know that patents and trademarks are like gold; they can be sold for huge amounts or licensed to other companies and individuals, providing new revenue streams. Even very small companies are benefiting from this new wave of enthusiasm for IP. A small company with an important patent can find itself being acquired for many times its earnings.

But intellectual property also has a downside, especially knowledge assets. If your company owns an asset like a building, you can be fairly comfortable that no one is going to steal it. By contrast, you can't be certain that no one is going to steal your software code. Similarly, you can usually get at least some return on your investment with a hard asset like a building. But preserving the value of your knowledge assets is a totally different story. That's what I talk about in this chapter — strategies for protecting your brilliant entrepreneurial inventions, from the better mousetrap (at last!) to the perfect company logo.

# Patenting Your Better Mousetrap

What exactly is a patent? A patent grants an inventor a proprietary right — the right to *exclude others* from making, using, offering for sale, or selling the invention — for 20 years from the date on which the application for the patent was filed in the U.S. At the end of the 20-year period, the patent goes into public domain, and anyone may produce and sell it.

Today, patents are enjoying a tremendous resurgence of interest. Everyone, it seems, is trying to patent something. One woman tried to patent her own genes. Even the U.S. Patent and Trademark Office (PTO) has gone patent crazy, issuing to itself Patent 5,885,098 for a "spiral patent office," which is the new patent office that looks something like New York's Guggenheim Museum.

Do you have any idea which invention receives more patent applications than any other? Why, it's that better mousetrap, of course. The first patent was issued in 1903. Even today, the PTO receives at least 40 applications a year for patents on the mousetrap; but of the 4,400 patents issued, only the original inventor has made a profit off his patent.

Being able to patent your product, an aspect of your product, your process, or your business model (how you make money) gives you a distinct competitive advantage for a time because it theoretically creates a clear field for you to introduce your product and establish your brand before others can copy what you did. As the rest of the chapter explains, however, what is theoretically true and lawful isn't always what happens.

## Timing is everything

Many inventors and entrepreneurs wait until they're ready to file for a patent to document and protect their inventions. That's a big mistake. From the first day you conceive an invention, it is vital that you date, sign, and state the purpose of any documents related to that invention. Having your signature witnessed also adds strength to your claim. Keeping any records that can assist in proving your first-to-invent claim in a safe place is a good idea. In fact, I recommend (as does the PTO) keeping your records in a bound document.

## De-fizzed

In the United States, only the original inventor can file for a patent; that is not the case in most other countries. The difference between the U.S. and most countries is that in the U.S., the *first to invent* has *first right* to file for a patent. In other countries, the *first to file* has first right. But don't think you can invent something and then take your time about filing for a patent.

I once had a student who developed a new kind of bottle stopper, ensuring that the fizz would stay in sodas as long as the stopper was in place. He talked to a patent attorney, and the plan was to file for a patent in the early 1990s before provisional patents (I talk about those later in the chapter) were possible. Prior to provisional

patents, inventors filed simple disclosure statements with the patent office, giving notice that as of the filing date, the inventor exercised his rights to this device.

Well, the busy attorney neglected to file the disclosure document until my student reminded him. Later, when they applied for a patent, they discovered that someone on the other side of the country had already filed for a patent on the same type of device, preventing my student from obtaining a patent. Had the attorney filed the disclosure document right away, my student probably would have been declared the first to invent. Yes, timing is everything.

Avoid leaving blanks in your descriptions, and try to avoid erasures and line-out mistakes. If you're working on a computer, make sure that everything you do is date-stamped by the computer and shows the progression of your work. You may also want to print out a hard copy, sign it, date it, and have it witnessed, because you can change dates on computer-generated documents.

## Is it patentable?

Your invention must meet several criteria before the PTO will consider it for a patent.

✔ **Inventions require classification.** An invention must fall into one of five classes:

- Process type (industrial or technical)
- Machine
- Articles of manufacture
- Composition of matter (chemical compositions)
- New and useful improvement of any of the preceding four classifications

Combined, these classes include almost everything made by humans and the processes to make those things. You cannot patent laws of nature, physical phenomena, or abstract ideas.

✔ **The invention must be new and not contain prior art.** You cannot patent your invention if it was known or used by others, or patented, or described in a printed publication anywhere in the world before you invented it or more than one year before you applied for a patent. So, the bottom line is that if you're going to talk about or use your invention in public, filing for a patent immediately helps you avoid the risk of not being able to file at all.

✔ **The invention must be not be obvious.** An invention must be sufficiently different from what has been used by (or described to) someone having ordinary skills in the area of technology related to the invention. For example, you can't patent an invention that merely substitutes one material for another or changes the size of the invention.

✔ **The invention must have utility.** This means that your invention must be useful. It can't be whimsical.

## Types of patents

In general, the patent office grants two types of patents: utility and design. Utility patents are the more common type. They protect the functional parts of machines or processes in addition to software that drives machines. Some examples are toys, film processing, protective coatings, tools, and cleaning implements. A utility patent is valid for 20 years from the date of application.

Design patents cover ornamental designs for an article of manufacture and protect only the appearance of an article, not its structural or functional features. The design patent is valid for 14 years from grant and, unlike a utility patent, requires no fees to maintain.

The U.S. Patent Office also recognizes plant patents, which are granted to anyone who has invented or discovered and asexually reproduced a distinct and new variety of plant. The patent is granted for the entire plant.

You may also obtain a life-forms patent. This type of patent covers altered human genes, microbes that break down crude oil, and so on.

### Patenting small inventions

Beginning in 1995, the PTO began offering the option of filing a *provisional application for patent (PPA)*. This kind of patent protects small inventions whose inventors need more time to talk with manufacturers about building them. The PPA is less costly and much easier to file than a regular patent. It also establishes an early effective filing date in a patent application and lets you use the term *Patent Pending* on the invention. The date on which the PTO receives your written description of the invention, drawings, and your name determines the filing date.

The advantage to a PPA (beyond the ease of filing and lower cost) is that it gives you an additional year on the term of your patent. The PPA is abandoned by law 12 months after the filing date, so you must file an application for a nonprovisional patent within that time. Be aware that you can't file a PPA on a design invention.

### Issuing new "business method" patents

When two Internet companies unveiled their patents in August 1998, shock waves of discomfort were sent through the business world. It wasn't the mere fact that they had the patents as much as it was the nature of those patents. No, Priceline.com and Cyber Gold Inc. hadn't patented technology or products; they had patented their business models. In essence, Priceline and Cyber Gold were saying that they had invented new ways of doing business, and that if anyone wanted to use them, they had to receive a royalty. Priceline claims that it created the first reverse auction for airline tickets. Cyber Gold Inc. developed a system that automatically pays consumers to look at advertising.

You can patent a business method if it meets the criteria of being novel and having utility, but this type of patent is so new that no one really knows what the eventual outcome will be. Concerns that the PTO is moving closer to patenting concepts rather than technology or industrial inventions could open a Pandora's box of problems. Only time will tell whether the business method patent will hold.

## The patent process

The patent process is well defined, so following it on your own is an option. In fact, plenty of books show you how to patent your own invention. But I don't recommend that course. The examiners and attorneys at the PTO speak a language that only a patent attorney can decipher. When you consider that whether you are issued a patent depends on how well you state your claims in the patent application, hiring a good patent attorney to help you through the process is worth your time and money.

Patent attorneys are specialists, so don't hire your basic business attorney to file your patent application. Furthermore, if you intend to file for foreign patents, know that requirements vary from country to country, and typically, only a specialist in patent law is able to successfully wade through the morass.

### *Filing a disclosure document or provisional patent application*

As I discussed earlier in this chapter, filing a disclosure document with the PTO establishes a date of invention that becomes part of your patent record in case your invention receives a challenge later on. You can obtain a disclosure document on the PTO's Web site, www.uspto.gov. You can file this simple form without an attorney.

Don't rely on the old advice about mailing a dated description of the invention to yourself by certified mail. That tactic has no value to the PTO.

Many attorneys today advise inventors to file a PPA and not worry about the disclosure document. The PPA requires a more elaborate description of your invention such that someone could replicate what you've done. The disclosure document does not. Yet filing the PPA allows you to use the words *Patent Pending* or *Patent Applied For,* which give notice to others that you can exclude them from making or selling an invention like yours. Filing a PPA costs $75 for a small entity — a small price to pay to protect your hard work — but you have to file for your regular patent application within 12 months.

### *Filing a nonprovisional patent application*

The formal patent application contains a complete description of the invention, what it does, and how it uniquely differs from anything currently or previously existing. The application requires you to furnish a drawing of the invention — unless your invention deals with compositions of matter or some processes — that must show every feature that you specify in your claims.

In the claims section of the application, you describe in detail (specific enough to demonstrate the invention's uniqueness, but broad enough to make it difficult for others to circumvent the patent) the parts of the invention on which you want patents.

After receiving the application, the PTO conducts a search of its patent records for prior art, which can take up to three years. During that time, the public does not have access to your application, so your invention secrets are protected.

For an idea of what you're up against, you can conduct an initial patent search on your own by going to the PTO's Web site at www.uspto.gov.

The PTO contacts you when it completes the records search, stating whether it accepts all the claims, accepts only some of the claims, or denies the application. You can appeal a denial.

Most inventions receive a denial of at least one claim on the first round. You may then rewrite that claim, addressing the issues raised by the PTO before resubmitting it.

While the PTO is processing your patent application, you may display *Patent Pending* or *Patent Applied For* on your invention, but understand that these phrases have no legal effect. They indicate only that you have filed for a patent. Patent protection doesn't begin until the PTO examiner accepts all the claims and issues a patent.

As a side note, patent examiners specialize in certain categories of inventions, so they're usually familiar with the prior art in their areas of expertise. For example, I met a patent examiner whose specialty was inventions related to hydraulics, and that's all he did.

If your patent application is rejected, even after modifications, you can appeal to a board of patent appeals within the PTO. If your appeal doesn't succeed before the board, you can appeal to the U.S. Court of Appeals for the Federal Circuit. Of course, the appeals process can take years, and by then, you may have lost the window of opportunity to commercialize your invention. Failing to obtain a patent doesn't mean that your product doesn't have market potential; it means that intellectual property will not be one of your competitive advantages.

Filing for a utility patent costs $345 ($155 for a design patent) if you're a small entity. The issued patent costs $605 for a utility patent ($215 for a design patent). Remember that these fees do not include the cost of attorneys, which is usually substantial.

Once your patent is issued, you must mark your product with the word *Patent* and the number of the patent. If you fail to do so, you may not be able to recover damages from an infringer. On the other hand, if you mark a product as patented or patent pending when it isn't, you have broken the law and are subject to penalties.

Be aware that once your patent is issued, it becomes a powerful document that you must protect against infringers. If you allow people to infringe your patent, you can lose it. I discuss infringement of intellectual property rights later in this chapter.

### *Protecting your rights in foreign countries*

If you're planning to export your product and want patent protection outside the U.S., you need to file applications in each of the countries in which you plan to do business. Your U.S. patent is not valid outside the U.S. Patent laws in other countries differ in many respects from U.S. laws. For example, if you publicly discuss your invention prior to filing a patent application, even in the U.S., you may be barred from filing for a patent in a foreign country. In addition, most countries require that the product be manufactured in that country after three years.

Under the Paris Convention for the Protection of Industrial Property, each of the 140 adopting nations, including the U.S., guarantees to the citizens of all member nations the same rights in patent matters given to its own citizens. Likewise, within 12 months of first application in one member country, you enjoy first right to file in any of the other member countries. Check with a good patent attorney who's experienced in international agreements when you are first considering patenting your invention.

You must obtain a license from the Commissioner of Patents and Trademarks before you can apply for a patent in a foreign country.

# Copyrighting Your Original Work of Authorship

Copyrights protect original works of authors, composers, screenwriters, and computer programmers, published and unpublished. In general, a copyright does not protect the idea itself but only the form in which it appears. For example, if you compose a piece of music but don't put it down on paper or record it on some medium like a compact disc (essentially, it's just in your mind), it isn't protected.

The Copyright Act gives the owner of copyrighted material the exclusive right to reproduce, prepare derivative works, distribute copies of the work, or perform or display the work publicly. Copyrights are registered by the Copyright Office of the Library of Congress. Effective January 1, 1978, a copyright lasts for the life of the holder plus 70 years, after which it goes into public domain.

## Claiming copyright

To protect your original works of authorship, the work must be in a fixed and tangible form and contain a copyright notice (although the latter is not required by law) so that a potential violator cannot claim innocence because there was no notice. Your notice should contain the word *copyright* or the symbol © and provide the year of the copyright along with the complete name of the copyright holder, as in "© 2000 John Doe."

You are not required to register with the Copyright Office to obtain full protection under the law, but doing so is a good idea. You need to submit an application, the required fee, and a complete copy of an unpublished work or two complete copies of a published work. Here are some advantages to registering your copyright:

✔ It establishes a public record of your copyright.

✔ Before you can file an infringement suit, the copyright must be registered.

✔ If you register before or within five years of publication, your registration will establish evidence in court of the validity of the copyright and of the facts you've presented in the certificate.

✔ If you register within three months after publication of your work or prior to an infringement of your work, you will be able to claim statutory damages and attorney's fees in court.

## *Things you can't copyright*

According to the Copyright Office of the Library of Congress, `www.loc.gov/copyright/circs/circ1.html#wwp`, the following cannot be copyrighted:

✔ Works that have *not* been fixed in a tangible form of expression (for example, choreographic works that have not been notated or recorded, or improvisational speeches or performances that have not been written or recorded)

✔ Titles, names, short phrases, and slogans; familiar symbols or designs; mere variations of typographic ornamentation, lettering, or coloring; or mere listings of ingredients or contents

✔ Ideas, procedures, methods, systems, processes, concepts, principles, discoveries, or devices, as distinguished from a description, explanation, or illustration

✔ Works consisting *entirely* of information that is common property and containing no original authorship (for example, standard calendars, height and weight charts, tape measures and rulers, and lists or tables taken from public documents)

The courts have not comfortably settled the scope of copyrights for software. Originally, copyright protection extended to the "structure, sequence and organization" of a software program — in other words, its look and feel. But in cases stemming back to 1992, the courts allowed people to copy program flow, intermodular relationships, parameter lists, macros, and lists of services. In fact, in one case it was held that you could actually copy a complete program if doing so was the only way to get at the unprotected ideas inside the program.

Well, that opened up a can of worms, and by 1997, the courts were effectively reversing some of their earlier rulings. In April 1999, the courts said that Connectix Corp. had infringed on the copyright of Sony Computer Entertainment Inc. when it copied the PlayStation software code to extract the unprotectable content, which is another example of the importance of registering your copyright *before* an infringement occurs.

# *Protecting Your Logo: A Trademark*

A *trademark* is a symbol, word, or design used to identify a business or a product. For example, Apple Computer uses a picture of an apple with a bite out it followed by the symbol ®, which means *registered trademark*. You may have also seen the term *service mark*. This term identifies the source of a service rather than a product. Throughout the chapter, I'll use the term *trademark,* but the discussion applies equally to service marks.

Owning a trademark gives you the right to prevent others from using a confusingly similar mark; however, you do not have the right to prevent others from making or selling the same goods and services under a different mark. Only a patent can provide that level of protection.

You can claim trademark rights after actually using the mark or filing the proper application to register the mark with the PTO. The application states that you intend to use the mark in commerce. Like copyrights, you don't have to register to establish your rights or begin using a mark, but federal registration provides benefits beyond those of merely using the mark. A federal registration entitles you to use the mark nationwide and presumes that you are the owner.

You can apply for federal registration by

- ✔ Filing a use application if you began using a mark in commerce beforehand.
- ✔ Filing an intent-to-use application if you haven't used the mark in commerce, entitling you to put ™ after the name you are trademarking until you register the mark.

Two rights are associated with trademarks — the right to register and the right to use. In general, if you are first to use a mark in commerce, or you file an application with the PTO, then you have the right to register the mark. The right to use a particular mark is more complex. If two people use the same mark in commerce and neither has registered it, only the courts can decide who has the right to use the mark.

Trademark rights can last indefinitely if you continue to use the mark, but the actual term is ten years. You can renew the registration as many times as you like if you continue using it.

Between the fifth and sixth renewals of the trademark, you must file an affidavit providing information required to keep your registration alive. Otherwise, it will be canceled.

Like other intellectual property, federal registration protections apply only in the United States and its territories. Protecting your mark outside the U.S. means registering it in all the countries in which you want protection.

# The special case of domain names

Since about 1995, the United States Patent and Trademark Office (PTO) has received an increasing number of applications for marks composed of domain names — the letters and numbers identifying computers on the Internet — mainly from computer services and Internet content providers. When you apply to register your domain name as a trademark or service mark, you are subject to the same requirements as any trademark applicant.

A domain name is part of an overall Uniform Resource Locator (URL), which is essentially an address for a site or document on the Internet. The domain name also consists of a second-level domain — a "dot" — and a top-level domain (TLD). The wording lying to the left of the dot is the second-level domain; the wording to the right is the TLD. So, in the URL www.amazon.com, amazon is the second-level domain and com is the TLD. The http:// is the protocol used to transfer information. And www refers to the World Wide Web, a graphical hypermedia interface for viewing and exchanging information. The two types of TLDs are generic (.com, .net) and country (.eu, .au).

When you apply to trademark a domain name, neither the URL nor the TLD is included, because both are universal to all domain names. You can register a domain name only if it functions as a "source identifier;" that is, it doesn't serve merely as an address to access a Web site, but actually identifies the services provided or the product being sold, like wine.com or books forkids.com.

Trademarking domain names is a relatively new area for the PTO, so seek the wisdom of an experienced attorney.

# Guarding Your Interests

Trade secrets generally include sensitive company information that can't be covered by patents, trademarks, and copyrights. Trade secrets include recipes, ingredients, source codes for computer chips, customer discounts, manufacturer costs, business plans, and so forth. The only method of protecting trade secrets is through contracts and non-disclosure agreements that specifically detail the trade secret to be protected. No other legal form of protection exists.

# Contracts

A contract simply is an offer or a promise to do something or refrain from doing something in exchange for consideration, which is the promise to supply or give up something in return. So you are asking your employees to not reveal your company's trade secrets in exchange for having a job there (and not getting sued if they do reveal them).

In addition to using contracts with employees and others who have access to your trade secrets, make sure that no one has all the components of your trade secret. For example, suppose you develop a new barbecue sauce that you intend to brand and market to specialty shops. If you're producing in large volumes, you obviously can't do all the work yourself, so you hire others to help. To avoid letting them know how to reproduce your unique barbecue sauce, you can do three things:

- Execute a contract with them binding them to not disclose what they know about your recipe.

- Provide them with premixed herbs and spices so they don't know exactly what's in the recipe.

- Give each person a different portion of the sauce to prepare.

Protecting trade secrets isn't easy. You may not realize it, but your feasibility study and business plan are forms of trade secrets. The forms in which you present them are copyrightable, but the actual ideas are not, so they are trade secrets.

## Nondisclosure agreements

Many entrepreneurs try protecting their ideas through a *nondisclosure agreement (NDA)*. An NDA is a document that announces the confidentiality of the material being shared with someone and specifies that the person or persons cannot disclose anything identified by the NDA to other parties or personally use the information. Providing an NDA to anyone you are speaking to in confidence about your invention, business plan, or any trade secret is a good idea. Without it, you have no evidence that you provided your proprietary information in confidence; therefore, the PTO will consider it a public disclosure, that is, no longer confidential.

You definitely want to work with an attorney when you construct your NDA, because it must fit your situation. Generic NDAs do not exist. If you want an NDA to be valid for evidence purposes, it must include

- Consideration, or what is being given in exchange for signing the document and refraining from revealing the confidentiality

- A description of what is being covered (be sure this is not too vague or broad)

- A procedure describing how the other party will use or not use the confidential information

Whom should you have sign an NDA? Anyone who will become privy to your trade secret.

- ✔ **Immediate family.** Spouses, children, and parents do not usually require NDAs, but it wouldn't be a bad idea to have them sign one anyway.

- ✔ **Extended family and friends who will not be doing business with you.** To meet the consideration requirement for the NDA, you typically offer $1 in compensation.

- ✔ **Business associates or companies with which you might do business.** Consideration in this case is the opportunity to do business with you. For example, if you show your business plan to a manufacturer who might produce your product for you, the consideration is the potential of producing the product and receiving compensation.

- ✔ **Buyers.** Buyers typically don't sign nondisclosures because doing so may preclude them from developing something similar, or they may already be working on a similar concept. For example, toy manufacturer Mattel Inc. will not sign NDAs from inventors because they have a large R&D department that continually works on new ideas for toys. Chances are they're working on something that will be similar enough to potentially infringe on an inventor's product.

The truth is, an NDA is only as good (and reliable) as the person who signs it. Fighting a violation of an NDA in the courts is difficult and expensive, so when you're ready to talk about your invention, be careful whom you talk to.

# Strategies for Protecting Your IP

In 1998, patent-licensing revenues to companies, governmental agencies, and universities exceeded $100 billion. Expect them to exceed $500 billion by 2005. No wonder so many entrepreneurs are looking for ways to exploit their intellectual property to get a competitive advantage!

This new way of thinking about IP differs from the past, when companies managed their IP by defending their rights from infringement and making sure they kept up the maintenance fees so they wouldn't lose the patent. Until recently, companies never thought about the value IP can bring the company. Many found out through a majority of recent mergers and acquisitions that occurred because IP was perceived as valuable. Today, defense contractors license technology to toy manufacturers, and NASA technology has wound up in multiple consumer products. The potential is limitless. In this section, you discover that you should consider intellectual property as an asset to promote and defend.

In this new environment where IP is part of nearly every company's competitive advantage, whether it's a brand or a breakthrough technology, every entrepreneur needs to consider how to effectively manage its IP.

## Offensive strategies

One of the more important offensive strategies that you can tap is licensing your intellectual property to other companies or licensing intellectual property that your company needs to fulfill its strategies from other companies. A *license* is a contract between parties that permits the use of IP in exchange for money or other consideration. It is essentially the link between an inventor and a revenue stream from the commercialization of the technology. I'll consider licensing from the two perspectives: acquiring and marketing IP licenses.

### IP acquisition

You may have several reasons for acquiring the IP that someone else owns.

- ✔ **You need their IP to enter a market that you wouldn't be able to enter otherwise.** For example, you want to create a business of memorabilia based on blockbuster films. You need to license the rights to use the brands and characters of those films before you can do business.

- ✔ **Your technology needs exceed your resources.** Why reinvent the wheel? If someone else owns a technology that you need to use to carry out your business concept, try licensing it. Doing so is a lot less expensive than trying to invent around it.

- ✔ **You need another company's technology to supplement your own.** Patent pooling is becoming a major thrust today in high technology industries where you can't do what you want to do without trampling on someone else's rights. For example, when PCs use audio and video signals beyond conventional text and graphics, companies will find themselves stepping on technologies originally invented in the electronics industry. Many industries, especially in the new media area, are finding that they may have to resort to patent pooling to untangle the web of IP.

When you acquire IP from someone else, you should definitely check on the licensor's ability to transfer the IP, experience with licensing IP, and overall track record in licensing IP. You may want to consider talking with other licensees to see how their relationships with the licensor went. If you're the first licensee for this IP, you ought to be able to get some concessions. Critical questions you want to address include the following:

- ✔ Does the IP meet your needs?

- ✔ Does the IP work as claimed?

- ✔ Is the IP owned completely by the licensor? ( You want to make sure this won't be a sublicense — the licensor has licensed it from yet another party.)

✔ How much of an upfront fee and royalty will you have to pay?

✔ What will the manufacturing costs be?

✔ How critical is time to market?

✔ Are there any performance guarantees?

### Licensing your own IP

When you're planning to license your own intellectual property, consider how you're going to market it so that companies know it's available. Here are some actions you want to take:

✔ Begin by documenting exactly what you're licensing so that the licensee has no misconceptions about what is included.

✔ Decide how to value your IP. How much money is it worth for you to license it?

✔ Who is more likely to license your IP and why?

✔ What is your liability?

Always conduct extensive background checks on any potential licensee, including credit checks, security clearances, and ability to perform. In one case, a company found that its licensee, which was involved in a U.S. public offering, had an international client that was implicated in a financial and political scandal overseas. In another case, a company discovered that agents of its licensee had a history of making payments in violation of the Foreign Corrupt Practices Act.

Your licensee represents your company indirectly by using your IP. Make sure to choose wisely; a poor choice may come back to bite you.

### The license agreement

The license agreement (much like a partnership agreement) is an essential part of any licensing arrangement. In general, a license agreement spells out the terms under which the agreement will be executed — the duties and responsibilities of the parties involved. Here are some of the components of a good license agreement:

✔ **Grant clause:** This clause states what specifically is being delivered and discusses issues of immunity, exclusivity, and the right to sublicense.

✔ **Support services:** Definitions of what, if any, support services will be provided by either party should be included.

✔ **Confidentiality clause:** This clause defines the term for secrecy, the period during which royalties will be paid, any restrictions and permissions, how the agreement might be terminated, and issues related to the transfer of information to foreign governments.

- ✔ **Payments and fees:** You have several choices of how to get paid for your license. You can get a lump sum up front based on the usable life of the IP, or, preferably, you get an upfront payment and a royalty as a percentage of sales. Royalties are better because judging the life of IP and estimating sales several years down the road are difficult, if not almost impossible. Taking a lump sum payment certainly doesn't always match the life of a patent, so you can end up shortchanging yourself. Other forms of payment include equity, which is usually tied to an initial public offering (IPO), cross-licensing, and most favorable licensee.

- ✔ **Grant-forward and grant-back clauses:** A grant-forward clause provides that any improvements you make on your IP are automatically provided to your licensee. Likewise, any improvements your licensee makes are also available to you in a grant-back clause.

Many other issues are dealt with in the license agreement. You definitely want to consult an attorney with experience in licensing agreements, because putting such an agreement together is not something you should do on your own.

## *Defensive strategies*

In an earlier section of this chapter, I explained that you must defend your patent (prosecute infringers) or risk losing it. If someone doesn't have the right to make and sell your invention or other form of IP but does so anyway, that person has infringed upon your IP rights. Be aware that the government is not going to defend you. IP rights do not protect you from infringement; they give you the right to sue the infringer and enjoin or close down the infringer's operation. A court of law decides infringement cases, and you'll be happy to know that courts generally tend to side with the small inventor, particularly in cases where the infringer is a large company. To make sure that you have the best chance of winning such a case, prove the date of your invention by

- ✔ Recording all details of lab work
- ✔ Dating and signing every page — having it witnessed by an objective party
- ✔ Printing out your company data once a week, and then signing and dating it
- ✔ Binding your data in a permanent notebook
- ✔ Keeping the notebook in a safe place
- ✔ Keeping all letters, documents, and so forth related to the invention

CASE STUDY

# It was a dark and stormy night . . .

Defending your intellectual property can be an expensive and time-consuming process. One of the classic infringement cases involved the man who developed the technology for the intermittent wiper blade on automobiles. Bob Kearns's inspiration for the invention came to him one night while he was driving in a severe thunderstorm. He wondered why wiper blades couldn't function like an eyelid and blink.

In 1963, Kearns began working on the prototype for what was to become the intermittent wiper blade. He installed the prototype in his car and then made arrangements to demonstrate it to engineers at Ford. They were mildly interested and told him that he needed to cycle-test it to see if it would achieve 3 million cycles without problems. After meeting their test, Kearns returned to the engineers only to discover that they were no longer interested. Surprised but undaunted, Kearns approached a friend who supplied parts to the auto industry and assigned the rights to the patent to him in exchange for paying for the patent process and paying Kearns royalties plus $1,000 a month to continue R&D on the product.

To Kearns's amazement, in 1969, Ford introduced the intermittent wiper blade — Kearns's design — without ever having talked to Kearns again. In 1974, GM followed, with Chrysler doing the same in 1977. By that time, Kearns had reacquired his patent rights and filed suit against Ford in 1978. This action began a 12-year battle to bring the suit to trial. After the jury found in Kearns's favor, Ford offered to settle for $30 million, but Kearns didn't think it was enough and turned it down. A second trial awarded him $5.2 million, and finally they settled at $10.2 million. The Chrysler case ended in 1992, and that gave Kearns an additional $11.5 million. But he had paid a heavy price — more than 23 years of his life devoted to his invention and protecting his rights.

Kearns's case is not unusual. Small inventors often have their rights infringed upon by large corporations or by foreign corporations that make the product in their own country, where the patent doesn't apply, and try to market it in the U.S., where it does.

Beyond the obvious, how do you know when someone has infringed your patent? You look at the claims on which your patent is based and compare them point by point to the accused infringer's device or process. If they match, bingo! The courts can also find an infringement under the *doctrine of equivalents,* which states that if the infringing device or process is sufficiently equivalent in what it does to a patented device or process, an infringement has occurred.

If your infringement case is successful, the federal court will either enjoin the infringer, preventing further sales of the device by him or her, or mediate an agreement between you and the infringer that gives you royalties in exchange for allowing the infringer to sell the device.

Look into insurance that can help you pay the costs of fighting an infringement case.

Yet another problem that forces inventors into protecting their rights is a company that licenses an invention but doesn't use it, essentially keeping it out of the marketplace usually to protect its own invention from competition. To protect against this form of infringement, set specific performance targets in your license agreement. Doing so makes the licensee achieve a certain agreed-upon level of sales by a certain point in time or face losing the license. Performance targets also prevent the licensee from keeping your invention out of the marketplace, which in turn helps you to maintain your patent.

If you find yourself on the other side of the issue — that is, you are accused of infringing on someone's patent rights — take steps to fight the accusation by

✔ Challenging the validity of the patent

✔ Challenging the owner's rights to the patent and look at expiration dates

✔ Claiming that the alleged infringement was for private or experimental purposes only

You definitely want to obtain the services of a good patent attorney in any kind of patent infringement case.

# Chapter 9

# Getting Products and Services to Customers: Distribution

*In This Chapter*

▶ Tracking trends in distribution strategy

▶ Outsourcing your logistics function

▶ Using your distribution strategy to compete for markets

▶ Sorting out the consumer and industrial channels

▶ Checking your channels

*A* couple of reasons explain why distribution has become such an important part of any entrepreneur's competitive strategy.

First, mass customization (recall that mass customization, as defined in Chapter 8, is giving customers what they want, when they want it, and in the way they want it) requires that you find new ways of reaching your customers on an individual basis. Cable TV shopping, such as on the Home Shopping Network, came about because manufacturers needed a way to sell directly to the customer. E-commerce is perhaps the newest form of direct marketing via direct channels to the customer.

The Internet has precipitated massive consolidation in many industries by getting rid of intermediaries and collapsing distribution channels. Intermediaries are distributors, wholesalers, and retailers who come between producer and customer. Because the Internet is an open channel of communication with access to information at its source, customers connect directly with the source rather than paying more to an intermediary.

An increase in the popularity of low-cost distribution methods is the second explanation why distribution is gaining such prominence. Companies like Wal-Mart and Price/Costco pioneered a price-based distribution model, forcing manufacturers to change their operations so that they produce at lower costs and still make a profit. To many manufacturers, particularly those that deal in commodity products, survival means going direct to their customers via warehouse, factory direct, or e-commerce versions of themselves. Even companies that deal in information as their products often must position themselves as the low-cost providers.

In this chapter, you find ways of using an innovative distribution strategy to your advantage and become aware of current trends in distribution. I often tell entrepreneurs that big innovative opportunities usually are hiding in mundane, unglamorous areas where no one else is looking. I hope this chapter inspires you to look at distribution in a new light.

# Outsourcing Logistics

Distribution is about *logistics* — the movement of products and services from producers to buyers. But distribution is also about the way you market your product or service within your *distribution channel* — deciding, for example, how much of the channel you want to cover.

If you are a manufacturer, do you want to reach every possible distributor of your product? That approach is called *intensive coverage.* Alternatively, do you want to reach only retailers in a defined geographic area? That approach is called *selective coverage.* In addition, you can break *selective* down even further. If you are trying to project an image of luxury, for example, you might limit distribution to upscale boutiques, period. Although you can't escape decisions about your distribution channels, you can probably sidestep many of the details involved in logistics, at least for a while. For most entrepreneurial start-ups, having their own shipping department — a distribution center — is not within the realm of possibility because of limited funds. Consequently, most start-ups outsource their logistics needs to companies that specialize in providing that service.

Logistics consists of transportation, storage, and materials handling. Working with a good logistics service provider can ensure that you get the best rates and the most reliable carriers.

Today, finding all the major carriers online and even accessing logistics portals such as iShip (`http://home.iship.com/`) and Consolidated Delivery and Logistics (`www.cdlsf.com`) helps you discover your options. When it comes time to decide on a firm, ask yourself these questions:

- Can the company provide the services you need when you need them?
- How do this company's costs compare with other companies in the industry?
- What kinds of services do they provide?
- Does the company already deal with products like yours?
- What kinds of guarantees does the company provide to ensure that your products arrive at their destination in good shape?

CASE STUDY

## When Christmas delivery got stuck in the chimney

Your distribution strategy not only provides an enormous competitive advantage to your business in a market where everyone is innovating on the product/service side, but it also can be a matter of life and death. For e-commerce retailers, the results of the holiday season of 1999 show how important distribution can be. Consumers flocking to the Internet in numbers never seen before shopped for and purchased their holiday gifts online with a mere point and a click. And e-tailers delivered on their promises, making the buying process easy and fast.

What they didn't do such a good job of delivering to their customers was delivery itself. Most e-tailers forgot that a vital area of their business is fulfillment — getting the order packaged and out to the customer in a timely fashion. They hadn't planned well for the impact on their distribution systems. When the deluge hit, those systems failed. As a result, some of the e-tailers later failed, too.

# *Creating Your Distribution Strategy*

You can begin your distribution strategy quite simply by hiring outside companies to manage the physical handling and delivery of products. But that strategy is only one part of the picture. I always recommend to entrepreneurs that they graphically depict their options for distribution channels so that they can determine several essential factors, including

- ✔ The time from manufacturing to purchase by the customer. (You will also see the lead-time needed by each participant in the distribution channel.)
- ✔ The final retail price, which is based on price markups along the channel.
- ✔ The total cost of marketing the product, which also enters the pricing.

For example, suppose you're considering selling direct to retailers versus using a distributor as an intermediary. Your two options might look like Figure 9-1.

Figure 9-1 shows you that when using the indirect method, everyone along the channel who provides a service and adds value must be able to make a profit, so the cost to the end-user goes up. By contrast, the end-user benefits from purchasing direct from the manufacturer, but the manufacturer charges more than what it would have charged to the distributor because now it must assume many of the functions of both distributor and retailer. However, because the manufacturer doesn't need an expensive bricks-and-mortar site like the retailer, it passes those savings along to the end-user.

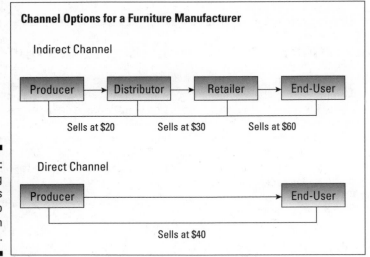

**Figure 9-1:**
Comparing the costs of two distribution options.

## When you have only one product to distribute

Most entrepreneurial start-ups launch with an initial product, not a line of many products. Those businesses obviously work on only one product at a time because they don't have the resources for developing several products at once. Entering the market on the strength of only one product and adding to the product list is generally the plan. As time goes by, the company starts making money.

However, finding a distributor willing to take on a company with only one product is difficult. Big superstores like Wal-Mart usually refuse to touch a company with only one product. The reason? If they're going to do all that paperwork, they prefer spreading the expense across a number of products from one source. What can an entrepreneur do to get distribution in a case like this? While exploring the possibilities, try

✔ Manufacturing your product and selling the first few to anyone who will buy, even at a discount so you can show some sales.

✔ Finding a catalogue that caters to your potential customers.

✔ Attending trade shows where you can demonstrate or show your product to buyers. In particular, try regional trade shows where participating is less costly.

✔ Asking people in the industry for recommendations. Trade associations and other organizations are good sources.

✔ Approaching the big retailers only after you've got all your ducks in a row. Preparing to mass-produce before you secure a contract of any size is a must; you don't want to risk losing a major customer because you weren't prepared.

✔ Steering customers who approach you directly to your distributor, once you've secured one. You don't want to alienate an important member of your channel.

# Distributing through Market Channels

Depending on the nature of your business, distribution of your product/service flows through either a consumer market channel or an industrial market channel, or sometimes both.

Businesses selling to end-users, or people who purchase goods and services at the wholesale or retail levels, are in the consumer market channel. Businesses that market goods and services to other businesses deliver products through industrial channels. So a manufacturer of production equipment markets to manufacturers who use this type of equipment in their processes. Similarly, an office supply company targets consumer businesses in a large downtown area — San Francisco, for example.

## Consumer channels

Within consumer channels, several choices are available for reaching your customers.

### Selling directly to customers

As discussed in the introduction to this chapter, selling directly means that no intermediaries come between you and your customers, and you take on all the responsibilities of typical intermediaries. Service businesses are usually direct sellers, but more and more, especially with the advent of the Internet, manufacturers are becoming direct sellers. You've probably visited factory-direct outlet malls where furniture, apparel, household, and other types of manufacturers sell goods to customers without intermediaries.

In general, manufacturers start by establishing traditional channel relationships with intermediaries, building brand-name recognition. That way, when they open direct outlets, they don't have to do much in the way of advertising to get people to visit. The Gap, an apparel manufacturer, is a good example of this strategy. It uses outlets for getting rid of excess inventory, slightly defective merchandise, and out-of-season merchandise. That way, its direct outlets don't compete against its retail outlets.

### Using retailers to get to customers

Retailers are the most common outlets for getting manufacturers' products to their customers. Attracting customers through their own marketing and promotional strategies is the retailers' responsibility. Of course, manufacturers must also support their retailers with special discounts and manufacturer promotions. But retailers incur the costs of a sales force and stocking enough product to meet demand.

When setting up a retail distribution system, manufacturers either use an in-house sales staff or hire independent sales representatives who work on commission. The job of these sales people is locating the appropriate retailers and arranging for product distribution.

### Using wholesalers and distributors to reach customers

Actually, the terms *wholesaler* and *distributor* are interchangeable in common usage, so for simplicity, I use *distributor* in this discussion. Distributors typically buy product in bulk from producers and then locate outlets for those products, freeing up the manufacturers for other tasks. Distributors are probably better at finding the best outlets because that's their core competency. Choosing a good distributor is still the job of the manufacturer. Remembering that you are entrusting the success of your product to this distribution company shows you what an important choice that is. Distributors provide many services, including

- ✔ Warehousing your products
- ✔ Advertising and promoting your products to retailers and/or end-users
- ✔ Providing special packaging and displays to outlets
- ✔ Training the retail sales staff
- ✔ Arranging transportation of goods to retail outlets and other customers
- ✔ Providing warranty or backup services
- ✔ Restocking retailers' shelves

Talking with your customers, suppliers, business consultants, and bankers who work with distributors can make the chore of finding a good distributor easier. Getting a referral from a knowledgeable source enhances your chances of making a good decision and selecting a company that is trustworthy, reliable, and interested in seeing your company succeed.

### Hiring manufacturers' reps to find customers

Manufacturers' reps are independent contractors whose job is finding outlets for manufacturers' products. They differ from distributors in that they don't purchase the products; instead, they act much like brokers or agents by bringing producers and retailers or other types of sales outlets together. They earn a commission on any sales they make. The manufacturer-rep relationship is not transaction based, however. Reps often work with a manufacturer for years, developing a territory. Usually a rep is responsible for that specific territory, so a manufacturer typically has several reps covering all the geographic markets it reaches.

# Industrial channels

With retail channels as the exception, businesses using industrial channels have the same options as those using consumer channels when selling direct or using the various types of intermediaries. With industrial channels, goods typically sell at wholesale prices.

You've no doubt noticed how powerful the business-to-business side of e-commerce on the Internet is. Today businesses purchase most of their supplies and raw materials online, saving time and money. If you're not doing business online, you may lose customers fast. Because customers can more easily shop and compare prices and services, your strategy for the online channel must consider prices and added-value services, thus distinguishing your company from others.

# Using Intermediaries

I talked a bit about intermediaries in the channel options section of this chapter, but now I want to address intermediaries from a strategic point of view. Intermediaries inhabit most distribution channels, even on the Internet. A portal site actually serves as an intermediary between the producer and end-user. The essential service that intermediaries provide is assuming tasks that don't fall within the core competency of the manufacturer. At the same time, they're also serving retailers by finding products that their customers need and want.

Here are the four primary ways you can use intermediaries as part of your distribution strategy:

- **Sharing the risk of *distribution*.** When a distributor purchases a product from the manufacturer and holds it in inventory for resale, the distributor is assuming the risk that it may not be able to sell all of the product it purchases.

- **Placing products into a *line* under a single product category.** For example, if your product is a new branded barbecue sauce, you may want it placed with a distributor who handles specialty food items. Thus, retailers that sell specialty food items are finding your particular product when they're purchasing other similar products from that distributor.

- **Breaking *bulk*.** Distributors usually purchase a product from manufacturers or suppliers in bulk. They then provide the added-value service of breaking the bulk product into quantities that their customers typically buy.

✔ **Being a source of customer/market information for the manufacturer.** You certainly don't want to produce more product than the market wants, yet you want to be ready if demand suddenly increases. Your distributor and other intermediaries can be a tremendous source of information about customer needs and preferences on a regular basis, because they're on the front lines when it comes to dealing with customers.

# Evaluating Your Channel

The best distribution strategy for your company is

✔ Reaching your customers in the most effective way

✔ Providing an appropriate final price for your product or service

✔ Providing service or backup service for customers

✔ Allowing you to focus on your core competencies

Although limiting yourself to one distribution channel isn't essential (having more than one is common), you don't want to cannibalize one channel by introducing a competing one. For example, if you sell your product through a distributor in a particular city, you don't want to open your retail outlet in that city, because doing so jeopardizes your distributor's sales. When looking at the attractiveness of a particular channel, be sure you consider whether customers readily use that channel and whether you can make a profit using that channel.

You determine the feasibility of a particular distribution channel in much the same way you determine the feasibility of a new venture. You want to see whether the channel creates a niche in the market, whether you can afford to use this channel, whether your customers will use it, and whether you can get your products to your customers quickly through this channel.

No one disputes that the profitability of a channel is important, but you need to look at the channel in terms of maintaining a high profit margin while selling your product at a price customers are willing to pay. If the margins in the channel you choose are slim, then that channel must produce a high volume of sales for you to make enough money to cover your overhead and still make a profit.

## The cost of the channel

The costs of your distribution channel consist of all the expenses related to marketing and distributing your product. Referring to Figure 9-1, you can see that although the cost of production may not change, the price to the customer changes based on how the producer chooses to reach the customer.

The manufacturer charges the distributor a price that enables the manufacturer to cover the direct cost of producing the product plus an amount for overhead and profit. The distributor adds in its costs when it sells to the retailer, and the retailer typically *keystones,* or doubles (at a minimum), its costs to the end-user. If you know that your end-user will pay only $50 for your product, and your intent is to use the indirect channel depicted in Figure 9-1, then you've got a problem. Using that channel raises the costs to the end-user to $60, and chances are you can't produce your product for less and survive.

Cutting out one of the intermediaries or going direct to the customer may bring the final price more in line with what the market says it will pay, but you won't be able to reduce the price to $20. Cutting out the intermediaries means that you now pay for marketing to the end-user and taking on tasks of the distributor and retailer. But you still can probably bring the price in line.

## Distributing to the superstores

Many entrepreneurs find homes for their products with superstores and discount outlets like Wal-Mart, Home Depot, and Toys 'R' Us. If you sign a contract with one of these stores, you almost instantly have national, and in some cases international, distribution for your product. These mass merchandisers account for more than 40 percent of all U.S. retail sales, which is amazing considering that they comprise only about 3 percent of all retail outlets. So these megastores are important outlets for small entrepreneurial companies looking to grow quickly.

But getting a contract with a superstore isn't as easy as you might think. It takes more than a great product; it takes a plan. Here's a four-step strategy that may help you get a foot in the door with your favorite superstore:

1. **Find and talk to the right person.** Don't waste your time talking to just anyone about your company and products. Find out who the decision maker (usually the buyer) is in your product area.

2. **Get a buyer to return your call.** If you're having trouble getting a buyer to return your phone call, try using a rep or participating in a trade show where the superstores look for new products. The Expo Guide Web site (www.expoguide.com) helps you find trade shows in your industry and market.

3. **Prepare your pitch carefully.** You must convince the buyer that you understand who the consumer is, who the competition is, how your product beats the competition, and how well the product sells.

4. **Prepare to deliver on your claims.** You must deliver on your claims if you do get a contract. The superstore may test your product in a few of its stores first, but if it does well, you may have to ramp up quickly, providing products for all the stores across the country. Being prepared for that means your systems and controls and the resources you need to produce that much volume must be in place. Other costs that you can consider here include where to locate. For example, if you decide to sell direct to retailers, then you may want to locate the manufacturing facility or distribution warehouses near major transportation hubs. Doing so helps in delivering products to customers quickly and as inexpensively as possible. On the other hand, if you are using distributors, your manufacturing plant can be located anywhere because you're shipping to a central distribution point.

## Using what works best to succeed

One of my former students produces a silk plant cleaner that he successfully sold into Price/Costco after demonstrating it to a buyer. It did well initially, but then sales began to slump. Fortunately, this entrepreneur stayed on top of things and discovered that the product did best when it was demonstrated, so that customers wandering the aisles of the warehouse superstore could actually see the value. So he hired a bunch of older women who were excited about the product and put them to work enticing customers. The approach worked, and the entrepreneur maintained his presence with the wholesaler. Sometimes the direct approach is the best approach.

## Channel coverage

When you have a start-up company, using intermediaries may be your wisest choice, because their expertise and contacts with customers help you expand more quickly into the market. Selling your products to just three distributors opens your access to hundreds of outlets at the retail level without increasing your staff or marketing budget. Considering what you might spend marketing and distributing your product to those hundreds of retail outlets individually, the bottom line is that distributors help your company achieve better coverage in appropriate markets than you can on your own.

## Distribution control

Basing your choice of distribution channels on the amount of control that you want to exert over your product once it leaves your site is important. If you have a product that requires a unique marketing strategy or demonstrations that convince customers to buy it, you don't want to use intermediaries who aren't willing to perform those tasks.

That very situation occurred with an industrial machine produced by my husband's and my company. We initially introduced the product through equipment rental outlets that were excited about it and were sure they would rent it often. Unfortunately, equipment dealers have the attitude that the customer will come to them because they need a certain product, so they don't do much in the way of advertising or promotion. When you have a brand new product that customers aren't familiar with, customers aren't going to come asking for it. Adding to the dilemma, ours is a product that wows people once they've seen it work, and equipment companies don't always demonstrate the products they have on the showroom floor. In short, your distributor has to be able to meet the needs of your product. If that's not possible, you have to find another route to the final customer.

# Chapter 10

# Putting Together Your Start-up Team

● ● ● ● ● ● ● ● ● ● ● ● ● ● ● ● ● ● ● ● ● ● ● ● ● ● ● ● ● ● ● ● ● ● ● ● ● ● ● ● ● ● ● ● ● ● ●

### In This Chapter

▶ Selecting your partners

▶ Choosing the best attorneys, accountants, and other advisors

▶ Forming your boards

▶ Bootstrapping your way with outside talent

● ● ● ● ● ● ● ● ● ● ● ● ● ● ● ● ● ● ● ● ● ● ● ● ● ● ● ● ● ● ● ● ● ● ● ● ● ● ● ● ● ● ● ● ● ● ●

*I*f you're planning to start your new venture by yourself, think again. Teams, rather than solo entrepreneurs, are starting the most successful new businesses these days. And members of those teams are found in different geographic locations, or the teams may consist of groups of small companies. The point is that today's business environment is so fast-paced and complex that having all the know-how to pull a business together and launch it all by yourself is just too difficult.

Many people understandably prefer retaining complete ownership of their company, making all the key decisions, and not having to share the profits. But that attitude certainly limits your potential and increases the risks you take. Collaboration — with customers, suppliers, even competitors — offers many great reasons for forming a team to start your business. Here are some of them:

✔ You can share the enormous effort it takes to start the business.

✔ The business can continue even if one partner leaves.

✔ If your founding team covers all the functional bases in the business — marketing, finance, and operations — you go farther faster before bringing others on board.

✔ You gain more credibility with lenders, investors, and others if you have a team.

✔ You make better decisions as a team than as a solo entrepreneur.

# Finding Your Start-up Partners

When using a team to start your venture, the first place to begin looking for help is among people you know (friends, family, and so on). That tactic can be good, but it also can be bad. You obviously need to know your partners well so you can trust them — and your friends and family definitely fit that criterion — and you want to choose people who bring the skills and expertise you need to the mix.

Starting a new business can be a stressful and tiring experience even with family members and close friends to share the burden. If things start going wrong, you may lose more than your business; you may lose a friend. Entrepreneur wanna-bes beware! The old saying rings true: Money from family is the most expensive money you'll ever get, because if you lose it, you'll pay for it for the rest of your life.

Having said that, I nevertheless have started three successful businesses with my husband (and he's still my husband) and worked on multiple business projects with a close friend (and he's still a close friend), so it can work out if you know the rules.

## The rules with family and friends

When going into business with family or friends, you often must compartmentalize your efforts. In other words, leave business issues at the business and personal issues at home. I can tell you from experience that following that concept isn't easy. If you're experiencing a problem with the business, you tend not to put it behind you when you go home. On the other hand, trusting in a business relationship is critical, and you know (and trust) no people better than your friends and family. Here are some tips about deciding whether to include friends and family on your start-up team:

- Choose friends or family members because they have skills and expertise you need or contacts that can help make the business successful.

- Make sure that you all have the same or similar work ethics. If one of you is a Type A workaholic and the other a slacker, you're not going to work well together.

- Remember that friends and family don't view you or your business objectively, so if they are part of your start-up team, make sure that your advisory board is comprised of people who have more objective views.

- Agree on whom is responsible for what. For example, if your expertise is money, then your decision is the one that counts when you can't agree with your partner on an issue related to money. Similarly, if your partner's expertise is marketing and you have a disagreement on a strategy, your partner's wishes should take precedence over yours. That way you won't have any stalemates and you won't argue (at least, not much).

✔ If you're working with your spouse, make it a rule never to bring the business into the bedroom (for that matter, into any part of your home). Spending extra time at the office helps settle differences before going home. Your home represents a haven for you, not another battleground.

✔ If a friend or family member isn't working out as you had hoped, then it's time to bring in a third party who can either help you resolve the issue or be the one to suggest that this person needs to leave the business. That way, you at least have a chance of saving the personal relationship.

## Covering all the bases

Your goal is putting together a multi-functional team with a variety of strengths and skills. Ideally, members of the core founding team must have skills in the three major functional areas of any business: finance, marketing, and operations. Having access to a network that crosses these three disciplines is a distinct advantage for your venture, significantly increasing your overall information and resources. You will also have three financial statements to rely on when you need to borrow money or talk to investors.

No matter what type of legal organization you end up with (see more about legal forms of organization in Chapter 14), members of your founding team are essentially your partners. Choose wisely, because a partnership is like a marriage. Considering that you'll spend more than half of your time each day with these people, you better like, respect, and trust them.

Naturally, fielding the perfect team from the start isn't always possible. Maybe you haven't found the right person, or you have but he or she isn't available yet or may cost too much to bring on board before the company's revenues reach a certain level. In the latter case, staying in touch with that person is a wise choice. Time goes by quickly, and good people are hard to find. Besides, if your company's making an aggressive start and doing well, the person you've been eyeing may surprise you and come on board sooner than you expected by taking less money in salary for an equity stake in your venture.

## Putting everything in writing

I can't tell you how often I see entrepreneurs go into business with people they like and trust only to have things go sideways for one reason or another. None of us can predict what life may throw at us. That's why I always recommend signing a partnership agreement. Treating your business relationship in a business manner helps you avoid the grief that lurks down the road.

Just like prenuptial agreements, you may flinch at suggesting a written agreement to a friend or family member, but do it anyway, especially if you're not equal partners in the venture. I talk more about the details of partnership agreements in Chapter 14, but for now just accept that you should have one.

## Benchmarking the perfect team

So what does the perfect team look like? Compare your team against the following benchmarks or criteria:

- ✔ You have covered the bases with expertise in marketing, finance, and operations.

- ✔ Someone on the founding team has experience within the industry and preferably in a similar business.

- ✔ The team members have good credit ratings.

- ✔ At least one person on the team has been an entrepreneur with a successful business.

- ✔ The team has a network of contacts that include money sources and industry sources.

- ✔ The team members are focused on the start-up and passionately dedicated to making it happen.

- ✔ The team members don't have a lot of family responsibilities — mortgages, spouses, children, debt — making it difficult for them to go through the early stages without a salary.

# Forming a Board of Advisors

In the beginning, you typically don't have all the resources necessary to hire all the expertise you need. You certainly can't afford an in-house attorney or accountant, and you may be relying on Uncle Jim or Aunt Jane, who is willing to donate services for a time. A board of advisors comes in handy in these situations, bringing together people who believe in you and in what you're trying to do. The board members provide experience, guidance, information, and services, and many times play devil's advocate, pointing out potential flaws in what you're doing. They are, essentially, your reality check.

In general, your advisory board consists of attorneys, accountants, bankers, professors, consultants in various specialties, and others giving you needed advice and helping you find the people and resources you need to tap.

For the most part, boards of advisors serve without compensation (although that is certainly not always true). Many entrepreneurs offer a great dinner at meetings, which may be from two to four times a year. If possible, offering to cover your advisors' expenses for attending the meetings is expected, especially if they travel a great distance. Advisors expect that you may be calling them for advice from time to time, but don't abuse the time they're essentially donating.

In the following sections of this chapter, I look at various professionals your business needs to tap for advice and to hire for professional expertise.

## Yes, you need attorneys

When choosing an attorney, pick one for his or her legal (not business) expertise. Attorneys are professionals who typically specialize in certain areas of the law: tax, intellectual property, real estate, business, and so forth. Because not much about a new business is unaffected by the law, an attorney is an enormously valuable asset to have on your board of advisors and an expert your company needs to hire from time to time. Benefiting your company, an attorney can

✔ Advise you on the best legal form of organization for your business, whether it's a partnership, some form of corporation, or a limited liability company. Find out more about legal forms in Chapter 14.

✔ Advise you and help you prepare the necessary documents for intellectual property rights acquisition — patents, trademarks, and so forth.

✔ Prepare and negotiate contracts in a variety of areas.

✔ Help you comply with federal, state, and local laws and regulations.

✔ Represent you in any legal actions.

Finding a good attorney takes time. The best way to find the right one for your business is by asking people you trust for referrals, particularly those who own businesses and work with attorneys in areas that you'll need advice. After compiling a list of the attorneys who sound promising, arrange a time for an interview. Yes, I said interview them. You are looking for someone with whom you expect to have a long-term relationship, so finding an attorney with an understanding of your business and who's compatible with your style is important. Likewise, because your business is in the start-up phase, select an attorney who is willing to listen to you and spend the necessary time with you, while offering flexible fees.

Calling an attorney's office and noting who answers the phone and in what tone of voice tells much about an attorney. If the receptionist is rude, you may find that the attorneys have an attitude that may not make you comfortable. I remember interviewing one attorney for my business who spent the entire time we were talking playing with a paper clip and looking out the window. I finally stopped the conversation and said that I didn't feel comfortable that he understood my company's needs, thanked him for his time, and walked out. Life is too short to have to work with people who don't care about what you're doing, especially something as important as a new business.

Entrepreneurs often ask whether going with a small law firm (one to three people) is better than a mid-sized to large prestigious firm. If your business concept shows tremendous promise of becoming a large, highly successful business, a larger firm may take you on in the beginning, recognizing that the real benefit to them will come over time as your company grows. But you probably won't work with the partners (the owners) in the early stages. Instead, they'll probably assign you to a young attorney with less experience. The advantage of a larger firm, however, is that chances are it's a full-service law firm that can handle most of your specialized needs.

A small law firm may be more interested in getting your business and less intimidating to deal with. Small firms may even be more flexible about fees, but they can't be all things to all people. Smaller firms are limited, and better service is not guaranteed, because the one to three partners at smaller firms do all the work. You do, however, work with the most experienced people.

Unless you're willing to change lawyers as your company grows, consider the following in choosing a good attorney:

✔ Pick a firm with an excellent reputation.

✔ Pick a firm that can grow with your company and its changing needs.

✔ Pick a firm that is well connected in all the specialties within the law, so that even if they do not do. for example, intellectual property law in-house, they have a strategic alliance with another law firm that special-izes in IP law.

Make sure the attorney has malpractice insurance. You just never know what the future may hold.

## Accountants can help you survive

While your lawyer is your advocate and does what you want (short of breaking the law), your accountant is bound by principles and ethics (Generally Accepted Accounting Principles, or GAAP) that do not permit advocacy. Accountants deal with a vital area of your business — its financial health. Before your business starts, your accountant helps you set up and periodically maintains your books. Because accountants are expensive, entrepreneurs typically hire a bookkeeper to record daily transactions and do payroll. They visit their accountants quarterly or at tax preparation time.

In addition, your accountant sets up systems and controls in your business and alerts you to responsibilities such as tax withholding, federal deposits, and reporting requirements. Activities, tasks, systems, and controls that your accountant can assist you with include the following:

- Keeping employee records
- Preparing stockholder reports
- Preparing budgets
- Establishing inventory controls
- Issuing invoices
- Making collections
- Providing referrals for professional services
- Making payroll tax deposits
- Preparing financial statements
- Filing yearly tax returns
- Balancing the checking account
- Writing checks
- Verifying and posting bills

Once your business survives on its own — achieving a positive cash flow and beginning to make a profit — you may want your accountant to do an annual audit, making sure that your accounting and control procedures are working properly. During that time, you will need a physical inventory. If your audit accountant finds that everything is in order, he or she issues a certificate to that effect. If you ever decide to take your company public (do an initial public stock offering, or IPO) or sell it to a larger company, having at least three years of audited financial statements is essential.

When choosing an accountant, just like your attorney, find one who is used to working with entrepreneurs. They understand your needs and limitations and can be more flexible in terms of fees and time spent explaining things to you. The accountant who suits your needs will grow with your company and put you in touch with people who can help you.

Just like law firms, accounting firms have advantages and disadvantages based on size. You want to pick one that can grow with your business, has an excellent reputation, and can provide all the specialized assistance you may need either in-house or through a strategic partner.

## When your lawyer is an entrepreneur

Attorneys aren't often thought of as highly creative thinkers, because they work within relatively strict boundaries. But once in a while a law firm comes along whose partners think like entrepreneurs, recognizing a big niche in the market that no one has tapped. One such firm is Venture Law Group (VLG), the Menlo Park, California, firm specializing in representing high technology companies and the investment firms that support them. What is unique about VLG (and has stirred the ire of many traditional law firms) is that it treats its clients like business partners and often accepts equity as pay in representing its clients' start-up ventures.

VLG placed itself in the heart of the Silicon Valley venture capital community. During its five-year existence, the firm has commanded the respect of venture capitalists and entrepreneurs. VLG sees itself as a matchmaker, serving as an advisor to entrepreneurs and putting them in contact with the best venture capitalists in the world. It has redefined what a law firm does by providing almost everything an entrepreneur needs to enjoy a successful start-up.

VLG searches through the many business concepts it receives to find the start-ups with the most potential. In that sense, it acts as a venture capital firm. Then it often purchases a small equity position through its venture fund, VLG Investments. Next it builds a team of expert advisors chosen especially for their ability to help a specific start-up. Up to that point, VLG doesn't charge client fees — it's betting on the long-term success of the start-up. It helps the entrepreneur refine a business plan and do whatever is needed to ensure a successful launch.

Another way VLG distinguishes itself from other law firms is that the start-ups it works with all receive the input of the firm's senior partners. No one is relegated to a law clerk or beginning associate. As a result, VLG doesn't let its attorneys handle more than about 15 to 20 companies at a time, which is substantially less than most law firms.

VLG has found an attractive niche in the market where it can pick and choose from the cream of the crop of technology ventures and hold their hands all the way to success.

## *Your banker can be your friend*

An old saying states that bankers will give you money only when you don't need it. And many entrepreneurs have found that to be true. Entrepreneurs take risks, sometimes a great deal of risk. Bankers, by contrast, are generally risk averse. They are protectors of money, and they don't like spending it unless they're absolutely sure, beyond a shadow of a doubt, that they're going to get it back. That's why banks are not good sources of start-up capital.

But every business needs a banking relationship. That relationship, at least at the personal level, has become difficult as more and more banks reduce the number of branches they have in favor of ATM machines. Consolidations — mergers and acquisitions — in the banking industry, result in people moving around at a breathtaking pace. One month you have a great relationship with a banker, but the next you find that she has been moved to another location and you're starting all over again.

In the past, if you had a long-term relationship with a vice president of a bank, you had an easier time securing a line of credit or a long-term loan if your company needed it. Today, decisions are made by computers against benchmark criteria hundreds, even thousands, of miles away from your community. You can go through the entire loan process without ever talking to a human being. The lack of human contact makes it easier for the bank to turn you down if it finds something that doesn't quite match its criteria. In the past, a banker asked you about a problem and tried to work around it. Today, the bank merely sends you a notice denying your request.

Still, you need to deal with a bank because your banker is a source of information and is able to refer you to other people you may need to meet. He or she advises you on your financial statements and helps you make your capital requirement decisions. Again, be as careful about selecting your banker as you are about your attorney and accountant. Here are some steps to take in selecting the best banker for your business.

✔ Start by defining a list of criteria for your banker based on your business's needs.

✔ Talk to other entrepreneurs about which banks provide the best services for small businesses. Often that bank is a community bank, as opposed to a bank with branches all over the country. A community bank often is more predisposed to working with entrepreneurs, understanding the nature of entrepreneurial risk and more willing to participate with the entrepreneur in growing the business.

✔ Talk to your other professional advisors and ask for referrals to banks with which they have good relationships.

✔ When it comes time to interview your banker, find an officer with a rank of assistant vice president or higher, because that person is usually the one who deals with small businesses on a regular basis. He or she also has a certain level of authority to make decisions quickly.

## *Don't forget your insurance broker*

I can't tell you how many entrepreneurs forget about insurance when they're starting their businesses. It isn't surprising considering how many factors you think about with a start-up. Catastrophes and problems are not what you're focusing on when you're trying to get a business up and running. But the fact remains that you will need several of the following types of insurance:

✔ Property and casualty

✔ Bonding (to protect against not completing a job — common in construction)

✔ Product liability

- ✔ Personal liability
- ✔ Auto on your company's vehicles
- ✔ Unemployment
- ✔ Medical
- ✔ Errors and omissions
- ✔ Life on key management
- ✔ Workers' compensation

Your choice of insurance brokers is between major firms like State Farm or Allstate, and an independent broker who finds you the best deal among a variety of different insurance companies. Most large name-brand insurance companies carry the mainstream insurance — life, property and casualty, personal liability, and auto — but they may refer you to specialists for coverages like bonding and product liability.

Your insurance needs change regularly over time, so establishing a relationship with an insurance broker you trust is a good idea. A good broker looks out for your company, finding ways to save you money on insurance.

## Putting together an advisory board

For most businesses, starting with a board of directors composed of the founding team and one or two other insiders is acceptable. Your outside opinions then come from an advisory board made up of people with expertise and contacts that you need to tap. The board members are generally people who believe in what you're doing and want to be part of your new business.

### Understanding that advisors are not the same as directors

Boards of advisors counsel the founders but have no voting power when it comes to major company decisions and the hiring and firing of executives and officers. Likewise, advisory board members are not in the same position as directors of having to protect the interests of shareholders.

On the other hand, a board of advisors has a certain level of influence and still indirectly takes some control from the founders when it disagrees with plans and decisions they make. Others in the company probably respect the opinions of the advisory board and may pressure you, the founder, into seriously considering those opinions.

More than ever before, you can't always rely on the ideas and opinions of a bunch of insiders. If chosen well, your board of advisors serves as your eyes and ears to the broader world outside your business.

## *Making the pitch*

Getting someone to serve on your board of advisors isn't as easy as you might think. The question that entrepreneurs never ask themselves before approaching someone to be an advisor is: "Why would this very busy and successful person want to spend time on my board?" And if this person is going to spend the time, why wouldn't he or she prefer making decisions and affecting what happens to the company as a member of a formal board? Directors can oust the CEO, for example. And when it comes to the issue of advisory board compensation (today, advisors enjoy stock or stock options), entrepreneurs often stammer and stutter, hoping that potential advisors will work for free.

You can expect your *personal* board of advisors (I talk about this later in this chapter) to serve gratis (although dinner or lunch once in a while would be nice), but not your formal board of advisors for a start-up company. You want to be able to contact them when you need their advice, even between regular meetings. You can usually get by for a few hundred dollars a meeting if you make your meetings prompt, organized, and relatively short, and you don't abuse your board members too often with phone calls.

Here's a strategy for approaching a potential board of advisors member:

1. **Identify the kinds of people you need on your board.**

   For example, you may want to find a strategic thinker who can help you draft your business and growth plans. You may need a specialist in *angel funding* (funds that come from a private investor — see Chapter 14) who can get you into that network. Or, if your business is labor intensive, you may need a human resource expert.

2. **Interview candidates by telephone.**

   Present candidates with what you're looking for. The interview also adds a personal touch to your request.

3. **Follow the phone interview with a letter.**

   Give the candidate overviews of your company and the board and its responsibilities.

4. **Follow the letter with a telephone invitation.**

   Ask the prospective board member to visit your company (and other board members).

When you finally meet face-to-face with a board member, find out what really motivates that person to serve on your board. Listening to the kinds of questions he or she asks is one way to get at what you really want to know — the candidate who spends a lot of time being concerned with how much you're going to pay may be doing it just for the money. Another way is to ask some pointed questions of your own:

> ✔ As a board member, whom do you believe you are representing?
>
> ✔ What have you accomplished as a board member for other companies?
>
> ✔ What do you see yourself doing on this board? What will you contribute?

If you happen to be lucky enough to find a candidate who barrages you with questions about the company and shows genuine enthusiasm for the possibility of working with you, grab that person. Such candidates are rare. Likewise, the candidate who challenges you with difficult questions and makes you squirm a little is worth grabbing up. Board members help you and your company grow. You don't want a bunch of "yes" people.

# Forming a Board of Directors

An advisory board provides advice and counsel and serves much like a consultant to an entrepreneurial venture. A board of directors, composed primarily of outsiders, is similar in some ways to an advisory board but quite different in others. A board of directors also provides advice and counsel, but its main job is holding management accountable for creating shareholder value and reaching established goals.

Several reasons point to why only about 5 percent of private companies have outside boards. Entrepreneurs don't usually like having "outsiders" evaluating their businesses and telling them what to do. In addition, a board of directors is an expensive proposition for a new company with limited resources.

If your company organizes as a corporation, you are required to have a board of directors. Typically, however, that board consists of the founders and maybe their attorney or accountant — pretty much an *insider* board composed of people who are owners or (in the case of the attorney and accountant) independent contractors hired to advise the company.

## Deciding when you need a formal board

Some entrepreneurs create a board if they expect to go through a challenging period and need significant advice, or when they prepare for an initial public offering (IPO). Others know that their companies are quickly growing; therefore, having a board of directors in place from the beginning is important.

Communication is the most important factor in the success of any board. Being privy to what's going on, the board moves the company forward. Your board of directors keeps your business on track if you choose wisely, but if you're too afraid of losing control of your company, you may end up choosing friends and family members or not having a board at all. Either approach can prove costly to your company.

A great board of directors with strong and respected people on it builds your company's credibility in the marketplace. A good board helps your business reach the capital markets and make its way through all the challenges of growth. Here are some factors to consider when establishing a board of directors for your business:

✔ Making about 75 percent of your board outsiders

✔ Finding people who have a rapport with each other

✔ Finding people who have broad networks of contacts

✔ Looking for people who complement insiders' strengths

✔ Making sure that your directors do you proud because your board represents your company to the outside world

✔ Finding honest people who have good problem-solving skills and integrity

Founders sometimes are burdened, especially during rapid growth, with operational details, the need to generate sales, and the problem of maintaining positive cash flow. Setting up a new board of directors under those circumstances may be difficult, so doing it before your business starts to grow is important.

Getting people to serve on your board today isn't easy, because boards often are sued for decisions made by management, and the frequency with which boards are being sued is increasing. Carrying directors and officers liability insurance (D&O) is a benefit that most candidates expect and deserve.

Paying directors a flat fee plus a per-meeting fee is typical, so the average board member may make about $35,000 a year. In addition, expenses are covered.

### Building your board

Here are some simple tips for building your board of directors:

✔ File a descriptive amendment to your certificate of incorporation.

✔ Meet every four to six weeks when your company faces important issues. In general, however, quarterly meetings are fine.

✔ Include only five to seven board members if you want more effective decision-making.

✔ Pay travel expenses and up to $1,000 a meeting to attract better people. Providing a small stock-option package may be necessary if doing so is standard for your industry.

✔ Treat your board with professional courtesy and respect.

### Insiders versus outsiders

Outside board members have no direct connection to the businesses they serve. They are important when dealing with succession planning and capital raising issues, and they bring a fresh point of view to the company's strategic planning process.

Insiders, on the other hand, have complete knowledge about the business, are more available to the business, and have already demonstrated their effectiveness. On the negative side, however, insiders may not be objective about the business, and their opinions may not be independent.

## Creating a personal board — your mentors

One type of board that many entrepreneurs neglect to establish is a personal board. At least as important as any other board, the personal board is a handpicked group of people advising you on your career and personal growth. The people on this board are the mentors and role models you want helping you achieve your goals. Insiders are people you trust, who hold what you discuss with them in the strictest of confidence. Your mentors let you know when you're out of balance, micromanaging your business instead of delegating, and stuck in the mud instead of moving forward. Your mentors provide a safe place for talking things through before addressing your board of directors or business advisory board.

Put together a personal board of directors — two or three people who are role models for you and who can be your mentors. Then take them to lunch!

# Pulling Yourself Up by the Bootstraps

So you don't have the resources to hire the management staff you need to run your business. You're probably doing what most entrepreneurs do — bootstrapping. Begging, borrowing, or renting everything you need so you can get your business going, bootstrapping consists of all the creative techniques entrepreneurs use to start their businesses on limited resources. Here's a summary of the basic bootstrapping rules:

- **Hire as few employees as possible.** Employees are your company's single biggest expense.

- **Lease rather than buy.** That way, you don't have to invest a lot of capital up front.

> ✓ **Extend payments.** Talk to your suppliers about arranging longer payment terms for a time.
>
> ✓ **Try to get your customers to pay in advance.**

# The rules for independent contractors

The Internal Revenue Service (IRS) has specific rules that you must adhere to when using independent contractors. A 20-point test for independent contractors spells out the ways you know that a worker is an employee. Make sure that your independent contractor isn't doing any of these things. You should know, however, that even if you follow the rules to the letter, the IRS can still challenge you. Too many business owners have violated the rules, so the IRS is on the lookout. Here are the 20 points.

A worker is an employee if he or she

✓ Must follow your instructions about how to do the work.

✓ Receives training from you.

✓ Provides services that are integrated into the business.

✓ Provides services that must be rendered personally.

✓ Cannot hire, supervise, or pay his or her own assistants.

✓ Has a continuing relationship with you.

✓ Must follow set hours of work.

✓ Works full-time for you.

✓ Does the work on your premises.

✓ Must do the work in a sequence you set.

✓ Must submit regular reports to you.

✓ Is paid regularly for time worked.

✓ Receives reimbursements for expenses.

✓ Relies on the tools and materials you supply.

✓ Has no major investment in facilities to perform the service.

✓ Cannot make a profit or suffer a loss.

✓ Works for one employer at a time.

✓ Does not offer his or her services to the general public.

✓ Can be fired at will by you.

✓ May quit work at any time without incurring liability.

As you can see, the determination of employee versus independent contractor is not clear cut, so tripping up and putting your company at risk is pretty easy. The "Safe Harbor Rules" in the IRS Code provide a bit of relief. Basically they say that a worker will not be considered an employee if

✓ You have never treated the worker as an employee for tax purposes.

✓ You filed all the employment tax and information forms needed to establish an independent contractor relationship.

✓ You have a reasonable basis for treating the worker as an independent contractor (long-standing industry practice, past IRS audit that verified it, judicial precedent).

## Outsourcing savvy

One way to avoid having to hire so many employees is to outsource your needs to other businesses that have the expertise. Independent contractors own their own businesses; you hire them to do a specific job. They're responsible to you only for the results of their work, not the means by which they do it. Hiring good independent contractors can save you money because you pay them a flat fee and they are responsible for their own taxes, medical benefits, unemployment insurance, and Social Security tax. All these taxes and benefits combined amount to as much as 32 percent of the base salary.

Handling an independent contractor relationship with care is important, because you don't want to do anything suggesting to the IRS that this person is really an employee. Many entrepreneurs are caught hiring people to work in their businesses without withholding taxes or having appropriate insurance, thus treating workers like independent contractors when they're not. It isn't that easy. If you want to use independent contractors instead of employees, you should

- ✔ Get the advice of an attorney who can make sure you're following the law (see the next section).
- ✔ Execute a contract with the independent contractor specifically stating that this person is not an employee for state and federal tax purposes.
- ✔ Make sure that the independent contractor carries workers' compensation insurance and has the necessary licenses for the work he or she does.

If the IRS declares that your independent contractor is really an employee, you will be subject to back taxes, interest, and penalties. If the revenue folks are in a really bad mood, they may charge you with fraud.

## Leasing your staff

One of the newest ways to get the personnel you need for your business is leasing them through a Professional Employer Organization (PEO). This tactic is different from using a temporary service. The leasing company essentially becomes your human resource department, assuming responsibility for payroll, insurance, and so forth. Your employees actually work for the PEO for tax purposes. The PEO provides this service for a fee that ranges between 3 percent and 6 percent of the gross payroll. You submit a lump sum to the leasing company each pay period that includes the payroll plus the fee.

By leasing your staff, you not only reduce your costs, but you also avoid many personnel headaches, including time spent on employee-related paperwork. The latter is a real benefit, considering that the average small business owner spends more than 25 percent of his or her time on paperwork related to employees.

Before deciding to use a PEO, ask yourself these questions:

- ✔ Will the PEO help my business achieve its goals?
- ✔ Is the company easy to work with?
- ✔ Is the PEO a member of important industry watchdog organizations: the National Association of Professional Employer Organizations (HAPEO) and the Institute of Accreditation for Professional Employer Organizations?
- ✔ What is the PEO's financial track record?
- ✔ Can the PEO give client references?
- ✔ How are employee benefits funded? Are insurance coverages met?

When you review the agreement with the PEO, be sure that it allows you to cancel with a 30- to 90-day notice.

Even when you lease your staff, you bear the ultimate responsibility for any unpaid payroll taxes, and you could be determined to be the actual employer if you determine salaries, choose your contract employees, or fire your contract employees.

When you structure an agreement, make sure that you and your partner stand to gain from the partnership. If the partnership is a one-way street, it will not last, because the partner who is not benefiting won't have a personal stake in seeing it succeed.

# Forming strategic alliances

Strategic alliances are quite different from outsourcing with independent contractors. *Independent contractor* is an IRS designation for tax purposes and is essentially a worker for hire. By contrast, a strategic alliance is not an IRS designation but is a more formal and closer relationship between two companies. It is a type of partnership that can be implied through the way the partnership works or through a legal arrangement with a formal partnership agreement. Your strategic partners can be suppliers, manufacturers, or customers. Reducing expenditures for marketing, raw materials, R&D, and so forth, or joining together to do a specific project, are reasons for forming such a partnership.

In strategic alliances, the partners are stakeholders — regardless of whether they hold stock in each other's company — because each partner invests time and money into the partnership. If the project or arrangement fails, the partners stand to lose, so strategic partners are subject to significant risk. For that reason, choosing partners who can bear the risk is necessary. Before approaching a potential strategic partner, do your homework and make sure that your candidate has the following:

- ✔ **Excess capacity.** In other words, your partner shouldn't be working to the limit of its capacity given personnel and equipment. It should have room to grow.

- ✔ **Experience in strategic alliances.** If your partner has experience with a few strategic alliances, that company will be a better partner because it will know what works and what doesn't.

- ✔ **A diversified portfolio.** When a partner's capabilities and investments are narrowly focused — it has all its eggs in one basket — it can't bear the risk of investment in your company and the partnership. Diversity limits risks so that if one investment goes bad, it doesn't bring the whole company down.

- ✔ **Relative strength.** Choose a partner that is as least as strong a company as yours, preferably stronger.

# Chapter 11

# Assessing Your Start-up Financial Needs

• • • • • • • • • • • • • • • • • • • • • • • • • • • • • • • • • • • • • • •

## In This Chapter

▶ Figuring demand for your product or service

▶ Checking how deep your pockets have to be

▶ Reporting your finances

▶ Calculating how much capital you'll need to start

• • • • • • • • • • • • • • • • • • • • • • • • • • • • • • • • • • • • • • •

So, you're expecting to raise capital for your new business the good old-fashioned Internet way, before ever showing a profit. After all, plenty of money out there is as ripe for the plucking as your sexy new concept, right? And you're probably not too concerned about paying serious attention to your start-up capital needs.

Wrong! While a whole lot of money is, indeed, available to entrepreneurs with great concepts, investors are a whole lot smarter, savvy to the inner workings of e-commerce and what makes a good business investment. Investors aren't throwing money after concepts that can't show a solid revenue model and profits within a reasonable period of time — the way they once did.

With all the talk about change, two things remain constant — you still need to create value and make a profit. Likewise, you don't necessarily need a lot of money to start a winning business. Some of the legendary and certainly venerable old companies you recognize today started on a shoestring. For example, The Clorox Co. started when five men from Oakland, California, each threw $100 into a pot to start the company. Lex Wexner borrowed $5,000 from his aunt to open a small retail women's clothing store that eventually became The Limited. Apple Computer, Inc., began with $1,350 that Steve Jobs and Steve Wozniak raised by selling a Volkswagen van and a Hewlett-Packard calculator. Dominos Pizza was started with $900, and the list goes on.

Certainly *Inc* magazine proves every year that you can start with little or no money with its report on businesses that began with less than $1,000. Here are a couple of examples:

- ✔ In 1997, Bill Martin and Greg Wright took advantage of a fast Internet connection from their dorm rooms at their respective universities, paid $75 for a New Jersey partnership fee, $70 to register their domain name, $30 for the first month's hosting fee, and started the successful Raging Bull financial Web site www.ragingbull.com.

- ✔ In 1993, Michael Knowles borrowed $1,000 from a friend to found Seven Hills Security Inc. in Tallahassee, Florida. In fact, he started the business from a room in his home. Now the business employs more than 130 people and produces $2.1 million in revenues.

If you think you need a lot of money when starting a business, you can forget that notion immediately. In this chapter, you discover ways to calculate how much you'll need and reduce the amount of actual cash you'll need.

# Estimating How Much You Will Sell

One of the toughest jobs for any entrepreneur is forecasting how much of your product or service you will sell, particularly if you're introducing a concept that is brand new and without a direct precedent. Understanding when you actually start your business that the numbers you estimate for your financial forecast will probably not hold true is important. At least you'll be in the ballpark, and that's better than most entrepreneurs who aren't as careful about how they forecast their sales and expenditures.

Why do the numbers change, even if you're careful about projecting your demand and expenses? Here are two reasons:

- ✔ When designing and developing a new product, calculating accurate demand and cost figures is difficult during feasibility analysis, because you don't yet have a production quality prototype. The prototype typically costs substantially more than your mass-produced products will cost, but it provides a basis from which to estimate costs of components, parts, labor, and so forth. So, the sooner you have a physical prototype, the closer your estimates are to the actual costs when you start the business.

- ✔ When you're forming a service company, you typically base demand and cost estimates on other companies in the industry. Without inside information, getting those figures is hard.

# Getting a three-way fix on demand

Estimating demand is the first piece of the information puzzle that you must solve while beginning to calculate how much money you'll need to start your business. Given the difficulty of arriving at accurate estimates, many entrepreneurs use a process called *triangulation,* which means that they approach an estimate of product demand from three vantage points: their industry, their market/customer, and their own knowledge (see Chapter 6). To develop these estimates, I suggest

- ✔ **Talking to industry watchers, suppliers, distributors, and the like.** Reading trade journals and visiting outlets helps you find out the kind of volume you can expect from your type of product or service. For a service business, you can find out how many clients an outlet sees in a month's time. Sometimes proprietary information like client volume is best estimated through observation or from third parties like suppliers and competitors.

- ✔ **Talking to customers.** I can't emphasize enough how important customers are in developing your business concept and providing valuable information in determining demand for your product or service. You can even talk to customers of your competitors. They are more likely than your competitors to give you the information you need. Ask how often they buy, what they buy, in what quantities, and for what reasons. Never rely solely on what others have to say about your customers. You need to talk to them yourself!

- ✔ **Relying on your own knowledge.** Bring your own knowledge and experience in your industry to bear on your estimates. Visiting a competitor's site and observing who the customers are, what they do, and what they purchase is beneficial.

Using these three sources of information may enable you to arrive at a number for demand that is reasonably close to being accurate.

# Forecasting your sales

Because sales impact other numbers in your forecast — namely, your expenditures — calculate them first. If you are introducing a new product or service, you must find a suitable substitute product to use as reference for demand. For example, when compact discs were introduced to the market, estimates of demand were based on sales of cassette tapes, because the belief was that customers who bought cassettes may eventually all switch to

CDs. Otherwise, if you're introducing a derivative of a product or service currently in the market, you can use that product as your guide. Information that you need to collect includes:

- *Sell-in* to the retailer (if you're using a retailer). This is the amount of product you sell to the retailer.

- *Sell-through* to the customer. This is the amount of product that the retailer sells to the customer.

- Seasonality in the market.

- Growth rates in your product or service based on the market.

- Innovations that may enable you to charge more for the product or service.

- Innovations that may let you produce the product for less than competitors (therefore charge less).

I would caution that if you choose public or well-established companies as benchmarks for demand, you need to discount your projected volume of sales because you don't have the same brand recognition as these companies or economies of scale.

# Calculating How Much You Will Spend

Some of your expenditures vary with sales, so your job becomes easier. For example, inventory and marketing expenses often vary with sales. Other expenses may vary by season, by the number of employees, or by usage, as in the case of utilities. Some expenses like rent and lease payments are fixed and won't vary, remaining the same each month. Your accountant can help you determine which expenses are fixed and which are variable.

## Cost of goods produced

Manufacturing businesses deal with complex issues when forecasting expenditures. One important issue is called the *cost of goods produced* (COGP) — the price you pay for direct labor, materials, and factory overhead (inventory) when producing a product.

Most start-up ventures figure the cost per unit to produce and then apply that figure (expressed as a percentage) to a more detailed cost accounting model that includes raw materials inventory, work-in-process inventory, finished-goods inventory, total inventory, factory overhead, work-in-process flow in units, and weighted-average cost per unit. The result is a more accurate COGP estimate. But for now, you don't have to worry about all that fancy stuff.

Here's what a simple COGP calculation looks like:

| | |
|---|---|
| *Selling Price* = | *$60/unit* |
| COGP | |
| Raw materials = | 4/unit |
| Direct labor = | 25/unit |
| Factory OH = | <u>10/unit</u> |
| Total COGP = | $39/unit |

# General and administrative expenses

General and administrative expenses that are associated with running a business include selling expenses like advertising, travel, sales salaries, commissions, and promotional supplies, and fixed expenses like facility, equipment, and administrative and executive salaries. Using a percentage of sales to project G&A expenses isn't smart, because some of these expenses are fixed and others are variable. To be as accurate as possible, I suggest breaking out the details of each of these expenses in separate statements and transferring the totals to your financial statements. That way, your financial statements don't become cluttered.

## Taxes

The last thing you'll consider is taxes (everyone tends to leave taxes until the end). You need to account for payroll, and state, federal, and in some instances local income taxes, as well as a variety of other taxes that are payable at varying times of the year. Calculating your income taxes, you prepare an income (profit and loss) statement so you know how much taxable income you have. I deal with the income statement in an upcoming section. In general, figure that taxes can amount to about 40+ percent of taxable income. Failing to account for taxes may cause serious cash flow issues for your business.

# Preparing Financial Statements

For purposes of the feasibility analysis, the only financial statements that really matter are the income statement and the cash flow statement. Ask any entrepreneur what the most important financial figure is (in any business), and he or she will tell you that it's cash. Cash is undoubtedly the lifeblood of any organization — not profit, but cash. The old saying rings true, "You can't pay your bills with profit, only with cash." Calculating your cash needs, you need to prepare an income statement, a cash flow statement, and a break-even analysis.

When you prepare any financial statement, you want to include *notes* or *assumptions,* explaining how you arrived at the figures in the statement or any unusual or non-recurring expenses, in particular, like the cost of setting up a booth and displaying your products at a tradeshow. In general, every line item in your financial statement references an assumption, explaining the premise for the number.

## Calculating profit and loss — the income statement

The income statement reports the profit or loss made by your business during a specified time. You usually calculate this statement first because you need profit totals (taxable income) to figure taxes for the cash flow statement. Taxes appear on the cash flow statement when they are paid. If your business is a sole proprietorship, Sub-chapter S Corporation, partnership, or Limited Liability Company, you don't show taxes on your cash flow statement because taxable income passes through to the owners to be taxed at their individual rates. I discuss legal ways to structure your business and their tax implications in Chapter 14.

Start-up ventures often do not show a profit in the first year or so because generating sales takes time and paying initial start-up costs usually sets the business back for a time. How much time it takes to make a profit is a function of the type of business and the strategy it uses. So, how do you forecast sales, profits, and cash flow, when you know your business is not going to earn a profit for several years? Many Internet companies face this dilemma, struggling to appear viable while they are burdened with enormous marketing expenses — to attract customers to their Web sites — and an inability to generate enough sales to show a profit.

For the most part, investors treat e-commerce a bit differently than traditional businesses. Investors are more interested in the size of the market and whether the concept will *scale out,* that is, grow to reach a mass market. So, the value of what you're forecasting is directly related to the size of your potential customer base rather than to the traditional profit projections. In fact, investors in Internet businesses often don't even care whether you include financials beyond revenue projections, because they will essentially determine what your financials look like.

More important perhaps is addressing key uncertainties in your financial projections. What are weak points that can cause your house of cards to tumble? How are you dealing with these weak points? And yet, forecasting sales and expenses as accurately as possible and justifying them is necessary. Look at Figure 11-1 for an example of a typical manufacturing business's income statement.

The basic formula to calculate profit and loss in a business is

*Revenues – Expenses = Net Profit before Taxes*

You can see in Figure 11-1 that Perfect Products' revenues ($440,875 for the year) come from sales of its product, Widget 1. The income statement presents the variable costs, or the COGP. I separated out labor within the COGP, showing the addition of one employee in Month 8 to handle the increasing demand projected for the product.

## Variable costs and gross profit

The difference between revenues and variable costs (or COGP) yields a company's gross profit. For the year, Perfect Products expects gross profit of $195,986, representing 44 percent of gross sales for the year ($195,986/ $440,875). Understanding gross profit as a percentage of gross sales is important. About 44 percent of every sales dollar pays the direct costs of making Widget 1, meaning that about 56 percent of every dollar is left over for paying overhead (general and administrative expenses or operating expenses) and making a profit.

## Fixed costs

The next section in the statement includes fixed costs, operating expenses or overhead that you must pay at a constant rate no matter how much product you're producing. Advertising expenses are a notable exception with a fixed percentage (3%) that varies with sales.

This section also includes an entry for depreciation. Improvements that Perfect Products made on its facility became an asset. The cost of that asset can be spread out, or depreciated, over a number of years (typically the useful life of the asset), essentially recovering the cost of the asset. Perfect Products' $10,000 improvement to its rented space depreciates over five years, thus one-fifth of the depreciation expense can be taken in the first year, or $167 per month, the amount that appears on the income statement. I advise you to check with your accountant about the most appropriate depreciation method for a particular asset.

**Perfect Products**

| | Premise | Month 0 | Month 1 | Month 2 | Month 3 | Month 4 |
|---|---|---|---|---|---|---|
| | Number of units sold | | 17 | 30 | 60 | 120 |
| **Revenues** | | | | | | |
| Widget 1 | | | 2,125 | 3,750 | 7,500 | 15,000 |
| **Total Revenues** | | | 2,125 | 3,750 | 7,500 | 15,000 |
| **Variable Costs** | | | | | | |
| COGS | 33% of Sales | | 701 | 1,238 | 2,475 | 4,950 |
| Labor cost | 2 employees @ $16/unit | | 544 | 960 | 1,920 | 3,840 |
| | 1 employee@$16/unit | | | | | |
| **Total Variable Costs** | | | 1,245 | 2,198 | 4,395 | 8,790 |
| **Gross Profit** | | 0.41 | 880 | 1,553 | 3,105 | 6,210 |
| **Fixed Costs** | | | | | | |
| Salaries-Principals | 1,500 per month each | | 3,000 | 3,000 | 3,000 | 3,000 |
| Depreciation on improvement | | | (167) | (167) | (167) | (167) |
| Gen. & Adm. Expenses | | | 600 | 600 | 600 | 600 |
| Building Rent | Per 1 year lease | | 1,800 | 1,800 | 1,800 | 1,800 |
| Equipment Lease | | | 2,200 | 2,200 | 2,200 | 2,200 |
| Advertising | | | 64 | 113 | 225 | 450 |
| Insurance | | | 1,600 | 1,600 | 1,600 | 1,600 |
| Utilities | | | 510 | 510 | 510 | 510 |
| **Total Fixed Cost** | | | 9,607 | 9,656 | 9,768 | 9,993 |
| Total Costs | | | 10,852 | 11,853 | 14,163 | 18,783 |
| **Earnings Before Interest and Taxes (EBIT)** | | | (8,727) | (8,103) | (6,663) | (3,783) |
| Cumulative P & L | | | (8,727) | (16,831) | (23,494) | (27,277) |

**Figure 11-1:**
An income statement reflects a company's revenue and expenses and reports its profits or losses.

## Net profit

You can show three kinds of net profit on your income statement: net profit before taxes, earnings before interest and taxes (EBIT), and earnings before interest, taxes, depreciation, and amortization (EBITDA). For simplicity sake, I'm indicating only earnings before interest and taxes. If you make interest payments and have a corporate form in which you show taxes, you have the additional following lines on your statement.

- Interest expense
- Earnings before taxes
- Income tax expense
- Net income

You can see in the sample statement that Perfect Products makes its first profit from operations in Month 9. This statement doesn't, however, include start-up costs prior to the business being in operation. So, Perfect Products' break-even point, which I show you how to calculate later in the chapter, requires a higher sales volume because it also accounts for the start-up costs.

**Income Statement Year 1**

| Month 5 | Month 6 | Month 7 | Month 8 | Month 9 | Month 10 | Month 11 | Month 12 | TOTAL |
|---|---|---|---|---|---|---|---|---|
| 200 | 250 | 300 | 350 | 400 | 500 | 600 | 700 | 3,527 |
| | | | | | | | | |
| 25,000 | 31,250 | 37,500 | 43,750 | 50,000 | 62,500 | 75,000 | 87,500 | 440,875 |
| 25,000 | 31,250 | 37,500 | 43,750 | 50,000 | 62,500 | 75,000 | 87,500 | 440,875 |
| | | | | | | | | |
| 8,250 | 10,313 | 12,375 | 14,438 | 16,500 | 20,625 | 24,750 | 28,875 | 145,489 |
| 6,400 | 8,000 | 9,600 | 7,504 | 8,576 | 10,720 | 12,864 | 15,008 | 85,936 |
| | | | 1,848 | 2,112 | 2,640 | 3,168 | 3,696 | 13,464 |
| 14,650 | 18,313 | 21,975 | 23,790 | 27,188 | 33,985 | 40,782 | 47,579 | 244,889 |
| 10,350 | 12,938 | 15,525 | 19,961 | 22,812 | 28,515 | 34,218 | 39,921 | 195,986 |
| | | | | | | | | |
| 3,000 | 3,000 | 3,000 | 3,000 | 3,000 | 3,000 | 3,000 | 3,000 | 36,000 |
| (167) | (167) | (167) | (167) | (167) | (167) | (167) | (167) | (2,000) |
| 600 | 600 | 600 | 600 | 600 | 600 | 600 | 600 | 7,200 |
| 1,800 | 1,800 | 1,800 | 1,800 | 1,800 | 1,800 | 1,800 | 1,800 | 21,600 |
| 2,200 | 2,200 | 2,200 | 2,200 | 2,200 | 2,200 | 2,200 | 2,200 | 26,400 |
| 750 | 938 | 1,125 | 1,313 | 1,500 | 1,875 | 2,250 | 2,625 | 13,226 |
| 1,600 | 1,600 | 1,600 | 1,600 | 1,600 | 1,600 | 1,600 | 1,600 | 19,200 |
| 510 | 510 | 510 | 510 | 510 | 510 | 510 | 510 | 6,120 |
| | | | | | | | | |
| 10,293 | 10,481 | 10,668 | 10,856 | 11,043 | 11,418 | 11,793 | 12,168 | 127,746 |
| | | | | | | | | |
| 24,943 | 28,793 | 32,643 | 34,645 | 38,231 | 45,403 | 52,575 | 59,747 | 372,635 |
| 57 | 2,457 | 4,857 | 9,105 | 11,769 | 17,097 | 22,425 | 27,753 | 68,240 |
| | | | | | | | | |
| (27,221) | (24,764) | (19,907) | (10,803) | 966 | 18,063 | 40,487 | 68,240 | |

# Forecasting your cash flow

Without a doubt, the most important financial statement for entrepreneurs is the cash flow statement, because it depicts the company's *liquidity* and shows when your company will achieve a positive cash flow based on revenues. Cash flow statements are also important to your bankers and investors, predicting your company's ability to generate the positive cash flows that are needed to meet its obligations.

The simplest way to explain the cash flow statement is to imagine it's like your checkbook. In your checkbook you log your deposits, *cash inflows,* from paychecks, clients, and other sources, and the checks you write, *cash out-flows,* to pay your expenses. The difference between the two tells you whether you have a positive or negative cash flow. In Chapter 19, I show you how to prepare a more complex but informative cash flow statement, describing changes in cash flow over time. A simpler version is shown in Figure 11-2.

### Perfect Products Pro Forma

| | Premise | Month 0 | Month 1 | Month 2 | Month 3 | Month 4 |
|---|---|---|---|---|---|---|
| | Number of units sold @ $125/ea | | 17 | 30 | 60 | 120 |
| **Sales Forecast** | | | | | | |
| Widget 1 | | | 2,125 | 3,750 | 7,500 | 15,000 |
| **Total Sales Forecast** | | | 2,125 | 3,750 | 7,500 | 15,000 |
| **CASH INFLOWS** | | | | | | |
| | 70% COD | | 1,488 | 2,625 | 5,250 | 10,500 |
| | 30% collection of 30 days | | 0 | 638 | 1,125 | 2,250 |
| **Total Cash Receipts** | | | 1,488 | 3,263 | 6,375 | 12,750 |
| **CASH OUTFLOWS** | | | | | | |
| **Upfront Cash** | | | | | | |
| Deposit-Rent | 1 month in advance | 1,800 | | | | |
| Equipment down-payment | | 2,200 | | | | |
| Permits | | 1,737 | | | | |
| Property Improvement | | 10,000 | | | | |
| Initial Supplies | | 1,500 | | | | |
| Insurance down-payment | | 1,600 | | | | |
| Computer | | 2,500 | | | | |
| Advertising | | 2,000 | | | | |
| Misc. | | 1,000 | | | | |
| **Total Upfront Cash** | | 24,337 | | | | |
| **Variable Costs** | | | | | | |
| COGP | 33% of Sales | | 701 | 1,238 | 2,475 | 4,950 |
| Labor cost | 2 employees-paid by unit Add 1 employee by unit | | 544 | 960 | 1,920 | 3,840 |
| **Total Variable Costs** | | | 1,245 | 2,198 | 4,395 | 8,790 |
| **Fixed Cost** | | | | | | |
| Salaries-Principals | 1,500 per month each | | 3,000 | 3,000 | 3,000 | 3,000 |
| Gen. & Adm. Expenses | | | 600 | 600 | 600 | 600 |
| Building Rent | Per 1 year lease | | 1,800 | 1,800 | 1,800 | 1,800 |
| Equipment Lease | | | 2,200 | 2,200 | 2,200 | 2,200 |
| Advertising | | | 64 | 113 | 225 | 450 |
| Insurance | | | 1,600 | 1,600 | 1,600 | 1,600 |
| Utilities | | | 510 | 510 | 510 | 510 |
| **Total Fixed Cost** | | | 6,774 | 6,823 | 6,935 | 7,160 |
| **Total Cash Expenditures** | | | 8,019 | 9,020 | 11,330 | 15,950 |
| **Net Cash In / Out per Month** | | | (6,532) | (5,758) | (4,955) | (3,200) |
| Cash Balance-Beg. of Month | | 0 | 0 | (30,869) | (36,626) | (41,581) |
| **Cumulative Cash Balance** | | (24,337) | (30,869) | (36,626) | (41,581) | (44,781) |

In "Month zero", before operations commence, Perfect Products has big cash outlays. Capital needs will total $64,222. (See Fig. 11-5)

30% of sales will be on 30-day terms, slowing cash flow.

Separate "break-out" statements provide details on all these items.

**Figure 11-2:** This cash flow statement depicts the cash inflows (revenues) to the business and the cash outflows (expenses).

## Cash Flow Statement (Unfunded)

| Month 5 | Month 6 | Month 7 | Month 8 | Month 9 | Month 10 | Month 11 | Month 12 | TOTAL |
|---|---|---|---|---|---|---|---|---|
| 200 | 250 | 300 | 350 | 400 | 500 | 600 | 700 | 3,527 |
| 25,000 | 31,250 | 37,500 | 43,750 | 50,000 | 62,500 | 75,000 | 87,500 | 440,875 |
| 25,000 | 31,250 | 37,500 | 43,750 | 50,000 | 62,500 | 75,000 | 87,500 | 440,875 |
| 17,500 | 21,875 | 26,250 | 30,625 | 35,000 | 43,750 | 52,500 | 61,250 | 308,613 |
| 4,500 | 7,500 | 9,375 | 11,250 | 13,125 | 15,000 | 18,750 | 22,500 | 106,013 |
| **22,000** | **29,375** | **35,625** | **41,875** | **48,125** | **58,750** | **71,250** | **83,750** | **414,625** |
| | | | | | | | | 1,800 |
| | | | | | | | | 2,200 |
| | | | | | | | | 1,737 |
| | | | | | | | | 10,000 |
| | | | | | | | | 1,500 |
| | | | | | | | | 2,500 |
| | | | | | | | | 2,000 |
| | | | | | | | | 1,000 |
| | | | | | | | | 24,337 |
| 8,250 | 10,313 | 12,375 | 14,438 | 16,500 | 20,625 | 24,750 | 28,875 | 145,489 |
| 6,400 | 8,000 | 9,600 | 7,504 | 8,576 | 10,720 | 12,864 | 15,008 | 85,936 |
| | | | 1,848 | 2,112 | 2,640 | 3,168 | 3,696 | 13,464 |
| **14,650** | **18,313** | **21,975** | **23,790** | **27,188** | **33,985** | **40,782** | **47,579** | **244,889** |
| 3,000 | 3,000 | 3,000 | 3,000 | 3,000 | 3,000 | 3,000 | 3,000 | 36,000 |
| 600 | 600 | 600 | 600 | 600 | 600 | 600 | 600 | 7,200 |
| 1,800 | 1,800 | 1,800 | 1,800 | 1,800 | 1,800 | 1,800 | 1,800 | 21,600 |
| 2,200 | 2,200 | 2,200 | 2,200 | 2,200 | 2,200 | 2,200 | 2,200 | 26,400 |
| 750 | 938 | 1,125 | 1,313 | 1,500 | 1,875 | 2,250 | 2,625 | 13,226 |
| 1,600 | 1,600 | 1,600 | 1,600 | 1,600 | 1,600 | 1,600 | 1,600 | 19,200 |
| 510 | 510 | 510 | 510 | 510 | 510 | 510 | 510 | 6,120 |
| **7,460** | **7,648** | **7,835** | **8,023** | **8,210** | **8,585** | **8,960** | **9,335** | **93,746** |
| 22,110 | 25,960 | 29,810 | 31,812 | 35,398 | 42,570 | 49,742 | 56,914 | 338,635 |
| (110) | 3,415 | 5,815 | 10,063 | 12,727 | 16,180 | 21,508 | 26,836 | 51,653 |
| (44,781) | (44,891) | (41,476) | (35,661) | (25,598) | (12,871) | 3,309 | 24,817 | |
| (44,891) | (41,476) | (35,661) | (25,598) | (12,871) | 3,309 | 24,817 | 51,653 | |

Cash receipts lag forecast because of accounts receivable.

First year, positive cash flow of $51,653 — not bad!

Second employee hired to help meet growing demand for Widget 1.

Perfect Products breaks out of the red, makes first profit in Month 10!

One important difference between a cash flow statement and an income statement is that you record cash inflows and outflows when they occur in a cash flow statement. So, if you make a sale in January but you receive payment in March, the cash inflow is recorded in March. By contrast, recall from earlier in this chapter that you record expenses when they're incurred and revenues when they accrue in the income statement. So, if you made the sale in January, it is recorded in January's income statement. Perfect Products' cash flow statement is a good example.

### Cash inflows

You record cash inflows — all the money coming into the business from various sources — first in the top section of the cash flow statement. Multi-product companies may separately record revenues from each product, providing a better picture of how each is doing. Cash inflows consist of

- **Gross receipts on sales.**
- **Dividend and interest income.** This is money from savings accounts or other securities.
- **Invested capital.** This is money that the owners or others invest in the company.

Because we are trying to calculate start-up needs, the cash flow statement of Perfect Products is considered unfunded, which means that investment capital isn't included. Perfect Products produces one product — Widget 1 — and sells 3,527 units at $125 a piece in the first year for total sales revenue of $440,875. Notice, however, that total sales received are only $414,625. Why the difference? Well, 70 percent of sales are for cash, and 30 percent are collected within 30 days, thus creating accounts receivable. You have to show the cash when it's received, so in Month 1, you see that the company receives $1,488 on sales of 17 products, but the remaining 30 percent, or $638, is collected in Month 2, along with 70 percent of Month 2's sales revenue.

### Cash outflows

The next section of the cash flow statement records operating cash outflows (your disbursements or expenses). You notice several differences about this section, including a Month 0 column, which includes all of the *start-up costs* you incurred — everything that you put into the enterprise before even opening the doors. I explain these start-up expenses later in this chapter.

Variable costs, expenses that vary with sales or the volume of product you're producing, appear next. The COGP is a variable cost, describing what you produce in any given month in terms of inventory. This figure likely differs from the *cost of goods sold* (COGS) figure on your income statement because COGS includes sales out of inventory (products you have already produced and paid for) but not the cost of products that you add to your inventory. For example, if Perfect Products reduces its inventory by $3,000 this period, its COGP is $3,000 less than its COGS on its income statement.

Other entries to look for in cash flow statements include:

- ✔ **Sales, General and Administrative Expenses (SG&A).** SG&A include salaries, rent, equipment expense, utilities, and so forth. Remember that providing key totals in your statement and referring to a breakout statement for details won't clutter your financial statement or make it difficult to read. Likewise, remember that you list only expenses you have actually paid each period.

- ✔ **Interest Expense.** You actually pay out in interest this amount. Perfect Products shows no interest expense.

- ✔ **Capital Expenditures (Buildings, Major Equipment, Machinery).** When you purchase something major like a piece of equipment, you generally don't pay cash for it, so your cash flow statement reflects your monthly payments, while your income statement shows a depreciation expense because you trade cash for another asset that must be depreciated. See my discussion of income statements earlier in this chapter to understand depreciation.

- ✔ **Long-term Debt Reduction.** If your company takes out a loan, you need to pay it back. The interest portion appears in the interest expense section, while the principal reduction appears in long-term debt expenses. Perfect Products has no outstanding loans.

Existing companies that distribute stock may account for the distribution of dividends to owners in a section of their cash flow statement. Most entrepreneurial companies do not distribute dividends in the first few years because reinvesting their earnings helps the company grow.

## What's left

The final section of the cash flow statement displays the net change in cash flow (whether you show a positive or negative cash flow for the period you're describing) for the month. In any particular month, net cash flow applies to that month only. Below the line for net change is a cumulative cash flow line showing the cash balances at the beginning and end of the month. The final column displays the net change in cash position. Perfect Products plans to end the first year with a positive net cash flow of $51,653 — not bad for a start-up company!

# Planning to Break Even

One figure you want to know at the feasibility stage is how long it will take the business to break even, or when your sales revenue is equal to your total expenses. In other words, the break-even point shows when you recover the COGS and pay operating expenses. Dividing the total fixed operating costs by the contribution profit margin per unit (100% minus the COGS is what you have left over to pay your overhead expenses) gives you the number of units you need to sell to break even.

You can see in Figure 11-3 that Perfect Products has total fixed costs of $127,746 for the year and a contribution margin of 56% (100 – 44% COGP), which considered together make their break-even point at $228,117 in sales, or 1,825 units.

Now you're ready to consider how much capital it will take to start your business and, perhaps as important, what form that capital will take.

$$\text{Break Even Point} = \frac{\text{Fixed Cost}}{\text{Contribution Rate}}$$

$$\text{Contribution Rate} = 100\% - 44\% = 56\%$$

$$BE = \frac{127{,}746}{56\%} \qquad \frac{228{,}117}{\$125/\text{unit}}$$

$$BE = \$228{,}117 \qquad BE = 1{,}825 \text{ units}$$

**Figure 11-3:** Analysis tells you how much product you must sell to begin to make a profit.

# Figuring How Much Money You Need

No matter how many times I present a scenario to a group of students or entrepreneurs and ask how much money they think it takes to start a venture, they always come up with a big number. Most people think that it takes a lot of money to start a business. Understanding your needs and figuring out how to satisfy those needs sums it all up. Not everything about starting a business takes cash. So, figuring out what your expenditures to start the business are going to be is the first thing you need to do.

Returning to the financial statements, I'll explain how to prepare the cash needs assessment. In general, you prepare your cash flow and income statements without considering any funding from yourself, investors, or other sources. That way you can find out exactly how much money it will take, at a minimum, to start your business.

## Taking a virtual tour of your business

Listing all the needs of a start-up venture is pretty difficult if you haven't walked through the business and its various processes and activities in your mind. Without doing this little exercise, you can easily forget important steps that can adversely affect your estimates. So, take a virtual tour of your business and begin mapping out how you want your business to work.

Starting at the front door (that could even be the front door of your home), perhaps the first thing you see is a desk with a receptionist answering the phone while typing something into a computer and printing another document on a nearby printer. Okay, what do you know so far? You know that you need a receptionist, a desk (and a chair — the receptionist has to sit on something), a computer, a printer, a telephone, and various office supplies. And you've just begun! Here's a plan for completing the tour:

- Make your way through the business in the same way that an order moves through it. Who gets the order first, second, and so on?

- Where each activity takes place, note what that activity is, who performs it, and what equipment and supplies are needed to complete the task.

- If you are developing a product, consider all the tasks related to that development, including everything that goes into building the prototype and the final product.

- If you are outsourcing tasks, note that and calculate the costs.

- Continue the tour through the completion of order-taking, billing, collection, and post-sales services.

- Don't forget administrative tasks like payroll and accounting and general expenses like rent and utilities.

By now, you have a good sense of all the expenses relating to start-up and to the business once it's in operation. Double check the list, making sure you aren't forgetting something important like telephone service or a DSL connection (a high-speed Internet connection delivered over existing telephone wires).

I always recommend graphing the business process so you can see interrelationships and how everything comes together. Doing so sometimes makes it easier to figure out the best way to run your business. You can do this by creating a flowchart of the various processes in your business (product development, manufacturing, administration, service, and so forth) and how they interrelate.

## Looking at the money you will need to spend

Money is spent in many different ways as a business starts out. Knowing that you have alternatives when it comes to finding capital to spend for your business is important to an entrepreneur, providing you more flexibility and making it easier for you to discover ways to reduce your capital requirements. That may make the difference between being able to start the venture or not. Here are some of the types of expenditures you will encounter.

- ✔ **Capital Expenditures.** Simply put, capital expenditures are physical items like plant and equipment that have a useful life longer than a year.

- ✔ **Start-up Costs.** These are all the costs related to getting your business ready to function in the marketplace. If you are introducing a new product that you developed, your start-up costs will include your design, development, and prototyping costs. If you intend to manufacture your product, start-up also includes the costs of setting up a facility, installing equipment, and training personnel in production. You also must prepare some initial inventory.

  If you are offering a service, setting up an office and training personnel may be necessary. If you're leasing, deposits on utilities and your place of business are needed. If you're in the retail business, your start-up costs include preparing your storefront, training salespeople, stocking the store, and announcing the opening with some initial advertising.

  You can think of start-up costs as all those costs that occur prior to opening the doors of your business.

- ✔ **Operating Losses.** Rarely does a start-up business operate at a positive cash flow from the first day. Your revenues won't likely be enough in the beginning to cover all of your expenses. Calculating just how much you're in the red each month is important because you must find a way to cover that loss.

- ✔ **Fixed Costs.** Fixed costs are expenditures that don't vary with sales. They fall under the general category of overhead and include things like rent, salaries, and loan payments. The important thing to remember about fixed expenses is that if your sales decline, these expenses stay the same; therefore, generating enough cash flow is vital in covering your fixed expenses.

## Thinking about your business in stages

Many businesses don't need to have everything in place when they open their doors. They merely need enough to satisfy the initial customers who already believe in what they're doing.

You get your initial customers by involving them in the design and development of your product or service at every stage. Have your customers test your prototypes and give you feedback. That's the best way to make sure you produce something they want.

Knowing your initial customers' needs is why most entrepreneurs start businesses with low overhead, no employees (if possible), and leasing rather than buying equipment. Suppose you're starting a business producing and selling three-dimensional, educational maps designed for elementary school children to a company like Rand-McNally (one of my former students did this). You don't have a lot of money, but you do have a customer in hand — the map company — that will pay you as soon as you deliver the first order. With that assurance, you can contract with a manufacturer to produce the product and a packager/shipper to deliver the product, while you can handle the paperwork from your home office.

As you look toward building your customer base or increasing the size of your orders, you must think about the point at which you need to bring in an employee to manage your paperwork. If you're happy with your outsourcing arrangement, you don't ever have to bring all those tasks in-house. But, if you decide to add to your product line, you may want to hire someone who can design new products for you. Increasing the number of employees, bringing in an additional investor, adding equipment, increasing your facility, and so forth, are what I call activation points for changing the resources of your business. If you're forecasting your cash needs for the first year and then doing pro forma (forecasted) financial statements for three years, you need to decide when activation points will occur. You don't need to know exact dates; what you need to know is what will precipitate the addition, whether it is a certain sales level or when you enter a new geographic market.

# Putting It All Together

You now have enough information to assess the amount of capital you will need to start and operate your business to a positive cash flow. One way to do that is:

1. **List and total your start-up costs.**

   Remember that start-up costs are the costs you incur prior to starting the business. Group them by capital expenses (plant, equipment, patents, and inventory) and soft costs (deposits, labor expenses, and prepaid expenses).

## 2. Find your operating losses.

Look at the cumulative balance on your unfunded cash flow statement and see if your business reaches a positive cash flow from sales during the first year. If it reaches a positive cash flow in, say, Month 8, then you know you need enough cash to cover the losses to Month 8. If your negative cash flow goes into the second year, you need a way to cover all the losses through the point of positive cash flow in the second year.

## 3. Calculate a safety factor.

A safety factor is additional cash covering any mistakes you may have made in your estimates or an unanticipated event. How much you add depends on your industry and the regularity with which your customers pay. For example, you may choose to add six months of fixed costs as your safety margin.

As an example, Perfect Products' total start-up needs are shown in Figure 11-4.

| | | |
|---|---|---|
| Capital Cost | | |
| Computer | 2,500 | |
| Property Improvement | 10,000 | |
| | | 12,500 |
| Soft Cost: | | |
| Equipment Lease Downpayment | 2,200 | |
| Deposits | 1,800 | |
| Permits | 1,737 | |
| Insurance | 1,600 | |
| Advertising | 2,000 | |
| Misc | 1,000 | |
| Initial Supplies | 1,500 | |
| | | 11,837 |
| Upfront Cash | | 24,337 |
| Start Up Loss | | 20,554 |
| Safety Factor  (6 months fixed costs) | | 59,799 |
| **Total** | | **$104,690** |

**Figure 11-4:** Start-up capital requirements for Perfect Products include capital and soft costs, upfront cash, start-up losses, and a safety factor.

Perfect Products' start-up costs of $104,690 is a substantial sum for most entrepreneurs to come up with. Arriving at that total and knowing that you have no way of raising that kind of money, is there anything you can do? You can look at your capital expenditures. You're proposing a computer purchase of $2,500 and property improvements amounting to $10,000. In the first place, you don't have to pay cash up front for the computer. You could lease it or make payments. By making payments of $114 a month, including principal and interest, you can still own the computer within two years. As for the improvements, suppose you decide to sign on for a longer term lease in exchange for your landlord agreeing to split the cost of improvements with you. That reduces your cash outlay by $5,000.

Now that you have some confidence in reducing your cash outlay, try tackling a more difficult challenge. A majority of lease companies don't charge a down payment. With good credit, you can often sign an equipment lease agreement for no money down and with only monthly payments. At the end of the lease, you can choose to purchase the equipment for an agreed-upon payment.

The safety factor is something else you can adjust. How much you need depends on your industry and your confidence that you can generate sales. Suppose that a bit more research reveals that your projected sales levels are such that you feel comfortable reducing your safety factor to three months of fixed costs. Now have a look at what your new start-up capital requirements look like in Figure 11-5.

**Figure 11-5:**
Adjustments to purchases, leases, and safety factors considerably reduce capital requirements.

| Capital Cost | | | |
|---|---|---|---|
| Computer | | 0 | Make payments of $114/mo for 2 years |
| Property Improvement | | 5,000 | Split with landlord |
| | | 5,000 | |
| Soft Cost: | | | |
| Equipment Lease Downpayment | 0 | | |
| Deposits | 1,800 | | |
| Permits | 1,737 | | |
| Insurance | 1,600 | | |
| Advertising | 2,000 | | |
| Misc | 1,000 | | |
| Initial Supplies | 1,500 | | |
| | | 9,637 | |
| Upfront Cash | | | 14,637 |
| Start Up Loss | | | 20,554 |
| Safety Factor  (6 months fixed costs) | | | 29,031 |
| **Total** | | | **$64,222** |

What a difference? You've managed to reduce your start-up capital to $64,222. Now you can see the value of breaking out your start-up costs into the types of money you will need so you can find creative ways to reduce the actual cash you put out.

## *The one-minute financial plan*

In keeping with the idea that you should always have the most important information about your concept at your fingertips, here are the key factors you ought to be able to provide to a potential investor, banker, or partner:

- ✔ Total start-up capital required
- ✔ When the business will reach a positive cash flow
- ✔ Volume of sales or number of units sold required to break even

# Part III

# Creating a
# Company

The 5th Wave          By Rich Tennant

"It's quite a business plan, Ms. Strunt. It's the first
one I've read whose mission statement says,'...keeps
me out of trouble!'"

## In this part . . .

**B**usiness opportunities don't become reality without a
company behind them. This part shows you everything you need to know to create a great business plan and
start a company to execute that plan. You also discover
some strategies and tactics to help find good sources of
capital for your business.

# Chapter 12

# Getting Ready to Do a Business Plan

........................................................................

### In This Chapter

▶ Deciding whether your venture is feasible

▶ Understanding business plans

▶ Starting with a vision

▶ Getting your business plan ready

........................................................................

*T*he bottom line is that preparing and adhering to a business plan enhances the chances that your new venture will be a success. Yes, many successful businesses began without business plans, businesses like Crate and Barrel, Pizza Hut, and Reebok. So, it certainly is possible, but considering today's complex and fast-moving environment, you probably don't want to launch a new venture without having written a business plan, unless you're starting a simple, small business or buying a successful small business. A business plan forces you to think logically and carefully about your business model, and it reduces your risk of failure.

Yet, executing a business plan is not a guarantee of success. Even if you craft the most elegant business plan, you can fail if you haven't done the appropriate research proving that your concept is feasible.

In this chapter, you discover how a business plan can make it possible for you to be more successful as an entrepreneur by taking a feasible concept and turning it into a successful business.

## Drawing a Conclusion about Feasibility

In the first and second parts of this book, you get a pretty good idea of what it takes to analyze the feasibility of a new business concept. You start with the development of the concept itself, identifying the product/service, customer, benefit or value proposition, and distribution strategy. You investigate the big picture, the industry, discovering in what ways to support the feasibility of your concept. You analyze potential markets and customers determining what the demand for your product or service may be. And finally, you choose your distribution channel and calculate your start-up capital requirements.

At any point along the way, if you work on a real concept, you may conclude that the concept isn't feasible. Maybe customer numbers are too few, or your start-up costs are too high, or you discover some regulations that make it difficult for you to do business the way you want. The more likely scenario, however, is that you find out your concept is feasible and now you must decide under what conditions you're willing to move forward with this new venture.

# *Looking at the Who, What, Where, and Why of Business Plans*

If a feasibility study is your way of testing your business concept, the business plan is the tool that helps show you how to execute your concept. You don't build a home without a set of blueprints. Similarly, you don't build a business without a plan.

In addition to including all the information that you develop for your feasibility analysis (see Chapter 4), a business plan discusses the operational, organizational, and financial management of a new business. In general, a business plan serves four purposes:

- **It's a reality check for you.** The business plan gets you into the details of the business in a way that the feasibility analysis did not. Sometimes those details reveal previously unforeseen problems. If the problems are significant enough, you may decide (even this early in the project) against starting the business. Knowing when to back out of a project isn't considered a negative; it's an important part of the planning process. Halting the start of a business before you expend all your time and money is far better than charging ahead and hoping things turn out OK.

- **It may reveal new opportunities on the operational side of the business.** The feasibility analysis did not focus on the operations of the business the way the business plan does. As you delve into the organizational and operations plan, you may discover innovations that you didn't think of before. In fact, you may find that your concept is more exciting than you ever thought. For some entrepreneurs, feasibility analysis is something they must do so they don't make the mistake of starting a business that has a poor chance of succeeding. Nevertheless, they pour their hearts into starting a company. They envision the culture, the way the business looks, and the kind of people who work there as more exciting than the product or service. That's okay. As you'll discover in Chapter 17, most great companies get a start because an entrepreneur wants to build a great company, not because he or she has a great idea.

✔ **It's a living guide to your business.** The business plan details all aspects of your business so that anyone reading it has a thorough understanding of how your business operates. I call it a living document because it always changes, responding to changes in the environment. I have never met an entrepreneur whose business plan predicted precisely what actually happened when the business started. Keeping your business plan in a secure area on your Web site and making changes as they happen so that you always have a current version of your plan available are not bad ideas. At a minimum, I recommend updating your business plan quarterly in the first year and then semiannually thereafter.

✔ **It's a statement of intent for others.** The business plan is not just an internal document; it is also of great interest to others — investors, bankers, potential management, strategic partners, suppliers, and lessors. Later in this chapter, I address the specifics of what these third parties are interested in when they read your business plan.

# Addressing the needs of your audience

Many different groups of people are interested in seeing your business plan. In this section, I discuss some of those people so that you have a good understanding of what you need to convey in your business plan. Remember that each reader looks at your business plan from a different perspective and has different needs that he or she wants to satisfy. Your business plan addresses those needs.

### Investors

Investors are more interested in the quality of the founding team and factors that predict growth. Why? Investors want to increase the value of their investment during the period of time they invest in the business. They want to know what deal structure you're offering, or how much of an equity interest they have and how they can liquidate their investment — sell their shares — at some future date. They also want to know if your management team has a proven track record and can make the venture successful.

Entrepreneurs often make mistakes with their business plans when considering potential investors. Examples of common mistakes include:

✔ **Projecting growth that exceeds the capability of the founding team.** Maybe you're lucky enough (or unlucky enough) to come up with a concept that has the potential for rapid growth early on. Assuming this kind of growth attracts investors is natural; however, if you don't show how your management team can handle that kind of growth, you actually discourage investors from considering your business. Rapid growth can be a deadly time for a new venture, especially if you don't have the systems, controls, and professional management in place to guide it. Furthermore, projecting high levels of growth and not achieving them make investors unhappy.

✔ **Trying to be a jack-of-all-trades.** How attractive to an investor is presenting a complex business concept, when you intend to do everything yourself? Not very attractive at all! Investors are nervous about investing in a company with a solo entrepreneur. They prefer teams comprised of people handling all the major functions of the business.

✔ **Projecting business performance that exceeds industry averages.** Face it. Why would an investor believe that your new company outperforms existing industry leaders? It just isn't going to happen. Projecting figures that are at or slightly below industry averages is a better approach, because you can then provide investors with a strategy for exceeding industry averages in the future.

✔ **Underestimating your need for capital.** Investors can readily recognize when you're trying to do something on too much of a shoestring budget; they've been down that road many times before. They don't see you as being frugal or conservative; they see naiveté on your part.

✔ **Confusing strategy and tactics.** As you can see in an upcoming section, strategies define the overall focus of a business. Tactics are the means and methods by which you implement those strategies. So if an investor asks what your strategy is for growing the company at 30 percent per year for the next three years, and you respond with "advertising on the Internet and attending trade shows," you quickly lose that investor's confidence because you responded with tactics.

✔ **Focusing too much on price.** It is rarely possible for a new venture to compete on price in a market comprised of established players. Building economies of scale in production take time, and you can't lower prices until you cover your costs. Investors know this, so they are more interested in your bundle of competitive advantages as a way of differentiating your business in the market.

✔ **Being proud of not investing cash in the business.** While I am a big proponent of bootstrapping, you won't attract investors to your business unless you have invested cold, hard cash in it. Sweat equity doesn't count — it's expected. Investors figure that if you invest your life's savings or mortgage your home, you're willing to take a big risk and not likely to take the easy way out and walk away. They also reason that you're probably trying harder to make the business a success.

### Bankers/lenders

The needs of bankers and lenders differ from those of investors. Bankers and lenders are more concerned with how you can repay the money they loan to you, so they look at your gross margins (revenues – COGS = gross profit/ revenues). If your gross margins are slim — 5 percent to 10 percent — you won't have much room to make errors because only 5 percent to 10 percent of your sales are available to pay your overhead and enable you to make a profit. Bankers also look at your cash flow projections, determining whether you can pay all your expenses and still have money left over at the end of the month.

Bankers look at your qualifications and may ask you to personally guarantee any loan they give you. Although you can try to avoid personally guaranteeing a loan, it may not be possible. More and more lenders are asking for personal guarantees from the founding team no matter how well financed the new venture is.

Here's a checklist of major concerns bankers and other lenders have when dealing with entrepreneurs:

✔ **Not supporting the amount of capital required.** You must show specifics about the amount of money you need and how you plan to use it. Justifying the amount with appropriate calculations and forecasts is essential.

✔ **Using the loan to pay off old debt.** Bankers, like investors, want to know that the money they're providing is going to have a positive impact on the business and is not just being used to pay off old debt or enable the founders to remove cash from the business.

✔ **Not having any assets to use as collateral.** Not all assets are equal. Some of your assets may actually have no value to the bank because they aren't worth anything outside the business in which they're used — for example, custom equipment. Bankers are looking for assets they can quickly and easily convert to cash or another use if your business gets into trouble.

✔ **Not demonstrating an ability to repay the loan.** Before approving a loan, lenders must know that your business generates enough cash to repay it. They look closely at your cash flow projections and the market research, determining whether your sales projections make sense.

✔ **Not showing the bank how it is protected in case of failure.** Lenders look to see if you have contingency plans for responding to unexpected events or downturns in the market. Again, they want to ensure that you can repay the loan no matter what happens.

✔ **Not demonstrating an adequate stake in the business.** Like investors, lenders want to know that you've taken an appropriate cash risk with this venture before they're willing to throw their cash into the pot.

### Future management

As your business grows, you may want to fill any gaps in experience and expertise by hiring professional management. A business plan lets these people see where they might fit in and gives them confidence when leaving their current situations to come on board. Potential key management will be interested in the operational and organizational plans, making sure that their skills and experiences are compatible with the company's needs.

# An all-purpose business plan outline

**EXPANDED EXECUTIVE SUMMARY** (6 page expanded summary as a separate document.)

**PROOF OF CONCEPT** (1 page summary)

**I. BUSINESS CONCEPT**

- Business Concept (Product/service, customer, benefit, distribution)
- Purpose of the business; why you're in business
- Core Values
- Description and uses, unique features/benefits of product or service
- The primary customer
- Spin-offs
- Environmental impact (if relevant)

**II. MANAGEMENT TEAM**

**III. MARKET ANALYSIS**

- Industry Description
- Target Market
- Competitors — Competitive Grid
- Your Product/Service Differentiation & Competitive Advantage
- Pricing

**IV. PROCESS ANALYSIS**

- Technical Description of Products/Services
- Status of Development and Related Costs
- Distribution Channels & Physical Distribution Plan

**V. ORGANIZATION PLAN**

- Philosophy of Management and Company Culture
- Legal Structure of the Company
- Organizational Chart

**VI. MARKETING PLAN**

- Purpose of Marketing Plan
- Plan to Reach First Customer

**VII. FINANCIAL PLAN**

- Summary of Key Points and Capital Requirements
- Needs Assessment Breakout (Hard costs, working capital, start-up)
- Break-even Analysis and Payback Period
- Plan for Funding

**VIII. GROWTH PLAN**

**APPENDIX** (organize and separate parts with tabs)

**FINANCIAL STATEMENTS**

- Assumptions for financial statements
- Proforma Financial Statements

**PROCESS PLAN SUPPORTING DOCUMENTS**

- Manufacturing or Operating Requirements and Associated Costs

**MARKETING PLAN SUPPORTING DOCUMENTS**

- Marketing Tools
- Media Plan
- Marketing Budget

**ORGANIZATIONAL PLAN SUPPORTING DOCUMENTS**

- Compensation Programs and Incentives

**CONTINGENCY PLAN**

**SUPPORTING DOCUMENTS**

### Strategic partners

The companies through which you outsource and with whom you have a strategic alliance are also interested in your business plan, because it tells the strategic partner how much potential growth it can expect from forming a partnership with your business. Strategic partners are more interested in your growth and marketing strategies, because they tell how much business the partner can receive from the relationship.

Count your major customers and suppliers among the strategic partners that are interested in your business plan. Both want to know that you have a well-thought-out plan, creating a big enough market for them as well. Suppliers check to see whether your business provides them with a new outlet for their products, and customers want to see how your business better positions their companies in the marketplace with new products and services.

## Using a guideline-outline

You can find plenty of guidelines for how to do a business plan. Some are more detailed than others, but they all feature basic components. In the sidebar "An all-purpose business plan outline," you can find an outline that is comprehensive, taking into account all types of businesses. You can modify it (add things and throw things out that you don't need) to suit your particular purposes. I discuss the guideline/outline components here in more detail.

Business plans used to be huge reports several inches thick, containing everything but the kitchen sink. However, much like the streamlining that business in general has gone through, business plans now are on a diet, much more concise and to the point. I explain more about the look of newer business plans in a later section. For now, here is what to put into a business plan.

### Starting with the feasibility analysis

The front part of the business plan is essentially the feasibility analysis. The difference is that by the time you prepare the business plan, you may have gathered more data or more recent information that you will want to substitute for outdated material in the feasibility analysis. Looking at the example outline (see the "An all-purpose business plan outline" sidebar), you can see that your work on your feasibility study takes you down to the *process analysis*. The financials you calculated for feasibility are a start, but by the time you prepare them for the business plan, you may have more data to include and you must produce a balance sheet.

### Process or operational plan

This section of your business plan presents a technical description of your product or service — engineering specifications where appropriate, a description of the prototype, and a depiction of the how your business will operate. Every business has processes to design and develop. Chapter 15 helps you design your business processes.

### Organization plan

This section of your business plan addresses the legal form of organization by which you are structuring your business — sole proprietorship, partnership, corporate form, or limited liability company. Chapter 14 provides you with guidelines for choosing the legal form for organizing your business that is best suited for you.

In the organization plan, you discuss your philosophy of management, present key management personnel, and deal with compensation and policies.

### Marketing plan

The marketing plan section of your business plan is quite different from the market analysis that you performed for your feasibility analysis. Your market analysis uncovered information about your customers — how they buy, when, where, how much — that helps you structure a marketing strategy to reach those customers. Your marketing plan includes your niche in the market, customers' perceptions of your company, and the tools you plan to use in reaching out to the customer. You can find out more about the marketing plan in Chapter 18.

### Financial plan

The financial plan forecasts the financial future of your company. Newer business plan formats provide summary financial figures and ratios within the plan itself and refer to a complete set of financial statements in an appendix. The well-designed financial plan demonstrates that all the claims you make in other sections of the business plan are supported by the financials in a way that says that your business can survive and grow over the long term. Chapter 19 helps you complete this section.

### Growth plan

In this section, you express your intentions about how you plan for your business to progress from start-up through the various growth phases. The growth plan presents key strategies for growth in the form of new products or services, new customers, or acquisitions. You can find out more about preparing a growth plan in Chapter 17.

### Contingency plan

Some entrepreneurs include a contingency plan in their business plan as a way of showing others that you recognize that everything might not go as planned. The contingency plan addresses how your company responds to changing market conditions, for example, what you expect to do if demand for your product is not as strong as projected. You can discover more about the contingency plan in Chapter 20.

### Appendixes

Business plans today are documents that are more concise. That means that the appendixes are longer. Appendixes contain supplementary information that is important but not vital to the business plan, such as resumes, job descriptions, lease agreements, maps, letters of intent, evidence of patents, designs, and complete financial statements.

### Executive summary and proof of concept

Although I am discussing the executive summary last (it's difficult to write without first completing the entire business plan), the truth is it may be the most important piece to the business plan puzzle. Most investors, bankers, and other interested parties look at the executive summary first, so if you don't grab their attention with it, they're not going to bother reading the complete business plan. In fact, many e-commerce ventures often receive funds based on expanded executive summaries (about six pages) that describe concepts, define customers, and establish market sizes, and the ability of businesses to scale out (a favorite term referring to an e-business's ability to grow and reach a mass market). These summaries are separate documents that you can provide without handing out your entire business plan. The expanded executive summary is a good way of gauging interest in your company before revealing all the details of your business plan.

 In the summary, an executive must immediately (within the first 30 seconds) capture the reader's attention. Developing a great concept statement that creates excitement and clearly presents your business idea is of utmost importance (if you need to review concept statements, revisit Chapter 4). Here's an example:

CompanyURL.com builds a link between online retailers and Internet consumers. Through its propriety software, CompanyURL.com allows customers to establish prepaid purchasing accounts, providing a safer, quicker, more efficient method to purchase goods or services from online merchants when they don't have or want to use credit cards to purchase online.

You can grab a reader's attention in many ways. You can use a key selling point or benefit that your business provides. You can introduce a problem and then show how your product or service solves that problem. In the earlier example, the problem is that the most common way of purchasing goods online is to use a credit card, but for many customers, particularly those in the 14–25 age group, credit cards are not available. They have to rely on parents. The solution to that problem is to set up a secure, prepaid account that the customer can access as needed. Solving a real problem will catch the reader's attention.

Most people who read business plans see a lot of them. You have to find a way to make yours stand out from the crowd. You can do this by giving your plan a professional appearance, providing a very tight and persuasive executive summary, and creating a business plan that is well organized, concise, and supported by good research.

The proof of concept is simply an even shorter executive summary at the front of your business plan. All on one page, it hits the major persuasive arguments that favor your business. *Proof of concept* is a phrase that traditionally refers to a prototype or experiment that proves that your invention can work. I broaden the use of the phrase here to include all those factors proving that your business concept works. The "Executive summary checklist" sidebar offers ideas to include in your executive summary and, even more concisely, in your proof of concept.

## Executive summary checklist

As you're preparing your executive summary and proof of concept, this checklist helps you make sure you include all the important points. Remember that discussing all these points in detail in your business plan is essential.

- ✔ Did you grab the attention of the reader in your opening sentences? Did your concept create excitement? Testing your opening on several people helps you discover its effectiveness.

- ✔ Did your business concept section clearly describe the purpose of the business, the customer, the value proposition, and the distribution strategy?

- ✔ Did your management team section persuade the reader that you have a team that can successfully implement the business concept?

- ✔ Did your industry/market analyses support your business concept and demonstrate demand for your product/service?

- ✔ Did your process plan demonstrate how the product/service can be be produced and distributed?

- ✔ Did the organization plan depict an effective infrastructure to facilitate the achievement of your business goals?

- ✔ Did your marketing plan demonstrate how your company can reach its customers and create long-term relationships?

- ✔ Did the financial plan convince the reader that your company has long-term potential and can provide a superior return-on-investment for its owners?

- ✔ Did the growth plan demonstrate the potential for reaching new markets, developing new products and services, and diversifying the company's offerings?

# *Getting Started with a Vision*

If you don't know where you want to go, any path will get you there. In fact, if you don't know where you're going, how will you know when you've arrived? The bottom line is that you must have a vision for your company. A vision is a picture of what you see as the future for your company. It's analogous to a rainbow. You can see it in the distance — it's where you want to be — and you keep moving toward it, but you never actually reach it. The Disney Co.'s vision is to "bring happiness to millions." Disney constantly strives for that but never actually achieves it completely.

As the entrepreneur or leader of the organization, it's your job to be the catalyst for a clear and shared vision. You can certainly succeed without a vision, but I don't recommend it. Research has found that vision seems to be the critical component to a company that endures over time. It's essentially the glue that holds everything together and gives the business a context in which to make important decisions.

You are no doubt quite familiar with enduring companies and products such as 3M's Scotch Tape and Post-it® Notes, Motorola's cellular phones, and Disney's animated films. These companies and others with vision survive economic shifts, changing technology, and changes in management because they have a vision that does not change.

The vision for your company comes from your core values — those things you hold to be true and are fundamental beliefs about what's important. Your company's core values reflect what you stand for, who you are, and they rarely change over time. For example, Merck, the highly successful pharmaceutical company, has core values which include preserving and improving human life, honesty and integrity, and unequivocal excellence in all aspects of their company. Nordstrom, one of the nation's top retailers, claims service to the customer above all else and continuous improvement in every aspect of their business.

One thing that's important to mention is that the core values of great companies are never about profits. They're always about ideals. Now, you may be thinking that you will be too busy figuring out how to start your business to concern yourself with something as soft and philosophical as core values. But, if you consider that all the number one companies in their respective industries put their core values in writing from the very earliest stages of their ventures, wouldn't you also want to do that?

Here are some suggestions for thinking about core values:

- Choose five or six at a maximum.
- Ask yourself, for each of your core values, if you can think of a situation where you may have to change one of your core values. If you can, then you probably haven't identified a core value.

✔ Make sure that your core values are communicated and accepted by everyone in the organization.

# Finding the Big Mission

A mission for your company is the one thing that will pull everyone together to reach a common goal. A mission is a clear and compelling goal that focuses the effort of everyone in the organization. It's a major goal that is achievable. It's a way of turning the broad purpose (the reason you are in business) into a goal. To have an effective mission, you must meet three requirements:

✔ The mission must have an end point. State the date when the mission will be achieved.

✔ The mission must be exciting and galvanize the energy of everyone.

✔ The mission must be measurable; that is, you must know when you've achieved it.

Here's an example of a good mission statement:

***To become a $1 billion company by 1980.***

This mission statement belongs to Wal-Mart Stores Inc. Sam Walton set that mission in 1977 and actually achieved $1.2 billion by 1980.

# Looks Count: Preparing and Presenting the Plan

No one gets excited about writing a business plan, because it takes so much time, energy, and effort. Business planning doesn't always work as logically and orderly as I've tried to show. Although you may be looking for industry information first, you're no doubt going to encounter important stuff to include in other sections of your plan. Don't be disconcerted when you find yourself confounded by information from all parts of your business plan at once. Here are tips for overcoming the toughest hurdle — getting started.

✔ **Know where to start.** The task can be daunting and the amount of information you need to collect overwhelming, but finding that first piece of information will lead to the next piece and the next. A hint: Everyone goes to the Internet first. Why not follow their lead.

✔ **Don't be discouraged.** Many entrepreneurs become discouraged when a particular piece of information doesn't just jump out and bite them. Rest assured, finding information tends to mushroom so quickly (sometimes it gets out of hand), and you find more information than you can imagine.

✔ **Answer key questions.** Organizing that pile of information sitting on your desk is the second hardest part of writing a business plan, so find out how each piece of information answers key questions about every section of the plan. Labeling folders with the key questions and filing the answers as you collect them makes the job go easier.

✔ **Always include sources.** Always be sure to include the sources of information you include in your business plan. You don't want someone asking, "Where did you get that statistic?" without the answer.

✔ **Use your outline to put the plan together.** Writing in a clear, concise style and making sure that the most important points stand out makes finding things easier for your reader.

## Making the plan look good

Looks count when you want someone to pay attention to your business plan. The trick is creating an attractive, professional looking plan that conveys the personality of your business without being too slick. I saw one business plan for an entertainment-based Internet company that was bound, full color on glossy paper. It must have cost thousands of dollars to produce. When I saw it, I had to ask, "If you can afford to create this type of business plan, why do you need me to invest?" Any investor criticizes the allocation of so much money when it isn't necessary.

Here are tips for making your business plan look professional and attractive:

✔ Spiral-bind your plan (use the good, vinyl coated stuff), so that it lies flat when it's read.

✔ Use excellent quality white or ecru paper, but do not enclose the paper in plastic — it makes the plan too thick.

✔ Use index tabs to separate major sections of the plan, so that it's easier for the reader to find things. Readers don't often start at the beginning of the plan and read to the end. They jump around a lot, so make it easy for them.

✔ Use a 12-point font in an easy-to-read character like Times New Roman or Arial.

✔ Use boldfaced headings and subheadings so they stand out, and use bulleted lists wherever possible.

✔ Put your company logo in the header section of every page.

✔ Make sure that you write clearly and concisely. A business plan is not the place for expository writing or expounding on your favorite topic at length. Prune excess words, and get someone you trust to read it and do the same. The more people you can have edit the plan the better.

✔ Number each copy of your business plan and slip a nondisclosure statement inside that you can hand to your reader.

✔ In the footer of every page include the following statement: "Copyright 2000 (Your Name). All rights reserved. No part of this plan may be copied or used without permission of its author." If you want to find out more about copyrights, see Chapter 8.

## Presenting your plan

If you're seeking capital from an investor you don't personally know, or from an investor group, don't be surprised about being asked to make a presentation of your business concept. The invitation to make such a presentation typically happens after potential investors read your business plan. Getting a look at you and your founding team is the purpose of the presentation. Investors enjoy seeing if you measure up under pressure. By no means a formal speech, once you introduce your concept and key arguments for its validity, the presentation turns more toward interaction. Here are tips to help you prepare for the presentation.

✔ **Check to see how long of a presentation your investors are expecting.** Nothing is worse than preparing to speak for a half-hour and finding out you have only ten minutes. On average, expect to speak uninterrupted for about 20 minutes. The main part of the presentation is the question and answer period, which will probably last longer than your presentation.

✔ **Grab your audience's attention in the first 30 seconds.** Appear genuinely happy for the opportunity when discussing your concept with your hosts. Check with them to see if they can hear you clearly and see your visuals. This will demonstrate your concern that they enjoy your presentation and they will feel more comfortable with you.

✔ **Don't use a lectern to speak!** Using a lectern may make you appear too stiff. Freeing yourself of this piece of furniture helps you gain a better command of the situation, making it easier for you to use visual aids and gestures.

✔ **Be careful not to pace or use any kind of repetitive movements.** Doing so may distract your audience from what you're saying, causing them to focus on what you're doing.

✔ **Whenever possible, demonstrate your product or service.** Product demonstrations create more excitement and make the whole concept more real.

✔ **Be sure to involve all of the founding team in the presentation.** Strength and safety come in numbers.

✔ **Practice, practice, practice.** Practicing in advance for your presentation helps you feel comfortable with the material so you don't have to use notes. You might try videotaping your rehearsal so you can review your presentation from the audience's point of view.

✔ **Brainstorm.** Compile a list of questions you think audience members may ask. Answering them helps you avoid being surprised by their inquiries.

✔ **Use visual aids but don't overwhelm the audience.** I remember the trouble one entrepreneur got into, setting up a computer-actuated, animated slide presentation on a timer so the slides changed automatically while he was speaking. He didn't give himself enough time to breathe, and by the time he finished (ten minutes faster than he thought he would), the combination of his rapid speaking and constant activity on the slide presentation left his audience out of breath, not quite understanding what happened.

### Answering questions

If you're thinking the presentation is the hard part, think again. Many entrepreneurs agree that the Q&A following the presentation is much more stressful, because investors love putting entrepreneurs on the hot seat and seeing how they respond. After all, starting a new business is a stressful activity (fun, but stressful), and investors rightfully want to know if you can handle it. They also like asking questions they've already answered, so they can see if you know what you're talking about.

Watch out for questions requiring precise (impossibly precise) responses or ones that are so broad that you wonder what the question actually is. Always asking for clarification if you don't understand the question is far better than appearing ignorant by answering the wrong questions.

One question that is most problematic for entrepreneurs is a complex question that contains several underlying assumptions. Here's an example of that type of question:

If you were to look at your venture and its market share before and after this potential investment, how would your market strategy have changed, and how much of your budget would you allocate to that change?

When you find yourself on the hot seat in a situation like this, have courage (maybe take a deep breath) and regroup — fast! If you choose, you can

- ✔ Attempt to restate the question in your own words, seeking confirmation that you heard it correctly.

- ✔ Ask the questioner to repeat his or her question, so that you're sure you heard it right.

- ✔ If you heard it right, then ask for a couple minutes to consider your response. You never have to answer without skipping a beat. Sometimes a pause is more effective, at least making you appear as if you're considering the best way to respond.

- ✔ Decide to respond to only one portion of the question — for example, the part about market share — and not commit to a specific course of action without first taking the time to thoughtfully consider your strategy. This type of response doesn't make you look indecisive; on the contrary, you're likely gaining the respect of your audience because you haven't made a precipitous decision.

If you're asked a question for which you don't have an answer, don't bluff. It may be a question your audience already has answered, or think they have. Instead, admit graciously that you don't have the answer at your fingertips, but you'll be happy to find it for them after the meeting.

If you *are* criticized for any aspect of your business plan (and expect that to happen), don't get defensive or attack your audience — you'll lose their respect immediately and may not be able to regain it. Instead, be gracious and remain cool. This may just be a tactic to see if they can get you to become flustered or angry.

## The one-minute business plan

If you had only one minute with an important person who could make or break your new venture, what would you tell that person about your business concept? This is an important exercise for you to master, because you will have many one-minute occasions to grab someone's attention. In fact, you won't often have more time than that. So here are the most important points:

- ✔ Your two-sentence concept statement with the product/service, customer, value proposition, and distribution strategy.

- ✔ Why you, and why now. Why are you the right person or team to do this, and why is the window of opportunity now?

- ✔ How you're going to differentiate your business in the market.

- ✔ How you're going to make money — your revenue model.

- ✔ Why you know there's demand for what you're offering.

# Chapter 13

# Finding Money to Start and Grow Your Venture

*In This Chapter*

▶ Making a money plan

▶ Using your own money first

▶ Looking for an angel this side of heaven

▶ Using venture capital

▶ Selling stock through an IPO

"*I* need money to start a venture" is usually the opening line when an entrepreneur comes to see me in my office. Most of the time, however, these entrepreneurs haven't done the homework they need to do before approaching an investor. But once I start my series of questions with them, they soon find out how badly they would have stumbled had they talked to an investor before they were ready.

Two major attitudes about start-up funds make the search for funds that much more difficult. They are

✔ The more money I get, the better. I can use as much as I can get.

✔ My business plan numbers are just estimates — the investor will tell me what I need.

If you're thinking like this, stop right now! First of all, why seek more investment money than you absolutely need? Every bit of capital invested in your business costs you some equity (ownership) in your company. Besides, having too much money may lead you to make poor decisions because you don't think as carefully as you should about how you spend that money.

Secondly, although it's true that your business plan financials are estimates, they had better be good estimates based on your research. Your investor may discount your estimate of rapid sales growth, but he or she wants to know that you've carefully considered all of your numbers and that they make sense.

In this chapter, you see how to raise capital for start-up and growth the smart way — and you start with a plan.

# Starting with a Plan

Before you talk to anyone — even your grandmother — about money, have a plan in place, a set of strategies for targeting the right amount of money from the right sources. Here are some guidelines for putting together a plan that works:

- ✔ Seek what you actually need, not what you think you can raise.

- ✔ Look at how your company grows and define the points when you'll most likely need capital.

- ✔ Consider the sources of money available to you at each stage.

- ✔ Make sure that the activities of your business let you tap into the correct source of money at the right time. For example, if you know that you are planning an initial public offering (IPO) in three years, start putting in place the systems, controls, and professional management that you'll need before the IPO takes place (I talk about IPOs elsewhere in this chapter).

- ✔ Monitor your capital needs as you go so that you don't have to return to the trough too many times. Every time you go back for another round of capital, you give up more stock in your company, and the percentage you own declines.

You can come out a winner if you prepare for your future capital needs. Just follow the lead of one technology company I know that produces custom productivity and e-commerce applications. This company keeps itself in a good position to raise capital by:

- ✔ Creating value in the form of long-term customers and great products.

- ✔ Running a profitable business.

- ✔ Keeping cash flow positive (see Chapter 19).

If you do these three things, you will probably not have difficulty raising growth capital whenever you need it. If you have a start-up venture, strive to achieve these goals from day one. In an upcoming section, I talk about where to find capital before your business starts.

# When you're financing a traditional business

Traditional businesses (non-Internet businesses) typically follow fairly pre-dictable financing cycles. Take a look at Figure 13-1 to see the stages of financing for a typical business.

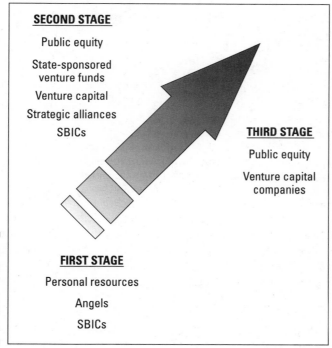

**SECOND STAGE**

Public equity

State-sponsored venture funds

Venture capital

Strategic alliances

SBICs

**THIRD STAGE**

Public equity

Venture capital companies

**FIRST STAGE**

Personal resources

Angels

SBICs

**Figure 13-1:** Three stages for financing the typical business.

First-stage funding is about getting seed capital to finish preparing the product and the business for launch. It's also the stage where you seek funding to begin operations and reach a positive cash flow. In the second stage, you're usually looking for growth capital. Your business has proven its concept and now you want to grow. Alternatively, your customers have demanded that your company grow to meet their needs (that's a nice thing when it happens). To successfully use second-round financing, you need to be out looking for capital in advance of needing it.

Third-stage funding generally results in an acquisition or a buyout of the company. It's the harvest stage for the entrepreneur who wants to take his or her wealth out of the business and possibly exit, or for investors who want to exit. In general, if you take on venture capital (a professionally managed pool of money), you are probably looking at a buyout or IPO within three to five years. That's because a buyout or IPO provides the cash your investor needs to get out of the investment.

## When you're financing for e-commerce

It's pretty easy to look at the funding stages of a traditional business, but the Internet has brought about some business models that don't fit those stages well, if at all. Internet-based businesses (whose primary location is the Internet) require a strategy that is part formula and part artistic achievement. Such a strategy is ill defined at best. And sometimes it's difficult to judge which concept is going to get funding before it launches, and which will have to bootstrap for a while to prove its concept. Drugstore.com is an example of a company that was funded on the concept alone before it went live on the Internet. By contrast, the founders of WebSideStory Inc., www.websidestory.com, a provider of Web-based audience analysis, had to prove their business model online before they received outside funding.

Grabbing early brand recognition from competitors online takes a lot of money, a professional management team, and the ability to grow in a hurry. If that's your business, here are some suggestions for maneuvering through the capital maze:

- **Don't take the easy money. You want smart money.** It's okay to fund a traditional business with money from friends, family, and lovers. Doing so isn't a good idea, however, when you're seeking early stage capital for an Internet concept. Who is funding your business is as important as how much they're giving you. Be sure that you associate with people who attract the right kind of money to your venture.

- **Get an introduction to the money source through one of your advisors.** Be sure you exercise due diligence (a fancy word for doing your homework — investigating the money source) on the investor to find one that has worked with your type of business before and has compatible firms in its portfolio that provide synergies with yours.

- **Don't get married on the first date.** Large quantities of money are available for great Internet concepts. If you have such a concept, you may have more term sheets (agreements listing what an investor is willing to do) than you know what to do with. It's tempting to grab the first term sheet under the assumption that the first is always the best. The agreement may be for the most money, maybe not, but the investor may not be the most compatible with your business. Compatibility is even more important than money, because the money source has a lot to say about what happens to your business. So, consider all your options before selecting one. Remember that the most important person to get to know in any potential investment firm is the partner you will be dealing with. If you don't have a good feeling about that person, you may want to look elsewhere.

✔ **Take the deal that moves you on to the next stage.** The biggest deal doesn't always win. What you're looking for is enough money to get you comfortably to the next round of financing and an investment firm that adds value to what you're doing in the form of introductions, contacts, advice, and so forth.

✔ **Get your Web site up as quickly as possible.** Don't wait for the perfect site; get up and running and start receiving feedback from potential customers. You need to keep the momentum going and collect data on the people who visit your site. This is important information to have when you talk to your investor.

✔ **Buy the best management you can get with your capital.** Investors are practically unanimous: The management team is more important than the business concept itself. When you obtain money, invest in the best management you can get. If you have to bootstrap with your own funds, seek a strategic alliance with a company whose great management you can leverage.

# Tapping Friends, Family, and Lovers

The majority of entrepreneurs — well over 70 percent — start their businesses with personal savings, credit cards, and other personal assets like the proceeds from second mortgages and sale of stock portfolios. Why is that? With all the venture capital and private investor money out there for the taking, why do you have to use your own resources? The answer is simple: Your new company is just too big a risk — it's unproven; you don't know for certain if the market will accept it. The only people who'll invest in your business at this point are people who know and believe in you.

But what if you don't have a network of friends and family willing to give you money, or from whom you prefer not to take money? What do you do then? One thing you do is bootstrap — beg, borrow, and barter for anything that you can from products to services to an office site. (Suggestion: Look at Chapter 12 to see how to reduce your start-up capital needs and lessen the front-end load.) One way to bootstrap is to avoid hiring employees as long as possible (employees are typically the single biggest expense of any business). Here are some other tips:

✔ Look for an office suite where you can share facilities and equipment with other tenants.

✔ Share office space with an established company that is compatible with yours. I know of a public relations firm that shared space with a friend's well-established advertising firm. In exchange for the space, the PR firm referred clients to the ad agency.

✔ To reduce cash needs, consider leasing rather than buying equipment.

✔ Barter with established companies for services. A friend of mine needed a wardrobe for a media tour when she was starting her business. She talked to a clothing designer and managed to get an entire wardrobe in exchange for promoting the label on her tour.

✔ Get your customers to pay quickly. Sometimes a new company can get customers to pay a deposit up front, providing capital for the raw materials you need to make the product.

✔ Ask your suppliers for favorable payment terms, and then pay on time. Those relationships become important to your business as it grows. You may find it necessary to request smaller amounts of credit from several suppliers until you establish your business.

If you do decide to take money from friends and family, do it in a businesslike manner. That is, have an attorney draw up a contract that protects both sides. Investing in a business venture is a risk and should only be undertaken by people who can bear to lose their investment, should that occur.

Family money is the most expensive money you'll ever use because you pay for it for the rest of your life!

# Finding an Angel

The second most common source of capital for starting and growing a business is an angel, also known as a private investor. Angels are members of the *informal risk capital market* — the largest pool of capital in the U.S. So, how do you find one of these gift-givers from heaven? Unfortunately, that's the hard part because angels tend to keep a lower profile than any other type of investor. Entrepreneurs typically find angels through referrals from someone else. That's why networking with people in your industry is so important when you begin thinking about starting a business. You need to build up a personal network to tap when it's time to look for private investment capital.

## How to spot an angel

I described angels differently in my first book about entrepreneurship. For one thing, I said that they were into the investment for the long haul. That was true, but times have changed; angel investors have, too. Today, angel investors look a lot like professional venture capitalists. Angels typically ask you for the same credentials that a venture capitalist wants:

✔ A business plan

✔ Milestones

✔ A significant equity stake in the business

✔ A seat on the board of directors

The similarity between an angel and a venture capitalist came about because of the long bull market in the late 1990s when venture capital funding reached astronomical levels. Flush with cash, the venture capitalist stopped looking at deals that were less than $3 million to $5 million, leaving the playing field wide open for angels to step in and do bigger deals than normal, with the promise of a quicker turnaround.

Angels used to be characterized as middle-aged, former entrepreneurs who generally operated solo and invested near their homes. They usually funded deals for less than a million dollars and stayed in the investment for several years. Today, angels come in all ages, even turning up among the twenty-something Internet crowd who hit it big with their first ventures. Angels also band together to increase the size of their investment pools and take on larger deals. Networks like The Tech Coast Angels and Berkus Technology Ventures, based in Los Angeles, California, consider themselves to be seed venture capitalists. They have become as sophisticated in their investment methods as any professional venture capitalist — exercising more due diligence and sometimes looking for a quicker return on their investment, often to the detriment of the business. In other words, they need to be cashed out of their investment before the growing business is in a position to do so. Entrepreneurs typically work with longer growth and performance horizons than venture capitalists and many of the new breed of angels. So their goals are often in conflict.

## How to deal with angels

In many ways, you deal with angels the same as you deal with professional venture capitalists. You start with a good referral from someone who knows the angel well. Then:

- ✔ **Make sure your goals and your angel's goals are the same.** Otherwise, you may risk the goals you've set for the business. Try to avoid an angel who wants to get in and out in three years or less. You can't build an enduring business in that timeframe. Besides, you need to find a way to buy out the investor at that point, and that may mean selling the business or offering an IPO, which may not have been your original plan.

- ✔ **Exercise your own due diligence (investigation, background check) on the angel.** Don't be afraid to ask for references from other companies the angel has invested in. Talk to those entrepreneurs to find out what their experience was.

- ✔ **Look for an angel who provides more than money.** You want contacts in the industry, potential board members, and strategic assistance for your business. These things are as important as money.

- ✔ **Get the angel's commitment to help you meet certain business milestones that you both agree on.**

## Getting ready to deal

One of the more important rules about negotiation is, "He who has the most information wins." Negotiating the best funding deal really is about 1) understanding the needs of the other party, 2) knowing what you want, and 3) knowing your alternatives if you can't come to an agreement. Here's a checklist of information you should have at your fingertips when you negotiate for funding:

1. How much money do you need for start-up and years one through five?

2. How will you use the funds?

3. What sources of money will you seek and why?

4. If you seek debt funding, what will you use as collateral?

5. Are you willing to personally guarantee the debt?

6. What funds have been invested to date and by whom? Are these funds debt or equity?

7. If you have received outside investment capital, what did the investor receive in return for the investment?

8. Which outside investors have you approached or will you approach? What were the results?

9. Under what legal form is the company organized and how does this help the principals and investors?

10. What tax benefits does the legal structure provide for the company, the principals, and the investors?

11. What is the financial vehicle being offered to the investors?

12. What is the payback period for the investor and the projected return on investment (ROI)?

13. What is the proposed exit strategy for the investors? The principals?

14. Have your financial projections been reviewed by an accountant?

15. What leases and loan agreements do you currently have?

# Daring to Use Venture Capital

Venture capital is a professionally managed pool of funds that usually operates in the form of a limited partnership. The managing general partner pulls together a pool of investors — individual and institutional (pension funds and insurance companies, for example) — whose money he or she invests on behalf of the partnership. Typically, venture capitalists invest at the second round of funding and are looking for fast growth and a quick turnaround of their investment. Consequently, their goals often conflict with the entrepreneur's goals for the company.

In the late 1990s, it appeared that all the rules about what a good investment is changed as venture capitalists began focusing on Internet companies and investing in ideas rather than intellectual property. They rushed to invest in companies like Amazon.com, Buy.com, and e-Toys, companies that weren't projecting profits for several years. But as stock valuations of these companies plummeted to near zero levels in late 1999 and early 2000, venture capitalists began rethinking their strategies. They didn't stop investing in Internet companies; they just started doing a better job of evaluating the opportunities.

What is still true about venture capital is that it funds less than 1 percent of all new ventures, mostly in technology areas — biotechnology, information systems, the Internet, and computer technology. To see how you may be able to use venture capital to your advantage, you first need to understand the cost of raising capital and the process by which it happens.

## Calculating the real cost of money

Raising money for your business, whether private or venture capital, is a time-consuming and costly process. That's why many entrepreneurs in more traditional businesses (non-high-tech or non-Internet) opt for slower growth, using internal cash flows as long as they can. But if you've decided to speed up your start-up or growth rate with outside capital, you need to have reasonable expectations about how that can happen. Here's what you need to know:

- ✔ Raising money always takes longer than you planned, at least twice as long. Count on it.

- ✔ Plan to spend several months seeking funds, several more months for the potential investor to agree to fund your venture, and perhaps six more months before the money is actually in your hands.

- ✔ Use financial advisors experienced in raising money.

- ✔ Understand that raising money takes you away from your business a lot, probably when you most need to be there. So be sure to have a good management team in place.

Start looking for money before you need it!

### Investors are fickle

Once you've found what you think is the ideal investor — you're compatible, you have the same goals for the future of the company, and you genuinely like each other — the investor may back out of the deal. That's right, after you've spent months trying to find this investor and even more time exercising due diligence (yours and the investor's), the investor may change his or her mind. Perhaps the investor stumbled across something unfavorable; more likely, he or she couldn't pull together the capital needed to fund your deal.

Always have a backup if you sense that the deal may be going sideways.

Investors often want to buy out your early investors, including your friends and family, typically out of the belief that first-round funders have nothing more to contribute to the venture. Investors also don't want to deal with a bunch of small investors. A buyout like this can turn into an awkward situation if you haven't explained to your early funders that it's a possibility. And if you don't agree to the buyout of the first round, understand that your investor may walk away from the deal.

### It takes money to make money

*It takes money to make money.* Truer words were never spoken. The costs of finding your investor, including preparing and printing the business plan, travel, and time, all are paid up front by you. If you're seeking a lot of money — several million — you probably need to have your financials prepared or reviewed by a CPA, and you need to prepare a prospectus, an offering document spelling out the risks and rewards of investing in your business opportunity. Again, these are costs you bear up front.

Once you receive the capital, the cost of maintaining it, ranging from paying interest on loans to keeping investors apprised of what's going on with your business, can usually be paid out of the proceeds. You'll also have *back-end costs* if you are raising capital by selling securities (shares of stock in your corporation). These costs include investment-banking fees, legal fees, marketing costs, brokerage fees, and any fees charged by state and federal authorities. The total cost of raising equity capital can reach 25 percent of the total amount of money you're seeking. You see it definitely takes money to make money.

## Tracking the venture capital process

The process that venture capitalists go through to analyze your deal, decide to make the deal, put together a term sheet, and exercise their due diligence can be quite complex and vary from firm to firm. In general, the process follows a predictable pattern, however. Before I show you the route, consider what venture capitalists are looking for.

A venture capitalist invests in your company for a specified period of time (typically five years or less) with the expectation that at the end of that time, he or she gets the investment back plus a substantial return, in the neighborhood of 50 percent or more. The amount of return is a function of the risk associated with your venture. In the early stages, the risk is high, so the venture capitalist wants a higher return. Later, when your business has proven itself and you're looking for second-round financing, the risk is less, so you have more clout in your negotiations.

The venture capitalist also probably wants a seat on your board of directors — a say in business strategy and policy.

### Approving your plan

The first thing venture capitalists do is scrutinize your business plan, particularly to see if you have a strong management team consisting of people experienced in your industry and committed to the launch of this venture. Then they look at your product and market to ensure the opportunity you've defined is substantial and worth their effort and the risk they're taking. If you have a unique product that is protected through patents, you have an important barrier to competitors that is attractive to the venture capitalists, who also look at the market to ensure a significant potential for growth — that's where they make their money, from the growth in value of your business.

If the venture capitalists like what they see, they'll probably call for a meeting at which you may be asked to present your plan. They want to confirm that your team is everything you say it is. (See Chapter 11 for presenting the business plan.) The venture capitalists may or may not discuss initial terms for an agreement at the meeting. It is likely they'll wait until they've exercised due diligence.

### Doing due diligence

If you've made it past the meeting stage, and the venture capitalists feel positive about your concept, it's time for them to exercise due diligence, meaning they thoroughly check out your team and your business concept or business as the case may be. Once they're satisfied that you check out, they'll draw up legal documents detailing the terms of the investment. But don't hold your breath waiting. Some venture capitalists wait until they know they have a good investment opportunity before putting together the partnership that actually funds your venture. Others just take a long time to release the money. In any case, you can certainly ask what the next steps are and how long they'll take.

One more surprise lies in store: It's unlikely that the money will be released to you in one lump sum. Study your term sheet carefully; for it probably states that the money will be released in stages triggered by your achieving certain predefined goals.

### Crafting the deal

Always approach a venture capitalist from a position of strength. If you sound and look desperate for money, I guarantee that you won't get a good deal.

Venture capitalists see many business concepts, but most of them aren't winners. Your power at the negotiating table comes from proving that your concept is one of the winners.

Every deal is comprised of four parts:

1. **The amount of capital to be invested**
2. **The timing and use of the money**
3. **The return on investment to the investors**
4. **The level of risk**

The amount of capital the venture capitalist provides reflects need. However, it also depends on the risks involved, how the money will be used, and how quickly the venture capitalist can earn a return on the investment (timing). The amount of equity in your company that the venture capitalist demands depends on the risk and the amount of the investment.

# Selling Stock to the Public: An IPO

The aura and myths surrounding the IPO (selling stock in your company on a public stock exchange) have grown with the huge IPOs undertaken by upstart dot-com companies that don't have an ounce of profit to their names. The glamour of watching your stock appear on the exchange you've chosen and the attention you get from the media make you forget for a moment all the hard work that led to this point and all the hard work that you can expect to follow as your company strives every quarter to satisfy stockholders and investment analysts that you're doing the right things.

It's no wonder so many naïve entrepreneurs announce their intention to go public within three years (if not sooner) of starting their businesses. If they knew more about what it's really like to launch a public company, these starry-eyed adventurers may think twice. I can't stress enough the importance of doing your homework — reading, talking to people who have done it — before making the decision to do an IPO. Once you decide to go ahead, you set in motion a series of events that have a life of their own. Yes, you can stop the IPO up to the night before your company is scheduled to be listed on the stock exchange, but doing so will cost you a lot of money and time, not to mention bad publicity.

An IPO is really just a more complex version of a private offering. You file your intent to sell a portion of your company to the public with the Securities and Exchange Commission (SEC) and list your stock on one of the exchanges. When you complete the IPO, the proceeds go to the company in what is termed a *primary offering*. If, later on, you sell your shares (after restrictions have ceased), those proceeds are termed a *secondary distribution*.

# Considering the advantages and disadvantages of going public

The real reason that many entrepreneurs choose to take their companies public is that an IPO provides an enormous source of interest-free capital for growth and expansion. After you've done one offering, you can do additional offerings if you maintain a positive track record. Other general advantages that companies derive from becoming publicly held are

- ✔ More clout with industry types and the financial community.
- ✔ Easier ways for you to form partnerships and negotiate favorable deals with suppliers, customers, and others.
- ✔ The ability to offer stock to your employees.
- ✔ Easier ways for you to harvest the wealth you have created by selling some of your shares or borrowing against them.

But becoming a public company also has several disadvantages that you should carefully consider. Some of them include:

- ✔ The cost exceeds $300,000, and that doesn't include the commission to the underwriter (the investment bank that sells the securities).
- ✔ The process is extremely time consuming, taking most of your week for more than six months.
- ✔ Everything you and your company do becomes public information.
- ✔ You are now responsible first and foremost to your shareholders, not to your customers or employees.
- ✔ You may no longer have the controlling share of stock in your company.
- ✔ Your stock may lose value because of factors in the economy even if you're running the company well.
- ✔ You face intense pressure to perform in the short term so that revenues and earnings rise, driving up stock prices and dividends to stockholders.
- ✔ The SEC reporting requirements are a huge and time-consuming burden.

Out of 3,186 firms that went public in the 1980s, only 58 percent were still listed on one of the major exchanges in 2000. As far back as 1993, the stock of only one-third of these companies was selling above its issue price.

## Deciding to go for it

If you've weighed all the advantages and disadvantages and still want to go forward with an IPO, you need to have a good understanding of what happens during the months that precede the offering. In general, the process unfolds in a fairly predictable fashion.

### Choosing the underwriter

You need to choose an underwriter that serves as your guide on this journey and, you hope, sells your securities to enough institutional investors to make the IPO a success. Like meeting a venture capitalist, you need to secure an introduction to a good investment banker through a mutual acquaintance and investigate the reputation and track record of any investment banker you're considering. Many disreputable firms out there are looking for a quick buck. You also want to find an investment banker who'll stay with you after the IPO and look out for the long-term success of the stock.

Once chosen, the investment banker drafts a letter of intent stating the terms and conditions of the agreement. The letter includes a price range for the stock, although this is just an estimate because the going-out price won't be decided until the night before the offering. At that point, if you're unhappy with the price, you can cancel the offering. You will, however, be responsible for some costs incurred.

### Satisfying the SEC

You file a registration statement with the SEC. Known as a *red herring,* this prospectus presents all the potential risks of investing in the IPO and is given to anyone interested in investing. Following the filing of the registration statement, you place an advertisement, known as a *tombstone,* in the financial press announcing the offering. Your prospectus is valid for nine months after the tombstone is published.

You need to decide on which stock exchange your company will be listed. Here are the three best known in the U.S.:

- ✔ American Stock Exchange (AMEX)
- ✔ National Association of Securities Dealers Automated Quotation (NASDAQ)
- ✔ New York Stock Exchange (NYSE)

The NYSE is the most difficult to qualify for listing. The NYSE and AMEX are auction markets where securities are traded on the floor of the exchange so that investors trade directly with one another. By contrast, the NASDAQ is a floorless exchange that trades on the National Market System through a system of broker-dealers from respected securities firms.

You may also want to look at regional exchanges like the Pacific Exchange and the Boston stock exchange. They are generally less expensive alternatives.

### Taking your show on the road

Many consider the road show to be the high point of the entire IPO process. It is exactly what it sounds like, a whirlwind tour of all the major institutional investors over about two weeks. The entrepreneur and the IPO team present the business and the offering to these potential investors, whom they hope to sign on. The goal is to have the offering oversubscribed so that it can be sold in a day.

One of the more important skills you can discover if you intend to go the IPO route (or seek money from any source) is how to talk to money people. These people have seen so many presentations from so many people begging for their resources that they are jaded. You have to work hard to capture their attention, and that's not an easy thing to do. Here are some suggestions based on the lessons taught by Jerry Weissman, whose company, Power Presentations, has been behind some of the most famous IPOs in history — Cisco, Yahoo!, and Compaq, to name a few.

- ✔ **Tell a great story.** Investors want to hear why this is the best investment opportunity they've ever seen. In short, they want to know what's in it for them, their return on investment. Entrepreneurs, by contrast, are more focused on what's in it for the customer.

- ✔ **The entrepreneur must tell the story.** Not only must the entrepreneur/CEO tell the story, but he or she needs to write it as well. No one has the passion for the business that the founder does, and that passion means a higher valuation for the business. So, tell your own story, and tell it with energy and passion.

- ✔ **Don't exaggerate your story.** Remember that investors have heard it all, so you need to tell them what makes your company stand out from the crowd. And don't hide potential problems or negatives your business may have. Recognize them and then tell investors what you intend to do about them.

- ✔ **Get their attention.** You can grab attention in many ways, but one of the best is to show your audience that you have a solution to a problem they're experiencing. For example, Scott Cook of Intuit (Quicken, Quickbooks) started his story with a question: "How many of you balance your own checkbooks?" Every investor raised his or her hand. "How many of you like doing it?" Not one hand was raised. He explained that millions of people around the world dislike that task, but he had a product that would solve the problem. That approach definitely caught the investors' attention.

### Dealing with failure

Once in a while, even when you've done all the right things, the IPO can fail, like the Texas company that developed a computer that would stand up to the toughest environments — places like machine shops and hot restaurant kitchens. When the founder decided to raise money through a first registered stock offering on the Internet, it was a long and costly undertaking (more than $65,000) to secure the necessary approvals from the SEC. But finally the company began selling shares through its Web site, its sights set on raising between $1.5 million and $9.9 million. The offering period was 90 days, and at the end of that time the company had raised only about $300,000. Attempts to do a traditional offering failed as well and the company filed for Chapter 7 bankruptcy. The total bill for the IPO was about $250,000, for which the company received nothing.

Just because you start an IPO doesn't guarantee that you'll finish it. Many entrepreneurs cancel their IPOs the night before they come out because they are unable to raise sufficient capital during the road show.

# Finding Other Ways to Finance Growth

Elsewhere in this chapter, I talk about equity sources of capital — selling ownership of your company in exchange for cash. But equity is not the only way to finance the growth of your business. Debt vehicles — IOUs with interest — are another way to acquire the capital you need to grow. When you choose this route, you typically hand over title to a business or personal asset as collateral for a loan bearing a market rate of interest. You normally pay principal and interest on the note until it's paid off. Some arrangements, however, combine debt and equity. For example, a debenture is a debt vehicle that can be converted to common stock at some predetermined time in the future. In the meantime, the holder of the debenture receives interest on his or her loan to the company.

Here are some of the more common sources of debt financing for growth.

> ✔ **Commercial banks.** Banks are better sources for growth capital than for start-up capital, because by the time you come to them, your company has, in all likelihood, developed a good track record. Banks make loans based on the *Five C's*: character of the entrepreneur, capacity to repay the loan, capital needed, collateral the entrepreneur can provide to secure the loan, and condition of the entrepreneur's overall financial health and situation. For entrepreneurs with new ventures, character and capacity become the overriding factors.

✔ **Commercial finance companies.** Also known as asset-based lenders, these companies are typically more expensive to use than commercial banks by as much as 5 percent above the prime interest rate. But they are also more likely to lend to a start-up entrepreneur than a commercial bank is. And when you weigh the difference between starting the business and not starting because of money, a commercial lender may not be that expensive.

✔ **Small Business Administration.** The SBA guarantees loans up to 90 percent and works with commercial lenders to deliver those loans. Because SBA-funded businesses tend to have a higher success rate than the average business, lenders enjoy working with the SBA.

✔ **SBA Express.** A new program, SBA Express aims to reduce all the paperwork associated with a traditional SBA loan. If you qualify at a bank, you can borrow up to $150,000 without going through the standard SBA application process. In fact, this program promises to give you a decision within 36 hours. Because the Small Business Administration only guarantees these loans to 50 percent of their face value, not all the SBA-qualifed lenders have signed on to the program.

# Chapter 14

# Starting with the Right Legal Structure

### In This Chapter

▶ Finding the right legal form for your business

▶ Using the sole proprietorship

▶ Choosing the partnership

▶ Electing the corporate form

▶ Looking for flexible forms

▶ Selecting the best legal structure

Choosing the legal form for organizing your business is one of the important decisions you must make before launching the business. Because of changing laws, entrepreneurs today have many more choices of how to structure their companies. Your need for capital and protection from liability are just two reasons why understanding the options available to you is so essential.

Those changing laws are also a good reason for seeking the advice of a good attorney or CPA to make sure that you're making the best choice for you and your type of business. This chapter gives you a solid background on what you need to think about before choosing a form and what you need to understand about of the various forms available to you.

## Deciding on the Best Legal Form for Your Business

All companies operate under one of four broad legal classifications: sole proprietorship, partnership, corporation, or limited liability company. Many entrepreneurs assume that the best entity is always one that lets profits pass through to the owners at their personal tax rate. They further assume that incorporating in your home state always is best. These assumptions can be wrong for some entrepreneurs and for some businesses. For instance, if you know that you want to do an IPO (initial public offering) within two years, you should probably form as a C Corporation because that is required to go public. If you're going to use venture capital, you probably want a C corporate form, and you may want to incorporate in California or Delaware. Those states have a substantial body of law in the area of corporate governance. Choosing the wrong entity when speed is of the essence (consider the case of Internet start-ups) can mean costly delays and lost opportunities.

## Understanding the factors that affect your choice

Understanding the various factors that come into play when you choose a particular form of legal structure is important. Seven factors affect your choice of structure. A summary comparison of these factors appears in Figure 14-1. Here they are in the form of questions you can ask yourself.

1. **Who will be the owners of the company?**

   If more than one individual owns the company, you can eliminate sole proprietorship as an option. If many people own the company, the C Corporation form is often the choice because it has an unlimited life and free transferability of interests. If you intend to have many employees, the C Corporation also lets you take advantage of pension plans and stock option plans.

2. **What level of liability protection do you require, especially for your personal assets?**

   Some forms protect you; others do not. It's a sad fact that too many businesses ignore the risks they face and don't acquire the correct forms of insurance. Just as you want to see the advice of an attorney and accountant as you develop your business, you also want to consider the advice of an insurance broker.

3. **How do you expect to distribute the company's earnings?**

   If you choose an entity allowing pass-through income and losses (partnership, S Corporation, or LLC), your earnings are distributed immediately without additional taxation. But in a C Corporation, only a salary or other forms of compensation are paid out pretax from the company to an owner.

4. **What are the operating requirements of your business and the costs of running the business under the particular form in question?**

   If you own a manufacturing company that uses a lot of machinery, you have different liabilities than a service company.

5. **What are your financing plans?**

   How attractive is the form to potential investors? Are you able to offer ownership interests to investors and employees? In general, if you're going to use venture capital, you need a corporate form. Most venture capitalists raise their money from tax-exempt entities like pension funds, universities, and charitable organizations. These organizations can't invest in companies that have pass-through tax benefits.

6. **What will be the effect on the company's tax strategy and your personal tax strategy?**

   This includes minimizing tax liability, converting ordinary income to capital gain, and avoiding multiple taxation, to maximizing the benefits of start-up losses.

7. **Do you expect the company to generate a profit or loss in the beginning?**

   If you think your company will lose money for the first few years (this is often true with biotech or other companies developing new products), then a pass-through option can be justified because you get to deduct your losses on your personal tax return.

# Going It Alone: The Sole Proprietorship

Would you be surprised to find out that more than 75 percent of all businesses operating in the United States are sole proprietorships? A sole proprietorship is a business where the owner is essentially the business; that is, he or she is solely responsible for the activities of the business and is the only one to enjoy the profits and suffer the losses of the business. Why do so many businesses start this way? Sole proprietorship is the easiest and least expensive way to form a business. If you're using your own name as the name of the business, all you need is a business license, some business cards, and you're in business!

Deciding to use another name for your business is only slightly more complex. For example, in the case of ABC Associates, you apply for a DBA, which is a *Certificate of Doing Business under an Assumed Name.* You can secure a DBA at your local government office. Securing a DBA ensures that two businesses don't operate in the same county with the same name.

## Advantages of sole proprietorships

I already mentioned that sole proprietorship is the easiest to start and least expensive form of organization, but it also gives the owner complete control of the company. You make all the decisions and suffer all the consequences, but the income from the business is yours and you're taxed only once at your personal income tax rate.

Many professionals, like consultants, authors, and many home-based business owners, operate as sole proprietors. Chances are the owners of your neighborhood café, pizza parlor, or shoe repair shop are sole proprietors.

| Issues | Sole Proprietorship | Partnership | S Corp. | Limited Liability Company | C Corp. |
|---|---|---|---|---|---|
| Number of owners | One | No limit | 75 | No limit | No limit on shareholders |
| Liability | Owner liable for all claims against business | General partners liable for all claims. Limited partners only to amount of investment. | Limited liability | Members liable as in partnerships. | Shareholders liable to amount invested. Officers may be personally liable. |
| Life of Business | Dissolution on the death of the owner | Dissolution on the death or separation of a partner unless otherwise specified in the agreement. Not so in the case of limited partners. | Continuity of life | Continuity of life | No effect |
| Transfer of Interest | Owner free to sell | General partner requires consent of other generals to sell interest. Limiteds' ability subject to agreement. | Subject to agreement | Free transferability of interests subject to agreement. | Shareholders free to sell unless restricted by agreement. |
| Distribution of Profits | Profits go to owner | Profits shared based on partnership agreement. | Profits go to owners. | Profits go to members. | Paid to shareholders as dividends according to agreement and shareholder status |
| Management Control | Owner has full control | Shared by general partners according to partnership agreement | Shared by owners/ shareholders | Rests with management committee (owners or those shareholders) | Rests with the board of directors appointed by the shareholders |

**Figure 14-1:**
This chart shows a summary comparison of legal forms of business organization.

# Disadvantages of sole proprietorships

For most entrepreneurs, the sole proprietorship form of organization is not satisfactory for several reasons.

✔ As a sole proprietor, you have unlimited liability for any claims against the business. In other words, you are putting your personal assets at risk — your home, car, bank accounts, and any other assets you may have. So, having business liability and errors and omissions insurance is extremely important. If you're producing a product, you'll need product liability insurance to protect you against lawsuits over defective products. If your company does work for other people (i.e. you have a construction company) you may be required to have bonding insurance to ensure that you complete the work specified in your contract. Because there are so many areas of liability and so many different types of insurance, you should talk to a good insurance broker. Check Chapter 11 for more discussion about insurance.

✔ Raising capital is much more difficult, because you're relying only on your financial statement. You are, for all intents and purposes, the business, and most investors don't like that situation.

✔ You probably won't have a management team with diverse skills helping you grow your business. You may have employees, but that isn't really the same thing. Putting together an advisory board of people with skills you need helps compensate for the skills you lack. To find out more about advisory boards, see Chapter 10.

✔ Because the survival of your company depends on you being there, if something happens to you or a catastrophe strikes. Legally, if the sole proprietor dies, so does the business, unless its assets are willed to someone.

If you intend to grow your business, organizing as a sole proprietorship is not a good idea, unless you're taking advantage of income and control benefits during the early stages of your business — for example, through product development.

# Choosing a Partner: The Partnership

A partnership is two or more people deciding to share the assets, liabilities, and profits of their business. Partnering is an improvement over the sole proprietorship because more people are sharing the responsibilities of the business and bouncing ideas off each other. Additionally, you now have multiple financial statements on which to rely and an entity that usually survives if one of the partners dies or leaves.

In terms of liability, however, you're raising the stakes, because each partner becomes liable for the obligations incurred by other partners in the course of doing business. This *doctrine of ostensible authority* works like this: Suppose one of your partners enters a contract on behalf of the partnership, purchasing certain goods from a supplier. That partner has just bound the partnership to make good on a contract even if the rest of the partners knew nothing about it. The one major exception is that personal debts of an individual partner cannot attach to the rest of the partners.

On the positive side, each partner uses any property owned by the partnership and shares in the profits and losses of the partnership unless otherwise stated in the partnership agreement. Partners don't have to share equally in the profits and losses. Ownership in the partnership can be divided in any manner the partners choose. The biggest issue with partnerships is that they often are fraught with conflict in much the same way as family businesses.

However, when you think about it, any business that includes a team of entre-preneurs, whether a corporation or limited liability company, has similar issues. The partnership agreement, therefore, becomes important from the beginning. I talk about partnership agreements in an upcoming section.

## Forming a partnership

You don't have to have a written agreement when forming a partnership; a simple oral agreement works. In fact, in some cases, the conduct of the parties involved implies a partnership.

Accepting a share of the profits of a business is prima facie (legally suffi-cient) evidence that you are a partner in the business, meaning that you may also be liable for its losses.

Partnerships come in several flavors. In most partnerships, entrepreneurs are *general partners,* meaning they share in the profits, losses, and responsi-bilities, and are personally liable for actions of the partnership. But, other types of partners have more limited liability, including:

- ✔ **Limited partners:** These partners' liability generally is limited to the amount of their investment.
- ✔ **Secret partners:** These partners are active in the ventures but are unknown to the public.
- ✔ **Silent partners:** These partners are usually inactive with only a financial interest in the partnership.

## The partnership agreement

I cannot emphasize strongly enough the importance of a partnership agree-ment. I often see people who claim, "We've been the best of friends for years; we know what we're doing," or "How can I ask my father to sign a partnership agreement?" How can you not? You must separate business from friendship and family, at least when it comes to structuring your company. This is a seri-ous deal. No matter how well you know your partner, you probably haven't worked with him or her in this particular kind of situation. You have no way of predicting all the things that can cause a disagreement with your partner. The partnership agreement gives you an unbiased mechanism for resolving disagreements or dissolving the partnership, if it comes to that.

Of course, consulting an attorney is necessary when drawing up an agree-ment, so that you're not inadvertently causing yourself further problems by the way a phrase is worded in the agreement or leaving something important out. The partnership agreement addresses the following:

- ✔ The legal name of the partnership.

- ✔ The nature of your business.

- ✔ How long the partnership is to last. Just like any contract, it needs a stop date.

- ✔ What each of the partners is contributing to the partnership — capital, in-kind goods, services, and so forth. This is the *initial capitalization.*

- ✔ Any sales, loans, or leases to the partnership.

- ✔ Who is responsible for what — the management of the partnership.

- ✔ The sale of a partnership interest. This clause restricts a partner's right to sell his or her interest to third parties. It provides, however, a method by which a partner can divest his or her interest in the partnership.

- ✔ How the partnership can be dissolved.

- ✔ What happens if a partner leaves or dies.

- ✔ How disputes will be resolved.

If you don't execute a partnership agreement, all partners are equal under the law.

# Going for the Gold: The Corporation

A corporation is a different animal entirely from the other forms of legal organization, because it is a legal entity under the law. Chartered or registered by the state in which it resides, a corporation can survive the death or separation of all of its owners. It can also sue, be sued, acquire and sell real property, and lend money.

Corporation owners are stockholders who invest capital into the corporation and receive shares of stock usually proportionate to the level of their investment. Much like limited partners, shareholders are not responsible for the debts of the corporation (unless they have personally guaranteed them) and their investment is the limit of their liability.

I address two major types of corporations in this chapter — the C Corporation (closely held, close, and public) and the S Corporation, which I discuss in the next section. Most corporations are *closely held corporations,* which means that their stock is held privately by a few individuals. A closely held corporation operates as any type of corporation — general, professional, or nonprofit. In a *close corporation,* by contrast, the number of shareholders you may have is restricted, usually to between 30 and 50 shareholders. In addition, holding directors meetings is not required. Such meetings are a requirement for a general corporation. The close corporation is not available in every state and does not permit you to conduct an initial public offering. Basically, a close corporation operates much like a partnership.

Doctors, lawyers, accountants, and other professionals, who previously were not allowed to incorporate, use professional corporations. This vehicle now lets professionals enjoy tax-free and tax-deferred fringe benefits. You should be aware that only members of the specific profession can be shareholders in the corporation.

In a professional corporation, all the shareholders are liable for negligent or wrongful acts of any shareholder.

By contrast, in a public corporation, stock is traded on a securities exchange like the New York Stock Exchange, and the company generally has thousands (in some cases, millions) of shareholders. Because I talk about public companies in Chapter 12, the focus here is on privately held corporations.

Three groups of individuals — shareholders, directors, and officers — make up the corporate structure. Shareholders own the corporation but they don't manage it. Shareholders exert influence through the directors they elect to serve and represent them on the board. The board of directors, in turn, manages the affairs of the corporation at a policy level and hires and fires the officers who are responsible for the day-to-day decisions of the company.

Public corporations in most states in the U.S. require only one director, but in other states, the number of shareholders you have determines the number of directors. For example, in one state if you have more than three shareholders, you must have three directors. However, you can always have more directors for many different reasons. (See Chapter 10 for a discussion about the value of a good board of directors.) If you are forming a corporation in a country other than the U.S., check with the local government to find out the requirements for boards of directors. The rules differ from country to country.

What is surprising for many is that corporations comprise only about 17 percent of all businesses yet they generate 87 percent of all sales. Part of this surprising picture is attributable to the fact that most entrepreneurs who intend to grow their companies choose the corporate form for its many benefits.

## Enjoying the benefits of a corporation

The advantages of a corporate form definitely outweigh the disadvantages. In another section, I mention that the owners enjoy limited liability to the extent of their investment (the one important exception is payroll taxes that haven't been paid to the IRS). By selecting the corporate form, you also can

- ✔ **Raise capital through the sale of stock in the company.**

- ✔ **Own a corporation without the public being aware of your involvement.** So, if you want anonymity, it's the way to go.

✔ **Create different classes of stock to help you meet the various needs of investors.** For example, you may want to issue non-voting *preferred stock* to conservative investors wanting to be first to recoup their investment in the event the business fails. Most stock issued is *common stock,* whose owners enjoy voting rights and share in the profits after the preferred stock has been paid.

✔ **Easily transfer ownership.** In a private corporation, you want assurances that your shareholders can't sell their stock to just anyone. In other words, you want to know who owns your stock. You can protect yourself by including a buy-sell clause in the stockholder's agreement. Usually, this clause specifies that the stock must first be offered to the corporation at an agreed-upon price.

✔ **Enter into corporate contracts and sue or be sued without the signatures of the owners.**

✔ **Enjoy more status in the business world than other legal forms because corporations survive apart from their owners.**

✔ **Enjoy the benefits of setting up retirement funds, Keogh and defined-contribution plans, profit sharing, and stock option plans.** The corporation deducts these fringe benefits as expenses that are not taxable to the employee.

## Weighing the risks

Every legal form has disadvantages and risks, and the corporation is no exception. Here are risks worth considering when contemplating using the corporate form.

✔ Corporations are much more complex, cumbersome, and expensive to set up.

✔ Corporations are subject to more government regulation.

✔ A corporation pays taxes on profits regardless of whether they are distributed as dividends to stockholders.

✔ Shareholders of corporations do not receive the tax benefits of company losses.

✔ By selling shares of stock in your corporation, you're effectively giving up a measure of control to a board of directors. The reality, however, is that the entrepreneur determines who sits on that board of directors in privately held corporations.

✔ You must keep your personal finances and the corporation's finances completely separate. You must conduct directors' meetings, and maintain minutes from those meetings. If you don't, you may leave your company open to what is known as *piercing the corporate veil,* which makes you and your officers liable personally for the company.

## Choosing the right legal form

Choosing the best legal form of organization can be a relatively simple task if you consider the type of business you have and what it's needs are. Let's try a hypothetical example.

Suppose your spouse is a highly paid executive for a major corporation, making possible your pursuit of developing a product you've been playing around with. You decide to set up a small business with a shop near your home. Because you're already covered for medical insurance by your spouse's company, you don't worry. However, you need to limit your liability, because you and your spouse have acquired a number of valuable assets. You realize that in any business dealing with products, some liability issues crop up and you want to make sure you're covered.

In the beginning, you expect losses as you purchase equipment, build your prototypes, and test them in the market. Once you launch your product, you probably have continuing losses because you're promoting your business and hiring new employees. But you have big plans for this business; in fact, within a year of introducing the product, you expect to need venture capital to be able to grow as fast as the market demands. You also see an IPO in your future.

The question is: What type of legal form should you choose?

*Analysis:* Developing a new product takes time, during which you are not bringing in any cash to the business, but you are spending a lot. Incubating in your garage as long as possible as a sole proprietor has a lot going for it, because it's the least costly form of organization. Your liability at that point is minimal; your product is not yet being used by anyone and you're not in the market. Once you move to an office and shop and hire some people to help you, the situation changes. Although you may still be incurring losses, you've increased your liability substantially. Because you don't yet have any revenues, however, you won't have to worry about taxes. At this stage, you may be considering the S Corporation form, giving you the protection from liability that you need but allowing you to pass the losses through to be used against your family income on your personal tax return. Although you can keep this form throughout the time that you're incurring losses right after you launch, don't forget that you intend to seek venture capital and must switch to a C Corporate form, the preferred form for investment purposes that is required for an IPO.

## *Where and how to incorporate*

You create a corporation by filing a certificate of incorporation with the state in which you do business and issue stock, making your company a *domestic corporation*. If you incorporate in a state other than the one in which you do business, your company is a *foreign corporation*.

In general, you want to incorporate in the state where you're planning to locate the business so that you don't find yourself working under the regulations of two states. When deciding where to incorporate, consider

1. **The cost difference of incorporating in your home state versus doing business as a foreign corporation in another state.**

   In general, if you're doing business mostly in your home state, incorporating there won't subject you to taxes and annual report fees from both states.

2. **The advantages and disadvantages of the other state's corporate laws and tax structure.**

   For example, in California, a corporation pays a minimum state tax regardless of whether it makes a profit. Colorado has no minimum state tax. Likewise, if you're incorporating anywhere other than your home state, and find yourself defending a lawsuit in the state of incorporation, you may incur the expense of travel back and forth during that time.

# Looking for Flexibility: The S Corporation, the LLC, and the Nonprofit Corporation

A number of different legal organizational forms offer flexibility for entrepreneurs in a variety of ways. In this section, we look at three: the S Corporation, the LLC, and the nonprofit. All the criteria used for making a decision about which form to choose apply here.

## Sizing up the S Corporation

Don't let the term corporation fool you. An S Corporation, for the most part, is nothing like a C Corporation. It is not a legal entity and does not pay taxes. Basically, S Corporations are financial vehicles for passing company profits and losses through to owners who pay income taxes at their personal tax rates. As a shareholder in an S Corporation, you may deduct any losses of the corporation on your personal income tax return, up to the amount you invested in the corporation. If you sell the assets of your S Corporation, you pay a tax on the amount of appreciation of those assets.

An S Corporation can provide employee benefits and deferred compensation plans. To qualify for S Corporation status, you must

1. **Form your corporation with no more than 75 shareholders, none of whom may be non-resident aliens.**

2. **Issue only one class of stock.**

3. **Ensure no more than 25 percent of the corporate income is derived from passive investments like dividends, rent, and capital gains.**

In addition, your S Corporation cannot be a financial institution, a foreign corporation, or a subsidiary of a parent corporation. If you elect to change from an S Corporation to a C Corporate form, you cannot go back to being an S Corporation form for five years.

S Corporations work if your business generates a lot of cash. If it doesn't, you can easily create a situation where you owe taxes on your profits, while the business isn't generating any cash to pay them.

In general, S Corporations work best

- ✔ When you expect to experience a loss in the first year or two, and owners have other income they can shelter with that loss.

- ✔ Where shareholders have low tax brackets (lower than the corporate rate), so the profits can be distributed as dividends without double taxation.

- ✔ Where your business may incur an accumulated earnings penalty tax for failure to pay out its profits as dividends.

## Comparing the S Corporation with the LLC

The Limited Liability Company (LLC) is the newest legal form of business organization, and while gaining in popularity for many entrepreneurs, it confuses the many choices they already face in structuring their companies. The LLC combines the best of partnerships (pass-through earnings) with the best of the corporate form (limited liability). LLCs have grown in popularity because they

- ✔ Limit liability for business debts up to the amount invested.

- ✔ Offer flexible management structure that allows members (the equivalent of shareholders in a corporation), or nonmembers they hire, to manage the organization.

- ✔ Allow the choice of being treated as a partnership with the benefits of pass-through earnings or as a corporation, whichever provides the lowest tax liability.

- ✔ Enable flexible distribution of profits and losses, meaning that you can divide them up any way you want among the members.

So what differences exist between an LLC and an S Corporation? Why would you choose one over the other?

- ✔ An LLC provides for an unlimited number of owners, whereas the S Corporation limits you to 75.

- ✔ An LLC permits you to include nonresident aliens, pension plans, partnerships, and corporations as members, whereas the S Corporation does not.

- ✔ LLCs can have different classes of stock, whereas an S Corporation is generally limited to one class.

You need two members to form an LLC in California, the District of Columbia, and Massachusetts. Expect other states to raise the number of members they require from one to two.

The members of an LLC are analogous to partners in a partnership or shareholders in a corporation. If the members self-manage, then the members act more like partners than shareholders, because they have a direct say in what happens within the organization. Stock in an LLC is known as *interest*.

If you're looking for more flexibility in what you're able to do, you would probably choose an LLC over an S Corporation.

## Making profits in a nonprofit organization

Let's dispel the biggest myth about nonprofit organizations first. You can make a profit in a nonprofit company; in fact, doing so is a good idea. What you can't do is distribute those profits in the form of dividends the way other legal forms do. A nonprofit, or *not-for-profit corporation,* is formed for charitable, public (in other words, scientific, literary, or educational), religious, or mutual benefit (as in trade associations).

Like the C Corporation, the nonprofit is a legal entity with a life of its own and offers its members limited liability. Profits that it generates from its nonprofit activities are not taxed as long as the company meets the state and federal requirements for exemption from taxes under IRS 501(c)(3). When you form a nonprofit, you actually give up proprietary interest in the corporation and dedicate all the assets and resources to tax-exempt activities. If you choose to dissolve the corporation, you must distribute those assets to another tax-exempt organization — you can't take them with you. Any profits you make from for-profit activities are taxed the same as any other corporation.

Nonprofit organizations derive their revenues from a variety of sources. They receive donations from corporations (these donations are tax deductible to the corporation) and others, conduct activities to raise money, or sell services (a for-profit activity). As entrepreneurs, founders of nonprofit, tax-exempt corporations can pay themselves a good salary, provide themselves with cars, and generally do the kinds of things you would do within a normal corporation, except distribute profits. Most entrepreneurs who start nonprofits do so for reasons other than money — for example, a driving need to give back to the community. James Blackman founded the Civic Light Opera of South Bay Cities, Redondo Beach, California, providing a cultural arts center for the community. The opera became the third largest musical theatre in California and has won many awards. Blackman's company also provides opportunities for physically and mentally challenged children to experience music and the theatre.

# Benchmarking Your Best Choice

 Now that you've gotten a good overview of what's available, Figure 14-2 offers a strategy for choosing the best legal form for your new business. Starting with the first question, work your way down, mapping an easy way to find your alternatives and organize your business.

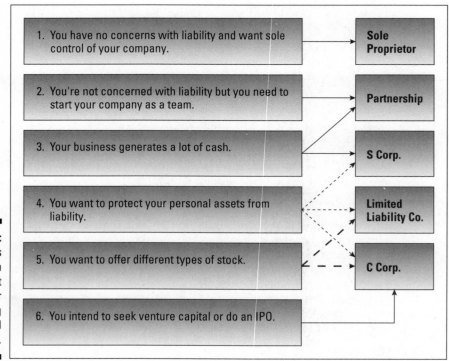

**Figure 14-2:** Six questions point you in the right direction for choosing your legal organization.

1. You have no concerns with liability and want sole control of your company. → **Sole Proprietor**

2. You're not concerned with liability but you need to start your company as a team. → **Partnership**

3. Your business generates a lot of cash. → **S Corp.**

4. You want to protect your personal assets from liability. → **Limited Liability Co.**

5. You want to offer different types of stock. → **C Corp.**

6. You intend to seek venture capital or do an IPO. → **C Corp.**

# Chapter 15

# Developing a Business Model for a Digital World

*In This Chapter*

▶ Building a bricks-and-mortar business model

▶ Trying the fast world of Internet business models

▶ Using several business models with one product or service

*B*uilding a successful new business takes a great team, customers, a value proposition, a product or service, resources, and a business model.

A business model simply describes the way you're going to make money with your business — certainly an important topic. In fact, discussing business models is a popular topic these days. Why? With the advent of technology — in particular, the Internet — during the past decade, new business models are popping up everywhere. With so many people trying to find a way of making money on the Internet and failing, investors are paying closer attention to the business model and demanding that businesses show a profit within a reasonable period of time for that particular kind of business.

## Producing Several Models from One Product or Service

Only your imagination and your ability to find a customer limit the number of business models you can create for introducing your product or service into the marketplace. One may do, but multiple models can be of great benefit to your company. In this section, you can find examples of products and services that have multiple revenue models.

## *Your consulting company*

Suppose you are a management consultant providing your expertise to mid-market companies needing help with their strategic planning. You help them create strategic plans, conduct seminars, do one-on-one CEO coaching, and general consulting. Business models you can consider include:

- ✔ Charging an hourly fee for situations where you're not certain of the time commitment.

- ✔ Having your client put you on a retainer, which entitles the client to an agreed-upon amount of your time.

- ✔ Taking a fee plus stock options in the company. That way you cover your expenses and still have a stake in the success of the business and an opportunity to benefit from capital appreciation.

- ✔ Charging a flat fee for seminars on your favorite topics.

Going one step further with this example, let's see how you can increase your revenue streams without having to do all the work — remember, making money while you sleep is one of the better business models.

"How do I do that?" you ask. Because you're an expert, you can write a great book based on your consulting experiences. Of course that's a lot of work, but if it's done well, it keeps on giving — even at night. Tape your seminars and sell the audio or videotapes. Once you've already done the work, all you have to do is find a variety of different ways of making it pay off.

I'm sure you can come up with even more creative models for a consulting company, or any other business you're considering.

## *Your software company*

Suppose you've come up with a new software program that helps small business owners manage all the activities of their businesses just like the big companies do with their enterprise management software. You can let the customer select the business model for you in one of the following ways:

- ✔ The customer uses the program free of charge, but a small window in the lower left-hand corner of the computer screen displays advertising while the program is running. In other words, in this model, your end-user isn't your customer. The companies that display their advertisements are your customers, and you receive your revenues from them.

- ✔ The customer purchases the program for a one-time fee that entitles the customer either to download it from your Web site or request delivery of a standard shrink-wrapped CD version.

> ✔ By continually coming up with new versions and enhancements, you
>   encourage the customer to purchase more from you — another stream
>   of revenue.

Going one step further with this example, let's say you also establish a Web
site for users of your program. There they can find additional information
and entertaining features. So how do you make money off that? Well, again
selling space for advertising is one way, but you can also charge a membership fee that puts your users into an elite club, perhaps giving them access to
personal application services that you host.

## Your movie theater

Suppose you own a small movie theater featuring films of independent film-
makers that are not distributed to mainstream theaters. You create a niche in
the market by serving hors d'oeuvres and drinks in the lobby before the
movie, in addition to standard popcorn, candy, and soft drinks. Consequently,
you have a regular stream of customers who enjoy this unique experience. So
how do you make money?

> ✔ You make money on admission. Because you're not competing with
>   mainstream theaters for the blockbuster movies, you can keep more of
>   the ticket money yourself. Mainstream theaters, after all, make money
>   on concessions, not tickets. Moreover, you provide added value by
>   including the hors d'oeuvres in the ticket price.
>
> ✔ You charge for beer, wine, and soft drinks, which have high margins, so
>   you make quite a bit on drinks.
>
> ✔ You charge for candy and popcorn on which you also make good money.

What other business models work for this concept? You can lease your facility during nonmovie times to organizations that want to present concerts,
speeches, seminars, and so forth. You can sign an agreement to display the
works of local artists in return for a percentage of any sales. You can, no
doubt, come up with many more business models, but I bet you never knew
that a movie theater could have so many possibilities.

## Your restaurant

Suppose you own a restaurant featuring Southwestern cuisine at reasonable
prices in an atmosphere worthy of a much more expensive restaurant. Your
customers like eating there not only because the food is great, but also
because members of your waitstaff have charming personalities and because
you enjoy walking around the restaurant greeting customers by name. Let's
see how you can build some business models.

✔ The obvious model is selling food and beverages, but if you have a bar, you have a good revenue stream off that. In most restaurants, alcoholic beverages, rather than food, bring in the most money.

✔ You provide a catering service, serving your cuisine at banquets and other events.

✔ You rent out your entire restaurant for special occasions.

Additional business models create revenue streams for your business. Suppose you have a signature drink that you concoct. You can arrange to produce and market that drink in bottles to supermarkets. You can develop a line of frozen foods from your repertoire and distribute them through specialty stores like Trader Joes. You can also charge for cooking lessons you conduct while your restaurant is closed to the public. If you let your mind wander, I'm sure you can come up with even better business models for restaurants.

# Looking for Another Gillette

The best business models have the easiest time getting funded, and that's important when you consider that most businesses seek outside sources of capital at some point as they grow. So what is the common denominator among the best business models? They provide consumable products and services so customers need to purchase them again and again. This strategy often is referred to as *the Gillette Method* after the famous manufacturer of razors and other products. The aim is selling the base product — the razor — relatively cheaply or even giving it away. Then customers who want to continue to use the razor must purchase razor blades that are not so cheap. Hewlett-Packard uses this strategy with its printers — selling them at low prices and making up the difference on printer cartridges and service contracts.

The best business models also provide for *multiple streams of revenue,* which means that your company makes money on a product or service that it sells through several different channels to different customers. The more revenue streams, the better, because if one dries up, you still have others you can rely on and your business won't be hurt.

In this chapter, you'll discover a variety of business models that are in use today. Each has advantages and disadvantages. Only you can determine which is the best for your business, but chances are you'll want to choose more than one.

# Improving on the Bricks-and-Mortar Model

Believe it or not, something positive needs to be said today about starting with a traditional bricks-and-mortar business. Consider that only about 35 percent of the population has Internet access, that leaves a huge chunk of customers wanting and needing to be served by some other method. Many people still enjoy shopping the old-fashioned way, trying on clothes, leafing through books, and wandering around furniture stores. Besides, recent events prove that having a traditional business in place — whether a retail or service business — and establishing a brand before offering it on the Internet has many advantages. The bricks-and-mortar approach means

✔ Your business has instant name recognition when it launches its site.

✔ Your business systems — accounting, purchasing, inventory, fulfillment, and so forth — are in place and proven.

✔ You already have a reliable revenue stream that carries you while your Internet site becomes profitable.

✔ You already have proven advertising and promotional strategies in place that you can leverage letting people know that you also conduct your business online.

In the next two sections on "Providing a service with an upside" and "Making money while you sleep," I talk about some new business models for services and products with bricks-and-mortar businesses.

## Providing a service with an upside

Traditional business models for service companies typically involve the entrepreneur doing the bulk of the work. After all, for the most part, customers hire entrepreneurs for their expertise. Service, by it's core definition, implies some human contact, which means it's generally not a business model that makes money for you while you sleep. *Making money while you sleep* is the mantra of my friend Paul Orfalea, founder of Kinkos, the biggest copy and printing service company in the world. He likes businesses that operate when you're not there, essentially 24 hours a day, seven days a week (the model I talk about next in the "Making money while you sleep" section). Unfortunately most entrepreneurs with service models don't often think in those terms, so they build their businesses entirely on what they and a few trusted employees or partners are able physically to do or provide.

More and more, however, we're seeing service entrepreneurs creating new business models that let them earn more than just their hourly wages or flat-fee arrangements. The following case study illustrates one such company.

The industrial design business is competitive, particularly in places like Silicon Valley and Route 128 in Massachusetts. One company that does work for such major companies as Silicon Graphics, Hewlett-Packard, and Motorola found that its margins were shrinking as more and more companies entered the field and as the cost of staying current with technology skyrocketed. The old business model was not going to work much longer. One thing the partners realized was that they were spending a lot of their time giving advice to start-up ventures — they were essentially acting in the role of a venture capitalist. That's when the idea for a new business model hit them.

Why not secure an equity stake in the companies they were serving rather than just a fee for service? They discovered the power of the multiple. For example, $1 received from a client for a service will never be more than $1, and once you subtract all the expenses, the profit is probably pennies. But if you take stock in a growing company, betting on their future success, that $1 can turn into $20. For these imaginative entrepreneurs, that was the way to go. And so far, it has worked well. Initially about 90 percent of their work was fee-for-service (a flat fee based on the service provided); it's now down to 60 percent, but their revenues have gone up substantially.

### Taking stock

Taking stock in your customers' companies does more than merely increase the value of what you do. It's about becoming partners with your customers in the venture. You now have a stake in the success of that company, so the company probably gets more value from your services because by nature you're more inclined to do more to protect your equity stake.

You can also take this strategy one step further. You can originate ideas for new products inside your design firm and bring in customers as partners to make those products happen — sort of an incubator for new products. Therefore, you create a niche that hasn't been served by venture capitalists who are usually more interested in bigger deals at later stages. Moreover, you've given your customers a resource they can't afford otherwise.

Many industries — engineering firms, consultants, public relations firms, and the furniture and toy industries, among others — use this business model. So how can you assess your service company to make sure that this business model is right for you? Here are some tips:

✔ Studying your industry carefully, identifying the business models that others are using. If no one uses the equity stake model, ask why. It may be that your type of business is not appropriate for this model, or it may simply mean that no one has tried it yet. If businesses in your industry are on the Internet, you can do a lot of your research there. Also check out industry trade magazines and entrepreneurial type magazines — *Inc., Entrepreneur, Fast Company, Fortune* — to find articles about companies and their business models. Most of these magazines have online versions that you can search by keyword. For more information on industry analysis, check Chapter 5.

✔ Connecting with a start-up or rapidly growing venture is where you're likely to find the possibility of gaining an equity stake. These companies are probably straining for resources and are gladly willing to give up equity rather than cash for what you can provide. The same industry research that I talked about above helps you spot some potential business you can approach.

✔ Determining that what you offer makes a significant contribution to the product or service your client is producing. For example, if your company provides bookkeeping or janitorial services, you're not likely to get stock because no matter how well your firm performs, it won't determine the success or failure of the client's firm.

✔ Creating a network of talented people in your service area that can pull together to produce a new product or provide a service to your clients. The entertainment industry uses this model because teams never seem to stay together for the long term. You can do bigger and more difficult — and more rewarding — projects this way.

✔ Doing your homework before you take an equity stake in a new venture. The old venture capital saying that only one in ten investments is a winner and that one pays for all the rest that don't make it is true. Don't let your excitement over equity cause you to make poor investment decisions.

✔ Not taking all stock. Be sure you also get some cash. Your customers respect your work more if they have to write a check each month.

✔ Making sure that your current business model is healthy enough to enable you to use the equity stake model.

Using the equity stake model has its risks. Before you jump in, ask yourself these questions:

✔ Is the market for the client's product as big as the client says it is? Does it really exist?

✔ Is the product meeting a real need in the market?

✔ Can the team make it happen? Do team members have the right skills, experience, and drive?

✔ How will you harvest your investment?

### Multiple products and services

Service entrepreneurs often limit themselves to thinking about various services they provide and forgetting the variety of products they can also offer their customers. Today, you want to think of your business as an information center for your customers. You want them looking at your business for as many of their needs as possible. So, your overall business model must apply multiple models generating many different streams of revenue. The first section of this chapter provides you with examples of various types of businesses and how you can produce multiple models from one product or service. Now I want you thinking about how many different products and services you can produce from one concept, because each product and service can result in several business models and revenue streams.

Let's look at a basic example, so you can see how you can turn a simple service concept into an exciting one with real possibilities. Suppose your basic business is providing landscape maintenance to your local community. Your business model involves having customers pay a fee for your service; the amount of that fee depends on the type of work being done. Now, take a minute and a piece of scrap paper to jot down at least three more products and services that you can add to the original one.

How did you do? If you came up with three, congratulate yourself, because you're much more opportunistic than the average person is. If you think of more than three, you definitely ought to consider becoming an entrepreneur, because it appears that you have a creative mind. Obviously this exercise wasn't designed in any scientific manner, so don't be discouraged if you came up with only one or two ideas. With a little practice, you can become quite good at generating opportunities. (To remind yourself of opportunity generation techniques, check out Chapter 3.)

Additional product and service ideas you may have written down for your landscape maintenance business include:

- Providing a unique line of imported plants to your customers.

- Giving seminars on in-house plant care at scheduled get-togethers in your customers' homes. Here you can either ask for a cover charge or sell products as a sideline.

- Setting up a local community Web site, providing answers to questions and a place for plant lovers to congregate. Collaborate with a local nursery to do this and charge a membership fee to suggest a place where you can get information that is not available anywhere else.

No matter what type of business you start, you will be able to find more than one business model to launch it.

## Making money while you sleep

The best of all worlds is a business that continues without you, freeing you to work on what you want to when you want. Product businesses are more often suitable for this type of business model, because owners don't usually do all the work, and once your product is out in various outlets, the cash registers can literally ring while you're asleep. That doesn't normally happen with a service company.

Wayne Huizenga, the founder of Blockbuster Entertainment — among several other billion-dollar businesses — likes a business model that provides a regular income, a rental income, for example. After establishing your initial inventory, you rent it over and over again, recovering your costs quickly. The rest is profit. You can see many examples of this business model in a variety of industries:

- Construction equipment leasing
- Car rentals
- Employee leasing
- Facility leasing

You probably hear a lot of talk about the information age, that ours is an information economy. Well, information can be both a product and a service. If you create a database of information that is valuable to a certain market, you sell that information over and over again, regardless of whether it's in a physical form like a book, software, or CD, or in virtual form over the Internet. Once you create the original product and set up your sales and distribution channel, it almost takes on a life of its own.

Software companies have jumped on the bandwagon that is the rental business model, providing hosted applications over the Internet to businesses that can't afford to purchase expensive software packages. The company literally rents the applications to users on a per-use basis or on a monthly basis.

With a product business, you can create additional revenue streams by adding services to your model, using the same kind of exercise you did in the "Multiple products and services" section. Now you can see why the boundaries between product and service companies are rapidly disappearing. You need to provide both to have a successful business today.

# Flying High and Fast with Internet Models

If you're already part of the Internet world as a user, you — like so many other people — may be asking yourself, "How can I make money on the Internet?" You read about others doing it all the time. Practically every magazine you pick up today has a story about the successful Internet entrepreneur who made it big before the age of 30. And there you sit at the ripe old age of 35 or 40 wondering why you're letting financial nirvana pass you by.

Well, here's the secret. The question isn't "How can I make money on the Internet," it's "How can I make money with my business?" The Internet is merely a vehicle, a tool, in the process of delivering your product or service, nothing more. And for some entrepreneurs, that thought conjures up a great place to start a business . . . it doesn't really deliver. One entrepreneur who loves collectibles thought it might be fun to make money selling unique items over the Internet. What a simple business concept — set up a great site, take orders, and you're in business, watching the money roll in. Right? Wrong!

What this enthusiastic entrepreneur didn't realize is how costly, complex, and time-consuming inventory management and order fulfillment (packaging and shipping) is. She found that her manufacturers had long lead times and most fulfillment companies were automated and set up for huge volumes, something she didn't have. Moreover, the fulfillment houses wanted about $9 a package to handle an order, and at that rate, she couldn't make any money and her customers would balk at the high price of shipping. In the short term, she solved her problem by hiring students to pack and ship her products through UPS; however, she knew that solution wouldn't work for long.

This entrepreneur is no exception to the rule. The fact is that many Internet e-tailers are not able to make money because their fulfillment costs are too high. And making money is something you have to do.

To make money with a business you need customers, a great team, a value proposition, a good product or service, money, and a business model.

Let's look at some of the ways you can do that with an Internet-based business.

## Taking a chance on clicks and hits

The first business model making an appearance on the Internet was probably the *clicks and hits* model where the company derives all of its revenues from advertising. That was in the good old days when advertisers didn't know any better and thought that people clicking onto a site actually read the banner ads, buttons, and so forth. Of course, now we know that for the most part they don't, which explains why this business model isn't successful in attracting investors.

The reason the model succeeded in the first place is because e-commerce was young, with few competitors, and advertisers feared that their competitors — other advertising firms — would beat them to the punch, acquiring the best sites on the Net. At the time, fewer sites got relatively more hits (visitors to the site), but today, with millions of sites, the number of visitors to any one site has proportionally decreased.

What does this mean to you? The clicks and hits business model has become the proverbial vicious circle. Attracting advertisers to purchase space on your site (providing you your revenue stream), you have to show that you're attracting the number of hits they require. To do that, you have to attract visitors and that means you have to spend a lot of money advertising both online and offline. Thus, the bulk of your investor money goes to customer acquisition.

But, remember, it isn't merely about hits, it's about click-throughs, or customers who actually click on the banner or button and link to the advertiser's site. If that isn't happening, advertisers are not interested in your site. In 1999, the Nielsen/Netrating Report, `www.nielsen-netratings.com`, indicated that click-through rates have plunged from 7 percent in 1996 to only 0.6 percent in 1999. That doesn't make advertisers happy.

Ask anyone in the know which Internet revenue model is the least effective as a revenue generator and you'll hear "the clicks and hits model." Public companies based on this model are feeling the pain as their stocks have dropped below initial public offering prices — many are now penny stocks.

If you still want to use advertising as a business model, make sure it isn't your primary business model, but rather one of several.

## Using a subscription-based model

The subscription model has proven successful for some companies. With this model, your customer pays a fee to access your site and use its services. It's similar to gaining access to a private club, giving you the right and privilege to use information that only members have. Fees typically are charged monthly, but, for example, *The Wall Street Journal* charges an annual fee to access its online journal and archives. In general, these sites are perceived as having a higher quality of target content and services than the average site.

Yet, not everyone is willing to pay for even the best information. As a result, entrepreneurs must change business models to survive. One such case is illustrated in the sidebar "Someone has to pay for it."

## Someone has to pay for it

You may have the greatest idea in the world, but if people aren't willing to pay you for it, you have no business — your business model doesn't work. One Internet firm provides health-care information to people with specific diseases through a subscription service. The focus was on serious chronic illnesses. Subscribers received personalized information based on information they provided the company about their disease. Essentially, each illness had a community site. The problem wasn't getting people to the site — customers loved the information they received and liked being able to communicate with others who share the same disease; the problem was getting them to subscribe to the service — less than 5 percent of the firm's trial customers subscribed, and it was about to run out of cash from initial investment capital.

With the status of the company in such dire straits, its founders decided to radically change the business model. They really didn't have a choice. After some brainstorming, the founders realized that they had collected valuable information about their subscribers. What if they dropped the subscription service and started selling real-time *aggregated* market research data on people with specific diseases to health-care companies and pharmaceutical firms? That would be a new business model, plus they could run advertising for their research customers — yet another source of revenue. They decided to go ahead with it. This new business model has worked so far, but it's too soon to know if the firm can succeed competing against major health-care providers that are starting to provide similar services. Still, the important lesson to be learned is that if your business model doesn't work, another one is bound to be out there that will. Remember, someone has to pay for what you offer.

## Growing a hybrid with clicks and bricks

Many Internet ventures that originally were virtual e-commerce companies selling products but carrying no inventory (they outsourced their fulfillment functions to bricks-and-mortar companies) are now being forced to become a combination Internet and traditional bricks-and-mortar company — hence the term *clicks and bricks*. For example, when Amazon.com first launched onto the Internet, it was designed as a totally virtual company linking with book publishers and distributors as its source of supply. Essentially the publishers and distributors would drop-ship orders to Amazon's customers (that means the books would go directly from the publisher to the customer). But when a bricks-and-mortar competitor like Barnes & Noble decided to play the e-commerce game, the rules changed. Amazon could no longer compete on fulfillment with Barnes & Noble's well-established warehouse and distribution system, so it was forced to invest in warehouse/distribution centers of its own.

Another challenge emerging for e-tailers who are trying hard not to become commodity sites is the recent introduction of shop-bots. Known simply as *bots*, they strike terror in the hearts of e-tailers everywhere. Bots are simply robots that search all the stores on the Internet for a given product and compare prices for you, producing the lowest price and the site that has it. That means the consumer never visits your site if the bot doesn't show that you have the best price. Bots force you to compete on price, not on value.

What all this means to an entrepreneur considering this business model is that Internet retailing is easy; distribution is hard. So, you may want to consider these tips for partnering with a good fulfillment company to keep your initial investment down.

- ✔ Get your fulfillment system in place before ever taking your first order. That way you won't disappoint your first customer.

- ✔ Consider your fulfillment needs. Do you have a perishable product? Is it fragile? Are you dealing in multiple products?

- ✔ Do your homework on the costs of setting up a fulfillment system in-house versus outsourcing. Find the best method at the lowest cost.

- ✔ Get referrals from other entrepreneurs on fulfillment houses.

- ✔ If you're outsourcing, choose your fulfillment house carefully. Make sure it's used to dealing with your type of product.

- ✔ Negotiate a deal with the fulfillment house where your costs go down as your volume goes up.

- ✔ Put someone knowledgeable in charge of your fulfillment functions.

- ✔ Always be honest with customers about the length of time it takes for them to receive an order. That means you better have a good relationship with a reliable fulfillment house or do it well yourself.

- ✔ If your products typically go to customers' homes, working with companies that regularly deal with home deliveries is a good option. iShip.com and HomeGrocer.com have good home delivery systems in place. Business shipments and some consumer shipments (Amazon uses UPS) do well with UPS, FedEx, and Airborne.

- ✔ Find a way to add value to your site so customers will purchase from you regardless of whether you also have the lowest price.

One way to create value is through building your brand, both online and off, so those customers trust you. Right now the e-tailers that are most successful have brand recognition — The Gap, Barnes & Noble, Nike, and so forth.

## Having it all with clicks and mortar

As more and more traditional bricks-and-mortar businesses go online, more and more entrepreneurs are opting to establish a presence in the real world before tackling cyberspace. The reason: Branding has become an important part of e-commerce strategy. If you create a brand that people love and trust in normal commerce, chances are they'll seek you out in cyberspace. Recent trends indicate that when a major company like The Gap or Cisco Systems now goes online, they outdo all the no-name Internet companies in a relatively short period of time. Cisco Systems, a business-to-business supplier of equipment for networks, sells more online than all the e-tailers put together. Companies such as The Gap and Victoria's Secret are profitable almost immediately while less well-known brands languish in unprofitability.

This pattern hasn't gone unnoticed by pure e-tailers like Zebramart.com, `www.zebramart.com`, a purveyor of luxury products. Zebramart plans to implement a reverse strategy, hoping its new bricks-and-mortar stores increase its exposure and legitimacy and enable it to provide better customer service.

## Thinking small

With the Internet bombarded by millions of sites, finding a niche that doesn't have a major player or an established brand is becoming more difficult. Many entrepreneurs are creating business models based on small niches — micro niches — in the market and doing quite well. I always say that you don't have to own a big company to bring a lot of money to the bottom line. One creative pair of entrepreneurs knew the futility of taking on such established brands in the job recruiting market as Monster.com and HotJobs.com, so they decided to focus — really focus — on a niche that was tiny. Their company, JobsinChicago.com, serves customers within an 80-mile radius of downtown Chicago. They're betting they can win because they know the area and the market better than anyone — certainly better than a company that's trying to serve the whole country.

Don't be afraid to carve out a small piece of a market that someone else is serving. Become the expert in that tiny niche, and you'll know those customers better than your competitors. Interestingly enough, the entire state of Maine has that philosophy about entrepreneurship. For years, they've been fighting to keep the major chains out and supporting locally owned micro-niche businesses that understand the Maine culture.

# Part IV
# Growing a Company

The 5th Wave                                      By Rich Tennant

"SINCE WE LOST THE DOLPHINS, BUSINESS HASN'T BEEN QUITE THE SAME."

# In this part . . .

$M$ost entrepreneurs want to grow their companies, but growth can be a dangerous time for a company if it isn't managed right. This part gives you the tools you need to organize your business for growth, develop a plan for growth, and make sure you're in a good financial position for growth. You also find out how to deal with those unexpected things that make life interesting as a business owner.

# Chapter 16

# Planning for Growth

· · · · · · · · · · · · · · · · · · · · · · · · · · · · · · · · · · · · · · ·

## In This Chapter

▶ Understanding the factors that affect growth

▶ Starting with some basic ways to grow

▶ Growing within a given market

▶ Growing within a given industry

▶ Moving outside your industry

▶ Going global

▶ Growing in the high tech world

· · · · · · · · · · · · · · · · · · · · · · · · · · · · · · · · · · · · · · ·

*I*f you're thinking the birth of a company and its early stages are the most perilous, I have news for you. They're not. I say that because if you plan for the start of your business and do all of the things we've talked about in other chapters of this book, chances are good that you won't be among the large number of entrepreneurs who fail. You're on your way to success, reaching the stage that causes the worst problems for many business owners — growth. Growth causes the kinds of problems that make the start-up phase so difficult. New business owners simply don't plan for it.

Growth is an inevitable outcome of a successful start-up, so why don't entrepreneurs plan for it? The main reason entrepreneurs forget to plan for growth is that they are so busy with the day-to-day effort of running their businesses that they don't stop long enough to raise their periscopes to see what's coming. Consequently, demand smacks them in the face. Because they don't have the systems and personnel in place to handle demand, they fumble around with it, and before you know it, the business is in trouble. Businesses and the entrepreneurs who start them look different when they're growing. The skills you need to bring resources together to start your business aren't the same as the skills you need to grow your business to the next level. You may need to bring in extra talent to make it to the next stage.

A good growth plan includes your goals, the strategies to reach those goals, and the tactics you use to execute those strategies. In this chapter, you find out about growth strategies that are available for your business.

# Identifying Factors That Affect Growth

When designing an effective growth plan, you first must understand all of the factors that affect your company's ability to grow. They start with:

- **Your intentions about your business.** You may be surprised to discover that business owners don't always want to grow their businesses substantially. They're perfectly happy running their little shops just the way they are, thank you. Probing a little deeper, you may find that the decision not to grow is rooted in fear. With a small business, you can pretty much control everything, but when your business grows rapidly, you begin relying on other people. For some entrepreneurs, delegating authority for their businesses to others is hard, like handing your child over into the care of someone else. Before your business can grow, you must want it to grow; it doesn't normally happen by itself.

- **Your ability to pull together the right team for growth.** No matter how much you believe in your growth strategy, you can't do it alone. You need a team of people as committed to your business as you are. Conveying your vision of company growth and convincing everyone to buy into it is critical to the successful execution of your growth plan.

- **What your target market looks like.** How much your company can grow is a function of the size of your market and the buying power of your customers. If your market is small and not showing signs of growth, achieving high levels of growth may be impossible. On the other hand, if your product or service has global potential, substantial growth is definitely within the realm of possibility.

- **What your competition looks like.** Why would anyone enter a market where giants play? Going head-to-head with the big guys is not a good strategic plan in most cases, unless you can create a niche in that market that no one else is serving. That way you can gain a foothold before the big companies find you. Older, stable industries are tough to grow unless you introduce an innovative product or new technology.

- **How innovative the industry is.** If your industry isn't known for its innovations, your company can gain a competitive advantage by introducing something new. On the other hand, if you're in a highly innovative industry like software, you must quickly produce a constant stream of innovations to grow.

- **The importance of intellectual property rights.** Not many industries exist today where intellectual property isn't critical to long-term success. Owning patents, trademarks, and copyrights is the key to entering some industries and providing barriers to entry for others. If you can't gain access to the intellectual property you need through licensing, it may be difficult to grow.

- ✔ **How predictable the industry is.** If you're in a predictable industry, differentiating your business from the rest can be more difficult. In an unpredictable industry like the Internet, you have more opportunities to find niches in the market.

- ✔ **Barriers to entry.** Your ability to grow your company is also affected by barriers to entry that others in the industry set up to keep you out. Those barriers can take the form of intense research and development, heavy expenditures in plant and equipment, contracts with key supply channels, or regulations, to name but a few.

# Starting with Some Basic Growth Strategies

Companies grow at different rates because of the factors we discuss in the previous section on "Identifying Factors That Affect Growth," but two common patterns describe most businesses — the normal and the accelerated growth rates seen in high technology companies. In this section, we look at the normal growth curve. Don't forget to check out accelerated growth in "Growing as a High Tech Company" later in this chapter.

Looking at Figure 16-1, you see the normal growth path for most businesses depicted in four phases. The length of time a business spends in any one phase varies. Some businesses spend a long time in start-up, trying to reach enough critical mass to allow them to grow. Others start growing rapidly almost from the beginning. Some businesses never reach what we would call *high growth;* they simply continue growing at a relatively stable pace, because of the market they're in or sometimes because entrepreneurs put brakes on their businesses to keep them from growing faster than their resources can manage. That's OK if you're meeting customer demand, but if demand far exceeds your ability or desire to meet it, you could be shooting yourself in the foot.

At each stage of growth, you and your business face differing issues and activities. The defining issues you find in each of the four phases are

1. **Start-up:**

   Here your concerns center on securing enough start-up capital, seeking customers, and designing an effective way to deliver your product or service. Your role is that of doing almost everything (including, sometimes, the janitorial work). Cash is important, because you never have enough of it.

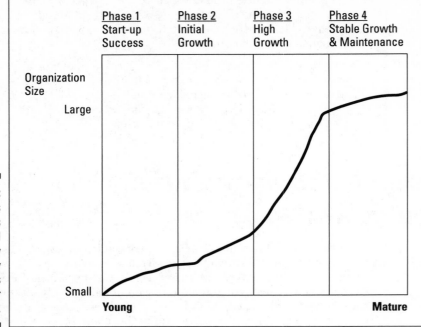

**Figure 16-1:**
As
companies
grow and
mature, they
generally
pass
through four
stages.

2. **Initial Growth:**

   You know you've made it through the first phase if you have enough customers to keep your business running with a positive cash flow. Now the
   question becomes, do you have enough cash flow to sustain the business while it's growing? Although your business is still small during this
   phase, you're still doing a lot of the work because you're keeping
   employees to a minimum. Nevertheless, it's stable, and if you wanted to,
   you could actually keep it running this way indefinitely.

3. **High Growth:**

   If you're an entrepreneur, you probably won't be satisfied maintaining
   your business at the level of initial growth, which is essentially where
   most small, lifestyle businesses remain. You probably want to expand
   and grow the business to the next level, but that takes a much more
   intense level of growth. Attaining high growth usually doesn't happen
   when using internal cash flows, so you must consider finding the
   resources you need to do it. (See Chapter 12 for suggestions on where to
   find financing for growth.) You also must:

   • Plan carefully for this type of growth, because it can quickly get away
     from you, depleting your resources before you achieve your goals.

   • Delegate more responsibility and perhaps even bring professional
     management on board. In high growth business, it's common to

find a management team in place that is different from the one that founded the company.

4. **Stable Growth:**

   If you succeed in passing through the high growth phase, your company can probably achieve a more or less predictable level of stable growth. Your company now has all the systems and controls found in a larger company. The danger at this point is complacency. You falsely assume that stable growth can continue indefinitely. Unfortunately, the market doesn't agree with you. If your company isn't in a relatively constant state of change, responding to and leading in the market, it may begin to lose market share. Companies can and do fail at this stage.

# Growing within Your Current Market

In general, most new businesses attempt to grow as much as possible within their current markets before taking on new markets. That kind of growth makes sense financially. Growing within your current market means increasing the number of customers and volume of sales to those customers. Let's look at the methods for doing that.

## Building out your customer base

One of the first growth strategies that businesses use is *market penetration*. You increase sales to current customers by doing a better job of advertising and promotion. You're gradually increasing the number and type of customers you serve. Suppose, for example, that you own a company that provides technology services to small businesses. You may extend your services to mid-sized companies or extend your reach beyond your current area. After solidifying each customer group, you move on to the next group.

Another way of achieving market penetration is by finding additional uses for your product, luring customers away from your competitors, and educating nonusers about the benefits of your product or service.

## Developing your market

When you use *market development* as your growth strategy, you're expanding your product or service market into a broader geographic area. For example, if your company starts on the West Coast, you may begin moving into the Midwest. One of the more popular ways of growing geographically is by franchising. You're no doubt familiar with the popularity of this strategy considering such famous franchises as Kentucky Fried Chicken, Golf USA, Kragen, and Burger King.

## *Franchising*

In franchising, you sell the right to do business under a particular name as well as the right to the product, process, or service. You provide training and assistance to your franchisees in setting up their businesses. Your franchisees pay you a fee and a royalty on sales of about 3 percent to 8 percent.

You provide your franchisee:

- ✔ A product or service with a proven market
- ✔ Trademarks
- ✔ A patented design, process or formula
- ✔ An accounting and financial control system
- ✔ A marketing plan
- ✔ Volume purchasing and advertising

Franchising isn't without risks, because it's essentially like starting a new business all over again. You need to document all the processes and procedures of your business in a manual for franchisees. You also must be careful about whom you select as your franchisees, because they represent you and your business's reputation. Franchises are costly propositions because of legal, accounting, consulting, and training expenses, and they take about five years to show a profit.

Not every business is suitable for franchising. While assessing your business, benchmark it against the following criteria:

- ✔ Do you have a successful prototype operation (preferably multiple outlets) with a good reputation and proven profitability?
- ✔ Do you have registered trademarks or other forms of intellectual property?
- ✔ Is your business easily systematized and replicated?
- ✔ Can your product or service be sold in many different geographic regions?

You need sufficient resources, sometimes in excess of $150,000, to develop an effective franchise program, and you must create

- ✔ A prospectus that details the franchisee's rights, responsibilities, and risks.
- ✔ An operations manual that explains in detail how the business works.
- ✔ A training and support system for your franchisees before they open their franchise, and an ongoing system after launch.
- ✔ Site selection criteria and architectural standards

You should always consult an attorney when setting up a franchise program to avoid errors that could result in litigation.

### Licensing

Licensing is another good way of developing your market without having to invest in additional sites yourself. Licensing works when you have intellectual property — patents or trademarks — that has value in the marketplace. You can license the right to use that intellectual property to others. For example, suppose you develop and patent a new kind of vacuum cleaner that revolutionizes the way people clean. You set up a company to produce a machine under your brand. But to grow, you also license the right to manufacture and distribute that technology outside the U.S. to one or more vacuum cleaner manufacturers that are doing business in other countries. That way you don't have to set up additional manufacturing facilities. Licensing is discussed in depth in Chapter 8.

## Developing your product

A third way to grow the current market is developing new products and services for the customers you have. The goal is selling more to your current customers because they are the easiest sales you have. The computer hardware and software industries are a classic example of this strategy. They regularly upgrade their products to newer versions, fixing bugs in earlier versions and installing new bells and whistles to entice their customers to purchase the upgrades.

Your customers are the best source of ideas for product and service innovations. Most of these ideas come in the form of improvements to existing products *(incremental innovation),* but once in a while you uncover an idea for an entirely new product that can be a tremendous source of growth for your company. These *breakthrough* products are not something you can plan. They usually surface during intense brainstorming sessions or when customers, suppliers, or employees suggest them. Breakthrough products usually require a much longer product development cycle and cost more to develop than incremental products

## Branding your company

One of your more important products — and many entrepreneurs don't realize this — is your company and what it stands for. Too many entrepreneurs focus exclusively on promoting their products and services and forget that their company images — their brands — are far more valuable assets than any products or services. If you establish brand recognition for your company, marketing any new products or services that you develop is by far easier. When customers associate your company name with quality, service, reliability, and great products and services, that brand becomes an umbrella under which you can add new ways of serving the customer.

The classic examples of the effectiveness of branding are apparel companies that don't design their own clothes but put their branding on articles of clothing they purchase from a commodity apparel manufacturer. Nike and Mossimo, among many others, purchase T-shirts from apparel manufacturers such as Hanes and print their logos on them. These companies find that customers actually pay more for the same T-shirt with a Nike design on it than for the same T-shirt with no design or the design of a lesser-known company.

Creating a brand is an essential part of developing new products and services. Actions you can take to start creating brand recognition for your company include:

- ✔ **Brainstorming all of the things that your company is good at doing.** What is special about your company? Do you offer the highest quality products? Do you have better service? Is your company culture unique?

- ✔ **Selecting two or three of your biggest strengths to serve as the focus of all of your marketing efforts.** Make sure customers see the strengths associated with your company's name again and again so that the two become synonymous. Monster.com, the job matching service, paints itself as a company that uses aggressive, cutting-edge tactics. Its commercials, featuring kids doing adult jobs and talking in the clichés of people in those jobs, sent a message that this company has a no-holds-barred approach to finding jobs for people who visit its Web site.

- ✔ **Deciding how your brand name will be used.** In a sense, you must create rules for the consistent use of your brand name. For example, make sure that the company name is always displayed with the product or service that you're promoting. If you want your company to be associated with the highest quality, you probably wouldn't promote it in an environment that is not perceived as such, for example, in a discount catalog.

- ✔ **Getting feedback from your customers.** Conduct blind tests with customers to see how they're responding to your branding efforts. Then adjust your strategy based on what you find out.

## Growing within Your Industry

Growing within your industry means expanding by acquiring or teaming with other companies in the industry and in your distribution channel. In this section, we look at three ways to take advantage of growth opportunities in your industry.

# *Moving vertically in your channel*

Your distribution channel offers opportunities for moving upstream or downstream in a movement known as *vertical integration.* (If you need to find out more about distribution channels, see Chapter 9.) When you move upstream in your channel, you gain control of your suppliers by acquiring them, by securing exclusive contracts, or by starting a supply outlet of your own. Gaining control of upstream activities in your channel is popular with companies using a just-in-time approach to production. Doing so enables them to receive raw materials and supplies exactly when they are needed without carrying an inventory. This control saves time and money and significantly reduces the cost of production.

When gaining control of downstream activities in your channel, you're controlling the distribution of your product by either selling directly to the customer — for example, you purchase a retail or wholesale outlet — or acquiring the distributors of your products.

What you can control is a function of where you are located in the distribution channel. As a retailer, for example, you already control the downstream portion because you sell directly to the consumer. You can control your sources of supply upstream as a way of growing within your industry. Likewise, if you're a supplier, the only upstream activities you're able to control are the actual sources of raw material (in other words, lumber mills for lumber and paper goods or cattle ranches for meat to resell) or the distributors from which you get your supplies for resale.

# *Moving horizontally in your channel*

You can also grow within your industry through *horizontal integration,* or by acquiring your competitors or starting a competing business. Suppose you own a theme restaurant catering to customers who like sports. Your restaurant is located in the northern part of the city. One way you can grow into other areas of the city is to acquire one or more of your competitors that are located where you want to be.

Another way to grow horizontally in your channel is to manufacture your product under another label, reaching a different customer segment. For example, some established high-end apparel designers reach the mass markets by producing a line of apparel under a different label, a strategy that also is common in the major appliance and grocery industries. Major retailers like Vons and Sears regularly put their brands on products made by others expressly for that purpose.

## Creating a network in your industry

The newest way to grow is developing strategic alliances with others in your industry, so that you focus on what you do best and rely on your network for everything else you need. These alliances enable you to work with the best suppliers and distributors, grow more rapidly, keep your unit costs down, and develop new products more quickly. Another benefit is that because investing heavily in fixed assets no longer is a necessity, you can devote those resources to finding new competitive advantages.

Even if you have a service business, you can take advantage of this strategy by forming strategic alliances with companies that are the best in accounting, payroll, telemarketing, and data processing.

# Diversifying Outside Your Industry

Intuition tells you that you need to exploit all of the opportunities in your current market and industry before jumping outside to foreign territory in the form of a new industry. However, entrepreneurs have succeeded in using a diversification strategy early in the growth process. Situations in which such a strategy makes the most sense include these situations:

✔ You have excess capacity or spare resources that aren't in use. Making use of them provides a new revenue stream for the company.

✔ Your customers are asking you to provide them with products or services that are outside of your current industry.

✔ You foresee major changes in your industry forcing you to look outside for your growth.

## Capitalizing on the synergy of like businesses

The easiest way of diversifying so that you make the most of what you already have is to find products or businesses that are technologically similar and complementary to your business. This is called *synergistic diversification*. For example, a restaurant chain may acquire a bakery to bring down the costs of supplying baked goods to its chain. A sporting goods store may acquire a batting cage business as a promotional opportunity for its baseball equipment and apparel.

## *Acquiring an unrelated business*

When you acquire businesses that have no relationship to your core business, it's called *conglomerate diversification*. That's a mouthful that may give you pause before you try it. You do not want to become a conglomerate without ensuring your core business is in a healthy position, because no synergies exist between the two businesses; they operate like two completely different entities. So, why try conglomerate diversification? Because sometimes, it enables entrepreneurs to gain control of a business function that can ultimately help them. Examples of conglomerate diversification are

- ✔ Purchasing the building in which you have your offices and becoming a landlord to other businesses to which you lease your excess space.

- ✔ Acquiring a travel agency to manage all of the travel plans of all of your busy sales people, saving money by bringing that function in-house.

Whenever you acquire another business, particularly one that is completely different from yours, working with someone who's experienced in mergers and acquisitions is a necessity. You'll also want to ask

- ✔ Are the cultures of the two companies compatible? Don't focus only on financial and operational synergies.

- ✔ Are the leadership styles of management compatible?

- ✔ Will you be better off a year from now having acquired this business?

# *Going Global to Grow*

The truth is that you don't have to take your business global to be a success, but in today's marketplace, avoiding global influences is pretty hard. And if you do business on the Internet, you've become a global business whether you wanted to or not. So, I would say that the question isn't "Should you go global?" but rather "When should you go global?" Several reasons why you need to consider the global marketplace in your growth planning are

- ✔ The Internet brings the world to your doorstep. You may find that your best suppliers, distributors, and customers are located in other countries.

- ✔ The Internet also brings your competitors to your doorstep. Today, even if you have a local business, your competitors can pounce on your market from anywhere in the world with the click of a mouse button and the overnight delivery capability of companies like FedEx and UPS.

- ✔ Shortened product lives and costly research and development force your company to enter more than one major market to start out just so you recap the costs of product development more quickly. The global marketplace is a major supporter of businesses introducing new products.

✔ You may find new markets for your products that are losing their luster here in the U.S. You may also find complementary products produced in other countries that you can add to your product line.

✔ Exporting to countries governed by the North American Free Trade Agreement (NAFTA) (Canada, Mexico, and the U.S.) is attractive because of the elimination of trade barriers. Similarly, the Uruguay Round of GATT (the General Agreement on Tariffs and Trade) reduces or eliminates tariffs among 117 countries and improves patent and copyright protections.

✔ You can find untapped markets in new arenas like China and Vietnam.

## Deciding if you're ready

Most new businesses don't begin exporting until they establish their businesses domestically, because global markets present entirely new issues that must be dealt with. Likewise, most entrepreneurs with start-ups are busy enough just establishing their products and services in the domestic market. In the case of my company and its PowerSource product, a huge potential in the international market was projected, but before taking that leap, the machine's components had to be redesigned to meet electrical and other requirements in different regions of the world. Doing that right now takes important resources away from our focus on building our presence in the domestic market.

Research points to certain business attributes that serve as precursors of greater success for businesses deciding to go global. Ask yourself whether you or your business has the following attributes:

✔ You've had a global vision from the inception of your business.

✔ You have a management team with international experience.

✔ You have a strong international network of contacts you can tap.

✔ You have a new technology that other countries don't have.

✔ You have a unique intangible asset in your business such as know-how that no one else has.

✔ You can derive additional products and services from your core technology.

✔ You have systems and controls in place that will work in the international environment.

You also need to know that exporting is a long-term commitment. You may not make money for some time, so you must be in a position to suffer the losses for a while.

# Finding great global markets

The world is a big place when you're figuring out where to sell your products and services. Some countries are friendlier to U.S. products than others. The International Institute for Management Development and the World Economic Forum, as well as the *1999 World Investment Report* from the United Nations, suggest ten countries that are good places to start looking. In alphabetical order, they are

- **Australia** — stable region, growing, low inflation, and good resources.
- **Brazil** — receiving a lot of foreign investment, but tariffs are high.
- **Canada** — the largest trading partner of the U.S.
- **Germany** — the largest economy in Europe.
- **Hong Kong** — a duty-free port and on its way back.
- **Japan** — formerly closed markets are beginning to open.
- **Netherlands** — largest U.S. trade surplus. Open trade and investment policies.
- **South Africa** — the best place in Africa to do business.
- **Taiwan** — healthier than most Asian countries right now and the eighth largest trading partner of the U.S.
- **UK** — they speak English and are a natural beachhead in Europe.

One good way of starting your search is consulting the *International Trade Statistics Yearbook of the United States,* which is available at any major library (you have to pay for a CD-ROM that contains all the data). Using the SITC (Standard Industrial Trade Classification) 4-digit codes found in the book, you can find information about demand in specific countries for your type of product or service. The reference book also includes a 10-digit harmonized system that provides a way to classify commodities sold in international trade. In fact, if your shipment exceeds $2,500, you must find out the 10-digit number for tracking purposes.

When looking at demand for U.S. products, the three important pieces of information you'll find are

- **The dollar value of worldwide imports of a specific product to a specific country.** Here you can find out how much each country is spending on products like yours.
- **The growth level of imports over time.** You are looking for countries where import demand levels exceed worldwide averages.
- **The share of total import demand for U.S. products to a country.** What you're looking for is a country where total import demand for U.S. products exceeds 5 percent. Lower figures suggest tariff issues.

## Getting help

Moving into the global market is not something that happens without a great deal of planning and effort. Most companies wisely put all of their systems and controls into place before they venture out into international waters.

U.S. brands, while familiar to people in the U.S., are not always recognizable in other countries. Couple that with desires and preferences of foreign buyers that can be different from those of U.S. buyers, and you see that you need plenty of research on the purchasing habits of the customers in the region you're trying to reach.

Many resources are available to companies wanting to export goods abroad. A few of them are

✔ **Trade missions.** Trade missions are tours of particular regions of the world that are organized by the U.S. Department of Commerce to help U.S. companies find good connections with trading partners and customers in other countries. These tours are a great way of making first contacts with the right people. The DOC provides several types of trade missions to businesses.

- **Specialized trade missions** focus on specific product lines and are designed for producers of those products.

- **Seminar missions** provide technical presentations for companies with technological or sophisticated products that need to connect with appropriate representatives in the foreign country.

- **Matchmaker trade delegations** are for new exporters or companies new to the world of international trade. Lasting a week, company representatives typically visit two foreign countries where they meet with customers, distributors, and so forth.

✔ **Trade fairs and exhibitions.** International trade fairs are a good way to test your products in an international environment without even leaving the U.S. They are also a good way to meet potential distributors and suppliers.

✔ **Catalog shows and video catalog exhibitions.** This is the least expensive way of promoting your products in the international arena. You send your product literature to the appropriate Department of Commerce agency, and it displays the material at exhibitions in U.S. embassies and consulates. The video version is excellent for machinery and other products that cost a lot to ship to a normal trade fair.

Uncle Sam's interest in helping you export your products overseas is evident in the wealth of resources available to exporters. A portion of that wealth includes:

- ✔ **The Export-Import Bank of the United States** www.exim.gov provides loans to small businesses, helping them extend credit to potential foreign customers and provides insurance to protect exporters if a foreign customer defaults on a purchase contract.

- ✔ **The U.S. Trade and Development Agency** www.tda.gov actually pays companies to develop business plans for foreign development projects that benefit American exporters. The goal is to create markets for U.S. exports. If your company has a product or service with export potential, read *Pipeline* at the agency's Web site. Summaries of project feasibility studies are available there.

- ✔ **The Department of Commerce** www.doc.gov helps you find the most appropriate region of the world for your products and set up booths at selected trade shows frequented by agents for various industries and countries.

- ✔ **Overseas Private Investment Corp.** www.opic.gov is a federal agency offering political risk insurance and loans to help U.S. businesses of all sizes invest and compete in 140 emerging markets and developing nations worldwide.

- ✔ **International Trade Administration** www.USAtrade.gov is a global network of trade professionals helping business owners reach their international goals. It's sponsored by the Department of Commerce.

## Using the Internet to go global

The Internet gives every business with a Web site an instant global presence. No quicker way of reaching another country with information about your company and its products and services exists, but that doesn't mean that you'll instantly attract customers to your site. Furthermore, even if you attract them to your site, how do you deal with cultural differences that are exacerbated by the ease with which you can communicate via the Internet? You may want to ask yourself the following two key questions if you decide to go global via the Internet:

- ✔ How do I know if I'm attracting potential global customers to the site?

- ✔ How can I make my site more globally user friendly?

Technology has made answering the first question easy. Your server statistics reports (your Internet Service Provider provides these to you or will give you the tools and password to access them yourself) can tell you what's happening at your site, helping you determine whether you're getting global visitors to your site. Looking at the Domain Report tells you that visitors with `.com`, `.org`, `.net`, or `.edu` extensions to their domain names usually (but not always) are based in the U.S. When you start seeing extensions that you don't recognize like `.ca` (Canada) and `.uk` (United Kingdom), you know that you're reaching the rest of the world. That's a start. If you really want to hit the international market, you need to invest some time and money into a globally user-friendly site. But, in the meantime, you can immediately encourage international visitors to consider doing business with you by:

✔ Including all of your contact information: toll-free and direct phone lines (be sure to include the country code and area code. For the U.S., the code is 1), fax, and e-mail. Many international customers prefer fax and e-mail because they're easier to deal with through different time zones, and many international customers have an easier time reading English than speaking it.

✔ Including your customer service hours on the site. Don't forget the time zone. Spell it out in full (PST=Pacific Standard Time), because not everyone is familiar with U.S. time zone acronyms.

✔ Remembering to write your dates, the way most of the world writes dates — as day-month-year. To avoid problems, write out the date as February 5, 2000, or 5-Feb-00, completely avoiding confusion.

✔ Stating clearly on your site whether you sell products only in domestic markets so you don't confuse or disappoint your international visitors. If you are planning to sell internationally in the future, let your international customers know that their visits to your site and their feedback are appreciated and will speed up your ability to justify selling internationally.

# Growing as a High Tech Company

As I said at the beginning of this chapter, the growth pattern of high technology businesses often differs from that of other businesses. Let me clarify. Within the technology sector, companies grow more traditionally because the technology is a natural outgrowth of previous technology, while companies that are experiencing hypergrowth generally are introducing a new technology that finally reaches critical mass. They are pioneers within their industries. It is the latter type of company that I refer to in this section.

## Finding the early adopters

The first stage in the life cycle of a business is defined by the introduction of the product to the early adopter market. These are people or businesses that always purchase the latest technology as soon as it hits the market. Many times they serve as beta testers (beta refers to a second-stage prototype — alpha is the first stage) for the product, giving their feedback to the company in exchange for benefits.

Although the early adopters are a small group, certainly not large enough to sustain a company in terms of sales, they provide an important opportunity for the company to work out all the bugs before demand increases. The company can't stay in this stage too long, however, before it must do what it takes to gain mainstream acceptance of the technology.

## Getting to mainstream adoption

Geoffrey Moore, author of *Crossing the Chasm* and *Inside the Tornado,* asserts that somewhere between the early adopter and mainstream adoption stages of technology lies what he has coined as *the chasm* — when early adopters have used the technology long enough to grow tired of it, but mainstream customers are still not comfortable with it. Crossing the chasm to have a chance at mainstream adoption, a company needs to create a bunch of niche markets in which the technology is adopted. The goal is to rack up as many niche markets as it takes to gain enough momentum to drive the product into what Moore calls *the tornado.*

The tornado is a period of mass-market adoption — when everyone decides that your technology is the best and they all switch to it. The tornado produces a flood of demand that can't be met. This situation is quite unlike what faces most entrepreneurs, who are always looking for ways to *create* demand. In this case, everyone wants what you have, so you can set marketing aside for the moment and focus on production and distribution. At this point, process is what counts. You can worry about developing customer relations later. Right now, all they want is the product.

## Surviving mainstream adoption

If your company makes it through the tornado, it must shift gears again, becoming more customer focused and looking for ways to sell more products to the customers you gained from the tornado. Now, marketing comes back into play. Several important rules about coping with a hypergrowth situation are

✔ You must be willing to attack the competition ruthlessly. Your goal is to become the industry standard. It's really a life or death situation.

✔ You can only become the market leader by expanding quickly, even at the expense of the customer. Remember that prices on technology always come down, so you have to increase volume to make money and that comes from selling to every type of outlet possible.

✔ You must focus on process above everything else, making sure you have your partners, and production and shipping mechanisms in place before hypergrowth occurs. Once you've hit hypergrowth, it's all about execution.

✔ You must always drive to the next lower price point. Hewlett-Packard executes this strategy extremely well, always becoming the first to hit a new lower price point on a product. That way they gain customers who are waiting for that price point first. If you don't play the lead in grabbing the lower price point, you'll lose customers to your competitors.

## Not everyone survives a tornado

Not every company that experiences a tornado of mass market adoption survives it. The classic story of Sony 15 years ago is one such case. Sony found itself in a tornado with its Betamax technology for VCRs. Sony decided to seize control of the tornado by refusing to license its new technology to other vendors. When it was unable to keep up with demand, vendors rejected Sony Betamax tapes and adopted VHS technology, which was a different way to read the tapes over the tape heads. The rest is history. That's why you're using VHS tapes in your VCR rather than Betamax tapes. Remember that you must get your technology out to as many users as possible to reach critical mass and stay there. That may mean partnering with others to make sure you can meet demand when it hits.

# Chapter 17

# Organizing Your Business for Growth

· · · · · · · · · · · · · · · · · · · · · · · · · · · · · · · · · · · · · · · · · · · · · · · · · · · · · ·

## In This Chapter

▶ Moving into the managerial mode

▶ Moving faster and with more flexibility

▶ Finding and retaining good employees

▶ Recruiting for e-business

· · · · · · · · · · · · · · · · · · · · · · · · · · · · · · · · · · · · · · · · · · · · · · · · · · · · · ·

*I*n a business world running at Internet speed, how you organize your company and how you staff it with the right people become critical issues that can either facilitate your company's growth or ensure that it can't grow. When your company goes beyond survival mode and enters a rapid growth mode, cash flow remains a vital issue, but staffing and systems begin competing for your attention. The challenge becomes how to balance limited resources against the need to take on more staff. Needless to say, in your planning for growth, you also must plan for the potential addition of employees and management to your team.

Furthermore, as your organization grows, you must maintain the entrepreneurial spirit that got you to this point, because that spirit is essential to your company's ability to navigate in a fast-moving global environment. You no doubt know about shifts in management style occurring during the past several years. More and more companies have abandoned the top-down, chain-of-command hierarchical structure for more fluid structures that encourage employee empowerment, participation, and open-book management styles. That's because businesses find that rigid structures don't respond well to fast-changing environments. In fact, the more rigid management styles often cause businesses to break down.

In this chapter, you discover many techniques for creating a winning organization and positioning it to respond rapidly in a changing environment.

# *Moving from Entrepreneurship to Professional Management*

The success of your growth strategy depends on your ability to move from entrepreneurial to professional management. Adapting doesn't mean that you leave your entrepreneurial spirit behind — far from it. What changing to professional management means is that the skills you need to rapidly grow your company are quite different from the skills you need to start your company. In fact, sometimes the skills that launch your venture — taking a risk, controlling attitude, bootstrapping, and so forth — can propel it out of control during a rapid growth cycle.

Most entrepreneurs don't have strong enough professional management skills; rather, they are by nature resource gathers, when what the company needs most as it grows are people who can manage resources. The reality is most entrepreneurs don't enjoy the management aspect of business, so they leave it to others who are better at it. Look at Table 17-1 for a snapshot of the two points of view: entrepreneurial and managerial.

| Table 17-1: | Entrepreneurial View versus Managerial View |
|---|---|
| *Entrepreneurial View* | *Managerial View* |
| Motivated by opportunity — resource acquisition | Motivated by resources — resource management |
| Risk management | Risk avoidance |
| Revolutionary — breakthrough actions | Evolutionary — derivative actions |
| Unpredictable environment with limited resources | More predictable environment with committed resources |
| Rented, leased, borrowed resources | Owned or employed resources |
| Flat organizational structure — team approach — empowered employees | Hierarchical organizational structure — chain of command |

As you see from Table 17-1, entrepreneurs are driven by an opportunistic attitude, while managers are generally driven by the need to manage resources. They are typically given a budget within which they must strive to stay. By contrast, entrepreneurs aren't limited by resources; they can always go out and find more.

Similarly, entrepreneurs tend to break the rules and create brand-new ways of doing things. Managers, for the most part, work in a more evolutionary fashion, building on what already exists, improving and refining it.

Entrepreneurial organizations are generally flat, which means that they don't involve layers of management. Everyone works together as a team, quite unlike the layers of management found in most large organizations.

If you're making the transition from entrepreneur to professional management:

✔ Recognize that a change in your management structure must take place before growth begins.

✔ Get help putting formal decision systems in place that give more people authority and responsibility over major decisions for the company. Bottom line: Give up some control.

✔ Make sure that any functions of your business that are critical (life and death) to the success of the business are not in the hands of only one person. If that person left, you'd be in big trouble.

✔ Carefully evaluate your growth strategy and make sure that the systems and procedures you have put in place match your strategies.

✔ Establish a board of directors, if you don't already have one.

## *Discovering your company's culture*

Every company has a personality, a distinct way of doing things that you recognize the minute you spend any time at all inside that company. This distinct personality is known as corporate culture, and it has become an important competitive advantage for most businesses. While you describe a company culture in your handbook or allude to it in your promotional activities, you see it mainly in the daily interactions of the people who work in your company.

Culture is important for two reasons:

✔ It gives people in your company a sense of purpose and propels them to achieve the company's goals.

✔ It is a reflection of the implementation of your company vision.

I worked with a manufacturer that epitomizes the benefits of a strong corporate culture. This company is fanatically customer driven. Walk onto the floor of its assembly plant, pick out anyone to talk to, and I'll bet that within one minute, you'll hear the word *customer* from that person. Everyone in that organization, from the janitor to the president, knows what he or she does to contribute to customer satisfaction. They all know that it's the customer who pays them.

That kind of cult-like culture is found in many successful companies like Southwest Airlines, UPS, and Intel Corp., to name a few. When employees are committed to the vision and culture of the company, they can accomplish nearly impossible feats. For example, one company's product development team had to develop an innovative new computer to try to save their company from the depths of a financial crisis. During the process, the team discovered that the software piece for the computer was far behind schedule and might cost them their market opportunity. The three engineers assigned to the project spent an entire night trying to resolve the software problem. They succeeded in completing two or three months of work in one night. That kind of effort doesn't happen without a commitment to the company.

How do you know what your company culture is if it isn't obvious? Make sure that what you find out matches what you *want* your culture to be. If it doesn't, it's time to do something about it. Asking the following questions can help you begin to think about the kind of culture you have in your organization:

- Does your company work in teams or individually?
- How does your company deal with change?
- How does your company deal with failure?
- How does your company make decisions? Who makes the critical decisions?
- How do you prioritize work?
- How do you share information inside and outside your company?
- Do you take a long-term or short-term view of decision-making?
- How do you make sure you have competent employees?
- How do you encourage diversity?
- How are employees treated? What does your company's vision say about employees?

Your company's culture is part of its competitive advantage. Employees as well as customers need to recognize and promote your company's culture and competitive advantages. If it's strong like the culture at Southwest Airlines, which makes up for its cattle-herding approach to loading passengers with its wacky, irreverent flight attendants and ground crew, customers may choose to deal with your company just because of its customer-oriented culture.

## Developing a human resource policy

The human capital side of your business affects everything your business does; it is the heart and soul of the business. Your vision, culture, core values, and goals affect policies that you develop to guide human resource decision-making. The changing role of organizational management also impacts the way you as the entrepreneur make decisions. While a detailed discussion of all the new principles of management (check out *Managing For Dummies*) isn't possible, key management principles for the new marketplace promote:

✔ Using self-directed teams rather than departments, functions, or specific tasks. This strategy empowers employees and focuses everyone's energies on company goals.

✔ Focusing on core competencies — those things the company does to create value.

✔ Including the customer in everything the business does, from product design to marketing to service. Everyone in the organization needs to know the customer.

✔ Providing rewards based on team effort above rewards based on individual effort. If you reward individuals when you're trying to encourage teamwork, your employees become confused.

✔ Sharing company information with employees so they can use it to provide input and feel a vested interest in the success of the company.

# The truth about successful companies

Think you know what makes a successful company? Answer these five true/false questions:

1. In general, the greatest and most enduring companies started with a great idea.

2. Great companies have charismatic leaders.

3. The driving force in great companies is shareholder wealth or profit.

4. Great companies do not take big risks.

5. Most people would be comfortable working for a great company.

All five are false. But if you answered true to some, you're not alone. These statements represent five of the biggest myths about what makes a great company. In their research, which became part of their best-selling book, *Built to Last,* Jim Collins and Jerry Porras studied the number one companies in every industry, comparing them against the number twos. They discovered

1. Few of the great companies started with a great idea; in fact, most were not even successful in the beginning. Sony Corp. started by producing rice cookers and failed at several products before beginning a stream of breakthrough products like the magnetic tape recorder in 1950, the first all-transistor radio in 1955, and the Sony Walkman in 1979, to name only a few.

2. The great companies did not have charismatic leaders heading their teams; instead, they had entrepreneurs who wanted to build a great and enduring company. How many readers would recognize the name of William L. McKnight — probably few if any. Yet, he was at the helm of one of the most innovative manufacturing companies of all time for 17 years — 3M Corp.

3. The driving force in the great companies is adherence to their purpose and core values above shareholder wealth or profit. Every one of the great companies had written vision statements and clearly articulated core values that they held to religiously.

4. The great companies didn't plan for everything. They took risks when their intuition told them it was time.

5. In general, the great companies hold so firmly to their core beliefs and the company culture that develops from them that anyone who doesn't fit into that culture has a difficult time surviving in the organization.

These management principles are well-suited for entrepreneurial businesses with limited resources working in this fast-paced market. In fact, they are more successfully implemented in start-up companies for which you can hire the right people for your company's culture.

# Organizing for Speed and Flexibility

Throughout this book, I talk about the importance of planning, of having a plan for start-up, for growth, and later on, for your exit from the company. But having a plan doesn't mean that you know what the future will bring. It's pretty obvious nowadays that we don't know what the future has in store except more of the same — change. So how do you plan for change? You build a flexible organization that quickly responds to change without the need to totally reorganize.

More and more, new business models that never existed before have entrepreneurs looking for new ways to do old business and taking advantage of the low overhead and speed of doing business on the Internet. These new models require a different way of organizing when examples of these new organizational forms aren't always out there to guide innovation. So, in the true spirit of what they're all about, entrepreneurs must make things up as they go.

When your company organizes in a way that it can respond to whatever is thrown at it, you must

✔ Invest in technology that can handle a big surge in growth; don't invest only for what you need right now.

✔ Train your current employees how to orient new employees that you'll need to bring on board in the future. That way, if you have to hire many people quickly, they can be assimilated into your business culture without disrupting workflow.

✔ Not take success for granted. Like Andy Grove, CEO of Intel Corp., be paranoid. Keep your periscope up and constantly scanning the horizon for competitors, for a change in demand, or for a shift in market conditions.

✔ Design an organization that operates in a constant state of change. That way, you'll never have to completely reinvent it, and you'll always be ahead of the game.

## Organizing around teams

Teams are a vital part of any company, whether the business has just opened or has existed for 50 years. Studies show that organizations learn and grow at the team level, not at the individual level. That's because teams that work in collegial environments, sharing a company vision, become aligned in their purposes and goals, thus benefiting the company.

# The pay plan that nearly wrecked the team

One business owner I know realized almost too late that a compensation policy he had established for his company nearly destroyed the teamwork he had so carefully crafted. The entrepreneur thought he could energize his crew of salespeople by instituting a commission program on top of their sales salaries, but he was wrong. In fact, the new policy caused a number of problems. Salespeople no longer shared information or collaborated with each other to gain more sales for the company, because that might reduce their own commissions. At times when one salesperson followed up, helping the customer of another salesperson, dissension became evident. Furthermore, other employees — in shipping and other support areas of the business — who were not on the commission plan felt slighted.

Recognizing his mistake, he quickly revamped his program to include the other employees in addition to salespeople, offering everyone the possibility of an extra month's pay plus monthly bonuses rather than the commission system. The by-product of this new strategy is that it encourages teamwork and creates a win-win situation for everyone.

Promoting team interaction is often easier with a start-up company, because you can't get the company going unless everyone shares their knowledge. If you're not careful, however, as the company grows you can lose some of that entrepreneurial team spirit, and getting it back is hard work.

One entrepreneur I know avoids that trap by documenting her company's best practices so that she can bring everyone — including new hires — up to speed. She identifies four documents that detail the company's best practices and ensure that employees are able to work together as a team. They are:

- ✔ **The training document.** This document spells out for everyone what his or her knowledge-sharing obligations are to everyone else in the organization. The job of managers is to set performance benchmarks, reward achievement, and provide to employees the resources they need to do their jobs, while the job of employees is to take charge of designing and implementing training programs.

- ✔ **The vision statement.** The vision statement indicates that everything the company does must make a positive contribution to great food, great service, and great finance. All the decisions that employees make are guided by the vision.

- ✔ **The training questionnaire.** This survey helps management target training efforts by identifying the expectations of employees and understanding the metrics for determining when and how those expectations are met.

- ✔ **The training skills document.** This document outlines skills an employee must acquire by several designated points in time. It also discusses the resources, help, and training that the company provides to assist employees in achieving their skills targets. The training passport is a record of that achievement.

# Taking your company online

Regardless of whether you decide to start a pure Internet company or take your bricks-and-mortar company online, you face organizational issues that you didn't have before. Jupiter Communications studied the top 100 Web sites, finding that fewer than half of the top 100 sites have their roots in traditional businesses. Yet, about 59 percent of online commerce is conducted on the sites of companies that have bricks-and-mortar locations. That means a large share of traditional businesses that haven't already gone online may want to consider doing so because the perceived value is present.

You have several organizational options to consider when you think about bringing the Internet into the mix. One option, of course, is an organizational structure that doesn't include the Internet as a distribution channel. For some businesses, this is a perfectly viable option, because in some instances, having a Web presence won't necessarily enhance your business. If you have a local business based on face-to-face contact with your customers — a restaurant or boutique — you may not be able to justify the time, expense, and maintenance costs of a Web site in terms of the value it brings to your customers and your business. But, if you find that most successful businesses in your industry are using the Web in a variety of ways, from advertising to selling products to business-to-business purchasing, you may find that you have to develop a Web site just to stay competitive.

Three other organizational options offer varying degrees of potential to entrepreneurs who are deciding what role the Internet will play in their businesses. They range from testing the waters with a marketing approach to going all the way and developing an independent Internet business.

## Marketing runs your Internet strategy

Some companies run Internet projects as extensions of their current business practices, using existing people and departments — for example, putting your marketing people in charge of the Internet. This often is an entry strategy for many businesses, because it lets them test the waters before they jump in headfirst for a swim. For that reason, treating an Internet project as a mere extension of an existing business is more of a short-term solution with the disadvantage of being operated like a pet project rather than a permanent part of the organization. With marketing running the show, technology people don't want to commit their human capital and finance people don't want to contribute their budget dollars. So this structure does not encourage cross-functionality. Nevertheless, it is a start if you must conserve capital.

## Internet business unit inside the company

Some companies establish independent business units that focus on creating the company's Internet presence. That kind of unit has its own budget and is free to do what it wants, but it serves as coordinator for anything that relates to the Internet for the entire company. ESPN.com and CNNfn.com are examples of sites that are independent business units inside their parent companies.

The problem with this approach is that you run the risk of confusing the customer when one unit of your business takes your brand in a direction different from the rest of the company.

### Independent Internet business unit

In this structure, you form a separate Internet business unit that focuses on the Internet channel but carries a consistent brand message for the company. With the separate business unit, you don't risk compromising your brand but you still reach your customers who use many channels to purchase their goods and services. The result: You gain a competitive advantage over pure Internet companies and pure bricks-and-mortar companies. This structure is probably more effective, because it is cross-functional and team-based, and thus is inherently more flexible and capable of rapid response to change. Everyone within an organization must think about the Internet and how it affects what he or she does.

The Gap launched its Web site in late 1996 and introduced full e-commerce capability in late 1997. After only two years, it became the leader in brand awareness in the clothing industry. Its site now attracts four times the traffic of its two most popular bricks-and-mortar stores, and the site carries The Gap brand to the Web in a consistent and recognizable way as a separate Internet business.

# Finding and Keeping Great People

Ask any company owner what the most difficult issue he or she faces is and you'll hear, "finding and retaining good employees." In a volatile marketplace, great employees come at a premium, and keeping those employees can be almost a daily task in some industries like high tech. Yet, many entrepreneurs aren't effective at recruiting and hiring top talent because during start-up, they usually had a close-knit team that satisfied all the functions of the organization and worked well together under a common goal. Bringing new people on board is sort of a shock to the system, because they don't always fit neatly into the culture and ways things are done. But, bringing new people into the organization doesn't have to be such a culture shock if you spend the necessary time and effort to find the right people.

The question of when to add new people to the team is paramount. Some companies take the approach of doing it when it becomes obvious that they have to — when it's clear that it's time to delegate authority and bring in professional management to give the organization some structure. One company I know, founded by a husband and wife team, decided to bring in help when employees began working 80-hour weeks. Because the company was established with a good track record, it was in a great position to hire the best people. This strategy can work if your original founding team has the skills to carry the company to the point of generating enough revenues to allow it to hire more people. In fact, this strategy is probably the most common.

Another strategy is to start your company with a professional management team. In other words, you hire the best people you can — those who have had experience running large companies — with the resources you have, then add more later on. One software company did this by hiring key management to handle all the major functions of the business. They kept their flat, entrepreneurial feeling by making sure that no one reported to any of these management people. Many high tech and Internet companies start with a professional management team in place because they seek venture capital at an early stage and expect to do an IPO. In both cases, professional management is critical.

Your need to bring on additional management will be a function of:

✔ Your ability to delegate responsibility and authority

✔ The resources you have for hiring the best

✔ Your company's need for more structure and the skills of professional management

## Recruiting the right people

Recruiting is the task among all the aspects of the hiring process on which entrepreneurs probably spend the least amount of time. And that is surprising, because the recruiting process determines whether you ultimately get the right person for the position you want to fill. Entrepreneurs often find someone to fill a job rather than someone with the potential to fit in well and grow with the organization. Part of the fault for that slipup lies in the way they announce the opening for the position. If you describe a position solely in terms of skill requirements and function, you'll probably find someone who's looking for a job rather than a career. Young entrepreneurial companies need people who can perform several functions and work as a team. The following tips help you effectively find the right people for your needs:

✔ **Have a marketing plan for attracting talent.** Just like your marketing plan creates awareness for your business, you need a marketing plan to catch the attention of the best candidates for the positions you want to fill. That plan spells out your strategy for proactively going after the type of people you need — in simple terms — what kind of person you're looking for, where you can find him or her, and how you're going to approach that person.

✔ **Identify your best employees.** Most entrepreneurs can profile their best customers, but can they profile their best employees? Knowing the characteristics, skills, experience, and attitude of your best employees helps you look for those traits in your new hires. If you know what you're going after, you're more likely to find it.

✔ **Be creative about where you find talent.** Some companies are so concerned about hiring new people who immediately fit in with their corporate culture that the first place they look is through their current employees. Put the word out about the positions you're trying to fill. Chances are people who are recommended to you by your current employees are in a better position to fit right in from day one because your employees know exactly what you're looking for and probably won't recommend someone who doesn't fit your needs. Other places to look are professional associations, personal recommendations from your professional advisors, universities, and recruiters.

✔ **Define what makes your company and the open position unique.** Remember, you're marketing this new position and making sure that a potential candidate understands the benefits of coming to work for your company. Are you offering: Better pay? More flexible work hours? Opportunities for advancement? A company culture second to none? If you want to ensure that you position your company correctly, research what job seekers in your industry value.

✔ **Establish a talent channel.** Over time you'll discover the best resources for recruiting, so keep in touch with them even when you're not recruiting. You also need to keep your company name in the limelight by associating with the local college or university, sponsoring community activities, and writing articles for trade journals.

## Finding your team

Depending on the type of position you're looking to fill, you can find the people you need by:

✔ Getting referrals from current employees and others you work with in your industry. This is the best resource.

✔ Hiring a human resource consultant who targets the best places to find people and guides your selection process. You may also consider finding one who can serve on your board of advisors.

✔ Recruiting at vocational schools, colleges, and universities.

✔ Checking public employment offices.

✔ Using private employment agencies (also called headhunters).

✔ Tapping into location organizations and trade associations.

✔ Using temporary help services.

✔ Checking Internet bulletin boards like Monster.com.

✔ Scanning want ads from papers like *The Wall Street Journal.*

### Demonstrating your advantages

You'll encounter competition for the best people in any field, so having a good sense of the unique benefits of working for your company is important. Small companies are attractive for many reasons. A few of the reasons include that:

- ✔ You can make decisions directly impacting the company.
- ✔ You can move more quickly into positions of responsibility in the company.
- ✔ You can work in a more flexible environment.

### Developing an effective job description

Before beginning your search, you need a good job description — essentially guidelines for you and a potential candidate about the requirements for a particular position. Some of the things you may want to include in your job description are:

- ✔ What level of education and work experience do you need? I recommend that you state these as "desired" levels rather than required. You still screen out candidates who don't come close, but you also have the opportunity to look at people who may not have the exact education and experience you seek that may, nevertheless, be best-suited for the position.

- ✔ A list of the duties and responsibilities of the position so that the candidate knows what's expected. Be careful, however, not to be so precise that you neglect to leave open the possibility for more flexibility in tasks.

- ✔ The name of the person to whom the candidate will be responsible.

- ✔ An explanation of the personal characteristics that you're looking for, including such things as communication skills, self-motivation, ability to work in a team, and so forth.

As you design your job description, keep in mind that the Equal Employment Opportunity laws prohibit discrimination based on age, sex, color, race, national origin, religion, and so forth during the recruiting and hiring processes. For example, your job description or application can't require a photograph of the applicant, unless the position requires certain physical characteristics (usually this would be for something like modeling or acting, not most business situations).

## Choosing the right candidate

Your selection of the best person for the position is the result of a combination of studying a job application form and resume and conducting an interview. The application and resume are good screening tools, but exercise caution because applicants tend to overstate their qualifications and achievements. Factors to check out in a resume are

- ✔ The length of time an applicant spent in any one previous position. Does it seem reasonable to you or did the applicant seem to move around a lot?

- ✔ Does the applicant's prior work experience match your needs?

- ✔ Does the appearance of the resume suggest that the applicant is serious about his or her career. If a resume is poorly prepared, with errors, I won't consider the candidate. If the job-seeker can't take the time to do a resume right, when the stakes are high, how careful will he or she be with a normal workload?

- ✔ Did the candidate emphasize skills and experience that are relevant to the position?

Contacting the references provided with an application and finding out more about the candidate is important before conducting an interview. However, your final decision about a candidate may come during an interview when you can observe his or her nonverbal and verbal skills. In person, you have the opportunity to sense whether the candidate fits in with your company culture.

---

## Employment laws you need to know

You need to be aware of important employment laws when you recruit and hire new employees. Eight of the more important laws to know about are:

- ✔ You must pay women and men the same for the same work (Equal Pay Act of 1963).

- ✔ You cannot refuse to hire, promote, train, or increase pay based on race, color, sex, or national origin (Civil Rights Act of 1964 — applies to companies with more than 15 employees).

- ✔ You cannot discriminate against persons between the ages of 40 and 70 (Age Discrimination Act of 1973).

- ✔ If you have a federal government contract of $50,000 or more, and 50 or more employees, you must actively recruit and hire the handicapped (Vocational Rehabilitation Act of 1973).

- ✔ If you have a federal contract in excess of $10,000, you must make an effort to employ and

advance qualified disabled veterans (Vietnam Era Veterans Readjustment Act of 1974).

- ✔ You must examine documents of all candidates to ensure that you don't hire illegal aliens (Immigration Law of 1986).

- ✔ If you have 15 or more employees, you can't do any testing to screen out the disabled or someone related to a disabled person (Americans with Disabilities Act of 1990).

- ✔ You must prove that any discriminatory practices in which you may engage are job related and required to operate your business (Civil Rights Act of 1991).

Knowing about and adhering to these laws is important. In a time of increasing litigation and regulation, not doing so can be costly to your business.

## Avoid these questions

The EEOC (Equal Employment Opportunity Commission) has released the following guidelines regarding questions that may *not* be asked before hiring someone.

✔ **What is your age?** Only in the case of a young applicant can the employer ask if the person can prove he or she is of legal age after hiring. In other cases, age questions like "When did you graduate from high school?" are not permitted.

✔ **What church do you attend?** No questions regarding religion of the applicant or the applicant's family are allowed.

✔ **Do you have children or plan to get pregnant?** Questions regarding personal family plans or living arrangements are not permitted.

✔ **Have you ever been arrested?** "Have you ever been convicted of a crime?" is permissible.

✔ **How is your health?** "Do you have any condition that would prevent you from doing your job?" is permissible.

✔ **You have beautiful skin; where are your ancestors from?** Questions about ancestry, heritage, culture, and so forth are not permitted.

One change is that if your candidate is in a wheelchair, for example, you may ask what accommodations are necessary to hire this person.

During the interview, ask questions that explore whether the person can provide the skills your company needs and can work well with others. Be sure to spend the majority of the interview, however, asking questions that probe the candidate's character. Putting the candidate into a hypothetical situation forces him or her to make decisions that reveal character. For example, "You become aware that someone on your team has been revealing critical information to a friend in a competing company. What would you do about it?" Or, "What do you like to do in your spare time?" Getting someone to talk about their life outside of work often reveals a lot about their values and how they spend their time. Someone who has a lot of outside activities that take a lot of time may not be willing to work the long hours you may expect. Be sure to observe the candidate's body language as he or she responds to questions like these. It is often said that about 90 percent of communication is nonverbal.

You must be careful not to ask questions that are illegal to ask prior to the point of hiring someone. The sidebar "Avoid these questions" lists what some of those questions are.

# Recruiting an experienced CEO for an e-business

Today's Internet environment calls for changes in the way founding teams are put together. Many new e-businesses are started by young entrepreneurs in their early 20s who know technology and may have great business concepts, but they are not seasoned enough to take a venture through venture capital funding and an IPO and come out successfully on the other side. Compensating for their lack of experience, these young entrepreneurs seek out veteran CEOs, but successful company leaders are in short supply because of high demand by technology companies. If you're starting an e-business and need an experienced CEO, the more important characteristics that describe the candidate you need are that he or she is

- ✔ **A visionary.** In other words, the CEO candidate must see clearly where the company needs to be heading and must convey the confidence that this vision is right for the company.

- ✔ **Adaptable to change.** The environment for e-businesses is volatile and in a constant state of flux. A good CEO must be ready and able to quickly and effectively change the direction of the company.

- ✔ **Market driven.** Technology companies often fail because they focus on the technology instead of the customer. Customers must understand how to use your products and services or they will not purchase them.

- ✔ **Experienced.** The CEO must demonstrate that he or she understands markets and can effectively lead the company.

- ✔ **Well-connected.** In other words, he or she has good contacts. Who you know matters more today than ever before, because today's market-place is a collaborative one in which even competitors may have to work together.

Founding a successful e-business is about having a great professional management team in place. It can literally make the difference between a venture that grows successfully and one that languishes.

# Chapter 18

# Reaching the Customer

● ● ● ● ● ● ● ● ● ● ● ● ● ● ● ● ● ● ● ● ● ● ● ● ● ● ● ● ● ● ● ● ● ● ● ● ● ● ● ●

### In This Chapter

▶ Marketing one-to-one

▶ Developing your marketing plan

▶ Maintaining your best customers

● ● ● ● ● ● ● ● ● ● ● ● ● ● ● ● ● ● ● ● ● ● ● ● ● ● ● ● ● ● ● ● ● ● ● ● ● ● ● ●

*M*any people believe that the traditional role of marketing as the primary conduit to the customer has radically changed. Marketing is no longer an activity within a department of a business; you find it in every other functional area of the business, from research and development to operations and finance. This change happened because companies increasingly understand the value of focusing on the customer. When only one functional area of your business deals with the customer, you can't be customer focused.

As is true with every other area of business, technology dramatically affects marketing. I'm not saying that marketing, as a function, has become less powerful than before because it has been assimilated into other functions. On the contrary, marketing is an even more important and powerful part of the organization because it is part of everything the company does. Training everyone within an organization to listen to the customer puts the company in a stronger position to serve its customers the way they want to be served. The company can better determine what its strengths are and apply those strengths to the appropriate markets through the appropriate channels.

Marketing has changed for other reasons as well. Today, customers are more market savvy; they demand choice, quality, and superior levels of service, and they expect businesses to respond quickly to their fickle changes in tastes and preferences. They also demand customized and personalized products and services, which makes it difficult to mass market to nameless, faceless hordes of customers anymore. Today, you have to market to customers in the way they want, satisfying their specific needs, when they want them satisfied.

In this chapter, you discover how to build a marketing plan for your business that recognizes the changes that have taken place in the marketplace because of technology. You also find out how important branding is to your business's success in a marketplace where it's easy to get lost in the cacophony of competing products.

# Marketing to Customers, One at a Time

Organizing around customers is what marketing guru Don Peppers preaches. He also asserts that you must not treat every customer the same; you must create a learning relationship with each and every one of them and strive to keep your customers for life. Well, it isn't as simple as that, but companies everywhere are discovering the value of what Peppers professes.

For example, Federal Express learned that it could save money and benefit its customers at the same time by using the Internet to allow customers to track their own shipments. When a customer calls FedEx to inquire about a shipment, it costs the company $2–$3; in other words, the company loses money on the deal. It also takes the customer longer to get an answer by phone and he doesn't feel in control of the situation. But if the customer goes to the Web site to check on a package, the customer has an instant response and FedEx actually makes money by reducing costs. This is a learning relationship and a win-win situation for both.

Despite everything else your business may have (including money), customers are its most important asset. If you don't have customers, you don't have a business. So you need to build an environment where customers and your company can share information with each other and create value for each other. Developing these relationships takes a long time, so don't expect a quick return on your investment.

If you want your business to be successful at marketing, you need to

- ✔ Make marketing not merely a function but rather a way of doing business that permeates every part of the business.

- ✔ Design your products and services to meet the needs of your customers the way they tell you they want them. Giving customers exactly what they want means you actually spend less in marketing.

- ✔ Promote the character, philosophy, and culture of your company — in other words, the truth, not an image you want customers to believe.

- ✔ Build long-term relationships with your customers. The longer you retain a customer, the more profitable having that customer becomes, providing referrals, additional purchases, and savings from lower customer acquisition expenses.

A major side benefit to building customer relationships is that your customers won't automatically shift their allegiance to someone else when your company runs into a problem. Having a customer see your business through a negative experience actually strengthens the relationship because customers are not used to having businesses care about them enough to try to solve a problem. In this kind of relationship, your customers aren't merely a series of transactions.

## *Using the customer to build your market strategy*

When you have a one-to-one mentality, you build your market strategy around your customers, so you don't have to worry about your market share. It doesn't matter any more. You create your niche in the market serving the customers whom no one else serves and putting your company in the leadership position from which you set the standards for everyone else. Other ways to build your marketing strategy around your customer include:

- ✔ **Making sure your company positioning is based on how *you* want customers to view your company and its products and services.** Identical products, for example, can be perceived differently depending on who's marketing them. That's why, for example, customers will pay much more for a branded shampoo than for a generic, even though each has the same ingredients. The reputation and integrity of the company behind the product sells the product.

- ✔ **Building credibility for your company and its brand.** Invest in quality, service, and customer satisfaction to reap referrals from satisfied customers. Build trust with your customers by always delivering what you say you will.

- ✔ **Mass customizing with your key customers.** One entrepreneur I know supplies the products and services needed for developing resorts worldwide. He points out that if he understands the specific needs of a resort developer in the Middle East, he can suggest the best products and services and create a level of customer satisfaction that can't be attained with standardized products.

- ✔ **Finding out who your best customers are and making sure you keep them.** A good customer is worth his weight in gold — literally. As I said in the introduction to this chapter, the cost of customer maintenance goes down the longer that you keep your customers. In an upcoming section about "Keeping Your Best Customers," I discuss more of the specifics of keeping those loyal customers.

CASE STUDY

---

# Marketing in a split second

An excellent example of using technology to gain a competitive advantage is employed by Capital One Financial Corp., the credit card, investment, and financial services company. Imagine having a company where the telephones ring at a rate of one million calls per week. Managing that kind of traffic alone requires sophisticated computer systems, and Capital One has them. Before you ever hear the phone ring on Capital One's end, its computer has sprung into action.

In the split second after you punch the last digit into your telephone, Capital One's computer captures the phone number, identifies the caller, and predicts the reason for the call. The computer then selects the best customer service representative to contact for that particular call and speedily delivers approximately 12 pieces of information about the customer to the customer service rep. Included with that information are a prediction as to what the customer might want to buy and how the service rep can make the sale, once the original reason for the call has been resolved.

The amazing thing about this process is that all these steps take place in only 100 milliseconds. That's a tenth of a second. In less time than it takes for the second hand on your watch to click one time, Capital One's computer determines whether to roll out the red carpet to its valued customers in need of assistance or open the door for new ones wanting to give the company a try.

What you can take away from this example is that you must continually experiment with your customers and modify what you do based on what your customers tell you.

---

# *Using technology to build your market strategy*

The Internet isn't the only technology affecting the way companies market their goods and services. All sorts of technology — from database marketing to e-mail to desktop publishing — shape marketing strategies. For example, tasks that businesses once outsourced to print shops are increasingly brought in-house for preproduction work on the desktop. Technology facilitates innovation in ways that companies never previously dreamed about.

Because of technology, the emphasis in marketing shifts from products to information and solutions. Rather than selling mere products to customers, companies search for ways to solve customer problems with a bundle of products, information, and services that the customers often conceive. The value of this strategy is that product acceptance increases and costly redesign is often avoided.

Additional ways you can use technology to market more effectively include:

- ✔ Using e-mail to communicate rapidly and easily with customers, suppliers, and partners around the world.

- ✔ Using the teleconferencing or video conferencing capabilities of an application like Microsoft's *NetMeeting* on your computer or through outlets like Kinkos (where you can rent conferencing time) for international sales meetings to cut back on air and other travel expenses.

- ✔ Providing dial-up connections and laptop computers, so employees can work virtually anywhere in the world. This increases productivity and brings your company closer to your customers.

- ✔ Using voice mail to answer the phone, receive messages when you're not in the office, and obtain customer feedback.

- ✔ Using desktop publishing software to bring production of expensive promotional material in-house. You can even work on prepress designs on your desktop before sending them to a printer for professional bulk printing.

- ✔ Receiving updated information about equipment, supplies, and other industry information through links to CD-ROM or Internet services, which also can be a handy way to locate items that aren't normally carried in stock for your customers.

When you think about technology, remember that it isn't merely a tool to improve the way you do business or to free up your time to focus on the customer, it's also a driver of innovation and competitive advantage. Nevertheless, it can't replace personal contact with your customers, which is essential, and it can't replace your unique ability to make sense of a lot of customer information.

## Using the Internet to build a market strategy

The relatively new world of marketing online turns the traditional precepts of marketing strategy upside down. You can't sell *to* customers on the Internet; they sell themselves. After all, customers can easily comparison shop for consumer and business products online and decide for themselves what they want. The hard-sell, close-the-deal kind of salesmanship that prevailed for years in the traditional marketplace is totally alien on the Web. If that sounds like a problem for entrepreneurs trying to market their products and services, think again. Yes, you approach marketing from a different viewpoint, but you also reap greater benefits, because Internet customers tend to be more loyal once they've successfully done business with you. Remember that Internet customers still experience considerable fear and anxiety about purchasing online. They've heard too many stories about credit card identities being snatched from their owners by hackers tapping into online transactions. So, they're more likely to stay with a company they trust, where they are confident that their private information is secure. Consider the following six marketing strategies and examples from successful companies doing business online.

### Using information to brand your company

In traditional marketing terms, when you want to increase sales you create a pitch and broadcast it to the masses. On the Internet, however, that gets you nowhere. Most people don't read those ads, so you need to provide information that enables those customers to make their own choices. For example, look at Auto-by-Tel, www.autobytel.com, which links new-car buyers and dealers. You create a wish list for the car you want, send it to Auto-by-Tel, and it finds your dream car, tells you the wholesale price (no negotiations), and essentially gives you all the information you need to make an informed decision. Auto-by-Tel even delivers the car to you! So, as a company marketing online, you don't have to make a hard-sell pitch to win a happy customer; you just give them what they want.

### Creating positive public relations

Some companies excel at using their sites to generate positive public relations for their companies by satisfying their constituents, customers, suppliers, shareholders, and so forth. MiniMed, www.minimed.com, has good reason to celebrate what it does. The medical device company provides Website visitors with the latest about how to deal with a chronic illness like diabetes. Shareholders stay in touch with how the company is doing financially, and physicians find out more about the latest therapies. MiniMed effectively segmented its market and now serves each segment individually.

### Providing customer service

Under the old marketing paradigm, you provided customer service within the limits of your resources. On the Internet, by contrast, you realize that customers want instant satisfaction of their needs. Adobe, www.adobe.com, the software company, has taken 24-hour service to the max by providing people to answer e-mail questions any time of the day or night and offering a toll-free phone number so you can actually speak to a human being.

### Creating your image

People will visit your Web site if it's entertaining, lively, interactive, and constantly changing. One of the better examples, surprisingly enough, is the Ragu site (you know, spaghetti sauce), www.eat.com, where you talk to Web site spokeswoman Mama, who serves as your host. You can find her favorite recipes or even learn to speak a little Italian. It's a real cultural experience.

## Gathering customer information

Categorizing your customers is important, so you can serve their particular needs and anticipate what their preferences are. Sites like Amazon.com, www.amazon.com, track your preferences every time you make a purchase and suggest new products in which you may be interested. The more information customers give Amazon, the better Amazon can serve them.

## Don't forget the costs

With throngs of businesses rushing to put up Web sites and engaging in e-commerce, is anyone calculating what it costs to attract real customers to your site so that you have even a slight chance of persuading them to purchase something? To attract customers, Buy.com, www.buy.com, sells everything essentially below cost to compete in a market where price is essentially the only differentiating factor. But that's only one of the many costs of attracting customers to your site. The contrast between what traditional bricks-and-mortar and online businesses spend for customer acquisition is enormous.

The National Retail Federation reports that traditional department stores spend about 3.5 percent of their sales revenue on advertising. By contrast, Shop.org, www.shop.org, an e-commerce trade organization, reports that dot-com retailers spend an average of 76 percent of their revenues on acquiring new customers. While appearing to be extravagant, e-tailers claim that it takes more effort to grab customers' attention when you're one of millions of sites on the Internet than it does if you're a business with a real building in a great location. Consequently, these companies do anything they can to attract customers. However, on the downside, they don't always retain those customers to gain repeat sales. In other words, those businesses can't recoup their acquisition costs if customers don't buy again from them. By comparison, traditional retailers spend about 16 percent of their advertising dollars keeping current customers happy, while e-tailers allocate only about 3 percent.

Shop.org reports that the average acquisition cost for an e-tailer is $42 per customer. That cost comes down to $22 if the retailer has multiple channels of distribution like Victoria's Secret, which has retail outlets, a catalog, and a Web site. Jupiter Communications estimates that e-tailers spend anywhere between 1.5 and 2.5 times the actual price of an order to acquire that customer. So, if your customer pays $60 for an order, you're probably spending between $90 and $150 just to get that customer to the site to make that first purchase. If you don't find a way of nurturing customers to keep them coming back, you'll never recoup the acquisition cost.

If you're entering a market that has dominant players, estimates indicate you must spend a minimum of $10 million on advertising, and more likely $60 million, if you want to make a strong impression. Putting all this in perspective, AOL spent $808 million (17 percent of its revenues) in advertising for only one year.

Now, contrast what the *Inc.* 500 spend on sales and marketing with what we've been talking about for e-commerce. In February 1999, *Inc.* reported that out of its 1998 *Inc.* 500 group:

- 3% of the companies spent *less than 1% of revenues*
- 43% of the companies spent *1%–5% of revenues*
- 25% of the companies spent *6%–10% of revenues*
- 18% of the companies spent *11%–20% of revenues*
- 9% of companies spent *21%–50% of revenues*
- 1% of companies spent *more than 50% of revenues*

What can you do to keep acquisition costs down and customer loyalty up? Here are some tips:

- **Build your brand quickly.** The sooner you gain brand recognition, the sooner your marketing costs, as a percentage of revenue, typically come down. Don't just try to build your brand on the Internet. You must create awareness in offline situations as well.

- **Encourage referrals.** Referrals are the least expensive way to get new customers who are more likely to purchase and remain customers over the long term.

# Creating a Marketing Plan

Marketing includes everything you do to create awareness for your business and its products and services — the name you give your business, the features and benefits of your products and services, the way you deliver those products and services, where you locate your business, and the advertising and promotion tactics you use to get customers and keep them.

Think of your marketing plan as a living guide to your customer relationships, containing the goals, strategies, and tactics that you use to build your customer base. With a new venture, your goal may be creating awareness for your company and capturing those initial customers. Later on, you can create a marketing plan designed to grow your business to the next level.

An effective marketing plan is compatible with your overall company goals and has short-term as well as long-term objectives. A marketing plan takes time to play out.

One big reason marketing plans fail is that their creators don't stick with them long enough to see the results. Most marketing strategies don't provide immediate results. Expect them to take some time.

## Preparing to plan

An effective marketing plan is the result of preparation — not a lot, but some is necessary. Try following these important steps:

1. **List your marketing options.** Because so many ways of marketing to your customers exist, you must explore all the possibilities. Don't limit yourself to what you already know or even what your industry already does. Talk with other business owners, customers, and suppliers. Check out books and articles on successful marketing strategies that others have used. A strategy that worked well in another industry may also fit in with your industry.

2. **Start to think like a customer.** Take a look at your business and what you're offering from the customer's point of view. What would entice *you* to make a purchase? Richard Branson, the founder of Virgin Airways, looked at his service from the point of view of a passenger and designed his planes to meet their needs.

3. **Know your competition as well as you know your own business.** You have to know what others in your industry are doing so that you can find the gaps that your business can fill. In fact, one of the best tactics is becoming your competitors' customer.

4. **Rank the pros and cons of your options.** Of the many options you've collected, start by eliminating those that aren't feasible right now, usually because you can't afford them. Then rank your top ten choices based on how well they reach the customer.

Once you have completed these steps, you're ready to begin writing your marketing plan.

## Writing a one-paragraph marketing plan

One of the best ways to begin the task of preparing a marketing plan is to write a one-paragraph plan that includes all the elements of the complete plan. The advantage of writing a one-paragraph plan is that it forces you to focus on what's important and to determine what your key benefits are — those things that will grab your customers' attention. A good one-paragraph marketing plan looks like:

KosmoTrade assists furniture traders around the world by using an Internet-based portal. This marketing plan creates company awareness and name recognition in the marketplace where the target customer is any organization dealing with furniture. The plan specifically targets small exporters needing buyers in other countries or outlets for excess inventory and importers seeking new vendors under competitive conditions. This value-added e-solution reduces time and risk in finding new customers or suppliers. The company serves a niche market that targets smaller companies wanting access to worldwide business opportunities. Stakeholders view KosmoTrade as a professional, innovative, and customer-focused company with a quality-driven service. Initial marketing tactics include personal selling at industry events, partnering with similar organizations to exchange links and banner ads, listing with major search engines, developing a public relations strategy to create publicity, and generating traffic by providing useful information to the customers. The company uses an average 16 percent of sales to implement the marketing strategy.

*(Authors of this marketing plan: Christopher Besmer and Veronica Havranek, Top Ten Business Plan 2000, Greif Entrepreneurship Center, University of Southern California)*

Now, let's take it apart to see that it consists of:

- ✔ **The purpose of the plan:** What does the plan accomplish? In this case, the plan creates awareness for the company and brand recognition in the marketplace.

- ✔ **The benefits of the product/service:** How does the product or service satisfy a need or help the customer? The KosmoTrade solution reduces the time and risk in finding new customers or suppliers.

- ✔ **The customer:** Who is the primary customer? In this example, the primary customer is any organization dealing with furniture, specifically small exporters needing buyers in other countries or outlets for excess inventory.

- ✔ **The company's identity and product position:** How does the customer view the company and the product? In this case, customers see KosmoTrade as a professional, innovative, and customer-focused company with a quality-driven service.

- ✔ **The market niche:** What niche has the company defined? How does the company differentiate itself? KosmoTrade positions itself in a niche targeting smaller companies that want access to business opportunities worldwide.

✔ **The marketing tactics:** What specific tools can be used to create awareness and build customer relationships? KosmoTrade's initial marketing tactics include personal selling at industry events, partnering with similar organizations to exchange links and banner ads, listing on major search engines, developing a public relations strategy, and generating traffic by providing useful information to the customers.

✔ **The budget: What percentage of sales does marketing represent:** KosmoTrade spends an average of 16 percent of sales to implement the marketing plan.

Each of these parts can be explored and discussed more fully in your marketing plan.

## Defining your customer

In developing your marketing plan, you discover as much as you can about your customer. The more you know, the better you're able to provide what your customer wants. In traditional market research, you generally look at demographics and psychographics. Demographics are characteristics such as ages, income and education levels, and race, while psychographics include attitudes, intentions, values, and lifestyles. Companies like Mediamark Research, Inc., www.mediamark.com, and Simmons Market Research Bureau, www.smrb.com, conduct this type of research by taking random samples of the population to segment the market. Segmenting a market makes it easier to focus on the particular slice of the market that your company intends to serve. In general, the four market segments are

✔ **Product:** Certain products attract certain types of customers.

✔ **Geography:** Different regions have customers with distinct buying habits or tastes and preferences.

✔ **Psychographic characteristics:** Knowing that your typical customer has a specific trait, like a propensity to take risks, helps you design your marketing strategy to reach those particular customers.

✔ **Demographics:** You can segment the market down to the exact neighborhood in terms of what customers purchase, how often, when, and so forth.

You can also segment a market based on the bundle of benefits that you're providing the customer. For example, perhaps your customers look for the highest quality; moreover, they're willing to pay for it. That customer segment differs from customers that seek out the product as inexpensively as possible.

## Doing your market research

The best information you can receive about the customer is the information you gather by getting out and talking to potential customers. See Chapter 6 to take a look at techniques for researching your customer. Doing your own market research means that you get exactly the type of information you want when you want it.

Besides gathering information about your customers, you gain a sense of how customers view your product or service in relation to those of your competitors. Is your product more or less expensive or of higher or lower quality? Product positioning defines the product in terms of its benefits to the customer. Testing your product positioning with your customer is important, because you want to ensure that your customer sees your company and its product in the same light you see it. Test your product positioning statement with several different groups, including:

- **Peers:** Ask people you know to give you their opinions about your positioning statement and how they think the product will do.

- **Members of your distribution channel:** Talk to suppliers, distributors, retailers, and salespeople, who usually have definite opinions about product positioning.

- **Focus group:** Get feedback from customers through focus groups. Make sure these customers aren't the same ones who participated in the design and development of your product. You want unbiased opinions.

- **Test markets:** Check your product positioning by test marketing your product in a specific geographic area.

## Building and protecting your brand

Building brand loyalty nowadays is a difficult but not insurmountable task as long as you build your brand around your company philosophy rather than an image of your products. For example, associating your products with young, sexy, twentysomething people doing exciting things may sell products initially, but when you're building a brand for the long term, you don't want to fight a war of images. Companies like Smith and Hawkens and Starbucks Coffee communicate the philosophies of their companies by making them stand out from the crowd and breaking with the tradition of image advertising.

As you establish a brand name, you need to protect it. Of course, you want to trademark it (see Chapter 8 for more about trademarks). But that's just the beginning; you must protect it from people who misuse or use it incorrectly. Make sure that the media correctly refer to your brand. And when you're selecting your brand name, test it to make sure it does what you want it to do and isn't too similar to existing trade names.

## Packaging can perk up profits

Even packaging is a form of branding and marketing for your company, particularly if you sell consumer products. Carefully designing and testing packaging can mean the difference between a product that sells and one that languishes on the shelf. Declining sales pointed one gourmet cookie company in the South to its customers — major retailers like Neiman Marcus — who thought the packaging didn't fit in well with the rest of their gift items. The cookie company hired a design firm, spent $250,000, and as a return on their investment, saw their sales increase by 50 percent. Packaging tips that can help promote your products suggest that you:

- ✔ Make sure you recognize from the package what the product is — features, directions for use, ingredients, remedies for misuse, quality, and warranty.

- ✔ Make sure key benefits stand out — convenience, price, quality, and so forth.

- ✔ Put your company philosophy on the package — in other words, *customers are our most important assets.*

- ✔ On consumer products, make sure the customer recognizes the product from the package alone without reading anything.

## Pricing the product or service right

No matter how great your product or how well you package and promote it, if the price isn't right, it won't sell. Who determines the price of your product? The customer, of course. Customer perception of the value of the product or service ultimately decides the price. Other situations create guidelines that help you figure out how to price your product or service, including when

- ✔ **Demand is greater than supply.** When you can't supply all the demand for your product, you can price the product higher than market and then reduce the price as your ability to meet demand increases.

- ✔ **Price doesn't matter.** If people need or want your product and purchase it regardless of the price, you can charge a higher price. Generally, these are products, like gasoline, for which there is no real substitute.

- ✔ **You have a great deal of competition.** In this case, you reduce your price to meet or beat your competition.

- ✔ **Your product has unique features.** You may be able to charge a higher price if your product is unique.

- ✔ **Your product introduces new technology.** Again, you want to charge a higher price initially and then reduce the price as competitors enter the market.

- ✔ **Your product positioning will associate your product with a particular price.** For example, if you position your product as the do-it-yourself alternative, customers expect a lower price.

When considering the price of your product or service, take into account the level of sales and profit margin you want to achieve. Look at your costs to produce the product and what the market says the price should be, and then find a point that covers your costs, allows you to make a profit, and offers a correct perception in the marketplace. Examples of common pricing strategies include:

- ✔ **Cost-based pricing.** In this strategy, you add the costs of production and business operations to a profit margin, arriving at a market price.

- ✔ **Sliding on the demand curve.** You introduce the product at a high price in this strategy, and as you begin to achieve economies of scale and your costs decline, you can reduce the price accordingly.

- ✔ **Skimming.** When you have a product that no one else has and demand for it is high, you can enter the market at a high price until competitors force the price down.

- ✔ **Demand-based pricing.** Through market research, you find out what customers are willing to pay for the product, and price accordingly.

- ✔ **Penetration.** When you must grab much of the market quickly, you introduce the product at a low price with minimal profit. Once you have the market share you're after, you can gradually increase the price to match the rest of the market. Be aware that this is a costly strategy in terms of advertising and promotion.

- ✔ **Competition-based pricing.** With this strategy, you price your product in line with your competitions' pricing . . . higher if you are offering a valued-added service or feature.

- ✔ **Psychological pricing.** Your pricing position reflects an odd-even strategy. If you price your product at $10.99, customers perceive it as a bargain; if you price it at $11.00, they perceive it as more expensive.

- ✔ **Loss Leader Pricing.** You price your older products below cost to attract customers to your newer products.

You soon face pricing problems if your prices are always based on costs or always follow the competition, if your new prices are always a percentage increase over the previous year's prices, or if your prices to all your customers are the same. Pricing strategy must be flexible to meet changing market demands. Like anything else, prices are subject to change when the market fluctuates. Failing to modify prices when necessary can mean lost profits.

# Keeping Your Best Customers

Many entrepreneurs spend all their time seeking new customers and forget about taking care of the ones they already have. That's a big mistake. Although it's true that you have to build your customer base when your company is new, at the same time, you must work equally hard to keep the good customers you acquire. Here's why. Most companies lose about 25 percent of their customers annually. If you figure that acquiring a new customer costs about five times as much as maintaining an existing one, you realize a lot of money is going down the drain. About 65 percent of an average company's business comes from current, satisfied customers. In this section, you find out a variety of techniques for keeping customers.

# Creating your promotional mix

Promotion is the creative side of marketing. It deals with guerrilla advertising, publicity, sales, and personal selling tactics. Your choice of tactics is called the *promotional mix*, which differs from company to company, depending first and foremost on your budget but also on the type of business you have, your goals, and your target market.

Your promotional mix must include the input of everyone in your company and the tactics that convey benefits to the customer. Advertising and publicity are two of those tactics.

## Advertising

Advertising creates product and company awareness. Advertising is everywhere you look, from the sign in a store window to the billboard along the highway, from the drive-time radio spot to the prime-time TV slot. Advertising creates awareness but can't guarantee sales, because most customers aren't as swayed by advertising the way they used to be. Moreover, most entrepreneurial start-ups can't afford to compete in the advertising arena with bigger companies, so they revert to what are called *guerrilla tactics,* less expensive methods that target specific customers. In general, any advertising you do must

   ✔ Target your specific customer.

   ✔ Convey a positive image of your company.

   ✔ Reflect the vision and culture of your company.

   ✔ Ask for the sale.

*Asking for the sale* is one advertising accomplishment that many entrepreneurs forget about. You can do everything else right, but if you don't convince the potential customer to commit to the purchase, you have nothing.

Advertising provides several choices for you. See Figure 18-1 for an example of a media comparison chart. Your choice of media depends on your type of business and common practices within your industry. In general, you choose between print and broadcast media.

**Media Comparison Chart**

**Figure 18-1:**
This chart compares the effectiveness of advertising in various forms of media, from newspapers to television to the Internet.

| Type of Media | Advantages | Disadvantages | Hints |
|---|---|---|---|
| **PRINT MEDIA** | | | |
| Newspaper | • Broad coverage in a selected geographic area<br>• Flexibility and speed in bringing to print and changing<br>• Generates sales quickly<br>• Relatively inexpensive | • Reaches more than target market<br>• Difficult to attract reader attention<br>• Short life | • Look for specialized newspapers for better targeting<br>• Include a coupon or 800 number<br>• Locate ad on right-hand page above the fold |
| Magazines | • Can target special interests<br>• More credible than newspapers<br>• Longer life | • Expensive to design, produce, and place<br>• Doesn't reach as many people at once | • Look for regional editions<br>• Use a media buying service<br>• Use color effectively<br>• Check on "remnant space," leftover space that must be filled before magazine goes to print |
| **Direct Marketing** *(direct mail, mail order, coupons, telemarketing)* | • Lets you close the sale when the advertising takes place<br>• Coverage of wide geographic area<br>• Targets specific customers<br>• More sales with fewer dollars<br>• More information provided<br>• Highest response rate | • Not all products suitable<br>• Need consumable products for repeat orders<br>• Response rate on new catalogs is very small, about 2% | • Create a personalized mailing list and database from responses<br>• Use several repeat mailings to increase the response rate<br>• Entice customers to open the envelope |
| Yellow Pages | • Good in the early stages for awareness<br>• Good for retail/service type businesses | • Relatively expensive<br>• Only targets local market | • Create ad that stands out on the page<br>• Look at what attracts your attention on a page |
| Signs | • Relatively inexpensive<br>• Encourage impulse buying | • Outlive their usefulness fairly quickly and are no longer noticed | • Don't leave sale signs in windows too long; people will no longer see them |

## BROADCAST MEDIA

| Media | Advantages | Disadvantages | Tips |
|---|---|---|---|
| Radio | • Good for local or regional advertising<br>• Good if you have a product or service that is quickly and easily understood | • Can't be a one-shot ad, must do several—a series<br>• Can be expensive in high demand time slots | • Advertise on more than one station to saturate market<br>• Sponsor a national radio program<br>• Provide the station with finished recorded commercials<br>• Stick to 30 second ads with music<br>• Depending on your target audience, try for drive-time slots geared to commuters |
| Television | • Second most popular form of advertising<br>• People can see and hear about product/service<br>• Can target at national, regional, or local level | • Very expensive for both production and on-air time<br>• Must be repeated frequently to be effective | • Time based on GRP (gross rating points). Range is $5-$500 per GRP. Use only if can purchase 150 GRPs per month for three months.<br>• Seek help of media buying service |
| Cable TV Shopping | • Good for new consumer products<br>• Target the consumer<br>• Good products sell out in minutes | • Not a long-term strategy<br>• Only good for products between $15 and $50<br>• Product must be demonstrable | • Call network for vendor information kit<br>• Contact buyer for your product category<br>• Be prepared to fill an initial order between 1,000 and 5,000 units |
| Infomercial | • Good for consumer items that can't be explained quickly<br>• Good for impulse buy items | • Very expensive to produce<br>• Hit rate is about 10 % | • Most profitable times are late nights, mornings, and Saturday and Sunday during the day<br>• Test time slots and markets to confirm effectiveness |

## INTERNET

| Media | Advantages | Disadvantages | Tips |
|---|---|---|---|
| | • Can reach customers on a global level less expensively than direct marketing or mass marketing via snail mail<br>• Good way to create repeat customers by providing added value at the Web site | • Difficult to target your audience<br>• Difficult to capture attention of Web surfers<br>• Can be expensive to do well<br>• Need to do offline advertising to get customers to the site | • Look for Web partners who will let you place links on their sites<br>• Put your Web address on your business card and all offline advertising and promotion for your company |

### Publicity

The best way to promote your company is through free publicity, which is basically free advertising for a product or business through various forms of media. The key to getting free publicity is having a product or company that is newsworthy, that has a great story. Ben & Jerry's, the ice cream producer, won millions of dollars worth of free publicity with their tale of a company that issued a public offering for the people in its home state of Vermont. If you believe that your company has an important story to tell, try

- ✔ Writing to a reporter, suggesting the idea and then following up with a phone call. It's better if you initially get to that reporter through a referral.

- ✔ Issuing a press release that answers who, what, where, when, and why.

- ✔ Building a press kit that contains a press release, bios of the founding team, photos of the key people in the story, background information, and any other media about the business.

By making the reporters' jobs easier, you're more likely to get them to write something about your company. If an article is written, be sure to get reprints that you can use in your advertising and promotion.

## Building relationships

To build relationships with customers, you need more than a mere collection of information. You need a dialogue with your customers either by phone, by e-mail, interactively over the Internet, or in person. The point is that the dialogue must be a two-way conversation if you're going to obtain any useful information. For making your relationship building efforts more effective:

- ✔ Do not attempt to sell every time you talk to your customer. Let them know that sometimes you call just to see how they enjoy their dealings with your company.

- ✔ Be sure to provide voice mail, so customers can leave messages or voice complaints after business hours.

- ✔ Put up a Web site where customers can post or send you their ideas and thoughts.

### Developing a customer information file

One of the more important support components of any customer relationship program is the customer information file (CIF). It contains all the information you collect over time about the customer. Beside the normal contact information, you'll want to include:

- ✔ How recently the customer made a purchase

- ✔ How often the customer purchases

- How much the customer spends on average per purchase
- How much the customer spent during the past six months or year
- Where purchases were made and how
- Any purchases returned and why
- Method of payment and debt history
- Types and dates of promotions the company sent to the customer
- Information gathered through dialoguing with the customer
- Customers' perceptions about the company's products, versus competitors

### Rewarding the best customers

Don't expect to build long-term relationships with all your customers once the number of those customers becomes large. Do your best, but remember that as few as 24 percent of your customers account for 95 percent of your revenues, so you really want to make sure that you're taking care of that precious 24 percent. At the same time, you want to identify your worst customers, those that cost you time and money but never buy from you on a regular basis or those with a poor debt history. If you're keeping good CIFs — especially if you're using a relational database — finding the best and worst customers won't be difficult.

CASE STUDY

# Getting your company noticed

Guerrilla advertising approaches help your company become noticed in an ever-increasing crowd of competitors. Guerrilla tactics include:

- Sponsoring a special event. For example, one company presents a *business-after-hours* event, displaying its products to an invited group of professionals who can enjoy drinks and hors d'oeuvres. Another company sponsors a Little League baseball team, providing team shirts and trophies.

- Demonstrating your expertise in a particular area. One public relations firm creates awareness by developing a newsletter focusing on women who work in large organizations. Taking an often humorous approach, the newsletter captures a lot of attention.

- Giving your products away to people who can get you free publicity like celebrities and others with access to the media.

- Offering free information on your Web site, attracting visitors and keeping your current customers coming back.

- Being the first to do something. For example, one entrepreneur, who was the first to offer a coffeehouse in his Idaho community in 1992, continues to innovate with amenities like live entertainment and a cybercafe.

Two proven ways to reward your best customers so they'll keep coming back and referring other customers to your business are

- ✔ **Frequency programs or VIP clubs.** If you fly, you are no doubt familiar with frequency programs in which you receive mileage credits each time you fly. You can redeem the credits for airline tickets when you've accumulated enough. Because rewards increase with use, you have an incentive to continue using that airline. Other businesses successfully use frequency programs. For example, many drugstores use cosmetic cards that give the holder a discount after they purchase a certain amount of cosmetics. Pizza parlors often offer frequent user cards that entitle the holder to a free pizza after they purchase a certain number of pizzas. Still other businesses offer memberships that entitle members to special discounts and other benefits that regular purchasers don't receive.

- ✔ **Just-in-time programs.** Many businesses keep track of dates and special occasions that are important to their customers. Many program their databases to automatically send a message to the customer on a particular date (in other words, a birthday, anniversary, and so forth) or remind the customer of a special sale on something they typically buy. If you keep an up-to-date CIF, you have a good idea what your customer usually purchases.

## Give yourself a test

If you think you're doing everything right when it comes to taking care of your customers, ask yourself these questions:

1. Do you treat all your customers the same?

2. Do you have a learning relationship with your customers? Do you learn from them and they from you?

3. Do you keep your customers?

4. Is your business organized around customers?

If you treat all your customers the same, you're wasting time and money. Spend the majority of your marketing dollars on the 24 percent of your customers who provide that 95 percent of your revenues.

You create a learning relationship with your customers by listening to them and learning their needs and requirements. Successful computer companies like Dell are interested in knowing why you need a computer before they ever get to the question of how fast you want that computer to be.

Try never letting your customers go to someone else to satisfy their needs. You should have a huge network of contacts, so that once your customers have purchased from you, you can refer them to one of your strategic partners when they need something that you might not carry. That way your customers think of you no matter what they need.

Make sure that everyone in your company understands the needs of the customer and how they can help to satisfy them. In that way, your company becomes customer focused.

# Chapter 19

# Proving You Can Make Money: The Financial Plan

### In This Chapter

▶ Lining up the parts of a financial plan

▶ Developing financial statements

▶ Analyzing financial statements with ratios

▶ Managing your working capital and accounts payable

*F*inding out that you need a business plan with a good set of financial statements and projections won't come as a surprise to you when you want to seek funding from a bank or investor. But how many times have you heard of a business that started without much planning and with financial forecasts that weren't grounded in reality?

Take, for example, Ben & Jerry's Homemade, Inc., the now famous ice cream manufacturer. The two entrepreneurs projected their first year's sales at $90,000. Imagine how many ice cream cones they needed to sell to bring in that $90,000. Where did that number come from, anyway? Actually, they pulled it out of the air, because they needed a figure to work with when preparing their financials. In reality, first-year sales for Ben & Jerry's totaled $200,000.

Financial plans of most start-up businesses don't end up matching reality. And that may make you wonder why it's so important to go to so much trouble preparing them. The answer: It isn't what you discover from the results; it's what you discover from the process of planning your company's finances that's so valuable. Too many small business owners entrench themselves in the daily activities of their businesses, never taking time to take stock of where the business is and where it's headed. These owners manage their operations on a day-to-day basis without identifying any goals. Going through the process of planning your financial future organizes and focuses you on important factors about your business that you probably never knew about.

Another important reason for planning your company's financial future is to help it deal with changes. If, from time to time, you're evaluating your company's strengths and weakness, what's happening in your market and industry, and what your competition is doing, you're putting your company in a better position for discovering new opportunities and avoiding problems.

One scenario I've run across too many times involves a business owner who tells me she believes that her company is not generating enough cash flow. Although she's content that cash flow at least isn't in the red, when I ask her if specific expenses of the business are increasing, or if her accounts receivable level is changing, she doesn't know. So, that fact tells me that her concern about the condition of her company results from a lack of information. She doesn't know what's going on, and that can make anyone nervous.

In this chapter, you discover the steps needed to create a successful financial plan and ways to manage your cash flow so that your business stays healthy.

# Identifying the Components of a Successful Financial Plan

A successful financial plan is not just a matter of putting together some financial statements and ratios. That's fine if your goal is just to report on the status of your business. But if you want to create a financial plan that helps you build a healthy foundation for the future of your business, you need to do much more.

Consider the exploits of an entrepreneur with a small retail outlet who experiences three consecutive years of losses after two years of profits. After financing the business with as much as he was willing or able to scrounge up, this particular owner was thinking his business was not worth saving. He didn't know what was wrong.

Guess what! He didn't have a financial plan. Instead of waiting and wading through three excruciating years of losses, or until he saw no way out of the situation, a financial plan may have given him the answers he needed during the first year that he experienced a loss. This entrepreneur, however, was fortunate enough to find a way out. Seeking the helpful advice of a turnaround consultant (someone who specializes in saving failing businesses), he put together pro forma cash flow and income statements in addition to preparing a break even analysis. That information told him how much he had to sell to make the retail outlet work and how much he had to cut his operating expenses. By setting small goals to give himself a sense of achievement and tracking his most important financial numbers on a daily basis, within a matter of months, this entrepreneur's company produced a modest profit, and its future now looks bright.

## Starting with goals

Every good plan starts with goals. After setting the long-term, mid-range, and short-term financial goals for a company, every good plan needs strategies, or ways to achieve those goals. After developing strategies to meet a company's financial goals, a plan requires tactics, or tasks that you need to do to implement the strategies. The following table provides a basic example:

| | |
|---|---|
| Goal: | To become the number one company in the industry. |
| Strategy: | Increase sales by 20 percent each year for the next five years. |
| Tactic: | Introduce a new distribution channel on the Internet. |

Having goals focuses the energy and enthusiasm of an organization on specific targets and helps a company make better decisions. For example, if you're considering investing in a particular new product but it doesn't help you meet your overall goal, you may want to forego the investment.

Support for the goals of an organization from key decision-makers is critical, but those higher-ups don't necessarily have to be the originators of the goals. Many great company goals came from the bottom up.

The key is acceptance. Everyone buys into the goals for the company so that focus and energy are not dissipated.

Many business goals take the form of financial numbers like sales, profits, assets, and working capital. These are good jumping off points, because you obviously know when you achieve them; however, they must be combined with strategies for achieving them. One large company I work with is great at setting goals and defining outcomes for the organization, but officials there never talk about how they're going to reach those outcomes. Consequently, everyone has a different idea about how to reach the goals, and in the confusion, they never are achieved. Always associate a goal with a strategy.

## Looking at capital budgeting

Your *capital budget* — what you plan to spend on assets like plant, equipment, and office space — is really a financial plan to achieve your company's objectives and to allocate its resources among the many investments that you need to make. In capital budgets, you look for alternatives to determine the best use of your funds, so that you can optimize the returns for your shareholders — the owners of the company. You look at the *cost of capital,* which is generally the amount of interest, equity, or return on investment charged by the various sources from which you acquire the money.

Budgeting for *capital expenditures* is an important part of financial planning and your capital budget. Preparing your capital expenditures budget essentially sets up a plan to acquire and manage the assets of your company. You may have bootstrapped the start-up of your company with little or no assets, but over time, you need to add equipment, increase your office or plant space, expand your product line, or invest in other forms of long-term assets.

Capital expenditures differ from current expenses because the company benefits from them for more than a year (or one fiscal period if the company's business year isn't based on a calendar year). They are part of the following decisions to make or buy, lease or purchase:

✔ Is it financially better to lease that new truck than to buy it?

✔ Is it better for the company to invest in an automated assembly system or outsource to another manufacturer?

✔ Which projects should the company fund, given its limited resources?

✔ How many projects can the company take on at one time?

Decisions about research and development also fall into this category.

Because capital expenditures require more time and effort in the decision-making process, having an evaluation system in place for making such decisions is a good idea. You must weigh the cost of investing in, say, a piece of equipment, the length of time required to recoup the cost, the return on investment, and the alternatives to making a purchase. Typically, projects, equipment, and other capital items that have the highest return on investment are where you spend your precious dollars.

## Budgeting for operations

The *operating budget* is really a group of several budgets that all relate to the operations of the business:

✔ Sales budget

✔ Production budget

✔ Direct materials budget

✔ Direct labor budget

✔ Factory overhead

The operating budget is broken out into these sub-budgets, which make analyzing what's going on with the business and finding potential problem areas much easier. Take a look at five operating sub-budgets.

## Sales budget

The *sales budget* presents a forecast for your company's sales levels over the period of time that you're considering — usually a year. This budget is normally prepared first because sales affect every other budget. The steps you use to prepare a sales budget are

1. **Estimating the number of units you think you'll sell during the forecast period.**

2. **Estimating the sales price per unit.**

3. **Multiplying the number of units to be sold by the price per unit to arrive at an estimate of your sales revenue.**

You estimate sales price and units separately because they are correlated, meaning that as the number of units you produce increases, the price per unit often (but not always) comes down, and vice versa. If you want to find out ways to estimate sales, check out Chapter 11. See Table 19-1 for an example of what a sales budget looks like.

| **Table 19-1** | **Sample Sales Budget** | | |
|---|---|---|---|
| | *Year 1* | *Year 2* | *Year 3* |
| Projected Sales in Units | $10,000 | $15,000 | $20,000 |
| Sales Price per Unit | $16 | $14 | $12 |
| Total Sales | $160,000 | $210,000 | $240,000 |

## Production budget

The *production budget* presents your company's output measured in units of the products you're producing or purchasing for resale. The production budget is derived from the sales budget and projected demand. Of course, these two items never are perfectly matched, so you have to account for adjustments that are the result of overproduction or underproduction. Those adjustments are found in the inventory budget. See Table 19-2 for an example of a production budget based on the sales budget you saw in Table 19-1.

| **Table 19-2** | **Sample Production Budget** | | |
|---|---|---|---|
| | *Year 1* | *Year 2* | *Year 3* |
| Projected Sales in Units | $10,000 | $15,000 | $20,000 |
| Beginning Inventory | $1,500 | $2,500 | $500 |
| Units in Production | $11,000 | $13,000 | $22,000 |
| Ending Inventory | $2,500 | $500 | $2,500 |

### Direct materials budget

Using the production budget, you can estimate the direct materials you need and the cost of those materials. If you are producing several products, you want to separate them so that you can track each one to determine which are doing well and which aren't. The *direct materials budget* includes:

- Production in units
- Material needed per unit
- Total amount of material needed (units × material per unit)
- Cost per unit of material
- Total projected materials cost

### Direct labor budget

In the *direct labor budget,* you look at the cost of labor required to produce your products. You start by estimating hours of work per unit produced and then the dollar amount per labor hour. Multiply the two and you get the total direct labor cost.

### Factory overhead

The last budget you build depicts the costs related to *factory overhead,* including management salaries and facility costs — all the costs that you can't trace directly to the production of the product. These costs aren't as easy to break out according to the specific product, so they're often allocated in a way that makes sense for the particular type of business you're in.

## Financial forecasts and ratios

Your financial plan includes a complete set of financial statements:

- Cash flow statement
- Income statement
- Balance sheet

The cash flow statement is vital because it reflects the true financial health of the business — in other words its ability to pay its obligations. The income statement tells you if your business made a profit or suffered a loss during the period. The balance sheet gives you a snapshot of the business's net worth. You can find out how to build these financial statements in the next section.

Another important component of your financial plan is the ability to calculate ratios that provide you with a better understanding of what's going on in your business. Ratios indicate financial health and stability. In the section about "Using Financial Ratios to Judge Performance," you find out how to calculate several important ratios.

# Building the Financial Statements

Financial statements provide a great deal of information about the financial condition of a company. Everyone, from investors to lenders to employees, managers, suppliers, customers, and in some cases, the Securities and Exchange Commission, is interested in financial statements. The information in financial statements helps anyone who is interested decide whether to invest in a company, make a loan, or take a management position.

Looking at deviations from expected financial performance and differences from period to period also produce important information about a company's financial health. The information that key decision-makers within your organization require influences financial reports. For example, your marketing manager may want to see sales levels per salesperson to spot problems. Your production manager may use financial reports to evaluate the potential purchase of a piece of equipment designed to save time and money over the long term. At a higher level, the CEO may want to know how the company's international sales stack up in proportion to its total revenue picture.

## Reviewing the income statement

In Chapter 11, I talked about how to develop an income statement. In general, the formula for the income statement is:

**Revenues – Expenses = Net Profit or Net Loss**

See Figure 19-1 for an example of an income statement.

The income statement in Figure 19-1 shows that the sample company became profitable in 2000, but it doesn't say how healthy the company is in terms of cash flow. The Cash Flow from Operations statement provides that information. Looking at the differences between the two years can uncover potential problems. For example, sales increased by $150,000 but advertising declined by $2,000, which is counterintuitive and gives rise to questions like: Does this reflect more targeted and effective advertising tactics? Did the company sell more products to its current customers, bringing acquisition costs down? The answers require further research.

Total operating expenses increased by about 4 percent, while gross profit increased by 53 percent, which combined may be a good sign that the company is keeping its overhead under control while it grows. However, it can also be a warning that if the company continues to grow at its current pace, it must prepare for increases in overhead.

| | 1999 | 2000 | Difference |
|---|---|---|---|
| Net Sales | 500,000 | 650,000 | 150,000 |
| Cost of Sales | 350,000 | 420,000 | 70,000 |
| Gross Profit | 150,000 | 230,000 | 80,000 |
| | | | |
| Operating Expenses: | | | |
| Wages & Salaries | 55,000 | 59,000 | 4,000 |
| Rent & Lease Payments | 9,000 | 9,000 | 0 |
| Utilities | 7,800 | 8,403 | 603 |
| Insurance | 15,000 | 18,000 | 3,000 |
| Advertising | 12,000 | 10,000 | (2,000) |
| Vehicle Operation/Maint. | 35,000 | 35,000 | 0 |
| Accounting & Legal | 4,000 | 2,500 | (1,500) |
| Payroll Taxes | 7,600 | 8,900 | 1,300 |
| Depreciation | 2,970 | 3,300 | 330 |
| Total Operating Expenses | 148,370 | 154,103 | 5,733 |
| | | | |
| Net Operating Income | 1,630 | 75,897 | 74,267 |
| Less: Interest Expense | (4,620) | (5,445) | (825) |
| Net Taxable Income | (2,990) | 70,452 | 73,442 |
| Less: Income Taxes | (31,925) | (34,209) | (2,284) |
| **Net Income** | **(34,915)** | **36,243** | **71,158** |

**Figure 19-1:**
This sample income statement details how sales and expenses result in a company's net income.

# Developing the balance sheet

The balance sheet tells you the value of the business at a particular point in time. It takes into account the assets of the company, such as equipment, inventory, cash, accounts receivable, property, and patents. It also shows the liabilities or obligations the company has entered into, such as notes payable, accounts payable, wages and taxes payable, and installment loans. The owners' equity section presents the shareholders' residual interest in the company after the liabilities are subtracted from the assets. Shareholders' residual interest is reported in the form of common stock, preferred stock, and retained earnings. The basic formula of the balance sheet is:

**Assets = Liabilities + Owners' equity**

Take a look at Figure 19-2 to see an example of a balance sheet.

The first section of the balance sheet covers the assets, which represent the actual cost of the items listed. Current assets, those consumed within the year, are considered to be liquid. Fixed assets are the company's resources that have longer lives; they may be tangible items such as equipment and facilities or intangible such as patents and licenses. Fixed assets, with the exception of land, are displayed less depreciation. The value of land is not depreciated.

| | 1999 | 2000 |
|---|---|---|
| **Assets** | | |
| Current Assets: | | |
| Cash | 21,450 | 44,025 |
| Accounts Receivable | 42,533 | 90,090 |
| Inventory | 39,875 | 92,606 |
| Prepaid Expenses | 0 | 8,250 |
| Total Current Assets | 103,858 | 234,971 |
| | | |
| Fixed Assets: | | |
| Land | 49,500 | 49,500 |
| Building | 247,500 | 247,500 |
| Vehicles | 52,800 | 57,750 |
| Equipment | 33,000 | 37,950 |
| Less: Accumulated Depreciation | (34,650) | (37,950) |
| Total Net Fixed Assets | 348,150 | 354,750 |
| **Total Assets** | **452,008** | **589,721** |
| | | |
| **Liabilities & Owner's Equity** | | |
| Current Liabilities | | |
| Notes Payable | 34,831 | 62,700 |
| Accounts Payable | 20,130 | 27,904 |
| Accruals Payable | 3,762 | 6,088 |
| Total Current Liabilities | 58,723 | 96,692 |
| | | |
| Long-term Liabilities | | |
| Installment Loan Payable | 0 | 42,354 |
| Mortgage Payable | 181,500 | 174,900 |
| Total Long-term Liabilities | 181,500 | 217,254 |
| **Total Liabilities** | **240,223** | **313,946** |
| | | |
| Owner's Equity: | | |
| Capital Stock | 49,500 | 88,575 |
| Retained Earnings | 162,285 | 187,200 |
| **Total Owner's Equity** | **211,785** | **275,775** |
| | | |
| **Total Liabilities & Owner's Equity** | **452,008** | **589,721** |

**Figure 19-2:**
This sample balance sheet depicts the basic accounting equation — Assets = Liabilities + Owner's equity.

The part of the balance sheet that lists liabilities uses a similar format, showing current and long-term liabilities.

The important thing to remember about a balance sheet is that it must balance! In other words, the asset side of the balance sheet must equal the liabilities plus owner's equity side. Again, comparing balance sheets from one year to the next provides you with valuable information, because you find out

- ✔ If accounts receivable and inventory increase or decrease relative to sales during the same period.
- ✔ If debt financing increases or decreases during the period.
- ✔ If accounts payable are at an appropriate level relative to sales.
- ✔ If sales increase to such an extent that additional investment in equipment is necessary.
- ✔ If the business's operations are producing sufficient cash flow.

## Creating the cash flow from operations statement

Chapter 11 explains how building a simple cash flow statement helps you figure out how much capital you need to start a business, but equally important is the ability to plan and manage for cash, both now and into the future. This section demonstrates how to prepare a cash flow statement for a growing business.

Summarizing the process, the cash flow statement reports on the cash flow from operations, financing, and investing activities of the company for a specific period of time. Important factors to remember when you're thinking about cash flow are

- ✔ You must make sure that your company has enough cash to meet all its obligations.
- ✔ You must identify alternative sources of cash for times when it's needed, along with the forms and terms associated with using those sources.
- ✔ You need to forecast and plan for the financial requirements of your company's operations into the future.

Cash flow is not a measure of your company's performance; it's a measure of your company's health and ability to meet its obligations. You can have a healthy cash flow and not have a company that's growing and performing well within its market. Similarly, profit is a measure of performance but not necessarily of health and ability to meet obligations, since you can have a profitable company that doesn't have the cash to pay its taxes, for example.

When planning for future cash needs, you need to look at short-term and long-term needs. Short-term needs usually center on the timing and the amount of cash flow. So short-term planning is about managing cash inflows and outflows.

The typical planning horizon for short-term goals is one month. Some companies find, however, that because of the nature of their businesses, they need to manage cash flow on a daily basis. Maintaining sufficient cash on hand to cover shortfalls is a wise choice for these businesses, as well as for those for which the size of cash inflows and outflows is difficult to predict.

Long-term needs are usually related to the acquisition of capital assets like equipment and facilities and are based on long-term goals for the growth of the company.

Cash inflows include such things as cash sales and collected accounts receivable, while cash outflows consist of payments for inventory, payments of accounts payable, and payments associated with payroll taxes, rent, utilities, and so forth. All are activities related to operations. Non-operating cash flows come from bank loans, additional investments by owners, the sale of assets, payment of principal or interest on debt, dividend distribution, or the purchase of fixed assets.

## Preparing the statement

Once you prepare and begin operating with a cash flow statement in your business, you want to link the income statement items with changes in balance sheet items arising from normal operations from one period to the next. Take at look at Figure 19-3 to see an example of this statement. It's linked to the income statements and balance sheets that were discussed in the two previous sections.

If your eyes are crossing now from all these new financial terms and calculations, you may want to skip this next part, but be sure to discuss it with your financial advisor, because the cash flow statement is vital to your business's health.

For those readers who are ready to tackle the preparation of a cash flow from operations statement, I recommend that you have a calculator handy and make copies of Figures 1 through 3 so you can easily refer to them.

Let's look at the steps you need to take to prepare this statement.

1. **Adjust sales to a cash basis.**

   Note that sales for 2000 were $650,000, but they were not all cash sales; some were made on credit. On the balance sheet, you find that accounts receivable increased from $42,533 in 1999 to $90,090 in 2000, so it appears that the company extended significantly more credit in 2000. Extending that credit results in a cash drain for revenues the company didn't collect. Although sales increased, cash flow from sales did not. So you need to adjust sales down by the amount of increase in receivables.

2. **Adjust the cost of sales.**

   Your cost of sales is the cost of goods you actually sold in the accounting period. It is affected by changes in the level of inventory, which is reflected in the current assets on the balance sheet and by changes in accounts payable and current liabilities on the balance sheet. Notice on the income statement that in 2000, the company had a cost of sales of $420,000. Inventory increased by $52,731 and accounts payable by $7,774 (on the balance sheet). The increase in inventory is a cash outflow that doesn't show up in the income statement, so it must be added to the cost of sales. The increase in accounts payable means that the company was using supplier credit and keeping more of their cash. This increase is deducted from the cost of sales.

3. **Adjust the operating expenses.**

   Because depreciation is a non-cash expense that reduces revenue, operating expenses don't appear to be as much on the cash flow statement as they appear on the income statement. Similarly, accruals are unpaid obligations and are a current liability on the balance sheet, because they represent money retained in the company. So you must deduct the increase from the operating expenses. On the other hand, prepaid expenses are cash outflows that increase operating expenses. You must add the increase in prepaids to the operating expense figure.

| | | |
|---|---:|---:|
| Net Sales | 650,000 | |
| Less Increase in Accounts Receivable | (47,557) | |
| Net Sales Adjusted to a Cash Basis | | 602,443 |
| | | |
| Cost of Sales | 320,925 | |
| Plus: Increase in Inventory | 52,731 | |
| Less: Increase in Accounts Payable | (7,774) | |
| Cost of Sales Adjusted to a Cash Basis | | (365,881) |
| | | |
| Operating Expenses | 155,704 | |
| Less: Depreciation Expense | (3,300) | |
| Less: Increase in Accruals | (2,326) | |
| Plus: Increase in Prepaids | 8,250 | |
| | | |
| Less: Operating Expenses Adjusted to a Cash Basis | | 158,328 |
| | | |
| Taxes Paid | | (34,209) |
| | | |
| Cash Flow (Cash Drain) From Operations | | 44,025 |

**Figure 19-3:**
Cash inflows and outflows result in a company's cash flow from operations.

The results of these calculations show that the company was in a relatively healthy cash position. However, increases in the company's accounts receivable reduced its sales revenues for the period (the amount of cash it took in).

Whenever both inventory and accounts receivable grow at a faster rate than sales, the company needs to beware, because such situations signal a future problem.

A summary of the steps used to prepare a cash flow statement reveals

- An increase in accounts receivable reduces cash flow from sales.
- A decrease in accounts receivable increases cash flow from sales.
- An increase in inventory uses cash, while a decrease in inventory decreases the cost of sales.
- An increase in accounts payable decreases the cost of sales.
- A decrease in payables means that you've paid obligations, so your cost of sales has increased.

## The bottom line on cash

Regardless whether you plowed through the calculations on the sample cash flow from operations statement, here are a few simple rules to follow to ensure that your company's cash flow stays in the black:

- **Tighten up credit and collections.** Follow up immediately if a customer is late on a payment.
- **Set up a cash reserve for bad debts.** Have a cash fund to mediate the effect of unpaid receivables.
- **Take advantage of your suppliers' credit terms.** Always pay your bills on time, but don't pay too early. For example, if you're given 30 days to pay, don't pay on day 5. Keep your money on hand until close to the 30th day.
- **Offer cash discounts.** Provide cash discounts to customers for prompt payment.
- **Manage your inventory carefully.** Inventory you don't need costs you money. If you find that some inventory is not selling, cut prices and move it out to turn it back into cash.
- **Make cash surpluses work for you.** When you have more cash than you need (above your reserve for contingencies), invest it in a short-term certificate of deposit or in the stock market in reliable funds to earn money on it.

> ✔ **Keep payroll under control.** Having more people on hand than you absolutely need takes a lot of cash. Consider outsourcing some of your tasks to retain more of your cash.
>
> ✔ **Cut expenses.** Be careful not to spend freely when you do have a cash surplus; the bills follow quickly. Keep overhead expenses down because they are expenses you continue to pay even when sales decline.

# Using Financial Ratios to Judge Performance

Fortunately, many tools can help you analyze your company's health and even see how your company's attributes stack up against others in your industry or against your own company's performance from period to period. When analyzing financials, you'll want to look at:

> ✔ Sales growth
>
> ✔ Profitability
>
> ✔ Gross Margin (revenue less cost of goods sold, divided by revenue)
>
> ✔ Selling, general and administrative expenses as a percentage of revenue
>
> ✔ Profit earned on asset base (how much you earn per dollar of investment)
>
> ✔ Debt-equity ratio
>
> ✔ Seasonality
>
> ✔ Liquidity

Ratios provide a way of interpreting information from your financial statements in all the areas just listed. But, they *are* useful only if they compare one company with another or compare periods within one company to look for patterns of change. Although it's possible to produce ratios on everything you have in your financials, that would be a waste of time. You want to produce only those ratios that have the most value for your company within your industry. I categorize them into the three most common groups (liquidity ratios, profitability ratios, and leverage ratios) to give you a good start on your analysis.

When you compare your company against another in your industry, you'll probably be comparing it with a public corporation, because companies on the stock exchange are the only ones required to publish their financial statements. This is not a good comparison if you have a small business, because economies of scale and productivity levels are different for large, public companies. It is more likely that you'll use ratios to judge how your business is doing from one month, quarter, or year to the next.

CASE STUDY

## Comparing your business to the industry

Tilt-Up is an up-and-coming construction company located in Sydney, Australia. While it's a relatively small company by industry standards, its founders intend to grow the company and see it compete successfully with the major public and private companies in Australia.

Tilt-Up was interested in comparing its progress against established companies in the

construction industry on three measures: profit margin (gross profit/revenues), return on assets (assets/revenues), and long-term debt to equity (long-term debt/equity). The company created a comparison chart showing the results of their ratio calculations against those of the industry. Here's what it looked like:

| Gross Profit Margin | Return on Assets | Long-term Debt to Equity | |
| --- | --- | --- | --- |
| Tilt-Up | 3.0% | 5.3% | 2 (times) |
| The Construction Industry | 4.3% | 9.1% | 1 (times) |

Tilt-Up appears to be working on a smaller gross profit margin than the industry as a whole. Its 3 percent means that 97 percent of its revenues go to pay its direct costs of producing its products, while 3 percent of revenues are available to pay overhead and make a profit. The industry average is 4.3 percent, which means that the larger companies have cost advantages that come from experience and volume.

With respect to return on assets, again Tilt-Up has a smaller return than the industry at large. But on the matter of long-term debt to equity, Tilt-Up is doing better than industry averages because its equity is two times its debt whereas in the industry, a one-to-one ratio of debt to equity exists on average. What this means is that Tilt-Up is carrying less debt than most companies in the industry.

## Liquidity ratios

Liquidity ratios help you understand your company's ability to meet its short-term obligations and maintain normal operations — in other words, to stay alive. The more liquid assets your company has, the better, because liquid assets convert more easily to cash, and cash is what your business needs. Three good, easy-to-use liquidity ratios are

✔ **Current Ratio:** The current ratio is your total current assets divided by your total current liabilities. So if your business produces a current ratio of 2.02, it means that for every $1 in liabilities, you have $2 in current assets. That's good, because the higher the number, the more liquid your company is. Over time, you want to look for patterns of change in liquidity, so you can catch potential problems early.

✔ **Cash Flow as a Percentage of Net Sales:** With this ratio, you arrive at the amount of cash flow per dollar of sales generated by operations. If, for example, your ratio of cash flow to net sales is $.20, you are producing 20 cents of cash flow from every dollar of net sales. The higher the number, the more liquid your company. Note that if your company has a negative cash flow for the period, you won't be able to calculate this ratio.

✔ **Acid Test:** This is a popular and tougher test for measuring a company's ability to meet its current liabilities with its current assets. The reason this test is tougher is that it removes inventory (which is often difficult to convert to cash, especially if it's obsolete). To calculate this ratio, subtract inventory from your current assets and divide the remainder by your current liabilities. Again, the higher the ratio the better, although the minimum rule of thumb is a 1:1 ratio.

## Profitability ratios

With profitability ratios, you try to view profit from the standpoint of net income, return on investment, and return on equity. Here are three profitability ratios:

✔ **Profit Margin:** With this ratio, you use net income and net sales from your income statement to figure out the dollar amount that remains after subtracting all costs of operations from sales revenues. You find the profit margin by dividing net income by net sales. Compare the percentage you come up with against other similar businesses in your industry to determine whether you're operating your business efficiently.

✔ **Return on Investment or Return on Assets:** Using net income from the income statement and total assets from the balance sheet, you arrive at a percentage that represents the number of dollars of income earned per dollar of capital invested in the business. The higher the number, the greater the return.

✔ **Return on Equity:** You find this ratio by dividing net income by owners' equity to find out the amount of net income earned per dollar of paid-in-capital plus retained earnings, which shows the effectiveness of the use of investor capital.

## Leverage ratios

Leverage ratios measure the level of debt the company maintains. Usually, a high number suggests a riskier situation, because even though the earnings for the company can increase or decline, the debt payments normally remain the same. Two debt ratios that you can use to analyze your company's debt position are

✔ **Times Interest Earned:** This ratio looks at earnings from operating income that is generated to meet interest charges on debt. The greater the earnings relative to the interest expense, the less risky the company is. To calculate this ratio, divide earnings before interest and taxes by interest expense. If you get a number like 16, it means that earnings are 16 times interest expense. Watching this number over time helps signal potential problems.

✔ **Debt to Asset:** This balance sheet ratio measures the percentage of your company's assets that are covered by creditors versus the percentage that are covered by the owners of the company. You calculate this ratio by dividing total debt by total assets. For example, most manufacturers have debt to asset ratios between 0.30 and 0.70. Look at industry averages to see if your company is in the same ballpark.

# Cash Planning: Managing Your Working Capital

Working capital is the money you need to run your business and pay your employees on a regular basis even when your revenues aren't received or collected on a regular basis. Cash planning is vital to your business, especially when you're in the growth mode. The biggest reasons you want to plan ahead for your cash needs are so that you can predict when you might experience a shortfall and plan to tap resources outside your business to cover you until the revenues you expect materialize.

Unfortunately, many businesses don't plan for their cash needs; rather, they react at the last minute when something happens. That's a dangerous position to put your company in, because by that time, you may be too far into a cash crisis to recover. Besides, when you stop paying your suppliers because you're low on cash (and suppliers are one of the first groups small business owners neglect when things get tight), you discover that you've actually shot yourself in the foot. Suppliers who don't get paid usually delay shipments or put your company on a cash-only basis, and that only exacerbates the situation. And if you choose the route of trying to get emergency funding from your friendly banker, you send up a huge red flag that you don't manage your business's finances very well. The bottom line: You need to manage your working capital better and plan for your needs.

## Planning for accounts receivable

You have accounts receivable in your business when you choose to extend credit to your customers, which is something most businesses do. When you extend credit, you allow the customer to keep his or her cash longer, but you have to wait longer for yours — 30, 60, or 90 days is typical.

The secrets to successful accounts receivable management are watching deadlines carefully and being consistent and careful about collecting payments.

Mismanagement of accounts receivable can send a business into a tailspin from which it is difficult to recover. You can manage your accounts receivable effectively if you:

- Minimize the time between shipping, invoicing, and sending billing notices, so you *start the clock* as quickly as possible.

- Regularly review your customers' credit histories with your company, so you can spot problems before they cause irreparable harm to the company. *Age your accounts receivable* on a monthly basis at a minimum (aging is looking at the status of each account in terms of whether the customer is late on payments and by how much).

- Make sure you get credit applications from all new customers.

- Provide incentives to pay early. This is more typical in business-to-business transactions. You provide a discount for an early payment and an interest charge for a delinquent payment.

- Develop a policy for collecting overdue accounts.

### Developing a credit policy

Having an effective credit policy in place makes life much easier and makes handling of credit situations more routine. Your credit policy includes four parts:

- The conditions under which your company extends credit

- The criteria your company has for extending credit

- The length of time for which you will grant credit (in other words, 30 days, 60 days, and so forth)

- A collection policy for customers who fail to comply with your credit policy

### Judging a customer's creditworthiness

The following are examples of standards used by companies to judge the creditworthiness of a potential customer:

- Current debt is free of delinquent payments

- If consumer credit, the applicant has a full-time job

- Income level greater than your minimum requirement

- If consumer credit, applicant has a valid credit card

- If business credit, a Dun & Bradstreet rating of A or better

- A credit bureau report showing no delinquencies

### Collecting your accounts

On the collections side, you want to establish a policy and procedure that you use consistently without discriminating. The following example of a collection policy, which prescribes actions from mild to severe, is only a recommendation:

✔ When the account is ten days overdue, mail a reminder statement.

✔ When the account is 30 days overdue, mail another past-due statement.

✔ When the account is 45 days past due, call the customer.

✔ When the account is 60 days past due, notify the customer in writing that the account will be turned over to a collection agency if payment is not received within 15 days.

The important thing about this process is that it keeps the matter in the forefront, minimizing the chances that the unpaid amount will become a bad debt write-off. Ultimately, you must make the decision as to what the best course of action is for your business, but for the business to stay healthy, you must collect your debts.

### Financing accounts receivable

While you wait for customers to pay what they owe, you still have to pay your employees, purchase supplies, cover the rent and utilities, and meet all other routine expenses of running the business. That's why it's so important to know the *cash cycle* for your business. The cash cycle is the period that runs from the date you buy or produce your product for inventory to the date a customer pays you for it. You can estimate the length of your cash cycle and how much financing you need to support that cash cycle using the following method with its accompanying example.

Suppose your restaurant has an inventory turnover rate of 22 times per year, an average collection period of 30 days, an average payment period for accounts payable of 60 days, cost of sales of $200,000, operating expenses of $120,500, and depreciation expenses of $2,000. Here's how you would calculate the financing to cover the cash cycle:

1. **Figure your cash cycle, which is: (Inventory turnover in days + Average collection period) – Average payment period for accounts payable.**

   Note that inventory turnover is the number of times you sell out of your inventory per year. For example, restaurants turn over about 22 times per year. To figure the cash cycle for a restaurant, do the following:

   Cash cycle = [(360 days/22) + 20] – 30 = 6 days

2. **Calculate the average expenditures per day, which is: (Cost of sales + Expenses – Depreciation) ÷ 360 days.**

   Average expenditures per day = ($200,000 + $120,500 – $2,000) ÷ 360 = $884.72 per day.

3. **Determine your required financing, which is: Your cash cycle in days x Your average expenditures per day.**

   Required financing = 6 days (cash cycle) x $884.72 = $5,308.32 financing required to cover the cash cycle.

### Borrowing against your accounts receivable

Many businesses that deal with accounts receivable resort to borrowing against them to speed up the cash flow from those receivables. Commercial banks and finance companies offer two major types of receivable financing:

- **Collateral:** In this type of financing, you pledge your accounts receivable as collateral against a loan that the bank grants to you. Then your customers' payments are sent directly to the bank.

- **Factoring:** In this type of financing, you actually sell your accounts receivable at a discount to a factor (finance company). The factor then collects on them and gives you the money collected minus a fee.

### Setting up a revolving line of credit

The least expensive way of getting outside help is through a revolving line of credit from your bank. Assuming your business has at least a small track record of success, this may be a good source for you. How do you know how much to request when you go to your banker to ask for a credit line? To answer that question, you need to calculate your cash conversion cycle. Here's how you do that.

1. **Figure out how many days it takes your customers to pay you.**

2. **Calculate the number of days it takes to make your product.**

3. **Count the number of days your product sits in inventory before being sold.**

Now, let's suppose that the answers to those questions are 60, 30, and 30, respectively. Your cash conversion cycle would be as follows:

**60 + 30 – 30 = 60 days**

Next, you want to calculate how much money you need to cover those 60 days. To do that, you multiply your average daily sales by the number of days in your cash conversion cycle. So, for example, if your projected sales for the year are $1 million, here's how you find the amount for the line of credit:

**($1 million ÷ 365 days) × 60 days = approximately $164,340**

I say "approximately" because this figure is a benchmark. Other factors like how fast the company is growing, the impact of a new marketing campaign, and so forth enter into the picture and can cause that number to go up or down.

A seasonal business typically requires more cash during the busy season and less at other times, so you will need to work that out with your banker as well.

Now, what happens to your business if, all a sudden, your customers start paying in 90 days instead of 60? Your cash needs skyrocket to $264,510. If you're not prepared for the increase, it may spell disaster for your business. Check to see what the averages are for accounts receivable in your industry. You may find that you need to manage them better and collect on what's owed to you sooner.

Although it's possible to seek a line of credit at any time, bankers prefer to see you after your first profitable year.

## Managing your accounts payable

Managing your accounts payable is an essential part of total cash management. It involves timing and negotiation. When your business finds itself in a cash crisis, you may need to request an extension of an obligation to a vendor or lender. If that creditor agrees to the extension, you are not released from the obligation, but your cash at least temporarily becomes available. Through that extension, you have received *trade credit,* which carries with it terms that usually involve a cash discount — for example, *3/10, net 30,* meaning you get a 3 percent discount if you pay within 10 days; otherwise, you must pay the full amount within 30 days.

Let's look at this situation in real terms. Suppose you purchase something for $30,000. You have a choice. You can pay $29,100 on any day from one through 10 or the full $30,000 on days 11 to 30.

If you can take advantage of the discount, pay on the 10th day, but no earlier. If you can't pay until after the 10th day, then pay on the 30th day, so you have an additional 20 days to use your money.

Vendors have bills to pay as well and you want to establish a good relationship, because it helps you in the end. Ways you can take advantage of trade credit include:

- ✔ Paying early whenever you can and taking advantage of discounts.
- ✔ Paying COD (cash on delivery) whenever you can and then asking for an additional discount.

✔ Paying your bills on time but not so early that you lose the advantage of using your money.

✔ Choosing quality vendors who give you the longest terms possible.

✔ Contacting the vendor immediately when you find out you can't pay a bill on time. Your vendor will probably work with you as long as you don't ignore the situation.

✔ Staying on top of cash flow management even if it means doing it on a daily basis. You must make sure that you can meet all your business's obligations in a timely manner.

# Chapter 20

# Planning for Things That Go Bump in the Night

. . . . . . . . . . . . . . . . . . . . . . . . . . . . . . . . . . . . . . . . . . .

### In This Chapter

▶ Preparing for bad times

▶ Making your exit with grace and wealth

▶ Exiting a failing business

. . . . . . . . . . . . . . . . . . . . . . . . . . . . . . . . . . . . . . . . . . .

**S**omething interesting happened while I was writing this chapter. I had nearly finished it when I completely lost the file and the backup — presumably to some virus or corrupt file. Talk about things that go bump in the night! How appropriate that a catastrophe like this should happen as I worked on the chapter that focuses on the calamities that befall businesses.

No matter how well you manage your business, the unforeseeable happens. A key employee announces her departure with two weeks' notice. After several good months, your company suddenly experiences a big drop in sales. You get slapped with a lawsuit from a former employee who says he was wrongfully terminated. The list goes on and on.

While in general you can't predict the future, what you can predict with certainty are death, taxes, and change. Yes, I'll stake my reputation on the fact that change is a certainty in the future. The problem is that you don't know exactly what those changes will be. The challenge, therefore, becomes preparing for the unknown.

Another certainty is that at some point in the future you may decide to harvest the wealth you've created and leave your business. Making a graceful exit takes planning so that you don't hurt your business and you're able to reap the full rewards of what you've created. You find out how to do that in this chapter. Graceful exits, however, are not always possible, so you can also discover ways to terminate your business in a manner least harmful to you and your investors and creditors.

It certainly isn't my intent in this chapter to frighten you away from entrepreneurship. Life in all its many facets is full of change, so why should business be any different? And yes, you must prepare for change. In this chapter, I show you how. After all, with change comes opportunity, and that is a good thing.

# Preparing for the Unknown: When Bad Things Happen to Good Companies

When you deal with the public, other businesses, the government, your competitors, and anyone else who comes into contact with your business, something is bound to happen that you'd rather didn't happen. Circumstances like that are almost laws of nature that challenge your business from time to time. Sadly, most businesses suffer more than they need to when bad things happen, because owners didn't understand the challenges out there and didn't have a plan for dealing with change, regardless of whether the change was positive or negative.

I'm not suggesting that you need to think about all the things that can possibly go wrong with your business. That would be a waste of time. Instead, you want to consider the most likely things that can go wrong and focus on ways to deal with them. In this section, I take a positive look at some of the more common threats to your business and give you some tips for coping with them.

## Protecting your company from lawsuits

I'm sure you're well aware of the litigious society we live in. Hardly a day passes that you don't hear about some company getting sued by customers, shareholders, other companies, or the government. Remember the lawsuit aimed at McDonald's Corp. in 1994, when an 81-year-old woman won $160,000 in compensatory damages and $2.7 million in punitive damages after she was burned by the coffee she had purchased at the drive-through. She held the cup between her knees while adding sugar and cream, and it spilled. Her lawsuit claimed that the coffee was too hot. Later a higher court reduced the punitive damages to $480,000, still a princely sum. McDonald's Corp. can afford it; can your small business?

In addition to damage awards, the cost of dealing with lawsuits also hurts businesses. A nonprofit organization that raises and trains guide dogs for the blind was sued by a husband and wife for $160,000 in 1995, when a blind man who was still learning how to use his cane and dog accidentally stepped on and broke the woman's toe. Although the couple eventually dropped the suit, the nonprofit organization, which had nothing to do with the incident, still paid $10,000 in legal fees, not to mention untold hours dealing with the case.

To add fuel to the fire, your own employees may be your biggest threat. Employee lawsuits against former and current employers have increased dramatically. One reason for the increase is that employees can sue without it costing them any money. They hire an attorney who works on a contingency basis (the attorney is paid only if he or she wins the case), so they're not out any money. But they stand to gain a lot, particularly because many of the cases settle out of court. Even when a claim is frivolous, employers end up weighing the risks of going to court, spending thousands of dollars and hundreds of hours of time, and suffering the bad publicity in the press, with the advantages of settling. Just to put an end to their plight, employers often choose to settle. In fact, plaintiff's lawyers often take on these types of cases, even if it looks like the employer will settle for a quick yet paltry $50,000.

As you can see, fighting or even settling a lawsuit can be a costly proposition for a small business. But you can put your company in a better position to avoid lawsuits by:

✔ Carrying the appropriate liability insurance so that if you are sued, at least you're covered financially and won't risk throwing your business into a financial crisis from which it may not recover.

✔ Being extremely careful and cautious about the people you hire. The most important characteristics you need to look for in an employee are trustworthiness and character. Call the references you are given, and check out education and experience claims, which often are embellished or falsified.

✔ Keeping an accurate and current file on each employee. Your employee files must document all the events related to individual employees, including promotions, raises, performance evaluations, training, and infractions of company policy. Write in an objective and factual style, because the file may be viewed as evidence in court. For objectivity, more than one person needs to contribute to the file. Other contributors can include the employee's immediate supervisor, a manager in the employee's area, or anyone in regular contact with the employee.

✔ Putting in writing any communications that you have with your employees about job performance, regardless of whether it's good or bad. Be sure to note the dates and times when these communications occur, and more important, obtain a signed receipt from the employee confirming that he or she has seen your written communication.

✔ Watching your employees for signs of fatigue, mental illness, drug or alcohol use, stress, or aggressive behavior, which may signal potential problems that may eventually require dismissal.

✔ Taking seriously any complaints you receive about an employee and thoroughly investigating those complaints.

✔ Consulting your labor attorney first, if you find that you must fire an employee. The attorney examines your employee file to make sure that you are in the best position to complete the termination and to defend yourself against a potential lawsuit. You may not be aware that you can also be sued for negligence for not firing an employee, if that employee presents a danger to other employees.

While your chances of being sued may seem great, many companies actually manage to avoid lawsuits. One of my favorite companies has nearly 1,000 employees but has never experienced a wrongful termination suit, because the human resource director keeps excellent records, treats employees with honesty and respect, calls them in to talk to them several times to discuss any problems they're having, and warns them if they are facing potential dismissal. So even when she has to fire an employee, that employee leaves feeling as though he or she was treated fairly.

## *Handling a decline in sales*

Your company does well for several months when all of a sudden (or even worse, so gradually that you don't notice until it's too late), sales drop so low they no longer cover your overhead. If you're the typical entrepreneur, you respond first by slowing down your payments to vendors and other creditors to conserve your declining cash, and then you begin laying people off. When creditors and vendors start calling, asking where their money is, you stop answering the phone in the vain hope that all these problems will simply disappear. By now, you're panic stricken, which causes you to make poor decisions about the use of your dwindling resources. Your attitude: If you can just hold on for a little bit, things will get better. Unfortunately, what you've done is shoot yourself in the foot and actually make the situation worse.

What causes an entrepreneur to become so oblivious that he or she doesn't recognize what's happening in the market and puts the business at risk? The answer lies in all the different hats that entrepreneurs usually wear in their businesses. These hard-working stiffs are so preoccupied with surviving the day-to-day drudgery that they rarely spend time out in the market to find out what's heading in their direction.

You can definitely prepare for a decline in sales, because it's not outside your realm of control. Here are some tips to help you put your company in a good position to survive and actually turn around a decline in sales:

✔ If you're wearing a lot of different hats in the early stages of your business, whoever is keeping your books needs to hand you, at minimum, a weekly sales report so you can identify sales patterns for your business. This practice makes you aware of sales and enables you to immediately detect the signs of a decline. Search for the source of that decline and make necessary changes immediately.

✔ Do not reduce your prices. If you create products and services that your customers perceive as valuable at current prices, reducing prices only puzzles customers. The decline in sales may have nothing to do with price. Don't forget to warn vendors you deal with if you intend to be slower than normal in making payments for a while. Work out an arrangement with them, so you don't lose their confidence.

✔ Talk to your customers. They're your best source of information about why sales are declining.

✔ Make sure that a new competitor hasn't entered the market without your knowledge.

✔ Make sure that the quality of your products is still above industry averages.

✔ Control your overhead costs and reduce them if possible, especially where the expense does not produce revenue for the company. For example, are you able to sublease any portion of your office or plant space to another company? This will not only reduce your overhead but also give you another source of revenue. It's unfortunate, but the quickest way to reduce your overhead is to reduce the number of employees you have. Make sure, though, that you don't compromise your ability to produce and deliver your product or service.

✔ Make liquidity a top priority; that alone helps you ride out many bumps in your business life.

✔ If you haven't already done so, put a contingency plan in place that you trigger when you see the start of a downturn in sales.

✔ If you're too late to forestall a cash crisis, consult a debt negotiation company, crisis management consultant, or attorney who can help you work through problems with your creditors.

## Surviving the loss of a key employee

You must prepare for other businesses that may try to entice greatly talented personnel within your organization over to their side. If you have a high tech company, employee turnover can become a way of life, particularly if you're located in an area populated with many of your competitors — Silicon Valley and the Research Triangle Park in North Carolina are examples. Key employees can literally back out of their driveways one day and go left to their place of business, while the next day they back out and go right to work at a competitor's business. Frankly, that's one reason why Microsoft Corp. located its headquarters in Redmond, Washington, far away from the technology belts, where it wasn't under all the pressure of headhunters. Microsoft reasoned that it's more difficult for a key employee to make a decision to move if it means selling a home and relocating to a different state.

But, you can lose key employees plenty of other ways. As more and more executives travel globally, the risk of a fatal accident is greater, and of course, stresses of the market bring on more stress-related diseases. Have I made my point for succession planning?

Preparing your business for the loss of a critical employee means

- ✔ Carrying key-person insurance on vital people in your organization. Doing so helps you cover the cost of replacing that person quickly at a time when it may be financially difficult to do so. This type of insurance also helps to replace lost profits; provide the funds to recruit, hire, and train a suitable replacement; and pay a tax deductible death benefit to the employee's family. How much you need depends on how many of these needs you want to cover and the type of business you have. A good insurance broker can help you make a wise choice.

- ✔ Having your company's key employees train their replacements inside the company. That way if something happens, someone who knows the position is ready to step in.

- ✔ Working with a good succession consultant who can also step in on a temporary basis if a key person leaves your company.

- ✔ Cross-training personnel in key positions, so if someone leaves, someone else can take over.

- ✔ Conducting an exit interview to find out why a key employee has chosen to leave. Perhaps, as a result, you can prevent the same thing from happening in the future.

## Dealing with the economy and Uncle Sam

Always count on the economy and good old Uncle Sam to create situations that you, as a business owner, must deal with. Fortunately for you, both move at glacial speed, so you'll normally have plenty of time to prepare.

For example, how many times have you heard business owners complain that their businesses failed because of a recession? Does that mean that the business otherwise was destined to become a roaring success? That notion is just plain wrong. Recessions don't happen overnight — you have plenty of warning if you know what you're looking for. Right after World War II, the government began compiling information on patterns of change in the economy and developing key indicators of condition of the economy. The *leading index,* for example, consists of the Producer Price Index, the Consumer Confidence Index, and the Manufacturers' Orders for Durable Goods. That index typically declines for about nine months before a recession. Similarly, the *coincident-lagging index,* which is a ratio of the *coincident index* (consisting of employment, personal income, and industrial production statistics) to the *lagging index* (consisting of the Consumer Price Index and interest rate and unemployment statistics) declines for 13 months prior to the onset of a recession. Most indexes like the Producer Price Index are reported monthly. If you go to the U.S. Department of Commerce site at www.doc.gov, you'll find the latest economic indicators right on the home page.

If you start to recognize the typical signs in the national and regional statistics, as well as those in your particular industry, you have some time to prepare.

You are no doubt aware of the potential for tremendous fluctuations in the stock market. They seem to be unpredictable and for businesses whose lives depend on their companies' valuations, a precipitous drop in stock price can be devastating. But, even here, there are some warnings. Notice that public companies are careful about when they announce their quarterly earnings (or lack of them). They are also careful about what they say publicly because they know that investors in the stock market make rapid decisions, often based on a company or what analysts say about it. The Federal Reserve Board is another bearer of news (interest rates typically) that usually has an impact on the stock market. The fickle movements of the stock market are a discussion for another book, and don't usually directly affect private businesses unless they're heavily invested in the stock market.

Here's what you can do to be more proactive about responding to economic conditions:

✔ Move your company into a more liquid position, because cash is king when recession makes loans harder to come by.

✔ Plan to take advantage of opportunities to acquire assets that weren't affordable during a robust economy.

✔ Reduce your overhead to the minimum you require to run your business.

✔ Return to the bootstrapping techniques you used when you started your business — lease instead of buy, keep employees to a minimum, and borrow and barter wherever possible.

## *Coping with product liability*

As a manufacturer or business owner associated with the production of a product, you'll probably be sued at some point in your business life. The courts more and more appear to have shifted the burden of product liability away from the user and onto the manufacturer, a serious problem for business. Even if your product is of high quality and completely safe, with all the required warning labels ("Don't put your hand into the machine." "Don't run the machine in water."), someone is bound to carelessly misuse and abuse it and then blame the resulting injuries on you and everyone else in the distribution channel. Ways to avoid and prepare for product liability issues include:

- ✔ Making sure that you provide appropriate instruction manuals for your product, detailing how to correctly use and service it.

- ✔ Applying the required warning labels for your type of product. A good place to start is with the Occupational Health and Safety Administration (OSHA), the government agency that monitors workplace safety. The OSHA Web site is located at www.osha.gov.

- ✔ Making sure that you train dealers, distributors, and reps in the correct use of the product, so they can pass that training along to your customer outlets.

- ✔ Responding immediately to complaints from customers about your product and resolving those complaints so that your customer isn't inclined to take legal action.

- ✔ Promptly notifying customers if you discover a problem with your product that can result in liability and passing along your solutions so the customer can take care of the problem immediately.

- ✔ Establishing a safety panel responsible for reviewing safety requirements and establishing new ones as your business grows. The panel maintains records on all decisions about product design, testing, and evaluation, as well as any problems that occur.

- ✔ Exercising care not to claim anything in your advertising and promotions that implies a level of safety that your product does not have.

- ✔ Carrying product liability insurance, which covers your defense, any personal injury or property damage, but not lost sales or the cost of redesigning the product.

- ✔ Finding a qualified attorney you can go to if a product liability issue arises.

- ✔ The bottom line — design, produce, and deliver a superior product.

# Harvesting the Wealth with a Graceful Exit

Talking about an exit strategy may seem strange in a book about starting a company, but an exit or harvest plan is part of the overall strategic planning for your business. Using such a strategy certainly is a major change in the business, but if you don't know where you're headed, how will you know when you've arrived? Some entrepreneurs plan to never leave their businesses; others just enjoy the start-up phase and like to leave the management to other workers. Still others take the business to a certain stage and then leave. Whatever you decide is right for you, I assure you that at some point you'll want to harvest the wealth that your efforts and your company have created. You have many alternatives for doing this, and I'm giving you two of the best.

# Selling your business

If you're ready to move on to something else, or you're ready to make a change in your life or where you live, selling your business may be right for you. Doing so leaves you free mentally and financially to do whatever you want. But don't think that selling the business that you sweated blood and cried real tears to create will be easy. On the contrary, selling is one of the more difficult decisions you'll ever make about your business. Some entrepreneurs experience a sense of loss much like losing a loved one. Others experience a sense of exhilaration from the freedom of not having to think about the business every day, but then they realize they've lost their focus and don't know what to do next.

Never sell your business without knowing what you're going to do the next day, and the next, and the next.

In a perfect world, you know from the day you start your business that you intend to sell it at some point in the future. That way you make decisions that place your business in the best position possible to be sold. You make sure that your business makes a good profit (instead of showing no profit to avoid taxes, which devalues your business), and that you have good employees, solid customer and vendor contracts, superior sales people, and so forth. Knowing that you're going to sell, you want to build as much value as possible, so you have more to harvest from the sale.

Unfortunately, many entrepreneurs don't think that far ahead, so they may not decide to sell the business until six months before it happens. Then they have to scramble around to make their business look good.

## Who can help you?

With so many ways to sell their businesses, many small business owners rely on the services of a business broker or business opportunity broker who takes a commission from the sale just like a real estate broker. Owners of larger or high tech businesses are more likely to rely on an investment-banking firm that specializes in the sale of these types of ventures. An investment banker probably wants a retainer, which applies against the final fee for the sale of your business.

Using brokers isn't a necessity. You can advertise in your local paper if your business is more localized or in *The Wall Street Journal* if it has national or international appeal. However, much like finding a business you want to buy, the best buyers are found by networking with your attorney, accountant, and banker. Those professionals hear about buyers for particular types of businesses all the time.

### What do you sell?

First of all, you don't have to sell all the assets of your business. For example, you may sell all the equipment but choose to maintain ownership of the building and lease it to the new owner. Your buyer may not want to purchase all the equipment you have, so you'll have to find another buyer for what's left. Accounts receivable, inventory, and accounts payable are negotiable items, too. Never assume anything. Include an inventory of what you're selling to eliminate any possibility for error.

And be sure to check out your buyer, making sure he or she has the skills and financial resources to purchase your business and keep it operating at the same level of quality that you established. This factor is particularly important if your name has been associated with the business for a long time. An entrepreneur friend of mine experienced difficulties when she sold her chain of healthy food stores bearing her name to a larger company. The new owner didn't treat the customers with the same care and attention that my friend had insisted on when the company was hers. It isn't easy to see your name on something that no longer represents your values.

## Selling out but staying involved

You may reach a point when you want to take some of your investment out of the business to enjoy some things you've always wanted to do, yet you're not ready to completely leave the business. You can accomplish this in several different ways.

### Selling your stock

One choice you have is selling some or all the stock you hold in your company. Remember that selling stock applies only to corporations and limited liability companies. If you're in a partnership, you can sell your interest back to the partnership. If your company is privately held, you're probably governed by a shareholders' agreement that was drawn up when you formed the company, specifying how much of your stock you can sell at a given time, to whom you can sell it, and how its value is determined. A similar situation exists for limited liability companies whose members have interests rather than shares (see Chapter 14 for a review of legal forms of business organization).

If your company goes public, the job is much easier because you sell your stock on the open market, unless you're restricted by your shareholder's agreement. The SEC also has strict guidelines that you must follow if you own a substantial portion of stock in your public company.

If you succeed in creating a valuable company, your equity increases substantially, which means a big tax liability when you sell your stock. Be sure to discuss your strategy with a good tax attorney or an accountant.

# Becoming part of a roll-up

During the past few years, the marketplace has experienced a phenomenon that has taken on many names: roll-up, consolidation play, PacMan strategy, or buy-and-build. Here's how it works. A large company moves into a fragmented industry with a number of small mom-and-pop type businesses. The consolidator buys them up and puts them under one umbrella to benefit from economies of scale and centralized functions like purchasing, accounting, and human resources. The local management team usually stays on board, while the parent company builds a national presence.

The big payoff comes when the consolidator takes the company public in an IPO and then buys out all the owners. For small lifestyle-type business owners, selling to a consolidator is a way to reap wealth that the business never could have produced on its own.

You see all types of businesses participating in this phenomenon — towing companies, coffeehouses, candy makers, automobile dealers, and limousine services. Many family businesses consider this way of selling the business when no one in the next generation is ready to take over the business.

The two parts to this type of deal are

1. You, the small business owner, take stock in the roll-up company, join the management team, and bet that the IPO enables you to cash out. But, you must realize that IPOs occur only when the market is right for them. Solid deals always find a market, so make sure you're associating with a consolidator that has an excellent investment banking firm underwriting the deal. (See Chapter 14 for more about IPOs.)

2. You sell your company in the end.

So it's important that you know the roll-up company well and feel confident that it will be able to make the strategy work. You also want to ensure that the value placed on your company is fair.

An entrepreneur with a consulting firm was approached by a consolidator. The offer was tempting, but during the process of studying it and looking at his own goals, the owner decided to pass, preferring instead to grow his business under his control. Another entrepreneur with a chain of audiology clinics looked at her offer from a different perspective. She had spent a number of years building her business and was ready to spend more time with her family. Selling to the roll-up company gave her more freedom to do just that.

If a consolidator approaches your company, consider the offer carefully. Getting into the deal early is better, because you gain more negotiating power. Make sure your employees buy into your plan, because you need their help. Let them see how this move provides them with a better opportunity for career advancement. But more important, make sure that your customers won't be unhappy that the small company through which you treated them so well is now part of a large conglomerate. You can reassure them that you plan to retain your local identity as they benefit from your new buying power.

## Restructuring your company

Many entrepreneurs envision turning over leadership of their companies to a son or daughter and cashing out a rather significant portion of their investment. You can actually do this by splitting the original company into two businesses. You retain ownership of the part of the business that owns all the assets like plant and equipment, while your son or daughter owns the operations aspect of the business and leases the assets from you. For example, suppose you own a restaurant, but you no longer want to spend your days running the business. You give the ownership of the restaurant (the name, the operations, the employees, and so forth) to your daughter while you continue to own the building and the equipment, which you lease to her. Now you derive an income from the lease and you're still somewhat involved in the business without the rigors of the day-to-day management.

### Doing a phased sale

You've decided. You want to sell the business, but you must do it slowly because selling it lock, stock, and barrel will be too much of a shock to your system. You can make the sale less shocking to your system by phasing it out over a specified period of time, in say, two phases. Here's how it works:

- ✔ **Phase I:** Sell a portion of the business but remain in control of operations and continue growing the company to an agreed-upon point.

- ✔ **Phase II:** Finish the sale of the business at the prearranged price. The entrepreneur (seller) may stay on for the transition in ownership or leave as agreed upon.

A phased sale has advantages for the buyer and for the seller. You, the seller, stay on with the business, making sure it keeps moving in the direction you wanted it to go and getting your equity back so you have cash to do other things. The buyer, on the other hand, benefits from not immediately having to come up with all the cash to buy the business and from keeping you on board during the transition to ease typically nervous employees through a change in ownership. The buyer has the added advantage of being introduced by you to all the people he or she needs to know to run the business successfully.

Always involve an attorney in a phased sale, because it is more complex than a straight sale. Your attorney will ensure that you have a proper buy-sell agreement that specifies the terms of the purchase, the amount of control your buyer can exert during the time you're still in the business, and the amount and type of proprietary information that you must share with the buyer before the sale is complete.

### Structuring an ESOP

An Employee Stock Option Plan (ESOP) is another way you can cash out of your business over time as long as you have more than 25 employees. ESOPs are essentially tax-qualified pension plans or defined-contribution plans that have specific requirements. To qualify, your company needs to have

- ✔ Revenues of at least $3 million per year.

- ✔ An annual payroll of at least $500,000.

✔ The ability to cover the setup costs, which can run about $100,000 for legal, bank, and accounting fees.

✔ Assets that can be used as collateral for a bank loan, including inventory, accounts receivable, and equipment.

✔ Good cash flow so that the company can pay back the loan and repurchase stock of employees who leave the company.

Structuring an ESOP is fairly complicated and definitely requires the assistance of an attorney. Without going into great detail, this is how it works:

✔ Your company sets up a trust fund and deposits new or existing shares of stock that are allocated specifically for employees.

✔ Often the ESOP trust then takes out a bank loan, buying sufficient shares of stock to gain a minority interest of at least 30 percent in the company to trigger the capital gains exclusion. Then the ESOP company makes tax-deductible contributions of up to 25 percent of the participant payroll to the ESOP trust to repay the bank debt.

✔ The shares are then allocated to employee accounts.

✔ The cash the owners receive from selling their stock in the company is not taxed if it's reinvested in U.S. stocks or bonds.

✔ The cash-out price for the entrepreneur is based on the company's market value at the time.

One thing entrepreneurs often fail to realize is that with an ESOP, you must have a much more open environment with your employees in terms of providing them with information about the company's finances and operations. Your employees essentially become your partners, and the success rate of that partnership generally is good. About 71 percent of ESOP companies experience higher performance after the ESOP is put in place.

# When You Think You Can't Exit Gracefully

The fact that most entrepreneurs refuse to even consider that failure is a possibility proves they are the eternal optimists of the world. What you won't find when looking at most books about entrepreneurship is the slightest hint of a discussion of the topic of failure. It's almost as though talking about it will start a virus, causing many more businesses to fail. One of the more popular quotes among entrepreneurs comes from the movie *Apollo 13:* "Failure is not an option." But so does another famous quote that is probably more apt: "Houston, we have a problem." The problem isn't failure — that's an integral part of entrepreneurship; the problem is failing to know when to walk away. The shame is not in having a business fail; rather, it's in taking your family down with it, all because your pride would not allow you to quit. Failure is an option, and sometimes it's the only option.

Among the more successful entrepreneurs in our history who have failed are R.H. Macy, H.J. Heinz, and George Westinghouse, to name but a few. Just take a look at what recently happened to many Internet companies as an example of a new group of entrepreneurial failures. Failure is part of the entrepreneurial process. All the amazing new technology we have today might never have occurred if entrepreneurs hadn't encountered failures along the way.

Everyone handles failure differently. One entrepreneur divorced his wife, let his hair grow, and traveled across the country on a Harley. Another went on a spending spree. Yet another went into a deep depression. Ask entrepreneurs if they understand the risks they're taking when they start a business, and they always say yes. Ask if they realize they can lose their homes, their cars, and their savings accounts, and they say yes. But ask them if they believe that failure can happen to them, and their answer is a resounding no.

If you read this book all the way through, you increase your chances of avoiding failure — I can't guarantee you'll never fail, but I can say with some degree of certainty that you won't experience failure in the same way as the entrepreneur who didn't plan his venture well.

The best way to avoid your enemy (and in this case the enemy is failure) is to know your enemy. So in the next two sections, you're going to look at what remedies are available when you're on the brink of failure.

## Facing bankruptcy

The term *bankruptcy* sends shivers up the spines of entrepreneurs, because they want to avoid it at all costs. Contrary to the popular notion that you can solve all your problems by bankrupting out of your company and walking away, it just isn't that easy. Besides, if you have any ethics, you don't want to leave your vendors and shareholders high and dry, because it really is a small world, and you may need their help in the future.

What causes a business to reach the point of considering bankruptcy is not easy to identify. Typically, the immediately precipitating cause is the inability to pay off debt because of a lack of cash. But that lack of funds is only a symptom of a much deeper and more complex problem. I have a dear consultant colleague, Wes Zimmerman, who always says, "The tree grows from the bottom up, but it dies from the top down." How right he is. Whenever a business suffers or dies, look to top management to find the problem. The root source of a bankruptcy always is poor management — when the entrepreneur allows excessive debt to occur and overhead to explode, when he or she doesn't monitor the market, when things are done the way they've always been done, or when the business has union problems, supplier problems, and poor financial management.

The bankruptcy code has several sections. The two that relate to businesses are Chapter 11 and Chapter 7. Each is quite different in its approach.

### Reorganizing: Chapter 11

Chapter 11 isn't really a bankruptcy in the more common sense of the word. Rather it is a reorganization of the finances of a business with the agreement of its creditors so the business can continue to operate and pay off its debts. In cases where the creditors are confident that the entrepreneur intends to pay all debts, the entrepreneur can actually manage the reorganization without a court-appointed trustee. Here's how a Chapter 11 works.

The business owner files for reorganization and:

- ✔ Within 30 days, the owner and the creditors must meet to consider the status of the company and the steps it must take to reorganize so it can pay its debts and become viable again.
- ✔ The court appoints a committee, which includes the owner, to develop a plan for the reorganization.
- ✔ The reorganization plan must be submitted to the court within 120 days.
- ✔ Out of the total number of creditors affected by the reorganization, at least half must accept the plan.
- ✔ Once the court accepts the plan, the entrepreneur is discharged from any debts not listed in the plan.

Chapter 11 bankruptcy is the avenue you choose if you know you have the ability, given some time, to recover and pay off your debts.

### Liquidating: Chapter 7

When your business doesn't have the resources to pay its debts or any hope of securing them anytime soon, you'll probably resort to liquidating all the assets of the business and discharging most of your debt. I say most of your debt because you can't bankrupt out of payroll taxes that you failed to pay. They become your personal obligation until they are paid.

When you file a Chapter 7 petition, you request an *order for relief*. The court appoints a trustee to manage the liquidation of the business with the goal of reducing everything to cash and disbursing the cash to the creditors in order of priority. In general, secured creditors get paid first and then the priority claimants (administrative expenses related to the bankruptcy, wages, salaries, commissions, employee benefits, and so forth). Anything that remains after distribution to everyone who has a right to be paid goes to the entrepreneur. The entrepreneur's only exemptions from the bankruptcy are

✔ Interest in any accrued dividends up to the legal amount.

✔ The right to social security benefits, unemployment compensation, public assistance, veterans' benefits, and disability benefits.

✔ The rights to stock bonuses, pensions, or profit sharing.

If your business is a partnership, you're entitled to the exemptions given to individuals.

## Avoiding bankruptcy

Business owners have more control over a bankruptcy than you may think, because creditors naturally would rather be paid and they usually fare better in a restructuring of the debt than they do in a liquidation.

If you want to try your best to avoid bankruptcy, follow these tips:

✔ Don't rely on one major customer to generate the majority of your revenue — in other words, don't put all your eggs in one basket.

✔ Keep your overhead down to the essentials — those things that contribute to the generation of revenues.

✔ Stay as liquid as possible. A good rule-of-thumb is to have several months of overhead expense on hand.

✔ Pay attention to your relationships with your creditors. Be honest and forthright with them.

✔ Before you ever consider taking the bankruptcy route, seek the advice of a turnaround consultant who specializes in bringing businesses back from the brink of disaster.

## Stepping Back from the Brink

Turnaround consultants specialize in making unhealthy — even dying — businesses healthy again. They are true magicians who find positives in your business that you never thought about. They put you on a diet, help you establish small goals, and make sure you stay on track. From the experiences of turnaround consultants that I know, some tips for facing failure with grace (so that you can start again with dignity) suggest that you:

✔ **Find entrepreneurs who have *been there* and get their *done that* advice.** Unfortunately, when your business is failing, your family and friends are probably the last people who can help you. So you need to talk with people who've gone through what you're experiencing. Ask around. In general, entrepreneurs who fail and come back to experience success are more willing to talk about what they found out and to help you get back on your feet.

✔ **Fail fast.** If things go badly, don't drag it out. I know of entrepreneurs who stuck with a dying business for years while it sucked the life out of their families, friends, and their own health. You must focus on the fact that the business failed, that you did not, and that you still have the talent and skills to start again. That's important.

✔ **Give yourself a deadline.** Tell yourself that if your business isn't making a profit or generating a positive cash flow by next year, you're going to quit. That isn't easy to do, because entrepreneurs, you remember, are optimists, always thinking that a big order is just around the corner and agreeing with people who are telling them that their business is terrific. But when the numbers don't add up (and that's the real indicator), give yourself a deadline and stick to it.

✔ **Never comingle personal and business funds or assets.** If you lend your personal funds to your failing corporation and the company goes bankrupt, you must hop in line with the other creditors. Moreover, you may even have to return any repayment money you received in the year prior to the bankruptcy.

✔ **Never mess with the government.** Unless you want to risk losing your personal assets and have a debt follow you for the rest of your life, follow this guideline. Too many entrepreneurs in distress borrow funds from their payroll-tax and sales-tax accounts. Resist those temptations. Don't do it!

✔ **Keep your eyes on the next prize.** Opportunity is out there and you already know how to take advantage of it. This business was not your last opportunity, so start looking. I always say that things happen for a reason. Sometimes your best opportunity comes along because you were willing to leave behind a business that was draining you.

✔ **Do whatever it takes to pay back your investors.** They took the risk, yes, but if you pay them back, even if it takes a long time, they'll respect you and be there for you the next time you need them to fund an opportunity.

# Part V
# The Part of Tens

The 5th Wave    By Rich Tennant

©RICHTENNANT

"For 30 years I've put a hat and coat on to make sales calls and I'm not changing now just because I'm doing it on the Web from my living room."

# In this part . . .

*I*n this part, you find some of my best thoughts, including
motivating yourself to get started with a business idea,
using technology to grow your business, and even reasons
why you maybe *shouldn't* start a business. I finish this part
with the best industry resources on the Web to help you
gather competitive intelligence.

# Chapter 21

# Ten Reasons Not to Start a Business

**S**eems like everyone today is telling you to start a business — it's the only way to go. Why would you ever want to work for someone else? Well, I'm here to tell you that an awful lot of people should never start businesses. Are you one of those people? Take a look at ten reasons not to start a business and see what you think.

## Because Everyone Is Doing It

It does seem as though everyone is starting a business, from the paper boy down the street who just opened a Web-design shop on the Internet to the paper boy's mom who finally started the public relations firm she always wanted to have. And if they're not actually starting a business, they're talking about starting a business. Everyone seems to be playing with a concept of one sort or another. You hear it at cocktail parties and PTA meetings, at the local chamber of commerce and your local bank. While there's nothing wrong with all this wishing and hoping going on, it's certainly no reason for you to follow suit. The only reason to start a business is because *you* want to do it. Talking about starting a business is easy; actually starting a business is hard work. So make sure you do it for the right reasons.

## Because You Want to Be a Millionaire

Some members of media say that all you have to do is start a business and you'll instantly become a millionaire. Scan the magazine racks and you'll see what I mean. Headlines blare out "9 Millionaires Under 30," "10 Ways to Make

Your First Million." Half the time, the article asserts that generating a million dollars in sales makes the entrepreneur a millionaire, which is certainly not the case.

The truth is, easier ways can be found to make money than starting a business. Put your money in the stock market, long-term, and watch it grow as you relax with that book you've been wanting to read. I don't want to give you the impression that you can't become a millionaire by becoming an entrepreneur. Entrepreneurship is one of the last great ways to create substantial wealth. I just want to caution you that most successful entrepreneurs started their businesses for reasons that had nothing to do with money. Those reasons usually had everything to do with being passionate about their business ideas and wanting to turn them into the best businesses they could.

# Because You're Looking for a Secure Job

Maybe you just got laid off from your job and you figure, *why not start a business?* Actually, getting fired or laid off is a common precipitator of entrepreneurship. Sometimes, it takes that unexpected event to push someone to start the business he has always wanted to start. Many people start small businesses to create jobs for themselves, jobs that they believe will always be there (unlike the job from which they were just laid off). What they don't realize is that, on average, small mom-and-pop type businesses pay their owners less than they earned working for someone else, and they get the privilege of working seven days a week, twelve hours a day. What's more, they still don't have job security, because the failure rate of small businesses is quite high. If you're considering starting a business because you've just lost a job, use this book to help start an entrepreneurial venture that has the potential to provide not only a good salary but also wealth in the form of appreciation in the value of the business over time. That's a better investment.

# Because You Don't Want to Work for Someone Else

People who dislike working for someone else cite numerous reasons. They want independence — to do what they want, when they want, with no one looking over their shoulders and telling them what to do. They also don't like the idea of spending all their time working for the benefit of someone else, creating wealth for someone else to enjoy. Nothing is wrong with these reasons, but if they echo your thoughts, you may want to ask yourself whether it's the job that's making you feel this way — not the actual idea of working for someone else. Perhaps if you found a job that provided stock options or some other way to share in ownership and growth of the company you'd feel you have more of a personal stake in the job and the company. If you had a job that gave you a say in some of the important decisions of the company, you may enjoy the benefits of ownership without the headaches. Whatever the case, the fact that you don't enjoy working for someone else is definitely a sign that you should investigate other possibilities including entrepreneurship.

# Because You Just Came into Some Money

An entrepreneur with too much money can be pretty frightening. How can you ever have too much money to start a business, you ask? Because you have a lot of money available to you at the beginning, you don't make as wise decisions as when you have a limited amount of capital. The problem with being flush with cash is that if you lose money, you know there's more where that came from. A better plan is to formulate a business concept, test it in the market, and figure out how much money you need to start the business and take it to a positive cash flow on its own. By doing this, you may find that you don't need as much money as you have, and you can put the excess away for a rainy day or invest it in something else.

# Because If the Kid Down the Street Did It, So Can You

Many older adults are walking around shaking their heads, trying to understand all the twenty-something (and younger) entrepreneurs and their dot-com start-ups. Some of these older people with years of business experience are even being called upon to run the companies of founders half their age. The Internet and e-commerce seem to have given the advantage to youth and inexperience, while seasoned veterans of business struggle to comprehend the value of no-asset, no-profit enterprises. The kids make it look easy!

I caution you that no start-up is easy. If you sit dot-com whiz kids down and really talk to them about their experiences, you'll find that for many of them it wasn't as easy as the media made it sound. It was hard, but it was fun, and they wouldn't trade the experiences for anything.

# Because You Want to Give Everyone in Your Family a Job

Investors often run the other direction when they see a group of relatives running and advising the business — Uncle Jim is the attorney, Aunt Jane serves as the accountant, and so forth. To an outsider, this looks like you were going for cheap labor rather than getting the best people for your team.

And rather than clean house, a potential investor may just walk away. After all, plenty of easier opportunities are out there. Likewise, your children may have other ideas about what they want to do with their lives, and your *hot idea* for a business may not fit with their plans. Don't start a business to give your family jobs; start a business because you're passionate about a concept and want to make it happen in the most effective way possible.

## Because You've Got a Great Idea

Great ideas are a dime a dozen. You've probably heard the old adage, "I'd rather invest in a B idea led by an A team, than invest in an A idea led by a B team." Starting a business is about execution. You may have a great idea, but if you don't have the experience, knowledge, and persistence to make it happen, what's it really worth?

## Because It's Too Risky

Let's face it: Life is a risk. Driving a car, crossing the street, going to the parking garage at night, putting your money in stocks — all are risks that we take every day. Yes, starting a business entails risk, some of which you can calculate and some of which is unknown. You need to look at how much risk you can handle, while still keeping your sanity, and not hurting your family.

## Start a Business Because It's What You Most Want to Do

Okay, I threw you a curve, ending this list of *don'ts* with a *do*. That's because I want to end on a positive note. If you find yourself always making excuses for why you shouldn't, maybe you shouldn't be a business owner.

Entrepreneurial types tend to do just the opposite. They rationalize why they should start a business and discount any potential negative views. Nothing is wrong with listing all the pros and cons to starting a business. Go through all the *what ifs* and consider those negative scenarios. What it boils down to is, *Do you passionately want to start a business?* Do you think about it day and night? Do you run and rerun scenarios for how it can work (when you should be thinking about other things)? Are your friends tired of hearing you talk about *your business?* If those things are happening to you, then you have the entrepreneur's virus and the only way to cure it is to start a business.

# Chapter 22

# Ten Ways to Spark Your Entrepreneurial Spirit

*In This Chapter*

▶ Hanging out with the right people, at the right places

▶ Doing your research

▶ Doing something more — almost anything will do

**Y**ou've been talking about that great business idea for a long time now. You know you can do it; what's stopping you? Here are ten suggestions for helping you get some traction on your idea.

## Start Reading about Great New Businesses

Business magazines featuring entrepreneurs are among the most popular on the newsstands. If you want to inspire yourself with the possibilities, check some of my favorite titles:

✔ *Inc.* magazine, www.inc.com

✔ *Fast Company,* www.fastcompany.com

✔ *Entrepreneur,* www.entrepreneur.com

✔ *Business Start-ups,*
   http://www.entrepreneur.com/Magazines/MA_Issue/
   0,1388,117601,00.html

✔ *Forbes,* www.forbes.com

✔ *Fortune,* www.fortune.com, **and** www.fsb.com, **its small business site**

✔ *Red Herring,* www.redherring.com

# Join a Community Business Organization

Almost every community has an organization where you can meet and talk with other business people. If you get involved, you'll have no trouble finding people who offer encouragement to you for taking the next step in starting your business. You'll also find people who can help you take that step. One highly respected community organization is Rotary International, a humanitarian group of business people who dedicate themselves to improving the community, providing scholarships and other benefits. The advantage of Rotary is that wherever you travel in the world, you are likely to find a local chapter of Rotary. Angi Ma Wong, an intercultural communications consultant, travels all over the world. When she arrives in Singapore, for example, she looks up the local Rotary to see when their next meeting is. At the meeting, she is sure to come in contact with the most important business and government leaders in the community. And they are all willing to help another Rotarian in any way they can. To become a member of Rotary, you need to be nominated by a current member. If you don't know anyone who is a member, start by joining your local chamber of commerce and the various trade organizations for your industry. Chances are you'll find a Rotarian in one of these organizations as well. Besides, this is a great way to start to feel comfortable about wanting to become a business owner.

# Hang around a University Business School

Nowhere will you find a larger hotbed of entrepreneurial activity and new business start-ups in the earliest stages than at a university, particularly in its business school. That's because most colleges and universities now have courses in entrepreneurship that prepare students for success as entrepreneurs. Talk to the faculty in these programs about finding a student or students to help you do a feasibility study or business plan. Getting some energetic, motivated students on your team is one way to jump-start your business venture. You can also inquire about seminars and courses in such things as feasibility analysis, business plan writing, and technology commercialization, to name a few. Schools often offer these opportunities through their extension programs to people from the community who are not registered students. The environment alone is enough to get you enthusiastic about sharing in the excitement of entrepreneurship.

# Tell a Friend

I guarantee that if you announce to a friend that you intend to start a business, that friend will ask how it's going every time you meet. The need to report progress should be enough to motivate you to make headway. Nothing is better than to have a friend keep nagging you about your great idea — that's what friends are for!

# Do a Feasibility Study

Doing a feasibility analysis (described in Chapter 4) is a great way to become comfortable with your business concept and feel more confident about moving forward. A feasibility study helps you define the conditions under which you are willing to proceed. If those conditions look good, what's stopping you? Get out there and do it!

# Leave Your Job (or Get Laid Off)

Leaving your job is a pretty radical step, but some entrepreneurs can never quite get up the courage to start the businesses they've been dreaming about without having a cataclysmic event push them into doing it. One of the big reasons the 1980s are called the Decade of Entrepreneurship is that so many people were laid off because of downsizing by big corporations. Some of the suddenly unemployed even started new companies to compete with their old workplaces. Leaving a good job is a major decision that must not be taken lightly, and it needs to be considered only after you've done your homework on the business concept that you want to execute. You can do all the feasibility work for your new business while you're still at your job and not leave until you're ready to devote full attention to the new business.

# Discover an Industry

Immerse yourself in an industry and find out everything you can about it. Talk to all types of business owners, suppliers, distributors, and industry experts. Become *the* expert on your industry and soon you'll find the opportunity that's right for you. Because you've made important contacts in the industry and understand how the industry works, your knowledge motivates you to give your new business a shot. (Take a look at Chapter 5 if you want to find out more about what's involved in researching an industry.)

# Spend Time with an Entrepreneur

What better way to inspire yourself to start a business than to spend time with someone who has done just that? Spend a day with an entrepreneur you admire — perhaps someone in your favorite industry. Shadow that person, observing what entrepreneurs do on a day-to-day basis. Entrepreneurs love to talk with fellow entrepreneurs, especially budding entrepreneurs. Your chosen entrepreneur can give you personal advice based on his or her experience on how to get started, what pitfalls to look out for, and how to balance your personal and business lives. Besides, entrepreneurs are great cheerleaders, and your entrepreneur may say just the right thing to motivate you to start your life as an entrepreneur. If you took my earlier advice to join a community organization, chances are you'll have the opportunity to meet several entrepreneurs at various events. One of them just may be the perfect one to shadow.

# Find a Mentor

When you're starting a business for the first time, it's wonderful to have someone you can turn to when you need advice, when you're frustrated or discouraged, or when you want to share a small win. Mentors come in all shapes and sizes, but the best mentors are ones who believe in you and can be honest with you, who introduce you to important people you need to meet, and who pick you up when you fall down. A mentor may be someone who has had a successful business in the industry in which you're interested or someone whom you admire regardless of whether he or she happens to have experience in the same area as you. That's why it's so important to network, get out there and meet new people, because you never know when you'll meet your mentor, the person who ultimately starts you on your way.

# Do Something — Anything

"Just do it!" became the mantra of the twentysomething generation, but it remains a timeless reminder for anyone thinking about starting a business. That moment comes when you must say to yourself, "Just do it!" Leap into your opportunity with both feet and start doing something that makes your business happen.

File for your DBA ("doing business as") or your incorporation papers with a business name. Set up your home office to accommodate the new business until it's ready to move to a more formal site (or like many entrepreneurs today, keep your business at home and operate it virtually over the Internet). Get your domain address for the Web. Have some business cards made up. It doesn't take much to start to build a little critical mass of activities so that you feel like you're honestly in business.

# Chapter 23

# Ten Ways to Use the Internet to Grow Your Business

*In This Chapter*

▶ Finding a host for your Web site

▶ Becoming a virtual business

▶ Cultivating customers around the world

The Internet plays an important role in any business you choose to start. You can't get around it. Although you may choose not to have an e-commerce business, you still want an Internet presence, because customers and others in your industry expect it. Here are ten ways to use the Internet effectively to grow your business.

## Get Started Quickly

You can be in business almost as quickly as you can say, "My Web address is *mybusiness.com.*" Many well-known Web companies can serve as host for your site, if it isn't too big. Some even enable you to add a store if you want to sell products along with your services. For only about $100 a month, for example, Yahoo! Store, www.store.yahoo.com, gets you up and running in less than an hour. You can display photos of your products online and let your customers pay by credit card. You'll also get great reports on your most important information like your best selling items, where your customers are coming from, and many other useful statistics. What's more, you'll be located next to such venerable companies as Sony Pictures Entertainment, FTD Flowers, NASA, and FAO Schwartz.

So, what's your excuse now?

# Become a Virtual Business

Technology gives entrepreneurs a new option for running a business — creating a virtual company over the Internet. More and more entrepreneurs realize that they don't have to invest in bricks-and-mortar operations, hire a bunch of expensive employees, and carry a lot of costly inventory. By outsourcing all of the functions of the business, savvy entrepreneurs are becoming conductors of virtual orchestras of strategic partners who stay in touch with one another via the Internet. What's more, from the first day a company goes live on the Internet, it looks as big and important as any major company. Take, for example, AgInfoLink, the brainchild of Texas rancher Anne Anderson. Frustrated in her efforts to pull together an alliance of cattle ranchers to produce steaks of consistent quality and tenderness to supply to restaurants, becoming a virtual company made sense, because the people she needed to work with were spread from Argentina to Canada and her product, a digital tracking system, could be provided over the Internet. Now she tracks beef from the ranch to the refrigerator and everyone in her supply chain is linked to her private Intranet (a kind of Internet that is accessible only through her company).

# Join a Network of Business Colleagues

You don't have to go far to find an organization that can help you get in touch with others in your industry. Whether your business involves consulting, producing products, selling to consumers, or any of thousands of other enterprises, no doubt exists that at least one trade organization focuses on you, and you can find it by logging on to the Internet. For example, the National Federation of Independent Businesses (NFIB), `www.nfib.org`, is the largest advocacy organization representing small businesses. If you're a manufacturer, the Consumer Electronics Manufacturer Association, `http://www.ce.org`, may be right for you. Most trade association sites provide benefits to their members including industry news, informational articles, conference and seminar information, discounts, and other services.

Informally, plenty of online sites provide forums where you can meet and greet other people in your industry. The best are usually managed and conducted in a professional manner. These forums provide the additional benefit of international visitors, who give a different perspective to the discussions. Go to the Forum One site on the Web at `www.forumone.com` to search for a discussion group in your area of interest. For example, *Fast Company,* the highly successful business magazine, serves as host to a variety of forums. Go to `www.fastcompany.com/fasttalk/` to see the categories of forums. Most business organizations and business periodicals maintain forum sites.

# Stay in Touch with Your Customers

With your company on the Internet, you have the ability to stay in touch with your customers 24 hours a day, 7 days a week. With all that time available, you have no excuse not to find ways of getting as much information from your customers as possible. Set up a database to trap your customer information and give you the ability to mine all the gold there is in it. Make the database accessible to everyone and make everyone responsible for finding ways to satisfy the customer. But, be sure to create an interesting site so that customers want to linger there, and give them incentives for providing their views on products, services, and so forth.

Your customers are your best source of new product/service ideas, so find innovative ways to tap into them. Industrial waste cleanup guru, New Pig Corp., `www.newpig.com`, hosts a contest every year to find the cleanest companies in the U.S. Customers of New Pig from all over the country send their "dirty stories" in an effort to win cash, a stunning pig statuette, a handsome plaque, and a *Good Clean Fun Pack* of pig paraphernalia. In addition, the winners' stories are posted to the Web site for all the world to see. It's all good, clean fun, and it has made New Pig Corp. one of the more successful companies in the U.S. Look at Chapter 6 to get more ideas for staying in touch with your customers.

# Communicate with Your Strategic Partners

Technology makes it possible for you to have business partners located at great distances from you and still communicate relatively easily through e-mail, phone, videoconferencing, and the Internet. Depending on your communication needs, the technology you need is affordable. You can create a Web site dedicated to your partners and provide them with access to information they need to do what you want them to do. You can set up a dashboard on your computer to display information they provide to keep you up-to-date on what they're doing for you. Later on, you may want to develop an extranet or virtual private network to connect you and your partners like a virtual company, so that communications become instantaneous.

# Gather Competitive Intelligence

With an Internet connection, you open the doors to the biggest database in the world. You can find literally any piece of information you want in some form on the Internet. It may not always be free, but if you need it, someone out there provides it.

Today, it's easier than ever to stay in touch with what's going on in your competitive market — as easy as clicking on your competitor's Web site or going to one of the many government or proprietary sites to find the latest information on the economy and your industry. On most sites, you can even arrange to have the specific type of information you're interested in sent to your desktop on a regular basis via e-mail. Check out Chapter 24 to find some of the best resources for gathering competitive intelligence.

# Promote Your Company

The ability to bring in-house many of the marketing functions that you used to pay dearly for has been one of the greatest benefits of computer technology for small businesses. Desktop publishing software enables you to design and create brochures, newsletters, and business cards, and send them via e-mail to your in-house printer or to a bulk printing company. You can also quickly and easily publish these same promotional materials on your Web site. For small businesses with limited budgets, this ability to control the pre-production aspect of developing promotional materials has saved countless dollars and allowed these businesses to steer their limited dollars toward specialty advertising and promotion that they don't have the capability of doing in-house.

# Reach Global Customers

The Internet has shown us just how small the world we live in really is. All you have to do is put up a Web site and get that first e-mail from someone with a `.uk` extension on their e-mail address, and you know how far your business message can travel. But at the same time the Internet brings us all closer, it also creates problems for business owners who want to tap into those global markets but don't know how to communicate with their international customers. Fortunately, technology has come to the rescue in the form of companies that provide translation software permitting a user of your site to view it in his or her native language rather than ubiquitous English. Companies like Globalink, `http://www.globalink.com`, make it easy for your foreign customers to get to know you quickly and experience a level of comfort that makes them feel good about making that first purchase.

# Create an Intelligent Company

You can have all the technology in the world, but if it isn't giving you the information and knowledge you need to compete and succeed in a fast-paced environment, then it isn't doing the job it was meant to do. The goal of technology in your business environment is to help your employees and the company as a whole become more intelligent. Intelligence happens when everyone has access to the information they need to do their jobs and satisfy your customers. Installing a computer network that enables everyone to share files and access a central database helps you make quicker informed decisions, move faster without delays and errors, avoid duplication of effort, and generally, become a more effective company.

Technology is a serious investment, but if done right, it pays back the investment quickly in increased sales, efficiency, and productivity. You may want to check out my book titled *eBusiness Technology Kit For Dummies,* where you'll find out how to develop a technology strategy that works for your business.

# Develop New Products and Services

More and more, you'll see digital products and services in the marketplace — products created and delivered over the Internet . . . totally virtual products and services. Why? Because once you develop a digital product or service, your costs related to it essentially end. You have no inventory, warehousing, transportation, or intermediary costs. Plus, with the Internet, you can take advantage of product development partners anywhere in the world.

For example, Catriona Erler, a full-time gardening writer and photographer, used to make a living selling hard copies of articles and photographs to a small group of publishers. Today, she has digitized her business (and increased her profits) by putting everything online. Now she delivers digital photographs to publishers worldwide in near-real time via e-mail. Her clients look at her products online whenever they want, freeing Sarah to focus on coming up with more products. It's a win-win situation.

# Chapter 24

# Ten Best Resources for Gathering Competitive Intelligence

● ● ● ● ● ● ● ● ● ● ● ● ● ● ● ● ● ● ● ● ● ● ● ● ● ● ● ● ● ● ● ● ● ● ● ● ● ● ● ● ● ● ● ● ● ●

*In This Chapter*

▶ Hitting the streets for firsthand dope

▶ Becoming a customer of the competition

▶ Using the Web as your eyes and ears

● ● ● ● ● ● ● ● ● ● ● ● ● ● ● ● ● ● ● ● ● ● ● ● ● ● ● ● ● ● ● ● ● ● ● ● ● ● ● ● ● ● ● ● ● ●

*T*he assignment sounds awesome — find out everything you can about how your competitors see the marketplace where *you* want to operate. Gathering this competitive intelligence isn't that hard, however. You don't have to engage in corporate espionage to develop an accurate picture of your playing field. You only have to be alert and inquisitive and use all the resources that are freely available. Limiting this list to ten is purely arbitrary: Many more exist, and you can find them with your entrepreneurial initiative. Just give it a try.

## Pounding the Pavement

Each year the Greif Entrepreneurship Center at the University of Southern California gives an award known as the *Pound-the-Pavement Award*. It is given to the student who spends the most time in his or her industry, gathering intelligence by meeting and talking with industry insiders. This is a coveted award because the person who receives it is generally acknowledged as someone whose business concept has a high probability of success. That's because the best information you ever obtain about your industry and competitors is the information you gather yourself by hitting the streets and talking to key people within your industry.

Who are the people you need to talk to? Anyone is a candidate who does business in your industry, is part of your distribution channel (supplier, producer, distributor, and customer), or is an acknowledged industry watcher. The information you gather in this manner is valuable because it is the most current and has not been filtered by the media. While doing secondary research through journals, Web sites, and other sources is certainly important, you and your team need to do the bulk of your industry research.

# Shopping Your Competitors' Turf

One of the more effective ways to find out about your competitors' market strategies is to buy their products and services. When you make yourself a customer, you gain access to knowledge that you can't reach in any other way. By being a customer, you find out about the quality of your competitors' products and the way they treat their customers and handle problems. You get an inside view of what's missing in their strategy, which translates into an opportunity for you.

If you have any qualms about becoming your competitor's customer, remember that your competitor may already be a customer of yours!

# Skimming the Industry Journals

Several journals give broad views of industry activity from the points of view of industry watchers and analysts. Here are three:

- **Industry Week,** www.industryweek.com. This venerable magazine contains a wealth of articles on various industries. It also has two great tools:

  - The Business Services Matchmaker, which is an interactive business services directory that searches for firms in public relations, legal, accounting, human resources, Web development, and so forth, and ranks them based on your specific needs.

  - The Benchmarking Tool Kit, which lets manufacturers benchmark against 7,500 manufacturing facilities and access more than 100 case studies on manufacturing best practices. Best of all, they're both free.

- **Industry, Trade, and Technology Review** *(ITTR),* www.usitc.gov/ittr.htm. This is a quarterly staff publication of the Office of Industries. The reports provide analysis of important issues and insights into the global position of U.S. industries, the technological competitiveness of the United States, and implications of trade and policy developments. This is a good source if your business has an international component.

- **The Industry Standard,** www.thestandard.com/newsletters/. This magazine bills itself as the news magazine of the Internet Economy. It focuses on Internet businesses, offering articles, metrics on the industry, and a series of free newsletters.

# Surfing the Web

If your first instinct is to type the name of a company followed by dot.com as a URL in your browser, good move. Virtually all companies — certainly all that may be a competitive threat — have a Web site providing a ready source of company information, sometimes a great deal of information. You can supplement specific company and industry data by searching through the Web sites that follow.

## About.com

This large Web site, www.about.com, includes lots of information organized by industry and industry forums where you can meet and talk with other people in your specific industry. For example, if you go to the site and are interested in finding out more about the Internet industry, select that. Once you're inside an industry, all the links that appear on the page relate to that industry. So, if you're interested in statistics about industry size, growth rate, and so forth, click on it and you'll arrive at a page, http://internet.about.com/industry/internet/msubstatsref.htm, which gives you a wide-ranging selection of stats about that industry. You'll also find an events calendar for that industry.

## OneSource.com

One Source, www.onesource.com, is one of the better online sites for finding information on any industry. One Source's browser integrates various information types — textual and numeric, news and analyses, corporate and industry, regional and global — from the world's most respected data sources, and presents it in formats that make sense for your business. You can specify the kinds of reports you want to see, including industry information, company profiles, news, business and trade articles, research reports, executive profiles, and financial data.

## IndustryLink.com

This site, www.industrylink.com, provides links to any industry in which you may be interested. For example, suppose you're interested in the environmental industry. If you click on that industry on the home page, you are taken to a list of links to sites like the Environmental News Network, www.enn.com, and EnviroNet, which is a resource site for environmental professionals at www.enviro-net.com.

Remember that no one site has all the information you need, but each site you visit gives you clues to other sites that may help.

## Dun & Bradstreet

Dun & Bradstreet is well known for its credit reports on companies. This is a service for which you must subscribe and pay a fee. However, D&B has other resources on their Web site that are free and useful for gathering information on your market and your competitors. You can find the site at www.dnb.com/resources/menu.htm. In D&B's Economic Analysis and Trends section, for example, you find reports on business failures, start-ups, manufacturing, small business issues, and so forth.

## Hoover's Online

This is a massive site that holds the key to information on thousands of companies. Some of the information isn't free, but you can search for a particular company by name and get a lot of interesting data. Hoover's is found at www.hoovers.com. One of the more interesting sections is the IPO Scorecard, which lists the winners and losers each week from those companies that have done their initial public offering. You'll also find the latest business news.

## Lexis-Nexis

Lexis-Nexis is a proprietary database of information that bills itself as "the world's largest provider of credible, in-depth information," with more than 22,000 sources covering everything from legal and government to business and high tech at www.lexis-nexis.com/lncc/. It'll cost you (credit cards are accepted) to use this site unless you have access through your university library. The information you get through this database is filtered, which means that Lexis has experts who check on the credibility of the sources. So you can feel confident that you're accessing good information.

## Government Sources

- **Department of Commerce,** www.doc.gov. This site contains a wealth of information for businesses in a variety of areas. It's a great jumping off point to other government sites.

- **Office of Trademarks and Patents,** www.pto.gov. Here you can search for patents and trademarks owned by your competitors.

- **Small Business Administration,** http://www.sba.gov. This site contains an enormous amount of information, resources, and help for people starting businesses. Definitely check out this site.

- **Bureau of Economic Analysis,** www.polisci.com/exec/commerce/01529.htm. This site, which is part of the Department of Commerce, provides economic data on industries, including gross product by industry, cash flow, and input-output data.

# Index

## • *Numbers* •

1800Flowers Web site, 21
3M (Minnesota Mining and Manufacturing), 42, 181, 257

## • *A* •

About.com Web site, 347
Absolute Towing and Trucking, 37
accountants
  enlisting the help of, 134–135, 136–137
  tips for finding good, 137
accounts
  payable, 309–310
  receivable, 305–309
acid test, 303
activation points, 165
adaptation, 59
Adobe Web site, 274
advertising. *See also* marketing
  basic description of, 283–286
  comparison chart, 284–285
  cost of, 275–276
  effectiveness of, 283–285
  expenses, forecasting, 153, 155
  guerilla, 283, 287
advisory boards, 134–142
Age Discrimination Act, 265
AgInfoLink, 340
Agriculture Department, 94
AllBusiness Web site, 15
Allen, Bob, 27
AltaVista Web site, 69
Amazon.com Web site, 60–61, 65, 113, 194, 230, 275
American Association for Public Opinion Research Web site, 79
American Demographics Web site, 79

Americans with Disabilities Act, 265
AMEX (American Stock Exchange), 200
Anderson, Anne, 340
angel funding, 141, 192–194
AOL (America Online), 17, 275
Apple Computer, 149
Ashbrook, Tom, 52
assessments, personal, 46–47
assets. *See also* collateral
  and liabilities, accounting for, 296–298
  return on, 303
  used as collateral, 175
AT&T (American Telephone & Telegraph), 42
attorneys
  as entrepreneurs, 138
  enlisting the help of, 134–136
  tips for finding good, 135–136
Australia, 247
authority, doctrine of ostensible, 209
Auto Nation, 17
Auto-by-Tel Web site, 274
automobile insurance, 140

## • *B* •

back-end costs, 197
background checks, 193
balance sheets, 294, 296–298
bankers
  business plans and, 174–175
  enlisting the help of, for start-ups, 134–135, 138–139
  financing growth through, 202
  major concerns of, 175

bankruptcy, 324–326
Barnes & Noble, 230
bartering, 191–192
Batelle Memorial Institute, 42
bCentral Web site, 15
Bedoya, Edy, 66
Ben & Jerry's, 286, 289
Benchmarking Tool Kit, 346
benchmarks, 134, 218, 346
Berkus Technology Ventures, 193
Betamax technology, 252
bibliographies, 53
billing, 137, 163
biotechnology, 13
Blackman, James, 217
Blockbuster Entertainment, 17, 227
board(s)
  of advisors, 134–142
  of directors, 142–144, 192–193, 196
bonding, 139–140
Boston Duck Tours, 37
bots, 230–231
brainstorming, 42, 185, 242
branding, 62, 241–242, 274, 276
  basic description of, 280–282
  packaging and, 281
  pricing and, 281–282
Brazil, 247
break-even point, 162, 168
bricks-and-mortar business model, 223–227, 260–261, 340
budgets, 137, 291–292
*Built to Last* (Collins and Porral), 257
bulk, breaking, 127
Bureau of Economic Analysis, 348
Bureau of Labor Statistics Web site, 71

business concept(s), 176,
179–180
  basic description of, 47
  feasibility analysis and, 49,
    51–56
  which "scale out," 154, 179
  quick-testing, 50–51
  transforming opportunities
    into, 47–49
business models
  basic description of,
    219–232
  bricks-and-mortar business
    model, 223–227,
    260–261, 340
  clicks-and-bricks business
    model, 230–231
  clicks-and-hits business
    model, 228–229
  clicks-and-mortar business
    model, 231–232
  subscription-based
    business model, 229–230
business plan(s)
  angels and, 192
  basic description of,
    171–186
  company visions and,
    181–182
  elements of, 53
  executive summaries in, 53,
    54, 179
  importance of, 172–173
  investors and, 93, 192, 197
  mission and, 182
  one-minute, 186
  outlines, 176, 177–180
  preparing/presenting,
    182–186
  who, what, where, and why
    of, 172–180
Business Services
  Matchmaker, 346
Business Startups Web site,
  335
BusinessWeek Web site, 67
Buy.com Web site, 194, 275
buyer(s). *See also* customers
  bargaining power of, 61, 63
  patterns/habits of, 75,
    77–78
  switching costs, 62
buyouts, 189–190, 196

# • C •

Camera World Web site, 17,
  18
Canada, 247
capacity, 62, 202
capital. *See also* money;
    venture capital
  budgeting, 291–292
  cost of, 291–292
  expenditures, 161, 164, 165,
    167, 293
  finding, overview of,
    187–204
  first-stage funding, 189–191,
    195
  managing your, 305–310
  market, informal risk,
    192–194
  needs assessment, 162–165
  second-stage, 189, 196
  third-stage, 189–190
  underestimating your need
    for, 174
cash. *See also* cash flow
  cycles, 307–308
  discounts, 301, 409
  inflows, 157–160
  needs assessment, 162–165
  outflows, 157–161
  reserves, 301
cash flow. *See also* cash
  forecasting, 153–157
  management, 305–310
  as a percentage of net sales,
    304
  statement, 153–154,
    157–161, 166, 174, 294,
    298–301
casualty, 139–140
catalog shows, 248
Census Bureau Web site, 71
CEOs (chief executive
    officers), recruiting
    experienced, 267
Chappell, Jef, 97
Chapter 7 petition, 325–326
Chapter 11 bankruptcy, 325
chasm, use of the term, 251
chat, enhanced
    communication through,
    26–27

China, 246
Christmas delivery
    difficulties, 123
Chrysler, 119
CIF (customer information
    file), 286–288
Cisco Systems, 201, 232
Civic Light Opera, 217
Civil Rights Act, 265
clicks-and-bricks business
    model, 230–231
clicks-and-hits business
    model, 228–229
clicks-and-mortar business
    model, 231–232
click-through rates, 228–229
Clorox, 149
CNNfn.com Web site, 260
COGP (cost of goods
    produced), 152–153, 155,
    160–162
COGS (cost of goods sold),
    160–161, 162, 174
coincident
  index, 316
  -lagging index, 316
collateral, 175, 194, 202, 308.
    *See also* assets
Collins, Jim, 257
Commerce Department, 71,
    248, 249, 317, 348
Commissioner of Patents and
    Trademarks, 110
community business
    organizations, 336
compensation policy, 259
competencies, core, 97, 98,
    128, 257
competitive intelligence,
    68–72, 341–342, 345–348
Competitive Intelligence
    Guide Web site, 71
competitors. *See also*
    competitive intelligence
  attacking, 252
  basic description of, 12–13
  marketing plans and, 277
  pricing based on, 282
  researching, 67, 68–72, 84,
    151, 346
complexity, 62
concept, proof of, 54

confidence, importance of, 35, 37
confidentiality clause, 117
conglomerate diversification, 245
Conrades, Gus, 83
Consolidated Delivery and Logistics, 122
consultants. *See also* contractors, independent; outsourcing
  enlisting the help of, 134–135
  human resource, 263
  turnaround, 326–327
Consumer Confidence Index, 316
Consumer Electronics Manufacturer Association, 340
Consumer Price Index, 316
contingency plan, 53, 175–176, 179
contractors, independent. *See also* consultants; outsourcing
  contracts with, 146
  rules for, 145
contracts
  basic description of, 113–114
  independent contractor, 146
  nondisclosure (NDAs), 114–115, 184
  partnership, 133–134, 147, 148, 210–211
contribution rate, 162
control, giving up, 31
Cook, Scott, 201
copyrights. *See also* intellectual property
  basic description of, 110–111
  claiming, 110–111
  items which are not protected by, 111
core
  competencies, 97, 98, 128, 257
  values, 181–182

corporation(s)
  close, 211
  closely held, 211
  culture of, 255–256
  domestic, 214
  foreign, 214
  legal form of, 205–206, 211–215
Costco, 121, 130
Crate and Barrel, 171
creativity, 1, 33–44, 263
  enhancing, 41–42, 44–45
  making time for, 41, 44
  making your environment more conducive to, 44
Creativity Web Web site, 37–38
credibility, building, 271
credit
  policies, 84, 306–307
  ratings, 134, 167
  revolving lines of, 308–309
  trade, 309
credit card purchases, 180
critical mass, 252
criticism, sensitivity to, 35, 36
culture, of your company, 255–256
current ratio, 303
customer(s). *See also* buyers
  acquisition costs, 275–276
  base, building, 239
  business concepts and, 47–49, 55
  credit policy for, 306–307
  crucial role of, 13
  defining, in marketing plans, 279
  getting payments from, 145, 192, 301, 307
  hiring manufacturers' reps to find, 126
  identifying, 47, 271
  information, gathering, 275, 286–288
  keeping your best, 282–288
  learning from, 73–86, 273
  primary, identifying, 75, 77–78
  product development and, 95–96, 100

profiles, 82–83
  reaching, 269–288
  researching, 69, 77–83
  satisfaction, focus on, 255
  selling directly to, 125
  service, 250, 274
  staying in touch with, 341
  as strategic partners, 148
  tracking the preferences of, 275
customization, mass, 87–88, 121, 271
Cyber Gold, 107
CyberAtlas Web site, 71

• *D* •

Dahl, Gary, 36
DBA (Certificate of Doing Business under an Assumed Name), 207, 338
Debelak, Don, 39
debt
  to asset ratio, 305
  -equity ratio, 302–303
  reduction, long-term, 161
decision-making, 256
Defense Department, 93
Deja.com Usenet, 70
Dell Computer, 288
demand
  forecasting, 83–86, 150–152
  getting a three-way fix on, 151
  seasonal (seasonality), 84, 152, 302
demographics, 75, 279
depreciation, 155
Design Partners, 42
differentiation, 59, 64–65
DiMello, Tim, 29–30
direct
  labor budget, 292, 294
  materials budget, 292, 294
directors and officers liability insurance, 143
disclosure documents, 108
discounts, 301, 409
Disney, Walt, 44
Disney Company, 181

distribution channel(s),
    27–28, 85
  basic description of,
    121–130
  business concepts and, 47,
    49, 55
  consumer market, 125–127
  cost of, 128–129
  coverage, 130
  direct, 123–124
  evaluating, 128–130
  gaining access to, 63
  indirect, 123–124
  industrial market, 125, 127
  market analysis and, 75–76,
    85
  marketing plans and, 280
  moving
    vertically/horizontally in
    your, 243
  strategies for navigating,
    123–124
  using intermediaries,
    127–128, 129
diversity, encouraging, 256
dividend income, 160
doctrine of equivalents, 119
domain names, 113, 250
Dominos Pizza, 149
Dressmart Web site, 77
Drugstore.com Web site, 190
due diligence, 193, 196, 197
Dun & Bradstreet, 348

### • E •

early adopters, 251
Eat.com Web site, 274
EBC Computers Web site, 66
EBIT (earnings before
    interest and taxes), 156
EBITDA (earnings before
    interest, taxes,
    depreciation, and
    amortization), 156
economic data, 316–318, 348
economies of scale, 62
Edison, Thomas, 44
Education Department, 93

EEOC (Equal Employment
    Opportunity
    Commission), 266
Electric Library Web site, 70
"elevator pitches," 55
e-mail, 26–27, 28, 341, 342
  discussion groups, 70
  marketing through, 273
Emarketer Web site, 72
employee(s). *See also*
    consultants; hiring
  choosing the right, 264–266
  definition of, by the IRS,
    145, 146, 148
  finding and keeping great,
    261–267
  hiring the minimum
    number of, 144
  identifying your best, 262
  interviews with potential,
    266
  keeping files on, 313
  lawsuits, 313
  leasing, 146–147, 227
  legislation applying to, 265
  recruiting, 262–264
  stock option plans, 322–323
  surviving the loss of key,
    315–316
employment
  agencies, 21, 263
  laws, 265
end users, 75
Energy Department, 93
engineering, 23, 95–96
Entrepreneur Web site, 335
entrepreneurship
  basic description of, 9–20
  home-based, 15–16
  moving from, to
    professional
    management, 254–258
  personal goals and, 18–19
  recent changes in, 1–2
  recognizing, 10–11
  serial, 17
  traditional, 17–18, 189–191
  types of, 15–18
  understanding, 9–14
  virtual, 16–17, 340

entry
  barriers to, 30, 61, 62–63
  strategies, 64–66
EnviroNet Web site, 347
Environmental News
    Network Web site, 347
Environmental Protection
    Agency (EPA), 94
Equal Pay Act, 265
equipment(s)
  expenditures, as capital
    expenditures, 164
  leasing rather than buying,
    144, 165, 167, 191
equity stakes, 192, 225
equivalents, doctrine of, 119
ergonomics, 99
Erler, Catriona, 343
errors and omissions
    insurance, 140
ESPN.com Web site, 260
ethics, 136
e-Toys Web site, 194
Eureka Ranch Web site, 40
executive summaries, 53, 54,
    179
exit strategies, 318–323
expectations, quantifying, 84
expense(s)
  administrative, 153
  deducting, on your tax
    returns, 15
  equipment, 144, 164–165,
    167, 191
  general, 153
  projections, 150, 152–153
Expo Guide Web site, 129
Export-Import Bank of the
    United States, 249

### • F •

factoring, 308
factory overhead, 292, 294
failure
  dealing with, 202, 256
  finding opportunity in, 43
  knowing when to walk away
    in the instance of,
    323–324, 327

family members
  as investors, 190–191, 195
  as partners, 132–133,
    333–334
Fast Company Web site, 335,
    340
feasibility analysis, 49, 73,
    150, 153, 171–172
  basic description of, 51–56,
    337
  business plans and,
    177–178
feasibility decision, 53, 56
Federal Census Bureau Web
    site, 78
Federal Express, 50, 245, 270
Federal Reserve, 317
Federal Web Locator, 71
FedWorld, 71
finance companies, 203
financial analysis, 53, 56
financial plans. *See also*
    financial statements
  basic description of,
    149–168, 289–310
  building, 295–302
  business plans and, 176,
    178, 180
  components of, identifying,
    290–294
  feasibility analysis and, 53
  legal classifications for
    businesses and, 206–207
  one-minute, 168
financial statements. *See also*
    financial plans
  business plans and, 176
  preparing, 137, 153–161
  "Five C's," use of the term,
    202
fixed costs, 155–156, 164, 167
flexibility, 31, 258–251
focus groups, 82, 280
Forbes Web site, 335
Ford Motor Company, 43
forecasting
  advertising expenses, 153,
    155
  cash flow, 153–157
  demand, 83–86, 150–152
  sales, 150–152
  salaries, 153
Foreign Corrupt Practices
    Act, 117

foreign countries, doing
    business in, 109–110,
    245, 342
Fortune Web site, 335
franchising, 240–241
Free Websites Directory Web
    site, 97
frequency programs, 288
friends
  as investors, 190–191, 195
  as partners, 132–133
Fry, Arthur, 42
Fryer, Bronwyn, 17
fulfillment systems, 32, 231
Fun Cosmetics, 39
Furniture.com Web site, 21

• *G* •

GAAP (Generally Accepted
    Accounting Principles),
    136
The Gap, 232, 261
Garden Escape Web site, 21
GATT (General Agreement on
    Tariffs and Trade), 246
Gender, 11
General Motors, 119
genesis or founding team
    analysis, 53, 56
Germany, 247
Gillette method, 222
Global Link Web site, 342
global marketplace, 109–110,
    245, 342
goals, 18–19, 291. *See also*
    mission; vision
GORP.com Web site, 65
GoTo Web site, 69
government. *See also specific*
    *agencies*
  economic data, 316–317
  grants, 92–94
  relation of, to
    entrepreneurship, 12–13
  regulations, 63
  Web sites, 70, 71
grant clause, 117–118
grant-back clause, 118
grant-forward clause, 118
graphing business processes,
    163–164

Greif Entrepreneurship
    Center, 345
gross profit margins, 68, 155,
    174, 302
Grove, Andy, 258
growth
  basic strategies for, 237–239
  factors that affect,
    identifying, 236–237
  going global to promote,
    245–250
  high, 237–239
  as a high-tech company,
    250–251
  importance of, 14
  initial, 238
  organizing your business
    for, 253–268
  planning for, 53, 176, 178,
    180, 235–252
  rates, 152
  stable, 238, 239
  ten ways to use the Internet
    for, 339–344
guerilla tactics, 283, 287

• *H* •

habit, creatures of, 36
Hakuta, Ken, 36
Hall, Doug, 40
health
  insurance, 146
  personal, maintaining, 19
Health and Human Services,
    Department of, 94
Hewlett-Packard, 149, 224
hierarchical organization, 27,
    44
hiring. *See also* employees
  basic description of,
    262–266
  choosing the right
    employees, 264–266
  lawsuits and, 313
  leasing employees instead
    of, 146–147, 227
  manufacturers' reps, 126
  the minimum number of
    employees, 144
Hills, Gerald, 38
"hockey stick" growth, 84
Home Depot, 28, 129

home-based
entrepreneurship, 15–16
HomePortfolio Web site, 52
Hong Kong, 247
Hoover's Online Web site, 70,
348
horizontal integration, 243
HotJobs.com, 232
House of Representatives
Web site, 71
Huizenga, Wayne, 17, 227
human resource(s). *See also*
employees
consultants, 263
policy, 256–258

## • *I* •

icons, used in this book, 4
IDC Web site, 72
image, creating your, 274–275
*Inc.* magazine, 65, 66, 150,
225, 276, 335
*Inc. Technology* magazine, 17
income
statement, 153–157,
160–161, 294–296
tax, 156–157
independent contractors. *See*
consultants; contractors,
independent
industry
analysis, 53, 55, 59–72, 180
basic description of, 73
checking out the status of
your, 67–68
diversifying outside,
244–245
growth of, 67, 242–244
hostility of, 63
life cycles of, 59–60
mature, 68
researching, 66–72, 337,
346–347
structure, framework of,
61–64
threats to, 68
trends/patterns, 67
understanding your, 60–66

Industry Standard Web site,
72, 346
*Industry, Trade, and
Technology Review
(ITTR)*, 346
Industry Week Web site, 346
IndustryLink Web site, 347
information
customer, 275, 286–288
products and, breaking the
link between, 25
selling, 25
sharing, 26
transforming, into
knowledge, 24–25
using, to brand your
company, 274
InfoSeek Web site, 69
initial capitalization, 211
innovation, 14, 152. *See also*
inventions
differentiation strategies
and, 64–65
finding the right place for,
44
incremental, 241
instincts, 11
insurance
automobile, 140
brokers, 139–140
health, 146
liability, 139–140, 143, 313,
318
recommended types of,
139–140
Intel, 32, 255, 258
intellectual property. *See
also* copyrights; patents;
trademarks
basic description of,
103–120
infringements, 118–120
licensing, 114, 117–118
researching, 70, 71
rights, importance of, 236
strategies for protecting,
115–120
intelligence, competitive,
68–72, 341–342, 345–348
intensive coverage, 122

interest
expenses, 161
income, 160
Interior, Department of the,
93
International Trade
Administration, 249
International Trade Statistics
Yearbook of the United
States, 246
Internet
building market strategies
with, 273–274
business units, 260–261
enhanced communication
through, 26–27
open architecture of, 26
overall advantages of,
22–25
product development and,
97
ten ways to use, 339–344
time, concept of, 21, 23
using, to enter the global
marketplace, 249–250
using, for research, 66–72
interviews
with customers and
intermediaries, 82, 85
with job candidates,
265–266
Intuit, 201
Invent Resources Web site,
42
invention(s). *See also*
innovation
designing/developing,
88–90
getting outside help with,
42–43
licensing, 89–90
nurseries, 42–43
inventories, 85, 137
calculating expenses and,
152–153
cash flow statements and,
161
finished-goods, 152
managing, 301
work-in-process, 152

investors, 94–95, 160. *See also* venture capital
  business plans and, 173–174, 184–185
  exit strategies for, 194
  income statements and, 154
  paying back, importance of, 327
invoices, 137
IOUs, 202
IPOs (initial public offerings), 137, 142, 188. *See also* stock
  advantages/disadvantages of, 199–200
  angels and, 193
  basic description of, 198–202
  corporations and, 205–206
  roll-up companies and, 321
  venture capital and, 189–191
IRS (Internal Revenue Service), 145, 146, 148, 217. *See also* taxes
iShip, 122
ISPs (Internet service providers), 97, 250

### • J •

Japan, 247
Jdpost.com Web site, 38
job(s). *See also* employees
  candidates, choosing the right, 264–266
  descriptions, 264
Jobs, Steve, 149
JobsinChicago.com Web site, 232
John Makulowich's Awesome Lists, 70
Jupiter Communications, 260, 275
just-in-time programs, 288

### • K •

Kearns, Bob, 119
keystones, 129
Kinkos, 223, 273

knowledge
  relying on your own, 151
  turning information into, 24–25
Knowles, Michael, 150
Kohl, Jerry, 64–65
KosmosTrade, 278–279

### • L •

lagging index, 316
LavaBuns, 42
lawsuits, protecting your company from, 312–314
leasing
  employees, 146–147, 227
  equipment, 144, 165, 167, 191
Leegin Creative Leather, 64–65
legal classifications, for businesses, 205–218
  LLC (Limited Liability Company), 154, 205, 207, 216–217
  nonprofit corporations, 217, 312
  S Corporation, 154, 206, 215–217
  sole proprietorships, 154, 205, 207–209
lenders. *See also* bankers; loans
  business plans and, 174–175
  major concerns of, 175
leverage ratios, 304–305
Lexis-Nexis Web site, 348
liability
  insurance, 139–140, 143, 313, 318
  legal classifications for businesses and, 206–218
  product, coping with, 317–318
licensing, 120, 241
  intellectual property, 114, 117–118
  inventions, 89–90
life cycles, of industries, 59–60
life insurance, 140

lifestyle businesses, 14
The Limited, 149
liquidity, 157, 302, 303–304, 315
liquidation, 325–326
Liszt Web site, 70
Little, Arthur D., 42
LLC (Limited Liability Company), 154, 205, 207, 216–217
loan(s). *See also* bankers; lenders
  capacity to repay, 175, 202
  from friends and family, 191–192
  payments, 161, 164
  SBA-based, 93
  using, to pay off old debt, 175
logos, 184
Lycos Web site, 69

### • M •

McDonald's Corporation, 312
McKnight, William, 257
magazines, recommended, 335
mainstream adoption, 251–252
management
  adding additional, 262, 267
  effective, 253–268
  human resource policy for, 256–258
  organizing for speed and flexibility, 258–261
  teams, 175, 176, 180, 197, 258–259
manufacturers
  distribution channels and, 126, 127–128
  finding, 102
  product design and, 100–101
  researching, 102
  statistics on, 316
  as strategic partners, 148
Manufacturers' Orders for Durable Goods, 316

market(s). *See also*
    marketing
  analysis, 55, 77–85, 176
  defining, 72–77
  development, 239–241
  growing with your current,
    239–244
  leaders, 74
  narrowing, 74–76
  niche, 49, 65–66, 73–77, 278
  penetration, 239
  researching, 55, 77–85, 176,
    280
  segments, 74–76
  target, identifying, 73–77
  test, 78, 86, 280
  use of the term, 73
Market Insights Web site, 79
marketing. *See also* markets;
    marketing plans
  basic description of,
    269–288
  cost of, 275–276
  to customers, one at a time,
    270–276
  product development and,
    95–96
  in a split second, 272
  strategies, 68, 260–261,
    271–276
marketing plans, 53, 176, 178,
    180, 262. *See also*
    marketing
  basic description of,
    276–282
  one-paragraph, 277–279
  writing, 277–282
marriage, 11
Martin, Bill, 150
mass
  customization, 87–88, 121,
    271
  personalization, 87–88
matchmaker trade
    delegations, 248
materials/parts, sourcing,
    101–102
Mats, Yoshiro Naka, 44
maturity, of industries, 60

Mediamark Research Web
    site, 72, 279
medical insurance, 140
mentors, importance of, 144,
    338
Microsoft, 15, 273, 315
milestones, 192
Mina, Aleesandro, 18
MiniMed Web site, 274
mission, 182. *See also* goals;
    vision
models, business. *See*
    business models
money. *See also* capital
  calculating the real cost of,
    195–196
  as an enabler, 13, 49
  finding, for product
    development, 91–95
  plans, 188–191
Monster.com Web site, 21,
    232, 263
Montgomery, Donna Mae, 39
Moore, Geoffrey, 251
Moore, Gordon, 32
Moore's Law, 32
mortgage brokers, 21
Motorola, 181, 224
movie theaters, business
    model for, 221
MSN.com Web site, 69
Murphy, Bryan, 83

## • *N* •

NAFTA (North American Free
    Trade Agreement), 246
NASA (National Aeronautics
    and Space
    Administration), 89, 93,
    115
NASA Technology Web site,
    89
National Association of
    Securities Dealers
    Automated Quotation
    (NASDAQ), 200
National Federation of
    Independent Businesses
    (NFIB), 340

National Market System, 200
National Retail Federation,
    275
National Science Foundation
    (NSF), 94
NDAs (nondisclosure
    agreements), 114–115,
    184
Neiman-Marcus, 281
Nelson, Bill, 90
net profit, 156–157
Netherlands, 247
networking, 40, 225, 244
  organizations which
    facilitate, 340
  research through, 72
  start-ups and, 134
New Pig Web site, 341
Newman, Spencer, 65
NewsDirectory Web site, 70
newsgroups, 70–71
niche markets, 49, 65–66,
    73–77, 278. *See also*
    markets
Nielsen/Netrating Report,
    228
nonprofit corporations, 217,
    312
Northern Light Web site, 69
Nuclear Regulatory
    Commission, 93
NYSE (New York Stock
    Exchange), 200, 212

## • *O* •

obsolete, making yourself,
    28–29
obstacles
  clearing away, 37–42
  identifying, 35–37
Occupational Health and
    Safety Administration
    (OSHA) Web site, 318
Office Max, 30
Office of Trademarks and
    Patents, 348
office space, 191
OneSource Web site, 70, 347

open architecture, of the
Internet, 26
operating
budgets, 292–294
losses, 164, 166
operation(s)
plan, 53, 178
statement, 298–299
opportunities
being driven by, 14
finding, in failure, 43
finding, in the
unconventional, 43
researching, 67
testing, 45–46
transforming, into business
concepts, 47–49
order for relief, 325–326
Orfalea, Paul, 223
organization. *See also*
management
culture of, discovering,
255–256
managing your, 253–268
plan, 53, 176, 178, 180
Outdoor Adventure Online,
65
outsourcing, 30, 32. *See also*
contractors,
independent
calculating the cost of, 163
logistics, 122–123
product development and,
98
saving money by, 146
overhead, 165, 315
Overseas Private Investment
Corporation, 249

● *P* ●

packaging, 281
Panzarella, Jack, 16
Paris Convention for the
Protection of Industrial
Property, 110
partnership(s), 23–25, 27
contracts, 133–134, 147,
148, 210–211
with family members,
132–133, 333–334
with friends, 132–133

forming, 132–134
income statements for, 154
as a legal form, 205,
209–211
through strategic alliances,
148, 177, 244, 341
passion, importance of, 10,
31, 52, 201, 334
patent(s), 102, 104–110. *See
also* intellectual
property; Patent and
Trademark Office (PTO)
applications, 108–109
business method, 107
infringements, 118–120
licensing, 114, 117–118
process, 107
protection in foreign
countries, 109–110
for small inventions,
106–107
types of, 106–107
utility, 109
Patent and Trademark Office
(PTO), 71, 104–109,
112–113
payroll(s)
controlling, 302
leasing employees and,
146–147
stock option plans and,
322–323
taxes, 137, 146–147, 153,
327
Penta, Kristin, 39
Pentech International, 39
PEO (Professional Employer
Organization), 146
Persistence, importance of,
10, 31, 52
personal
board of directors, 144
liability insurance, 140
life, effect of entrepre-
neurship on, 19, 46–47
personality assessments,
46–47
personalization, mass, 87–88
Pet Rocks, 36
phased sales, 322
Pizza Hut, 171
Plank, Mathias, 77

PlumbNet Web site, 26–27
population changes, 84
Porras, Jerry, 257
Porter, Michael E., 61
Post-it® Notes, 42, 181
Pound-the-Pavement Award,
345
Power Presentations, 201
PowerSource machine, 99
PPA (provisional application
for patent), 106–108. *See
also* patents
Presley, Elvis, 37
Price Club, 28, 121, 130
Priceline.com Web site, 107
pricing
branding and, 281, 282
changes, 85
competition-based, 282
cost-based, 282
demand-based, 282
focusing too much on, 174
loss leader, 282
psychological, 282
reducing, 315
strategies, 69, 282
primary offerings, 198
prioritization, 256
PrivaSeek Web site, 49
problem solving, 35, 39–40
process analysis, 53, 176,
177–178, 180
Producer Price Index,
316–317
product(s)
benefits of, 47, 48, 55
breakthrough, 241
designing, 87–102
estimating sales for,
150–152
features of, 48
genesis of, 90
ideas, developing, 33–44
information and, breaking
the link between, 25
liability, 139–140, 317–318
multiple, 226–227
plans, one-minute, 102
protecting your, 103–120
/service development plan,
53, 56

product(s) *(continued)*
  sourcing your
    materials/parts for,
    101–102
  substitute, 63, 85
  zeroing-in on new, 88–90
production budget, 292, 293
productivity, increasing, 273
profit
  and loss, calculating,
    154–157
  margins, 68, 155, 174, 302,
    303
profitability ratios, 303
ProfNet Web site, 71
promotions, 283–286, 342.
    *See also* marketing
proof of concept, 179–180
property insurance, 139–140
proprietary factors, 63
prototypes, 86, 94–102, 150
  cost of, calculating, 164
  proof of concept and, 180
publicity, 286
public relations, creating
    positive, 274
purchasing. *See also* buyers;
    customers
  new ways of, 29–30
  product development and,
    95–96

• *Q* •

quality
  designing for, 101
  function deployment (QFD),
    100
questionnaires, 80–81, 259
QuickenMortgage.com Web
    site, 21
quiet period, 74, 76

• *R* •

RagingBull Web site, 150
Ragu Web site, 274
Rand-McNally, 165
random samples, 79
ratios, financial, 294, 302–305

reality checks, 172
recession, 316–318
record-keeping, 137. *See also*
    accountants; statements
recruiting, 262–264, 267
Red Herring Web site, 335
red herrings, 200
Reebok, 171
referrals, 263
relationships, building,
    287–288
Remarq Web site, 70
research and development
    (R&D), 13, 42–43, 67–68,
    91–95. *See also*
    researching
researching. *See also*
    research and
    development (R&D)
  competitors, 67, 68–72, 84,
    151, 346
  customers, 69, 77–83
  industries, 66–72, 337,
    346–347
  intellectual property, 70, 71
  manufacturers, 102
  markets, 55, 77–85, 176, 280
  offline, 72
  primary, 78–82
  public companies, 70
  secondary, 78–79
  the status of your industry,
    67–68
restaurants, business model
    for, 221–222
restructuring, 321–322
return
  on assets, 303
  on equity, 303
  on investment, 194, 303
revenue(s)
  multiple streams of, 222
  projections, 154–157
rivalry, 61, 64
Rogers, Manuel, 37
ROI (return on investment),
    194, 303
roll-up company, 321
Roney, Carley, 16–17
Roney & Partners, 16–17
Rotary International, 336

Rouse, Rolly, 52
Rubber Stamp Artist
    movement, 39

• *S* •

S Corporation, 154, 206,
    215–217
safety
  factors, calculating, 166
  requirements, 318
salaries
  calculating, 153, 164
  going without, during the
    start-up phase, 134
sales
  budget, 292, 293
  declines in, handling,
    314–315
  estimating/forecasting,
    150–152
  tax, 327
Sanchez, John, 38
"scale out," use of the term,
    154, 179
Scripps Ventures, 52
search engines, 69–70
seasonal demand
    (seasonality), 84, 152,
    302
Securities and Exchange
    Commission (SEC), 70,
    198–202, 295, 320
selective coverage, 122
sell-in data, 152
selling your business,
    319–323
sell-through data, 152
serial entrepreneurship, 17
service(s)
  bartering for, 191–192
  designing, 87–102
  estimating sales for,
    150–152
  marks, 112–113
  multiple, 226–227
  niche strategies for, 65
  protecting your, 103–120
  substitute, 63

Seven Hills Security, 150
SG&A (Sales, General and Administrative Expenses), 161
shakeouts, 60
Shin, Jack, 17, 18
shop-bots, 230–231
Shop.org Web site, 275
SIC codes, 67
Silber, Zalman, 34
Silicon Graphics, 224
Simmons Market Research Bureau, 279
skimming, 282
Small Business Administration (SBA) Web site, 78, 92, 93, 203, 348
Small Business Development Corporation Web site, 78
Small Business Investment Company (SBIC), 92
Small Business Innovative Research (SBIR), 93–94
Smart, Todd, 37
Smith, Fred, 50
Social Security tax, 146
software companies, business model for, 220–221
sole proprietorships, 154, 205, 207–209
Sony, 252, 257
South Africa, 247
Southwest Airlines, 255
speed
  importance of, 31
  organizing for, 258–261
SRI International, 42
stages, thinking about your business in, 165
Standard Industrial Classification (SIC) Index, 67
Staples, 30
Starbuck, W. H., 61
Starbucks Coffee, 10, 280
start-up(s)
  board of advisors, 134–142

board of directors, 142–144, 192–193, 196
contracts/written agreements for, 133–134
costs, 160, 164, 165–166
distribution channels and, 124
financial needs of, assessing, 149–168
government grants for, 94
partners, finding, 132–134
planning for growth and, 237–238
requirements, 53
taking a virtual tour of your, 163–165
teams, 31, 131–148, 173
STAT-USA Web site, 71
stock(s), 195, 197, 211–213, 215, 224–225. *See also* IPOs (initial public offerings)
  -holder reports, 137
  option plans, 322–323
  prices, fluctuations in, 317
  selling your, 320–323
strategic alliances, 148, 177, 244, 341
strategy, tactics and, confusing, 174
Streamline, 29–30, 49
StreetGlow Web site, 16
subscription-based business model, 229–230
success
  creativity and, 44
  definition of, 2
  elements of, 12
  truth about, 257
superstores, 129
supplier(s). *See also* vendors
  bargaining power of, 61, 63
  basic description of, 12–13
  payment terms with, 145, 192, 301, 309–310
  as strategic partners, 148
surveys, 80–81
synergistic diversification, 244

● *T* ●

Taiwan, 247
talent channels, 263
tax(es)
  contractors and, 145, 146, 148
  estimating, in advance, 153
  federal, 153
  home-based businesses and, 15–16
  income, 153, 156–157
  income statements and, 154, 155, 156–157
  legal classifications for businesses and, 205–218
  local income, 153
  payroll, 137, 146–147, 153, 327
  returns, preparing, 137
  sales, 327
  Social Security, 146
  state, 153
teams, 31, 131–148, 173
  adding new people to, 261–167
  organizing around, 258–259
Tech Coast Angels, 193
technology. *See also* Internet
  competitive advantage gained through, 23–24
  as a disrupter, 32
  turning information into knowledge through, 24–25
  using, to build your market strategy, 272–273
teleconferencing, 273
The Gap, 232, 261
The Limited, 149
TheKnot Web site, 16
Tilt-Up, 303
timelines, 53, 56
times interest earned, 305
TLDs (top-level domains), 113
toll-free telephone numbers, 250
tombstones, 200

tornado, use of the term,
251–252
Toys 'R' Us, 129
Trade and Development
Agency, 249
trade
credit, 309
fairs, 248
missions, 248
secrets, 113–115
shows, 52, 124
trademarks, 112–113. *See
also* intellectual
property
traditional entrepreneurship,
17–18
training, 164, 259
Transportation, Department
of, 93
triangulation, 83, 85–86, 151

### • U •

uncertainty, dealing with,
11–12, 62
underwriters, 200
unemployment insurance,
140, 146
United Kingdom, 247, 250,
342
United Nations, 247
United Road Service, 37
UPS (United Parcel Service),
255

### • V •

value
chains, 14, 25, 27–28, 188
creating, 257
propositions, 10, 47, 49, 55
VanGundy, Arthur, 40
vendors, 101–102. *See also*
suppliers
venture capital, 27, 189–190,
207. *See also* capital;
investors
angels and, 192–193
basic description of, 93, 194
companies, 52

deals, parts of, 197–198
process, tracking, 196–198
state-funded, 94
using, 194–198
vertical integration, 253
VHS tapes, 252
Victoria's Secret, 232, 275
video
catalog exhibitions, 248
conferencing, 273, 341
Vietnam, 246, 265
Vietnam Era Veterans
Readjustment Act, 265
VIP clubs, 288
Virgin Atlantic Airways, 43
virtual entrepreneurship,
16–17, 340
vision, 256, 267
basic description of,
181–182
statements, 259
VLG (Venture Law Group),
138
Vocational Rehabilitation
Act, 265
voice mail, 273

### • W •

Wacky Wallwalker, 36
Wal-Mart, 22, 121, 124, 129,
182
*Wall Street Journal, The*,
229–230, 263, 319
Walton, Sam, 182
Waste Management, 17
Web sites (listed by name)
1800Flowers Web site, 21
About.com Web site, 347
Adobe Web site, 274
AllBusiness Web site, 15
AltaVista Web site, 69
Amazon.com Web site,
60–61, 65, 113, 194, 230,
275
American Association for
Public Opinion Research
Web site, 79
American Demographics
Web site, 79

Auto-by-Tel Web site, 274
bCentral Web site, 15
Bureau of Labor Statistics
Web site, 71
Business Startups Web site,
335
BusinessWeek Web site, 67
Buy.com Web site, 194, 275
Camera World Web site, 17,
18
Census Bureau Web site, 71
CNNfn.com Web site, 260
Commerce Department
Web site, 71
Competitive Intelligence
Guide Web site, 71
Creativity Web Web site,
37–38
CyberAtlas Web site, 71
Dressmart Web site, 77
Drugstore.com Web site,
190
Eat.com Web site, 274
EBC Computers Web site,
66
Electric Library Web site,
70
Emarketer Web site, 72
Entrepreneur Web site, 335
EnviroNet Web site, 347
Environmental News
Network Web site, 347
ESPN.com Web site, 260
e-Toys Web site, 194
Eureka Ranch Web site, 40
Expo Guide Web site, 129
Fast Company Web site,
335, 340
Federal Census Bureau Web
site, 78
Forbes Web site, 335
Fortune Web site, 335
Free Websites Directory
Web site, 97
Furniture.com Web site, 21
Garden Escape Web site, 21
Global Link Web site, 342
GORP.com Web site, 65
GoTo Web site, 69
HomePortfolio Web site, 52

Hoover's Online Web site, 70, 348
House of Representatives Web site, 71
IDC Web site, 72
Inc.com Web site, 70, 335
Industry Standard Web site, 72, 346
Industry Week Web site, 346
IndustryLink Web site, 347
InfoSeek Web site, 69
Invent Resources Web site, 42
Jdpost.com Web site, 38
JobsinChicago.com Web site, 232
Lexis-Nexis Web site, 348
Liszt Web site, 70
Lycos Web site, 69
Market Insights Web site, 79
Mediamark Research Web site, 72, 279
MiniMed Web site, 274
Monster.com Web site, 21, 232, 263
MSN.com Web site, 69
NASA Technology Web site, 89
New Pig Web site, 341
NewsDirectory Web site, 70
Northern Light Web site, 69
Occupational Health and Safety Administration (OSHA) Web site, 318
OneSource Web site, 70, 347
Patent and Trademark Office (PTO) Web site, 71
PlumbNet Web site, 26–27
Priceline.com Web site, 107
PrivaSeek Web site, 49
ProfNet Web site, 71
QuickenMortgage.com Web site, 21
RagingBull Web site, 150
Ragu Web site, 274
Red Herring Web site, 335
Remarq Web site, 70
Shop.org Web site, 275

Small Business Administration (SBA) Web site, 78, 92, 93, 203, 348
Small Business Development Corporation Web site, 78
STAT-USA Web site, 71
StreetGlow Web site, 16
TheKnot Web site, 16
WebSideStory.com Web site, 190
WeInvent Web site, 42
Wrencheads.com Web site, 83
Yahoo! Web site, 45, 69, 339
Zebramart.com Web site, 232
WebSideStory.com Web site, 190
WeInvent Web site, 42
Weissman, Jerry, 201
Wexner, Lex, 149
Whitney Museum, 39
wholesalers, 85, 126
Wilson, Andrew, 37
Wong, Angi Ma, 336
workers' compensation insurance, 140
Wozniak, Steve, 149
Wrencheads.com Web site, 83
Wright, Greg, 150
Writers Alliance, 70

Xerox-Mail, 39

Yahoo! Web site, 45, 69, 339

● **Z** ●

Zebramart.com Web site, 232
Zimmerman, Wes, 324

# Notes